CW01021498

Conducting Beethoven

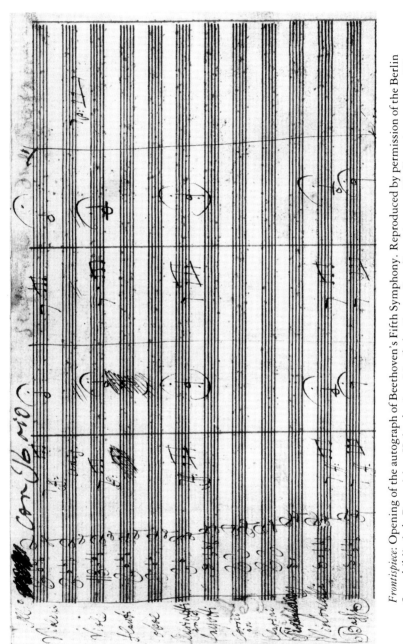

Frontispiece: Opening of the autograph of Beethoven's Fifth Symphony. Reproduced by permission of the Berlin Staatsbibliothek Preussicher Kulturbesitz, Musikabteilung. See discussion pp. 71 ff. and note to p. 73.

Conducting Beethoven

VOLUME I
The Symphonies

◄►

NORMAN DEL MAR

CLARENDON PRESS · OXFORD
1992

Oxford University Press, Walton Street, Oxford OX2 6DP
Oxford New York Toronto
Delhi Bombay Calcutta Madras Karachi
Petaling Jaya Singapore Hong Kong Tokyo
Nairobi Dar es Salaam Cape Town
Melbourne Auckland
and associated companies in
Berlin Ibadan

Oxford is a trade mark of Oxford University Press

Published in the United States
by Oxford University Press, New York

© Norman Del Mar 1992
The rights of Norman Del Mar to be identified as author of this work have
been asserted in accordance with the Copyright Designs and Patents Act 1988.

All rights reserved. No part of this publication may be reproduced,
stored in a retrieval system, or transmitted, in any form or by any means,
electronic, mechanical, photocopying, recording, or otherwise, without
the prior permission of Oxford University Press

This book is sold subject to the condition that it shall not, by way
of trade or otherwise, be lent, re-sold, hired out or otherwise circulated
without the publisher's prior consent in any form of binding or cover
other than that in which it is published and without a similar condition
including this condition being imposed on the subsequent purchaser

British Library Cataloguing in Publication Data
data available

Library of Congress Cataloging in Publication Data
Conducting Beethoven / Norman Del Mar.
Includes index.
1. Conducting. 2. Beethoven, Ludwig van, 1770–1827.
3. Beethoven, Ludwig van, 1770–1827. Symphonies. I. Title.
MT85.D336 1992
[v. 1. The symphonies.]
784.2′ 184145—dc20   91–29315
ISBN 0–19–816218–9.
ISBN 0–19–816219–7 (pbk.)

Typeset by BP Integraphics Ltd, Avon

Printed in Great Britain by
Biddles Ltd., Guildford and King's Lynn

For Jonathan with love
in the confident expectation that
he will disagree with most of it

Contents

◀▶

Apologia

◀▶

NOTHING might seem more presumptuous than to write a book detailing every thought, beat, and gesture in conducting the standard orchestral repertoire. Nor can such a book hope to have any universal validity; the art of interpretation must always by its very nature be a personal one, or it would immediately lose all freshness and turn into the merest mechanical imitation.

Nevertheless there has been a purpose in writing apart from the sheer enjoyment of doing so, which has been considerable—this being arguably a justification in itself: I believe I am not alone in devouring books and articles on subjects I already know a great deal about. It is immensely stimulating as much to agree as vehemently to quarrel with someone else on one's favourite hobby-horse.

If therefore I appear to be laying down the law in areas which are self-evidently a matter of opinion it is partly because nothing is worth stating unless one believes it implicitly and partly because it would be intolerable to read a treatise in which the author is endlessly sheltering behind defensive remarks such as 'in my view' or 'if I may be forgiven'.

It is also possible that my assertions may provide a starting-point for some budding conductor approaching one of these works for the first time. No doubt if he follows my precepts word for word he will produce my performance instead of his own. But if he is either prevented from making a blunder in front of the orchestra or inspired to consider a point which would otherwise not have occurred to him, he may have derived profit from seeing what I have to say.

One of the most important facets of conducting lies in mirroring in terms of real sound a visionary interpretation, the details of which already exist precisely in the mind. Indeed, the greatest problem of giving a première is that this idealized conception has to be rapidly built up during both study and rehearsals, without the advantage of previous experience, whether one's own or of earlier interpreters. In the case of standard repertoire, on the other hand, the reality of the music should pre-exist to such a point that the entire consciousness of the conductor is focused towards matching the live sound to the inescapable blueprint of 'how the music *goes*'.

But how this concept of an orchestral work's complete pre-existence is formed in an interpreter's mind remains widely controversial and even mysterious. It may be rooted in performances or, most suspect of all, in a recording heard and learnt in earlier years, even in childhood. The idiosyncrasies of such performances may have left indelible imprints upon a youthful artist's musical memory and imagination. However, should the conductor attempt to revive such fond memories of how a favourite work was first discovered, as often as not it will transpire that memory has played false after the lapse of years. Although many details will have retained their influence the nostalgic experience will reveal areas of disparity with the idealized memory, and hence the performance, of the young devotee turned mature interpreter. Such details of conception which have been retained come therefore as the result of instinctive artistic acceptance rather than blind imitation and need not be scorned or blushingly acknowledged in guilty acquiescence.

However, an additional consideration needs to be taken into account. Few conductors remain utterly true to a single interpretation over the whole span of a lengthy career. For one thing, taking the extreme, the passionate youth and the aged doyen may be the same person but are hardly the same artist; we change imperceptibly without realizing and our performances change with us. This is as it should be and the belief in the integrity of our vision is not invalidated thereby. No doubt if I had written this book twenty years ago, or if I were to write it twenty years hence, many of the views I express would be different. But at the moment I stand by them sincerely and with conviction, however much I concede the right of any other interpreter to dispute them to the hilt. And I would contend that in that very challenge may lie the value of the dispute—and hence of the book—to the conductor who takes issue with me.

It had been my original intention to compile a series of discussions of works from across the repertoire as I had occasion to conduct them and while they were thus fresh in my mind. But I was subsequently persuaded that it would be more satisfactory from the publication point of view to take the composers individually, to confine the first volume of essays to Beethoven, the second to Brahms, and so on—theoretically—until I drop. There is clearly some neatness in such volume-by-volume specialization although there would be no attempt to cover each composer's complete output, but rather to concentrate on the front line of the basic symphonic repertoire while at the same time avoiding any work I have not actually conducted in performance, however well I may know it.

I am beginning, accordingly, with Beethoven and of necessity the symphonies take pride of place. Volume Two will, I hope, follow in due course with the concertos, overtures, the *Missa Solemnis*, Leonora's Aria 'Abscheulicher' from *Fidelio*, and one or two other smaller but important repertoire pieces such as the violin Romances, before turning to further sets of volumes on Brahms, Tchaikovsky, Debussy, or whoever.

So then to the Beethoven symphonies, in respect of which I am by no means first in the field. Indeed, in discussing the problems of conducting the symphonies it would be a serious negligence, as well as a slur on the memory of a great Beethoven interpreter, not to take into account Felix Weingartner's classic handbook *On the Performance of Beethoven's Symphonies* published, admittedly some eighty years ago, by Breitkopf & Härtel, whose orchestral material remains to this day the standard edition of the scores and parts used throughout the world.

Eighty years is a very long time and inevitably views have altered considerably since Weingartner wrote, invalidating many of his opinions and seriously outdating one particular area of importance: his advocacy of Bülow's textual rewritings of Beethoven's instrumentation, especially in respect of the comparatively new chromatic horns and trumpets which had come to prevail by the turn of the century.

But much of Weingartner's artistry and wisdom transcends such anachronisms and needs to be placed once again on record, whether it is to be adopted or not—indeed however much it is now considered to be acceptable. Each and every present-day interpreter needs to make his own decisions in full knowledge of what were once considered to be judgements of artistic integrity by an accepted master during what was undoubtedly an era of great conductors.

One final word of pure practicality. I do not believe it possible to read the notes which follow without a score of the appropriate work alongside for constant reference and examination. My whole approach to any would-be reader has been on the assumption that he and I are examining our scores side by side and discussing the way in which the music is alive and existent within us.

In this respect, it seemed to me that the best way of directing the reader to any bars or places in the score was not by page references to the Breitkopf full scores, as Weingartner chose to do, but by bar numbers and occasionally rehearsal letters. There is obviously no foolproof method but virtually all modern editions of full or miniature scores have bar numbers and most full scores have the standard lettering. Where these differ and can cause confusion I have drawn attention to the variants and trust that the reader will take the trouble to co-relate his editions with mine.

N.R.D.M.

Hadley Common
December 1990

Symphony No. 1 *in* C *major,*
Op. 21

◄►

If the First Symphony is less often played than the later ones
this in no way implies any degree of inferiority or lack of mastery. Within its obviously lesser field of aspirations it is a wholly
successful closing item for a chamber orchestral concert as a
welcome alternative to a Haydn or Mozart symphony, or as
an admittedly rather substantial first item of a symphony concert
(like the Eighth, it is for example not infrequently used as the
curtain raiser, so to speak, before the 'Choral' Symphony).

I

Its first bars were once considered daring, and the striking wind
chords, punctuated by strong pizzicatos from the whole string
group, need to reflect that fact. Perhaps even today's audience
should be made to jump a little by the shock of the first chord.
There should be no real problem in getting good ensemble
between wind and strings by means of a clear quaver up-beat
in strict tempo.

The whole introduction is in principle beaten in 8 although
Beethoven's ♪ = 88 is too fast, like most of his metronome
marks; 72–6 is nearer to the breadth of pulse needed for the
cantando melodic line of the violins when bar 4 is reached,
although naturally this must be allowed to flow.

It is a good plan to beat out the quaver pulse during the held
wind chords of the opening bars, but not in the silences, strictly
measured as these must be. Moments of stillness in Beethoven,
of all composers, have a drama of their own which should be
maintained or even emphasized.

The lst violins' four-note arco chord in bar 4 is more significant than it appears at first glance, or in fact than it is sometimes taken to be. With its great spread, and it must on no account be played divisi, it is the clear precursor of the similar chord with an even more powerfully held top G near the beginning of the Fifth Symphony. Here it is only the dot that provides the link into the lyricism of the following bars, and the single quaver beat which this represents can all too easily be minimized. On the contrary, after the tutti has been taken off with the third beat the violins need to be addressed with a majestically sustaining gesture which forces the players to hold the note at a continued forte, perhaps even for slightly longer than the true value of that dot, before allowing it to melt into the warm singing piano with which they are joined by the 2nd violins at the lower octave, thus initiating the melodic effusion for which all that has happened so far is purest preparation.

In bars 5, 6, and 7 all the melodic strands should be encouraged to play with a truly cantabile quality, especially the violas (often neglected here) and the horns, whose descending phrase in bar 6 returns in diminution five bars later in one of the few solo phrases they enjoy in this early, rather careful, work of a master who was so soon to give the horns some of their most rewarding solos.

The tenuto marks in bars 8 and 10 will materially effect the style of the 8-in-a-bar beat. It would be an overstatement to suggest that a change could be made to crotchet beating; but the quaver pulse within each tenuto crotchet must cease to be perceptible, to be however consciously renewed in both bars 9 and 11, even though the latter in particular could seem to begin uneventfully. The horns' phrase, on the contrary, should continue a feeling of tempo marked in quavers even though the rhythmic pulse is suddenly only implicit, a subtlety which the style of the conductor's beating should indicate, leading to the strings' bridge passage which ends Beethoven's introduction.

This concluding bar 12 presents one of the few truly controversial points of this symphony, which concerns the strings' descending demisemiquavers. Since these might logically be held to correspond motivically with the similarly descending semiquavers of the succeeding Allegro (as in bar 18), a strong case

can be made for co-relating their speeds also, even if only approximately. Yet Weingartner advocates a reading in which the
demisemiquavers are played strictly, unvaryingly, in the tempo
of the Adagio molto, and there are certainly conductors who
still adhere to this view despite the very wide divergence in
speeds which this interpretation entails.

There is, moreover, a further factor to be taken into account.
Many European conductors believe in the dictum disseminated
particularly by pedagogues such as the late Hans Swarowsky.
At his well-known and greatly admired seminars for young conductors he dictated a formula whereby all tempi within a single
work were made to relate precisely. In the present instance,
for example, the tempo of the Allegro would correspond exactly
with that of the preceding Adagio molto with the new minim
equalling the old quaver. This highly questionable philosophy
disregards totally the fact that Beethoven's metronome marks
(whether one adheres to them strictly or not) make it plain
here that he intended the new minim to be considerably quicker
than the old quaver. However, Swarowsky's method would at
least retain some relationship between the demisemiquavers and
the semiquavers in question even though the one would be
exactly half the speed of the other.

One of the commonest alternative readings, favoured by
Weingartner, takes the bull by the horns and doubles the speed
of the demisemiquavers after a held double dotted crotchet, as
if Beethoven might have been writing in baroque notation. But
if the one reading is thought to be too pedantic, this other
is altogether too cavalier, and indeed a simple compromise is
ready to hand: the upper G dotted crotchet is sustained with
the stick together with the wind chord but without continuing
the quaver beat, almost in the manner of a fermata although
strictly for the correct duration, while the left hand then indicates the naturally falling figure which, starting correctly on
the 8th quaver beat of the bar, accelerates as it moves towards
the Allegro which emerges smoothly and logically, Beethoven's
$\downarrow$ = 112 actually conforming to the normally accepted tempo
for the movement.

The crescendo in bars 42–4 to the *ff* of bar 45 reads wrongly
since the whole orchestra has been *ff* already ever since bar
31. A sensible solution would be to drop to *f* at bar 41, the

violins at the beginning of the bar, the remainder at their re-entry after the crotchet rests.

There must be no change of pulse in going into the second subject at bar 52 but many conductors make a feature of later events such as the cadence in bar 68. The new forte material of bars 69–75 is then somewhat measured with a considerable pull back in bar 76. There is much to be said for this reading even if it could be thought a little over-romanticized. The section can sound ill-humoured instead of 'unbuttoned' (Beethoven's own favourite term) if played full tilt and the plunge into the quiet oasis of bars 77–84 will easily sound too abrupt. In any case the lyrical episode itself must surely be played at a more relaxed pace, with the grace-notes in the woodwind played short but on the beat, and a little affectionately. The gradual return to full tempo at the forte of bar 88 is made during the 3-bar crescendo of bars 85–7 (this all being repeated in the same way when the identical music is recapitulated in bars 221–41).

The *ff* of bar 94 (= 247) is a characteristic Beethovenian feature and needs to be both as sudden and as differentiated from the single *f* of the preceding bars as possible. It is a nice conceit for the conductor to be somewhat over-demonstrative in these anticipatory bars.

The repeat is by convention always taken, and rightly so; the 4-bar modulation back to C major for the return of the Allegro opening needs its logical fulfilment for the shock of the A major chord to take proper effect when in due course the second-time bars come round. Moreover the exposition is concise so that the mind and ear receive its restatement gladly. These corners are turned without variation of pulse, both when taking the repeat and when continuing with the development.

There is little doubt that the 1st violins should be *pp* in bar 131, in which case the flute should begin *pp* also. Perhaps a general diminuendo hairpin in bar 129 is the most practical answer. Unlike the subito fortes, which are a hallmark of Beethoven's style, subito pianos are less regularly so, and here there can be no betrayal of his intention in supplying the diminuendo.

The upper strings' *ff* in bars 134–5 need not be too ferocious, or the wind parts—especially the flute—will go for nought. More-

over, since the clarinets are just about to rest for no less than
25 bars it is worth featuring their entry as well. Beethoven is
still very conservative in his orchestral wind writing for clarinets, which is strange considering his adventurous use of both
clarinet and horn in the various chamber works of this period
such as the Septet.

Once again there should be no rubato of any kind when
approaching the recapitulation. Indeed the argument is so organized that the sense of arrival in bar 178–88 is immediately taken
over into a forward sweeping section so that it is only at the
sudden fall-back into the second subject that any feeling of relaxation is allowed at all. As a result there is, if anything, a suggestion
of animando during the chromatically rising chordal transition
section which is in sharp contrast to the fully secure tempo
of the exposition transition of bars 33 ff., a passage which Beethoven now short-circuits and which indeed never recurs throughout the movement.

The abrupt descent into the second subject in bars 204–5 contrasts strongly with the full close of the equivalent place in
the exposition (bars 51–2) and curiously lacks any diminuendo,
a little like the earlier instance of the kind in the development.
Here too the context does not at all suggest that Beethoven
intended one of his characteristic subito pianos, and a hairpin
down during the single bar 205 makes excellent sense, although
an argument might be maintained for keeping the intensity for
a further half-bar, the collapse being delayed until the descending
last four quavers.

There is no parallel in the exposition to those dissonant E♭'s
of the violas in bar 237. If they are right, and there seems no
justification for doubt, they may reasonably be brought out
a little with an anticipation of just the violas' crescendo and
a lean from the conductor in their direction.

The coda is played in strict tempo until the very last chord,
the final empty bar having no significance other than purely
structural. (A student did actually once commit the howler of
asking if one ought not to mark this silent bar with the stick.)
The 3-bar rest at the end of Schubert's Sixth Symphony is a
particularly amusing example of this kind of almost pedantic
accuracy of notation, which Beethoven is again careful to
observe at the end of the finale of this his first essay in symphonic

form. The delayed timpani entry in bar 289 is a dramatic stroke often overlooked and well worth featuring.

II

Sonata-form slow-movement repeats are more rarely observed than those of first movements or finales, even in Haydn and Mozart. The length both of the movement and of the work as a whole tends to become excessive, and in the present instance the remarkable *pp* fugato opening 15 bars lend themselves less effectively to restatement and there are no interesting first and second-time bars to add purpose to the practice—merely the simplest double-bar repeat sign. Beethoven himself seems to have been aware of the problem of proportion for he never prescribed a repeat in the slow movement of any of the later symphonies.

Beethoven's metronome mark cannot this time be taken seriously at all. ♪ = 120 is much too fast and flippant for so amiable an 'Andante cantabile' even allowing for the 'con moto'; ♪ = 88 is nearer, giving a gentle but nicely flowing pace. Beethoven neglects to say how far the crescendo of bar 16 (= 117) should go, or to what dynamic level; a sensible reading would be for the peak to be reached in bar 19, the sforzandos then being taken in a warm prevailing dynamic of, say, *mp*. Most important, of course, is for the *f* in bar 25 (= 125) to be subito.

Until quite recently there was never any thought of a problem over the thorny matter of co-relating the triplets and dotted rhythms, the timpani automatically continuing the sharp figuration established without inhibitions by the strings during bars 42–8. It would be hard to imagine anything more dreary, and unlike the vital artist we know the young Beethoven to have been, than for those bars to be bowdlerized into a soft-grained triplet-ridden section. Yet no less an interpreter than the conductor Erich Leinsdorf castigates the accepted readings of this movement as 'anti-musical' in his book *The Composer's Advocate*,* even going so far as to insist on changing the 1st violins' semi-quaver C♯ in bar 44 (= F♯ in bar 144) to match the rhythm of the lower strings, as one might in a Bach Suite. Of course, where bars 53–60 (153–60) are concerned, the answer lies in not

*Yale University Press, New Haven, Conn., 1981.

striving too hard to demonstrate the differences. After all, the
timpani rhythm becomes an essential feature in both the development and the coda and if the player has so worked at placing
his demisemiquavers after the triplets of the violins they can
easily turn into units of six instead of four (♩. ♪ ♪ as against
♩. ♪), which is as wrong in the one direction as a lazy triplet
semiquaver is in the other. As a result the strings (and bassoon)
would be condemned into perpetuating too tight a rhythmic
figure which, especially in the graceful coda, would be quite
disagreeable. Handled sympathetically these apparent differences can on the contrary be minimized to the point where
the listener becomes unaware of any problem, as would certainly
have been the case in Beethoven's day.

The climax of the movement patently occurs in the central
portion of the coda, prepared by the long build-up which is
itself punctuated by another typical Beethoven touch, the *subito*
p after a crescendo. (Here this is unmistakable as it occurs after
a previous *p*, but other less obvious instances will occur when
the crescendo initiates from *pp*.) Bars 180–1 in particular need
very warm and generous treatment, so that in this instance the
p of the graceful final section must come without a diminuendo
preparation. The *p* in the closing bars can perhaps have just
the least slackening of pace, a mere extra separation after the
staccato quavers, and with no suggestion of fermata on the last
crotchet.

III

The title Menuetto pays, of course, no more than lip service
to the dance form, and this is already an out-and-out scherzo.
Both in tempo and character there is no more need to bear
in mind the idea of a true minuet than in any of Beethoven's
subsequent scherzos. ♩. = 108, as printed, is a good tempo in
which there is every possibility for the *élan* suggested by the
marking 'Allegro molto e vivace', but it is a good idea to relax
a little for the Trio (no slower than ♩. = 92, however) which
otherwise sounds reckless and precipitate to the point of insensitivity.

Unusually, it is necessary to tell an orchestra at once whether or not the very brief first section of the Menuetto itself is to be repeated also on the da capo, a fairly prevalent custom at one time—like the Scherzo of the String Quartet Op. 18 No. 1 —although it is less so today. (Another such instance is the Scherzo of the Bizet Symphony in C.) An 'authentic' school of thought has, however, recently initiated a campaign to the effect that all da capo repeats should be taken in eighteenth-century works unless the words 'senza repetizione' are present. Fortunately this has not yet become universal practice.

Beethoven's dynamic marks are less than explicit in bars 16 and 18, where parallel drops to *p* must surely be meant, as in bar 12, for the violins. The *f* and *ff* in bars 17 and 19 then become angry retorts exactly like the *f*'s in bars 11 and 15.

IV

An air of mock solemnity should characterize the mighty fermata which opens the finale. This is, of course, quite different in kind from the gravity, not-at-all mock, with which the similar tutti *ff* G's open the Overture *Leonora No. 3*. The weight and intensity of that portentous statement would be out of place here, although superficially the six-octave deep unison of this opening appears equally imposing. The fermata may, perhaps, be deliberately held a little too long—say, some seven quavers— and summoned as well as sustained in somewhat theatrical style; there is, after all, not the slightest doubt that Beethoven is having fun during the whole of this introduction.

The fermata is then taken off before starting the violins on their gradually unfolding scale. The pulse should not stop, how- ever, so that the take-off gesture can legitimately provide a 'prep- aration' in tempo which will secure confident ensemble. This too will not spoil the joke, but on the contrary implies a decep- tive complacency which can be accentuated by over-scrupulous observation of the rhythms, phrasings, and dynamics. The subito piano of bar 5, on the other hand, needs the briefest hiatus at the barline, and the pianissimo which follows cannot but be played *pppp* and poco essitando. The second fermata must then again be taken off, but this time with an actual stopping of pulse, as indicated by Beethoven's indication 𝄽𝄾 . A tiny flick of the wrist will then launch the violins into the Allegro molto without fuss or difficulty. Nor will there be any ensemble problem here either so long as the violins are not kept waiting for too long, the new down-beat being deftly and accurately slipped in at their fourth semiquaver. This whole passage is a standard test piece for conducting exams or competitions.

Once again there need be no quarrel with Beethoven's metronome mark for the Adagio; ♪ = 63 is a perfectly sensible tempo. But the ensuing ♩ = 88 is simply break-neck for the finale proper, a much more reasonable pace being ♩ = 144. This main part of the movement is naturally beaten in 2, although the additional instruction '. . . e vivace' must never be lost to sight. This should inspire a sense almost of precipitoso at both letters **A** and **B** (bars 30 and 54) which should carry all before it for the duration of the exposition.

In bars **86–94** the wind may profitably be instructed to drop their dynamics between sforzatos, since theoretically they are still *ff* (or *f*, horns and trumpets) and if they are allowed to sustain at this level there will be no possibility of the all-important 2nd violins being heard.

As later in the Fourth Symphony the finale repeat should be observed; the first-time bars work excellently well and the return gives the movement a valuable degree of length and substance before the driving force is interrupted by jocularity during the development.

The gaiety itself is most infectious during bars 131–7 and the strings should be encouraged to play as lightly as possible. Then in bar 138 the crescendo brings an abrupt change of attitude. The four bars before letter **C** do not, of course, continue the crescendo, the *ff* bursting in ferociously in one of Beethoven's favourite *coups de théâtre*.

The parallel of bars 160–1 with bars 204–5 of the first movement could be thought to be disturbing; if indeed one inserts a diminuendo in that instance perhaps an analogous hairpin should be given to the woodwind here. Yet the *p* entry of the second subject might prove a reasonable justification in the first movement which does not necessarily apply here as there is no overlap of dynamics. At all events, whatever decision is taken in the earlier instance the present abrupt drop to *p* is both splendidly effective and highly typical of Beethoven's manner.

The trick of holding a tutti *ff* chord after the timpani has completed its roll recurs throughout Beethoven's output until as late even as the Overture *Die Weihe des Hauses*. The examples here (bars 235 and 237) are possibly the earliest and are less danger-ous in execution than, for example, the one in the C minor Piano Concerto last movement. But even these require a very positive sustaining gesture from the conductor to prevent some less alert member of the tutti from coming off as the timpani rolls stop with the down-beat.

The second fermata is cleared with a continuity-style beat which also gives the 2nd violins their entry, the coda accordingly beginning directly without a gap. In this way the final climactic statement of the first subject leads straight out of the fermatas and into the little march, so reminiscent of Mozart's, such as the one which ends 'Non più andrai' from *Figaro*, and which Beethoven conjures up as a surprise element to round off this happy first of his nine great symphonies.

Symphony No. 2 in D major, Op. 36

◄►

THE Second Symphony has the reputation of being the least played in the whole gamut of Beethoven's nine. Indeed, when during the 1920s and 1930s the symphonies were gradually making their first complete appearances on gramophone records the Second was the very last to appear. Undoubtedly also, except perhaps for a chamber orchestra, it is the hardest to programme, being too expansive for an opening item, appreciably more so than the First Symphony and even more than the Fourth or Eighth, and yet not weighty enough to close a symphony concert in the sense that the other odd-number symphonies do so signally.

Needless to say this has nothing whatever to do with quality. The Second Symphony is one of the warmest and most carefree of Beethoven's creations, coming at the end of his first period yet marking a significant stylistic advance on its single predecessor. It might indeed seem strange, considering the wealth of piano composition and chamber music Beethoven already had behind him, that this was only his second major orchestral work. Had he been another Mozart or Haydn it could have been his twenty-second, not his second, symphony. It was as if he somehow had precognizance of the epoch-making influence he was to bring to bear on the symphony as a genre, a development of the form as important and certainly more grandiose than that of his teacher, Haydn, still justifiably credited with being the 'Father of the Symphony'.

I

From the mature Haydn, more so than from Mozart despite the latter's superb examples, Beethoven inherited the tradition of beginning with a substantial slow introduction. Yet already here he inflates it to the proportions almost of an independent movement in its own right, certainly beyond anything either of those his great forebears envisaged as proper to the form, and nearly three times the length of the one with which he had preluded his own first example. The very start, therefore, must at once suggest a scale quite different from that of the opening of the First Symphony, already—one might say—producing a sense of occasion.

This is one of a host of related works whose openings pose analogous problems for a conductor in determining or indicating the value of the up-beat. Amongst others, the overtures to Mozart's *Magic Flute* and Rossini's *Barber of Seville* are obvious examples. In the present instance, however, a clear preparatory beat in strict tempo ought to allow no doubt about the length of the demisemiquaver since it corresponds exactly with the up-beat note five bars later where it arises out of the woodwind descending pattern. Nevertheless the orchestra is helped if the down-beat is given a kind of bounce to suggest the placing of the little note.

It is best to take the fermata off before starting the oboes and bassoons in such a way that the clearance gesture can give these players a preparation in the tempo to come. The introduction is then naturally beaten in six throughout as suggested by Beethoven's metronome mark, but his ♪ = 84 is surely appreciably too fast for Adagio molto; ♪ = 72 would give ample flow in view of the style of the first few bars as well as taking greater account of the quick-moving phrases to come; the 64th notes in particular will require melodic reality rather than being allowed to deteriorate into mere passage-work.

The notation of the violins in bar 7 has been known to cause controversy. The following approximates nearly enough to the widely accepted method of execution:

Ex. 1

Admittedly this shortens the F♯ and A slightly but if these notes are played strictly the effect is uncomfortable and pedantic.

In bar 11 the lower strings' quaver just before the *ff* might legitimately be marked *mf* bearing in mind the crescendo on the woodwind in this bar. The *ff* preparation to the new semi-quaver throbbing must be approached in absolutely strict tempo, the semiquavers themselves being taken firmly on the string until they turn into triplets in bar 17 when they can come half-off though still without being too short. The general dynamic level between bars 12 and 21 is certainly piano despite the greater restlessness of the second period (bars 17–21); there is thus no difference between the degree of piano in bars 12 and 17 after their respective crescendo approaches. But the sforzandos are nevertheless always strong and those of the horns (and oboes in their one answer of bar 18) especially so. In fact the horn dissonance in bar 22 can be quite startling and must be confidently played if it is not to sound as if the player has accidentally split the note.

In bars 25–8 the strings' triplets are now marked with dots and can be taken fully off the string in a gentle spiccato while the contrasting melodic passages can acquire a degree of warmth in the tone.

Care needs to be taken over ensemble in the violins' repeated D quavers at the first bars of the Allegro since these too are taken off the string and there is no direct relationship with the preceding tempo, as Beethoven's own metronome marks make clear. This Allegro, being much more brilliantly vivacious than the corresponding movement of the First Symphony, will be, unusually, even a shade faster than the printed mark of ♩ = 100, bearing in mind not only its splendid *élan* but also its generous proportions for a work of Beethoven's first period. This is a point which can obviously be emphasized if the repeat is taken, which is desirable if the length of programme will allow, as for example if the symphony stands alone in the second half.

There can be considerable urgency in the beat which will send the semiquavers in bar 37 scurrying, and moreover there can be no relaxation of tempo either at the second subject (bar 73) nor leading into it. (There seems to be a general *sf* missing in bar 70—cf. bar 242.)

At bar 93 the question may arise whether the lower strings' first A should not read A♯ by analogy with bar 265. If the players raise the issue there can hardly be any harm in making the correction but otherwise the error (presumably the composer's own) is barely perceptible.

In the following bar the *sf* semibreve in oboes and clarinets needs to be as strong as possible, supplying as it does a missing note on horns and trumpets. At the same time the entry of brass and timpani is rendered the stronger by the quasi-hiatus. (There is a striking parallel example of this in the finale of the Seventh Symphony.)

The drama is again heightened at bar 102 with changes in beat style so that the down-beat is primarily a cut-off gesture to be followed by the smallest syncopated up-beat for the strings' re-entry. The point towards which the music is progressing is the *ff* (subito) of bar 126, the six bars just preceding this whirlwind of a climax being uniformly piano with mere sharp jabs for the sforzandos, as in so many similar places in Beethoven, such as the 'Eroica' Symphony and the Overture *Leonora No. 3*.

A small problem of balance could arise in bars 153–7 if the passage is insensitively conducted. All the *sf* semibreves must be indicated with strong drops in volume while encouraging the woodwind who may otherwise become inaudible. Weingartner recommended a wholesale series of revisions including the interpolation of doubling clarinets, so remarkably omitted by Beethoven over the entire period (until indeed bar 170), but this changes the quality of sound in a way no longer considered acceptable. Then at bar 168 Beethoven's typical burst of tone becomes electric, to be followed by the horn fanfares of bars 166–9 which can be brought out with some challenging gesture.

It is important to make it clear that at letter E (bar 182) we are still within the orbit of the development, whose second section it is which is starting here. The empty beat is patently a point of repose and will be conducted as such, but without any suggestion of finality or sense of arrival. In this way it becomes perfectly natural when, after the brief regular statement of the second subject, the development takes off once again.

The alternating phrases of strings and woodwind are often played too perfunctorily. The last note of each group is not marked with the dot and the down-beats should therefore indicate the gently placed endings.

Bar 197 is yet another of Beethoven's abrupt fortissimos lead-ing to an equally abrupt collapse to piano (bar 212) after the 2nd violins' whirlwind passage which makes a splendid effect if dramatically featured with the beat. The return at letter F (bar 216) again needs absolutely no yielding of pulse.

It might seem strange that unlike bars 107–8 the flute in 279–80 remains at the lower octave. That something is thereby lost is undeniable but Beethoven's purpose must lie in the plunge of the 1st violins to the low G♯ in bar 281. As a result a new point is made when the flute is suddenly an octave higher for the ascending arpeggio in bar 282 which, reinforced by the horns, must have been intended to be the outstanding event.

The long coda grows naturally out of the closing bars of the reprise and carries the music powerfully forward to the climactic cadence of bars 336–40. After the violence of the *ff* interjections of bars 324 and 326 the score merely prescribes a continuing *ff* over the following fourteen bars and it might not seem too cavalier to suggest sacrificing a little of the intensity in the upper strings' quasi-tremolo to allow for a series of steadily rising dyna-mic markings at, say, bars 330, 332, and 335 with a general mark of *fff* at 336. The more gradual crescendo will also enable the chromatically ascending cello/bass-line to be given extra signifi-cance with strong accentuation, while other typically Beethove-nian touches can also be brought into prominence, such as the upward leaps in the violas in bar 326 (cf. the *Gewitter* movement in the 'Pastoral' Symphony) and that of the 2nd trumpet in bar 335.

A considerable air of triumph will then crown the movement as it careers headlong towards its close, the top C of the 1st horn (a high enough note even though it is only for horn in D) adding to the exultation. It is apparent that the single *f* at bar 350 is Beethoven's shorthand for *rf* and in no wise suggests a reduction in volume.

II

To have taken the first movement repeat certainly gives extra justification for the extended panoply with which it ends. But in addition it makes for better relative proportions with the slow movement, which can sometimes seem too expansive. This, however, may also be the consequence of undue indulgence in its pacing, the word 'Larghetto' being easily misinterpreted. It is an exceedingly rare term for Beethoven to have used, and applies more to the timbre and beauty of the opening, as suave and gracious a melody as Beethoven ever wrote, than to the grazioso character of the many subsidiary themes which follow (the English word 'gracious' being here deliberately contrasted with the Italian 'grazioso' which has an altogether lighter and more elegant connotation).

Nevertheless, even if the movement is consciously kept flowing—which at certain points along the way may be more easily said than done—Beethoven's ♪ = 96 will still prove too hurried for the warm geniality which is the Larghetto's prime quality; perhaps ♪ = 84 gives an acceptable compromise which will at the same time allow bars such as 15–16 to dance. Variations of style in the conductor's beat will be of inestimable value in keeping the movement buoyant, even dramatic moments such as the *ff* bar 46 needing a springy pulse if the second subject is not to emerge from it slightly more leaden-footed, an element which spells disaster to the sequential build-ups of bars 56–9 (and 62–5). The staccato semiquavers must here be taken off the string (which is by no means always done) unlike the repeated accompaniment notes of bars 32–40.

Bars 89–90, and their return in bars 254–6, continue to provide the chief hurdle of the movement with their surprisingly high horn writing (the later passage being for horns in A, so that the top notes are again top B's). A wonderfully imaginative piece of scoring, these high passages remain a considerable *bête noire* for horn players even in these days of wide-bore, or high-crooked instruments, whilst the legend remains green in older musicians' memories of Sir Thomas Beecham during a recording session spoiling a perfect take—after many unsuccessful attempts by his normally excellent hornists—by spontaneously murmuring 'Thank you, gentlemen' before the red light had gone off.

There should be not the least slackening of tempo as the lead into the development is effected. The start of this long section, although at first in the minor, is not hushed or mysterious, an atmosphere which should be kept in reserve for the build-ups of bars 108–14 and 118–25. In fact the dynamic marks at bars

100–7 are to a large extent incorrect. Nowhere in this first period should any instrument play less than *p*, while all crescendos drop back to piano within the space of a single bar, this being equally true of bar 105, although not so marked in the standard editions.

Bar 140, innocent as it appears on the printed page is an unexpected pitfall to the 2nd violins of most orchestras; the whole-tone jump to B♮ usually takes somebody by surprise and is indeed apt to sound strange unless played impeccably.

It seems likely that this is the first instance in orchestral music of horns changing crooks during the course of a single movement. Beethoven uses this innovation to dramatic effect when after a silence of no less than 32 bars to enable the change to be made, the horns—now in their high A crook—re-enter *ff* in bar 150. Hence these instruments should be highlighted and not only at their reappearance but also in their cadential figure of bars 156–8 which soars so beautifully in making the return to the reprise.

Rather curiously, perhaps, Beethoven also rests the clarinets for even longer during virtually the whole of the development, a matter of some 48 bars, even though they do not change instruments. His purpose in so doing is far from clear, but certainly attention should also be directed to their re-entry, two bars later than that of the horns.

The short coda can be very simply played in unvarying tempo to the very last note, even the 1st violins' two-octave descending scale in bars 260–1 being kept in a single position to avoid any sentimental shifts which would here disfigure a particular moment of beauty.

III

The Scherzo, bright and jovial as it should be, does not warrant too hasty a treatment, and ♩. = 92 works better than the printed ♩. = 100, the interchange between the violins and horns especially needing poise and clarity. With respect to finesse in dynamics it may be remarked that the *pp* in bar 33 must be subito, whereas in bars 51 and 52 the 1st and 2nd violins' entries may be given extra point—even marked up to *mp*—both to indicate the bar period and to give good measure to the decrescendo which follows.

There is much to be gained in starting the Trio appreciably more steadily—even as much as ♩. = 72—as this will point the contrast of the little woodwind tune as well as introducing a moment of gracefulness. The tempo is, however, only to be held back in this way for the repeated eight bars of the first section, after which the original Scherzo tempo should be resumed for the stormy passage which follows.

Here the violins play sul G and can with advantage start up-bow so as to bring out—with a down-bow at the heel—the furious *sf* at bar 94. One might also introduce a ‐‐ ‐‐ for the cellos and basses to emphasize their independent octave rise and fall in bars 101-3, a detail rarely audible and thus tending to remain a kind of private joke between conductor and players. The real leg-pull for the audience, à la Haydn, is of course bar 107 which can never be made startling enough.

It goes without saying that with the return of the Trio's little oboe tune in bar 109 there should be no attempt to reintroduce the slower tempo of its first statement, and the movement must end boisterously.

IV

There should be tremendous impetuosity too about the opening of the finale, the beat for which needs to be given with considerable flourish, a style which must contrast however with careful control for the 1st violins' after-phrase. No slowing up can be allowed for the melodic transition material at bar 26, a motif which strikingly anticipates the finale of Mahler's Fifth Symphony, much as the Trio of the preceding movement may be said to be the progenitor of the second Scherzo of Brahms's Serenade in D, Op. 11. Beethoven's numerous influences on his successors are extraordinarily wide and varied.

The essence of this finale, for which Beethoven's own ♩ = 152 is a very acceptable tempo, is in its abrupt accents and violent sudden *ff*'s sparked off by the conductor in his manner of direction. To make an extra point of this he should reduce his style to the smallest beat possible consistent with clarity for such hushed moments as bars 98–107 (= 282–93) and especially, of course, 336–71 in the coda which is again Haydnesque in its determination to make the audience jump out of their seats after so long a passage during which they should need to strain their ears to hear anything at all.

The 2nd violins' splendid upward rush in bars 390–1 (a device which Brahms again borrowed in the first movement coda of his Third Symphony—where it is, however, dramatic rather than jocular as here) may be hard to bring out unless classical seating is adopted, with the 1st and 2nd violins to the conductor's left and right respectively. This symphony benefits to a large extent from this formation, should occasion allow for it, bars 44–7 being an obvious additional example where the conductor's gesturing from one side to the other all adds to the fun of Beethoven's 'unbuttoned' mood.

If sudden fortissimos, such as bar 94, are to make their proper effect the preceding ten bars of forte with their attendant sforzatos can afford to be a little under-stressed by the conductor's manner of direction. The same naturally applies to bar 161, although here the preceding crescendo is itself very exciting with its typical touches such as the upward leaps of the violas in bars 151 and 153 and of the cellos and basses in bar 157.

In bars 165–7, and again 171–6, an extra effect can be produced by arranging for the horns and trumpets to drop in tone in each semibreve after the initial *ff*'s or sforzandos until bar 177 when for the first time a true fortissimo is maintained for four bars. Beethoven's renewed mark of *ff* is clear indication of his meaning and he has not yet come to use *fff* as he will when he reaches the Seventh and Eighth Symphonies.

Bars 282 ff. will be seen to be a little shorter than the parallel passage when it first appeared (bars 98 ff.), and can need extra care with the entry of the 2nd violins, who this time do not participate in the downward flips and are thus less well prepared for their upward staccato arpeggio. That first time also gave the 1st violins a crescendo which must be ostentatiously absent on this return. The pianissimos can be the merest whisper so that the last boisterous return of the rondo theme followed by its string of emphases will sound positively riotous.

The pauses are all quite long: bars 334–5 will need three bows from the strings, which will allow the piano fermata to be taken on a single up-bow. The *ff* fermata at bar 415 is perhaps not quite so long, but two bows will still be necessary.

Bar 432 is another palpable *fff subito* and the symphony ends in the highest possible spirits. No one could possibly guess that this happy work was written by Beethoven in the recent knowledge of his impending deafness and so soon after drafting the despairing letter to his brothers, the famous Heiligenstadt testament.

Symphony No. 3 in E flat,
Op. 53 ('Eroica')

◀▶

THIS symphony always carries with it the realization of its enormous significance. Not only is it at least half as long again as any prior symphonic structure but the intensity of its message was something totally foreign to its first hearers. Perhaps it is worth bearing in mind that at every performance there is someone in the audience who has never heard it before and for whom it should create an overwhelming impact.

Yet for so vast a canvas its orchestral resources are surprisingly modest, calling as it does for no more than one extra horn in excess of the forces required for its two predecessors. Indeed in modern halls with dry acoustics which fail to provide the warm, glowing resonance so necessary to encourage orchestral players to give of their best, it can be hard for the conductor to invest the sonority of the symphony with sufficient stature and power to satisfy the demands of such music. Many conductors of international repute, maybe partly for this very reason, aim to solve the problem, as well as adding prestige to their performances, by playing with fourfold woodwind and correspondingly doubled horns and trumpets. Weingartner, writing in 1907, already advocated doubling the woodwind in selected passages to compensate for the effect of the enlarged string sections of the post-romantic symphony orchestra. This, however, is a wider argument which will be of greater relevance when discussing the Ninth Symphony. Moreover, strange to say, this expedient merely dulls the clarity of the texture, however much it may increase the sheer volume, and obscures the boldness of Beethoven's addition of that extra horn, three horns being not only an unusual combination in itself, but handled by Beethoven with fascinating imagination throughout the work. It can even be unfortunate, therefore, that the effect is generally negated in its visual aspect by the presence of a bumper horn, thus presenting to the audience the present-day commonplace appearance of a four-horn section.

I

For so unprecedented an architectural span as the first movement already presents, it might have been expected that Beethoven would have provided yet a further enlargement of the introduction over and above that of the Second Symphony, itself a considerable advance upon the one which opens the First. Yet it was not until the Seventh Symphony that he took this step; the Fourth certainly has an introduction but it is relatively short, unusual and daringly experimental, and neither the Fifth nor Sixth symphonies can boast a single bar, both plunging directly into statements of the principal motif. The 'Eroica' also begins with the main theme, though preceded by two hammer-blows of the tonic chord; hence while Beethoven was eminently correct in considering the movement to be already so substantial as to need no introductory section, he nevertheless put in its place what one might describe as a preparation, balanced by two similarly enunciated E♭ chords of conclusion at the extreme other end of the movement.

With hindsight we today can recognize mighty spaced out chords as a prominent feature of Beethoven's style over the entire range of his works from *Prometheus* to the Overture *Die Weihe des Hauses*. But when the 'Eroica' was first heard, to start a symphony in this way must have been simply riveting, and these opening chords should be no less arresting in a present-day performance. To imagine how the symphony would sound without them one has only to turn to Mozart's early overture *Bastien und Bastienne* which amusingly anticipates Beethoven's use of an identical melodic formula.

If, then, these chords are to be imbued with such significance they will need not only great weight but perhaps a slightly wider spacing than would be dictated by the establishing of tempo in what is to follow. Thus the conductor's preparatory beats will be primarily concerned with meaningful sound quality, and will not suggest pulse either of crotchet or dotted minim (a factor which will inevitably affect the issue of ensemble for the 2nd violins and violas at bar 3).

Where the tempo itself is concerned, Beethoven's metronome mark of ♩. = 60 is so extreme that it could hardly be accomplished other than by beating 1-in-a-bar. In recent years this has actually been attempted, but the argument that protests the belittlement of both message and structure by such a method is a persuasive one, especially in view of Beethoven's constant use of powerfully cumulative sforzandos on the second and third crotchets which cannot be adequately conveyed as mere syncopations. Even the pulsating quavers in the third bar already mentioned need the guidance of a crotchet beat, however fluid. But at a tempo corresponding with Beethoven's ♩. = 60 such beats would be feverishly precipitate.

This is not to say, on the other hand, that a relentless heavy-footed three in a bar is the desired alternative. However much the crotchet must remain the basic unit there should always be a fluidity in the conductor's style to allow for the urgency and drive which are paramount in the structure. A sensible gait might be ♩ = 144 at which tempo the music will unfold naturally and which allows the orchestra to express both the strength and poetry of their lines, being neither rushed off their feet nor given leeway for undue sentimentality. Nevertheless there will also be places in which a suggestion of dotted-minim units can be beneficially used to lift the music off the ground, just as there are others where a relaxation into a true 3-in-a-bar will provide for a contrast of lyricism. It is in such flexibility that the art of interpretation will always reside; Brahms was ever at pains to emphasize this, even going so far as to insist that every theme within a single movement must be allowed to generate its own natural sense of pulse.

The succession of no less than twelve sforzandos during bars 25–34 suggests an overall increase of dynamic level; yet it is clear from Beethoven's markings in bars 23 and 27 that this whole passage remains in a general context of piano. Similar instances abound in Beethoven (Symphony No. 2, Overture *Leonora No. 3*, etc.) especially when they precede a *ff subito*. Here too there must be no premature anticipation of the mighty crescendo of bars 33 and 34 which heralds the first fortissimo of the work, and yet to underplay all those *sf*'s, like true sforzan-

dos in piano, is to mistake quite seriously the character in this
composer above all. A scrupulous marking of the passage in
line both with the stern literal-mindedness of today's orchestral
player and with Beethoven's patent intentions could be a series
of *fsfp*'s, in which case bar 35 will automatically begin piano
and thus prepare for the greatest possible surge of tone that
so brief a crescendo will allow.

The transition material at letter A (bar 45) is the first period
which can profitably be felt—though not beaten—in a dotted
minim pulse. If the tempo has degenerated too far to allow
for this, the conductor's approach has already become too heavy-
handed; bars 55–6, on the other hand, must be played with the
utmost emphasis on every fortissimo note.

Beethoven provided two overt points of formal demarcation;
the first is here at bar 57, the second the obvious one of letter
C (bar 83). It is the very stuff of which musicological discussion
is made to determine at what point the true second subject
enters. For long it was considered that it must clearly be the
contrasted section of bars 83–98, and the very fact of the difficulty
Beethoven experienced in formulating this passage is an indication of the importance it held for him. He seems even to have
completed the movement while leaving blank bars both here
and at the corresponding return in the recapitulation, which
explains why this section plays no part in either the development
or in the extraordinarily extended coda, for both of which he
found it necessary to invent an entirely new theme in its stead
(bars 288 ff.). In the event much of the continuity and forward
thrust of the music which grows out of the transition is directed
unequivocally towards letter C, giving the listener the instinctive
feeling that only here have we arrived at the outstanding corner
stone of the exposition. On the other hand there is undoubted
truth in the argument that it is the change of tonality which
is the determining factor in establishing where the second group
begins. On this basis it is bar 57 with its presentation of more
new material which deserves the place of honour, and in this
respect one needs to have taken note of Beethoven's choice
of this amongst his multiplicity of themes to occupy a place
of strategic importance at letter W (bar 677) just before the
very end of the movement. It must be initiated here therefore
in a manner which recognizes it as no mere passing episode

while the passage which follows it needs to be delivered with an almost savage intensity.

Bars 83–99 (and their return at 490*) provide the first major relaxation from the huge sweep of thematic evolution, amounting in fact to a kind of spiritual oasis. It is accordingly in no way damaging to the structural logic to relax the pace quite abruptly to perhaps ♩ = 126–120, allowing for fluctuations of phrasing.

Nevertheless, great care must be taken to prevent this period of calm from becoming self-indulgent. For example, after the natural tenutos demanded by the expressive sforzandos (bars 85, 89, 94) the tempo can be consciously picked up, especially by the basses when they provide the link to what follows. As a result the danger can be minimized of having allowed too great a rit. to have distorted bars 95–8 and hence the resumption of surging ahead in bars 99–109 will follow naturally, without giving the impression of a rescue operation.

The peculiar octave C's in the bassoons may have been an oversight on Beethoven's part resulting from a page-turn in the autograph. As they stand they appear to have no purpose and they could well be excised. But there is a contrary inconsistency if the passage is compared with the return, where there are indeed no octave F's in the bassoons at bar 504, but neither do the cellos and basses complete their phrase. This too can perhaps be brought legitimately into line by analogy.

In bars 109–12 the violas respond with *élan* to a conductor who shows his realization of their interestingly independent line; in the following four bars it is the flutes, clarinets, and 1st bassoon who struggle to make their *Hauptstimme* penetrate the texture. But whereas there is little one can profitably do for the violas other than encourage them to greater effort with a rueful smile, at bars 113–16 the 1st violins, horns and trumpets can reasonably be dropped to a 'poco *f*' (not piano as is sometimes heard, with very artificial effect), in which case an eleventh hour crescendo on the violins in bar 116 can be very exciting.

The period of the sledge-hammer blows is an obvious area

---

*The Breitkopf bar-count, followed here, continues through both first and second-time bars, unlike the first two symphonies. It is therefore four bars ahead of the numbering in, for example, the Eulenburg and Philharmonia miniature scores, from the development onwards (i.e. bar 156).

of danger for the conductor to become more demonstrative than would profit any orchestra. Nor would exaggerated histrionics be right for the meaning of the music; it is cold, concentrated fury which has to communicated, and this requires the utmost self-control. Naturally only the chords themselves are actually indicated, the silent beats being mere preparations. At the same time, there is no harm in placing the chords correctly (i.e. as 2; 1; 3, etc.) both as a precaution against accident and for one's own personal security—which can always be at risk if the blows are delivered as a succession of identical vertical beats.

After the last of these chords there can with advantage in most halls be a slight *Luftpause* to allow for some overhang of the tutti sound before the entry of the violas and cellos (or horns in bar 539). This is important not merely on practical grounds but because of the total change of mood, even the sforzandos now being expressive in character, a transformation which needs to be reflected in the style of the beat.

Some spacing is inevitable in so emphatically conclusive a bar as 147—three down-bows certainly—with a conspicuous restoration of tempo thereafter.

One of the major issues of the movement in the present climate of opinion is that of the repeat: until recently it was very rare to hear it observed. Amongst older generations of conductors Mengelberg stood alone in both playing and recording it. The exposition is on so large a scale that Beethoven himself specifically expressed the thought that it would be detrimental to subject the listener to so substantial a restatement. He is, however, believed by some authorities to have changed his mind, and a reprint of the Eulenburg miniature cites a letter from the composer's brother claiming that this rethinking was occasioned by numerous subsequent performances with the repeat restored. Certainly I recall with thoughtful respect the words of the Swiss conductor Erich Schmid, who told me how his orchestra in Zurich applauded, much to his delighted surprise, on his announcing that he would be observing the repeat.

However, the very fact that Beethoven himself was able to entertain both readings can arguably give each interpreter the right to freedom of choice, in the making of which he will have to weigh up a number of different considerations. One of these is certainly the length of the exposition, already discussed, although its relationship to the huge span of the whole movement needs also to be taken into account in balancing the proportions of the unusually extended development and coda, in which the exposition—the *Hauptsatz*, as the Germans describe it—could well require to be allowed its full weight.

Yet there is another element which so often tips the scales where this particular decision is concerned, that is to say the quality or interest of the first-time bars. Moreover the dramatic nature of the return itself may alter the character and significance of the opening bars of the work, as in the Fifth and Eighth symphonies. In this respect the first-time bars of the 'Eroica' are curiously conventional, even perfunctory, which in an otherwise so extraordinary movement may reasonably be thought to tip the scales in favour of their omission.

However, if the first-time bars are disappointing, those which lead on into the development are certainly not, being extremely atmospheric, leading the listener into realms of deep mystery and bewilderment from which it needs lightness of touch in bars 164–8 to provide the rescue. A slight rubato can then be made in bar 169 in order that the sforzando may give an expressive confirmation of the move to the new tonality of G major in which the development section now properly begins.

With bar 170 full tempo is now re-established with the appearance of the transition theme to which the new imitative sforzandos scattered amongst the strings and woodwind alternately lend a restlessness which will ultimately boil over. (Doubt is sometimes cast on the oboe's first B♮ in bar 179 but it is well authenticated as well as more satisfactory than the somewhat obvious change to A♮ by analogy with the surrounding entries.)

Meantime, however, two sudden drops in dynamic herald the first major episode (there can be no argument but that the *p* in bar 186 must be a piano subito, and that the omission in the oboe is the merest oversight).

Bars 190 ff. provide one of the most clear-cut examples of antiphony between 1st and 2nd violins, calling for the old classical seating of the strings with these sections placed on either side of the platform. This is rarely followed today and can only be insisted upon with the full co-operation of the leader of the 2nd violins since it introduces problems resulting in frayed tempers if either the section is unaccustomed to this seating or if it is markedly less beneficial to the surrounding repertoire. In any case for a satisfactory realization of the passage there is much positive gain if the conductor marks the parts with relevant alternations between *f* and *ff* as well as addressing the sections in turn to exact the maximum sharpness of attack from the descending figurations. At the return of the passage, however (bars 202 ff.) the conductor has other matters to attend to; nor is it any longer necessary to continue whipping up players who know exactly how much fervour is still required. It is rather the new sforzandos for the lower strings in bars 202, 204, and 206 which need attention. It is somehow particularly difficult to make these accents truly register as they should, and performances are rare indeed in which they can be heard at all.

The three-horn triads in bars 218–21 will produce a splendid ring if the players are made aware of the soloistic character of their role. The strings then take over for the *ff subito* of bars 222–3. (Note, by the way, the leaps up after the first notes, a typical Beethoven touch already noted in the Second Symphony and much to be exploited in the Storm of the 'Pastoral'.)

The gentler return of the transition passage, now a third lower in E♭, is emphasized by Beethoven's use of the clarinet to lead the sentences. Moreover, the cellos' *sf* lead (corresponding with bar 179) comes oddly a bar late, the soft-toned flute usurping their previous place of entry and thus often passing unnoticed, while the keenly attentive listener should be aware of a certain restlessness in the 3rd horn which leads to an outburst in bars 236–7. Although the rising phrase of the 1st horn derives from the imitative passage-work which has been in evidence since the beginning of the development, it here takes on a much stronger and more significant function. Thus both the 1st and 3rd horns must be brought out once again in a strongly soloistic manner with crescendos pointing towards their *sf*'s, the 3rd horn dramatically capping the top note of the 1st player.

Whether long or short, the recurring fugatos of Beethoven's output are always important. The 'Eroica' has many examples beginning with this in bars 240 ff. and whilst amongst the tersest of its kind it is also one of the most ferocious, and must be driven full tilt until with sharp leads for the rising woodwind phrases (the bassoons' is impossibly hard to bring out) the conductor turns vehemently to the lower strings whose violent descent carries the development into its terrifying central drama.

The purpose of such an unprecedented outburst must seem to lie in its huge architectural pile-up and not merely in the reiteration of sforzandos out of which it is constructed. A good solution in pursuit of this broader view is for each of the 6-bar periods to be thought of as characterized by a different orchestral colour. The initial phrase belongs to the trumpets (hitherto silent for 46 bars), the second to the woodwind—horns and trumpets being again notably absent, the third to the timpani whose re-entry, after a similar span to that of the trumpets, can be thunderous. The fourth phrase is at first dominated by the violins, the 2nds soon joining the 1sts, and indeed with the reassembling of nearly all the available forces the strings should now occupy the conductor's special attention. At the same time even the easily unobserved return of the clarinets can be turned into an event after their strange omission during the previous 16 bars, while bars 280–3 can surely be the turn of the 3rd horn, whose use and disuse are also of striking interest, and the reiteration of whose F's it is which precipitates the crisis of bar 284.

This is such a dramatic moment that the pounding strings need a stronger treatment than the printed *f* would suggest. A comparable passage with the identical problem occurs in the slow movement of Tchaikovsky's Fifth Symphony where the swinging pizzicato chords which succeed a breathless pause are marked as low as *mf*, and here, as there, it is more usual to play the chords with the utmost intensity. After a split second's freeze (no down-beat is given, of course) Beethoven's staccato crotchets are then forcefully evoked, the first six of which are all to be taken down-bow at the heel. This molto pesante will, of course, steady the pace to some extent, but with the resumption of normal bowing in bar 286 the tension is gradually relieved and tempo restored for the appearance of the new theme Beethoven was at pains to invent to fill the need created by his blockage in respect of bars 83 ff. (see above).

In keeping with the purpose of the new material, bars 288–341 represent a corresponding relaxation of intensity to the oases in the exposition and recapitulation, although in this section the tempo must be kept flowing, however much the unit of pulse is still essentially the crotchet; this is not graceful music, but expressive lyricism full of depth and beauty. Moreover, even the forthcoming central developing of the first subject must have a crotchet-dominated strength of purpose in its unison writing (the 3rd horn part is again soloistic in bars 320–6).

The modulation through G♭ major is a thoroughly Beethovenian purple patch requiring a new colour of tone quality, especially from the violins in bars 334–7. It is not only the style of beat, but something in the conductor's very facial expression which will coax the appropriate tenderness from the players. The music then withdraws to a hush for the development's final drama beginning with a meaningful glance towards the 1st bassoon.

The first important element to establish is the character of those stalking cellos and basses (every crotchet equally heavily pronounced in staccato) followed by exaggeratedly sharp sforzandos and immediate subito pianissimos (not *p*) especially in the violins. These drops can become gradually less extreme after the first three so that the crescendos can each start from a higher level. The interplay of woodwind and horns is fascinating as the tension once again builds up and can occupy the conductor to an increasing extent in the course of these 24 bars.

The fortissimo is, however, in no sense an arrival point, as is shown plainly by the violent cello/bass quavers of bar 369, and the wind's pillar-like dotted minims in the following passage cannot be allowed to check the momentum.

Here, at last, there does need to be a change in beat style, however much the pulse is consciously maintained, so that when the strings interrupt with their rising 3-note phrases these introduce stern reminders of the inner rhythmic element after bars in which this has been largely suppressed. The strings' phrases can thus be conducted with three equally wide beats in contrast to the statuesque held down-beats of the intervening bars, forte or piano alike. Then follow the four bars with a little more crotchet pulse to them, the second beat of each giving a syncopation jerk for the string quaver phrases, followed in turn by the bars with precise third beats for the pizzicatos.

The pairs of bars with their semiquaver tremolos, on the other hand, need no more than barely perceptible beats, the pulse being more thought than given, yet nevertheless in strict tempo throughout. Many violin groups find it convenient to take the pizzicatos in bars 385, 389, and 393—that is, those immediately adjacent to the *pp* tremolos—with the left hand, but if possible this should be discouraged as the more twangy sound is hard to avoid and can be ugly.

It is a nice idea to cue the notorious false entry of the 2nd horn with no more than a furtive glance in his direction whilst subduing the violins to an ever greater refinement of pianissimo to fulfil this, Beethoven's first use of *ppp*.

The horn itself should not be so soft as to sound tentative. With the inevitable hindsight of a twentieth-century background it is hard to understand the utter perplexity this admittedly daring stroke caused to even the greatest musical minds, not only of its own day but to such forward-thinking masters as Wagner himself who took the extreme step of changing the 2nd violins' A♭'s to G's in his performances of the work. Yet the concept of the $^6_4$ tonic chord being introduced in the form of the movement's *Naturthema* while the dominant seventh is still maintained is, after all, not so very extreme a dissonance, especially since it passes regularly enough into a general chord of B♭. Beethoven allowed himself still greater but similar clashes in the Piano Sonata 'Les Adieux', Op. 81, where the horn-like descending figures constantly slide to produce a succession of such dissonances.

The tutti *f* which interrupts the 2nd horn's quizzical interjection is often given too strongly. It is the succeeding *ff* in the next bar which is the real outburst heralding the return of the opening of the symphony for the recapitulation, and bar 400 should even come across slightly half-heartedly, as if momentarily thrown off-balance by the false entry. It is no wonder than Beethoven turned in perfect fury upon his acolyte Ries when that unfortunate accused the horn player of miscounting his bars.

In these days of chromatic brass instruments few audiences appreciate the care Beethoven took to allow his 1st horn time to change crook for the next solo and back again after it. The solo itself is the very essence of natural horn writing on the open notes of the F crook and pure joy to play in this way. Indeed much of the magic is lost if the valves are brought into use as they so often are these days, through the adoption of some other crook in the vain pursuit of absolute reliability.

Even the raising of the last G to Ab, dovetailing with the entry of the woodwind, can be most poetically effected on natural harmonics through skilful use of the hand in the bell to cover the otherwise sharp 13th partial.

Many 1st trumpet players automatically continue the melodic line at the upper octave in bars 446–8, and it is difficult to carp at such a measure in view of similar *Retusche* which are even more justifiable later. Amongst these may be cited the top Bb on the 1st flute in bar 520; composers as late as Schumann or Brahms (see the phrase near the end of the Andantino of the former's First Symphony) avoided the high Bb not because the note was unobtainable at the time but because its quality was shrill and its intonation unreliable. Today this is no longer necessarily so, and the distortion of the phrase becomes unwarrantable—'misguided piety' as Professor Tovey used to say.

The timpani outburst in bar 524 must on no account be overlooked and can be made riveting both by marking the group of semiquavers *fff* and by inciting the player with both eye and gesture. It should come over like a thunderclap.

Bars 555–60 at last reach utter calm, a moment which can be perceptibly savoured before it is to be rudely shattered. Yet it is not always recognized what a difference there should be between the nobility of the glowing Db major interruption of bars 561–2 and the paroxysm of anger with which the succeeding C major bars contradict the foreign tonality four bars later.

The entry of the 2nd violins then initiates the coda, a section of magnificently judged proportions, and it is this architectural aspect which is the conductor's chief concern in pacing its gigantic sweep of over a hundred bars to the culminating assertion of the principal subject and the great cadential apex of bars 675–6, followed in turn by the 'coda of the coda', as one might describe the last entry of the second subject proper.

There are, however, stepping stones on the way—both derived from the development—the first of which, especially invented as we have seen, is approached by some very delicate staccato work on the violins. If not interfered with (the conductor 'not getting in the way' as the players like to put it) this should present no problems, the tempo being maintained strictly, and once in motion will allow for the more important matter of shaping the conversation between the 2nd violins and solo oboe.

The violas too need featuring in bars 557–81 and there is much to be said for marking them up. Then in bars 581–4 the less movement the conductor makes the better apart from a single tiny flick of the wrist to help introduce the 2nd violins when they start their staccato.

A friendly glance to the 3rd horn pays dividends as he plays his version of the 'extra' theme on so many of what would have been stopped notes, a daring piece of writing for its day even though Beethoven covered his tracks by doubling the passage with the bassoon.

This stage of the coda then dwindles away to the lowest point before the last great upsurge. In these eight bars (599–606) it is the basses who need the smallest nods before each syncopated entry, lest for acoustic or other reasons they fail to synchronize perfectly with the staccato quavers of the violins which will usually be none too clearly audible across the platform.

Extremely softly as it should begin, there is more urgency in the striding section than there had been during its first appearance in the development, and it should now carry a feeling of suppressed excitement. The crescendo with its splendid interplay between the three horns is hardly more than anticipatory, so that the tempo will be urging forward marginally even as the corner is turned so lyrically by flute and violins into and through the great fourfold build-up of the principal subject. Here again it is the reiteration and cumulative experience of crotchet and quaver movement which brings about the fulfilment of Beethoven's towering structure.

Yet the fourth repetition of the theme—the trumpets' pealing statement—is still not the pinnacle, as Beethoven is keeping the mark of ff in reserve for the true apex of the whole movement in bars 675–6. As for the trumpets themselves, these present one of the relatively few places where there can be no purpose in preserving inviolate Beethoven's necessity to accommodate the limitations of his low-crooked instruments; for to reject the now long-established custom of allowing the trumpets to complete their culminating entries of the principal motif would be to give a woefully inadequate climax to this enormous movement.

Even now the end only comes after a surprise return of the second subject proper followed by bars in which heavy emphases on alternate beats lead to others in which the conductor must give the utmost weight to every beat of the bar. The two final chords will correspond as nearly as possible to those which opened the symphony.

II

The printed metronome mark of ♪ = 80 for the Marcia funebre is very nearly twice too fast for any interpretation which is to convey the epic quality of this music. There will naturally be variations of pulse during the many contrasted sections of the movement, but if the profoundly tragic opening and equally its return at the Minore of bar 105 are to be played with any realization of the music's sense of utter desolation it can hardly be taken faster than ♪ = 48. The proposition has been mooted that the movement represents a military ceremony and that Beethoven's metronome mark is thereby indicative of a slow crotchet pulse corresponding to the measured steps, two per bar, of a uniformed procession.

But whether or not one is able to embrace so unsympathetically martial a view of this deeply subjective music, it remains true that, at whatever tempo, allowance can be made for the normal ebb and flow of rubato in the melodic line which might weaken the inexorability of the funeral gait. It is a mass demonstration of sorrow which the movement is portraying, untinged by individual grief. There can be few works which portray this particular element of deep national mourning other than perhaps, the slow movement of Elgar's Second Symphony, composed as a tribute on the death of King Edward VII.

The basses' grace-notes in the opening bars present an immediate problem. According to Weingartner they should always come *on* the beat, to contrast with the corresponding little notes when printed as demisemiquavers. Weingartner even proposes that this differentiation be maintained in bars 106–7 where Beethoven, in the largely identical repeat of these bars, inexplicably writes demis instead of grace-notes. Yet this may cause one to reflect on whether Beethoven was much concerned about making any very marked difference between them, and so may on the contrary suggest that both must equally be taken before the beat. The grace-notes can then, if the movement is played at a true Adagio assai, come after, rather than together with, the up-beat demi of the violins' theme:

Ex. 2

Since the 1st violins, however, are at the opposite side of the platform, a certain duality of conducting technique will be essential, for while it is the shaping of the violins' phrasing which will continue to be the main preoccupation, at the same time the basses will need a special last second gesture each time, whether of eye or stick, if they are to fit in their up-beats correctly and together.

When in bar 8 the oboe takes up the melody it becomes at first hardly necessary for the conductor to do more than indicate the entries of the string triplet figures. Time beating is irrelevant, for the tempo continues unvarying and any good oboist will give more of his artistry if allowed a free rein. In bars 14–16, however, a little more guidance is advisable for the horn and clarinet entries as well as for ensemble during the decrescendo.

At bar 17, there should no longer be that quality of bleakness, but a new warmth in the string tone. The 1st violins' demisemiquavers require weight and need to be evoked with an intensity of hand and stick, just as the long notes in the next bar will require a sustaining style of beat, with a stiffening of muscles for the crescendo. Bar 20 is then characterized by a second beat cut-off followed by a peremptory double-gesture strongly maintained yet with no hint of a conventional fourth beat. Another sharp cut-off, with again no following beat until it is time to reintroduce the strings, should result in a horrified silence. The whole of this drama will have been enacted in a quite unusual rigidity of tempo, this of course including the silence during which the conductor remains totally motionless.

From bar 23 it is clearly the cellos who need featuring and who should play with great warmth even though it is only at bar 27 that Beethoven uses the word 'espressivo'; the violins in bars 25–6 play rather with what the Germans so movingly term *Innigkeit*.

Beethoven's sforzatos cannot be taken as rule of thumb any more than Mozart's *fp*'s. There will be instances in the Andante of the Fourth Symphony which equate with the examples here in bar 30, and again in bar 50, where they have been interpreted as different in kind from those in bars 58, 65, or 77, for example. In bar 30 in particular, the *sf* is to be treated as having duration as well as attack; that is to say, the piano in the following bar being subito after no more drop than, perhaps, to *mf*. This will include the 1st violins' demisemiquaver which, if bracketed in a single down-bow with the previous *sf* dotted semiquaver, will present no difficulty; bar 31 will then start up-bow at the point.

Bar 30 requires two weighty beats followed by none at all. A very soft re-entry indication on the fourth beat will then allow for a strong crescendo. The lower strings in the linking bar 36 should also be quite strongly directed. The winds' repeat of the subsidiary phrase can, if anything, be a little fuller still than the strings' first statement, warm as that was. A pinched sound on woodwind is not only disagreeable, but can often lead to one or other note failing to speak. The flutes' high entry in bar 45 suggests a full wind sound for its support, and the solo for 2nd oboe in bar 49 cannot afford to start too quietly if a confident decrescendo is to be given its full potential without the disaster which so often overtakes it.

The horns' *fp* in bar 41 is a shock and not always easy to control without sacrificing the strings' piano subito. It is best to concentrate the beat-style on the latter, but giving the horns an unmistakable sign that a strong accent is in no way out of place despite the drop in dynamic elsewhere.

Bars 56–9 are again to be played very tenderly and with the most beautiful tone the strings can supply. In bar 58 not all 2nd violin groups know of Beethoven's correction bringing the *sf* on to the second quaver and tying the accented G over to the third beat; they always much appreciate the change when it is pointed out to them.

The woodwind *f* is really a strong utterance in bar 60 and should be directed as such, giving the 2nd bassoon especial attention as he needs to use a very fat sound to support the weight of such a chord.

It is usual to accept that in principle subito pianos always require a hold-up of pulse, however slight. This cannot be allowed to apply to bar 67 which will otherwise interfere with the way Beethoven approaches the Maggiore. There should be no suggestion that with bar 68 an end has been reached and, owing to the preceding bar's staccato character, there is no difficulty in keeping strict time right through to the last note of the huge span, upon which the heavy cello/bass staccato quavers will then drive the music onward into the new section with resolute determination. Pesante as they are to be played, these quavers can even move imperceptibly forward, since the funereal leaden feet can now give way to a flowing tempo of not less than ♪ = 60; below this the triplets will become cumbersome, even ungainly.

Now the Maggiore does have more of a military air and the trumpets and drums come into their own especially, of course, in the concluding fanfare of bars 96 ff. But already in bar 78 the timpani roll can be thunderous and may be followed by a flamboyant gesture to the violins after what should have been quite a stern manner. For, during these climactic passages, the conductor's stance can emulate the erectness and self-discipline of a military commander. On the other hand, bars such as 82-3 and 86-7 show that Beethoven was enjoying himself in adding felicitous detail much as, a century later, Strauss amused himself when orchestrating *Der Rosenkavalier*, and hence a more civilian air of human good humour is not unbecoming.

The scene changes again quite abruptly with the *fp* in bar 101, and as the strings descend to the awesome *p subito* of bar 104 the tempo can imperceptibly broaden to arrive once again at the initial pace for the return of the Marcia funebre. This subito piano really can hold up the pulse, and to a marked degree, after the dramatic intensity of the previous crescendo. It can also legitimately be brought under the umbrella of Beethoven's sotto voce in the following bar.

The movement's opening is now restated but with a degree less stunned hesitancy than on its first occasion. Even the differences between bar 106 and bar 2 could be thought to support the idea that Beethoven wanted more feeling of continuity than at that grief-stricken outset of the tragic strains. Both the 2nd violins' and violas' longer harmony notes and the earlier re-entry of the cello/bass-line contribute to that sense of a new forward-thinking progressiveness, which is to be emphasized by the sudden upward thrust in the cellos and basses in bars 110–11, which can surely come forward out of the prevailing sotto voce.

Then, in momentarily relaxing the tension after the abrupt sforzato in bar 112, the tempo can be moved further forward through the striking entry of the solo bassoon towards the great fugato development. An entirely new style of direction is now needed as this strides ahead in a new and rhythmic ♪ = 69 which will be maintained inexorably without the least sensation of hurrying or broadening throughout its length.

In the build-up of power a series of vivid features need to be highlighted during its seven stages: the beat indicating the two half-bar stresses of the 1st violins should be given maximum edge (they are in fact the only sforzatos of their kind as the 2nd violins *sf* in bar 116 is an error); the countersubject on doubled woodwind should be made to grow in intensity as it passes from one group to another until it reaches the clarinets' version which will sound very penetrating; the horns' appearance, presaging that of the timpani, can be startlingly dramatic as it pinpoints the basses' long-delayed re-entry; the take-over of the countersubject on high violins and brass is then passionate (the delayed half-bar 2nd violin entry is an extra point of drama); the second formidable timpani roll of the movement needs to be electrifying and heralds the celebrated 3rd horn solo of bars 135–9, which should on no account be doubled, other than by the clarinets with which Beethoven supported it (a single first-class player can produce a more ringing tone, even without the need to snatch a breath at some ill-chosen point along its length, than any pair or group whose effect is simply different and coarser rather than stronger); and lastly a further statement on cellos and basses which, entering at a half-bar, is worth an especially powerful third beat for its initiation, punctuated as it is by the timpani. This, the seventh and final step in the ascent, then acquires the character of a link to the climactic passage which follows both by the piling-up of entries above it and by its extension to a 5-bar phrase.

The mighty pedal point of bars 145 ff. is emphasized by the

repetition of the basses' minims, re-enunciated in each bar unlike those of the horns. It is almost a universal tradition to allow the basses with a low C to double at the lower octave, but this is not necessarily a good idea. There is a sensation of upward lift to the passage, which the introduction of an extra dimension at the lower end of the tonal spectrum would tend to negate.

Although all wind and timpani drop away, it is naturally the strings' scrunch at bar 150 which is the culmination of this episode in the development, an attack the ferocity of which is maintained in the next bar though without having recourse to a succession of down-bows as in the parallel context in the first movement (bars 284–6). At last at bar 152 the power drains out of the music and the decrescendo begins already at a lower degree of intensity, which will be indicated with a down-beat of demonstrably less weight. The placing of the quavers and the handling of the cadence in bars 153–4 automatically allow the tempo to relax, though not to that of the beginning of the movement. It is not slowness of pulse which creates the atmosphere of the next bars but the sheer contrast of dynamic extremes. From the sotto voce, which is surely *pp* again rather than *p*, the sound should fade nearly to the limit of audibility.

If any member of the audience coughs or makes the slightest sound of any kind the conductor has failed to mesmerize them into the requisite degree of tense breathlessness; the less movement the conductor himself makes the better, and it is arguable that the subtlest use of fingers and eyes is the most the players need in the way of guidance rather than any conventional stick beats, however restrained. The pity is that some preparation is inescapable for the thunderous entry of the cellos and basses, to face whom the conductor will turn right round at the last possible moment, no up-beat in tempo being in the slightest degree necessary.

The 1st violins will have taken their high Ab at the point using hardly any bow; the following two bars need two bows for all strings in each bar, and the triplets which come after are taken heavily off the string. Nevertheless for all the clarity this gives, it is not unusual for the trumpets to find it hard to synchronize punctually. This will be especially true if there has been any looseness in the measurement of time during the drama of the previous bars, which are in no sense free recitative, so that any suggestion of fermata is out of order. It is therefore particularly important for the conductor to have counted to himself religiously through the bars of static minims, *pp* and *ff* alike, at a tempo of perhaps ♪ = 50. In bar 160 a new pulse will then be initiated with positive intent, the main weight of tone being in the cellos and basses. Then, once the triplet pulsations have been established, especial attention can be paid to the players at the rear of the platform for the sake of ensemble. The violins should be scrupulously maintained at a single forte, reserving their true strength for their upward rising arpeggios.

For all its weight and power of declamation the new outburst should not be too slow, even though it leads directly—and without further change of pulse—into the reprise proper of the movement's opening paragraph which as a result becomes appreciably faster than at first; ♪ = 63 will be found to be suitable both for the rhythmic figurations in which it is now clothed and for the funeral march theme itself on this, its third appearance.

The long-hallowed custom by which the basses descend to their low E♭, as given in the Leipzig Breitkopf edition of the parts, is obviously justified on dramatic-musical grounds, but is frowned upon in some critical quarters because of the unduly wide gap this leaves between the deep basses and the remainder of the string section. This is, however, easily remedied by making the basses divide to provide the missing note. A little pull-back in tempo is also dramatically called for during the descending triplets, which will lead to a slightly broader tempo for the vastly intensified return of the secondary phrase in bars 181-6. The warmest string quality should be evoked here, especially for the ascending 1st violin scale which can surely be played 'sul G'. As the string chord of bar 184 hands over to that of the wind in the following bar it is desirable to allow the least gap in order that the 2nd horn's sustaining pedal note can be heard.

With the relaxing of tension at bar 187 the more flowing tempo is naturally resumed and this can give rise to controversy over the strings' bowing style. The answer is likely to be a compromise between on and off the string, the first being too thick and heavy, but the latter wrong in character; players describe an in-between style, logically enough, as half-off, which can be a useful device both in piano and forte playing.

Bar 199 provides one of the many instances where Beethoven causes both tonic and dominant harmonies to be present simultaneously. Examples are to be found in the Seventh and Ninth symphonies, let alone the famous 2nd horn entry in the first movement of the present work. But whereas excited comments, and even 'correction', of the other offending places have at various times been occasioned, the dissonance afforded by the horns in this bar seems to have escaped notice.

The strange beginning of the long coda shares with Haydn's Symphony No. 101 the suggestion of a pendulum, or clock, even though their atmosphere and mood are of necessity totally different. There is none of Haydn's lightness of spirit here, and for all its apparent directness Beethoven's tick-tock will need to be interpreted in a stony, withdrawn manner if it is not to sound jaunty. The tempo continues with unyielding pulse as the music passes from the end of the reprise into the violins' staccato quavers which are now firm and on the string. There can be no hint of warmth and yet the tone must not be hard; above all, the sforzandos in bars 218 and 220 are hardly more than little jabs which should just clutch at the heart.

The pendulum then comes to rest at the first moment in the whole movement in which absolute calm prevails. For this a slightly steadier pulse can be adopted, although bearing in mind that the movement is far from over a feeling of continuity must still be preserved.

Bar 228 is surely the original source of inspiration for Mahler's obsession with a major-turned-minor chord as introduced first in the same tonality of C near the end of his Second Symphony's first movement, and then especially as a primary motto theme in the doom-laden A minor Symphony No. 6. Here Beethoven flanks it on either side with typical subito pianos, which need to be strongly emphasized but without hiatus of pulse, since they form part of the enormous cadential arch which only falls back to earth with the marvellously imaginative solo timpani stroke of bar 238, itself to be the opening of the next and final sentence.

The 2nd horn's low B's in bars 231-7 must surely be produced as muffled hand-stopped notes, several precedents for which can be found in Haydn and Mozart. Here they have the advantage of supplying an additionally sinister quality to this awesome passage.

The temptation to indulge an instinctive calando in bar 237 should be sternly resisted, as the last numbly tragic section calls for rhythmic unity at not too slow a tempo. The smallest beat consistent with clarity is all the conductor should allow himself in these paralysingly still bars, many superfluous beats being, if possible, suppressed altogether; in bar 240, for example, only the little click which initiates the 1st violin figure after the semi-quaver rest remains indispensable.

The wind need a strong and positive gesture for their sforzando in the penultimate bar, as do the upper strings for their forte chord, after which the last group of triplets in the cellos and basses can be made to enter after a little delay and allowed to lead back more slowly into the final fermata. But here a special gesture—or half-beat—is required, for which the players need to be very clearly alerted, or this can be a dangerous place for misadventure. There should be no gap in sound from the wind in their descending phrase which therefore must also have clear and positive direction. The last chord, in which the timpani is notably absent, should be held very long, after which there will need to be a substantial wait before continuing with the Scherzo.

III

Since the majority of Beethoven's own metronome marks are substantially too fast it is surprising to find one which for the first time is markedly on the steady side, considering the feverish excitement of this most dazzling of scherzos. A very staid reading would result from the printed mark of $\downarrow$. = 116 which might be stepped up reasonably to at least 126, though considerably swifter performances have been given which have been hardly less than revelatory despite inevitable sacrifices of clarity and accuracy.

The very start of the movement needs an exaggerated degree of expectancy on the part of the audience and players alike. Fear of initial faulty ensemble has in the past been known to have prompted even the greatest conductors to give empty bars, up to as many as four, by way of preparation; but this is not only an exhibition of unwarrantable mistrust of the players but kills the required atmosphere outright.

The movement, while mostly constructed in regular 4-bar periods, opens with a 6-bar phrase, balanced by another in bars 15–20. In between these comes the oboe solo in which Beethoven plays the first of his tricks on the listener which are such a feature of later symphonies such as the Fifth and the Seventh. The instinctive way to hear this phrase is in two irregular bar-lengths of 3 + 5, and this is endorsed by the figuration of the violas and cellos; but on its repetition Beethoven humorously puts matters to rights by introducing the octave doublings of flute and bassoon at the half-way point of the 8-bar phrase, and thereafter in the *ff* tutti development of the figure he reinforces this correction with successions of sforzandos, a typical instance of his use of humour, or perhaps benevolent bad temper, such as occurs again in the Trio, as will be seen shortly.

Bars 111–15 provide another 6-bar phrase, obviously introduced by Beethoven for emphasis, but the further example at the first-time bars is more subtle and needs to be clearly understood and directed as such, especially in organizing the re-entries of the 2nd violins and violas when taking the repeat.

The famous horn trio of bars 171 ff.* is sometimes thought to be controversial on the grounds that the only dynamic mark is *sf*. Since the strings' and oboes' answering comments are marked '*p*', and the horns' crescendo rises to forte as the first player jubilantly climbs to his top written C, it has been argued that the whole fanfare should start piano; indeed one Breitkopf printing of the score and parts actually adds that dynamic. Delicate, tasteful perhaps, as some might care to volunteer, it is however hardly in keeping with the truly heroic nature of such a fanfare, especially within the scheme of this particular symphony. Nevertheless it is true enough that it should not be rifted as is sometimes heard; nor should it be one jot steadier than the Scherzo upon which it breaks so dramatically. (The 2nd horn quavers present no problem regardless of speed as they will be double-tongued.)

In the second section of the Trio the bar phrase-lengths once

---

*Again Breitkopf counts through the first- and second-time bars, as also with the Trio itself. Hence at the beginning of the Trio Eulenburg readers need to subtract 4 from the bar-counts written above, and 10 from the return of the Scherzo.

again come into question. Strictly speaking from an analytical standpoint the whole section can be shown to fall into regular 4-bar periods with no adjustment needed until the second-time bars which create a 6-bar phrase when returning to the Scherzo proper. But this reckons without the shaping and accentuations of the phrases which are constantly organized so as deliberately to mislead the ear and mind of the hearer. Already in bars 201–2 the entry of the forte suggests a strong bar rather than the up-beat bar 202 really is. (Beethoven seems to have confused himself at this point as he wrote an abortive oboe entry for the repeat in bars 263–4.) But the succession of sforzandos and the alternate entries for strings and horns at bars 240 ff. produce so strong a suggestion of symmetry, putting these events on to the first bars of each 4-bar period, that it is less treacherous in performance practice to accept the reality of the syncopation by artificially creating 3- and 5-bar periods respectively out of bars 257–9 and 260–4 (the 2nd–6th of the first-time bars). The latter 5-bar period becomes, of course, one of 3-bars as well, when the second-time bars are taken, it being of particular importance to give a confident lead to the strings at this quite dangerous corner. I even recall the great oboist Terry MacDonagh asking me to be punctilious about giving him his cue at bar 275 as he had once, when principal player in the BBC Symphony Orchestra, missed it for Toscanini. And another world-famous conductor recently found himself put out of countenance, and without a straight answer during a masterclass, when suddenly confronted by his fledgling conductors with a question on the structure of this passage.

One other problem affects the text itself of the first-time bars. Weingartner asserts, without comment or justification, that the ties between the horns' dotted minims in bars 260, 261, and 262 to be found in some printings of the score and parts (both Peters and Breitkopf) are wrong and that the chords must be reiterated. This cannot be taken as self-evident, for a single sustained *pp* chord may well be represented to be the more logical reading and moreover creates a most beautiful oasis of stillness, however brief, before being swept away by the vigorous resumption of the Trio. The arguments in favour of the repeated chords, the version more generally accepted by present-day commentators and editions, stem firstly from the fact that the earliest sources do not show the ties, and then from the view that the

strings' and oboes' re-entry in bar 262 comes as part of a continuing pattern instead of jumping in from a kind of vacuum. But
it is precisely this kind of quasi-hiatus that Beethoven might
have desired, prepared as this itself has been by the already
held diminuendo 4-bar chord of bars 256–9, which on the repeat
leads to the hushed return of the Scherzo.

The four Alla breve bars create an atmosphere of fury and
need to be executed full-tilt. They alone might even provide
the motivation for a headlong pace in the movement as a whole.

Arguments have been put forward suggesting that in the total
absence of staccato dots the strings' crotchets in the coda might
with advantage be played legato on the string, creating an added
degree of breathless excitement in keeping with the chromatic
wind upward sighs. It is an attractive idea but is hardly likely
to have been Beethoven's intention. The conductor's style of
beat, on the other hand, may well change at the timpani *pp*
entry to suggest an abrupt feeling of apprehension, which
quickly changes back again at the horns' fanfare to one of exhilaration for the exultant last bars.

IV

The finale should follow soon enough to prevent relaxing the
tension; not absolutely segue that is to say, but without allowing
the orchestra to sit back and the audience to start coughing.

At the same time it should not start at too precipitate a tempo;
there is a heroism in these opening bars which can be negated
by any suggestion of sheer panic, and the stature of this extraordinary movement can be reduced if the startlingly unexpected
reworking of the Piano Variations, Op. 33 in the context of
this mammoth symphony appears to add gawkiness to ill-
humour instead of whimsy to strength.

Nor is there any need to accept the compulsion to adopt
a radically new tempo for the variations on the naked bass-line
at bar 12, as Weingartner does. Beethoven's metronome marks
are notoriously unreliable* but his $\downarrow$ = 76 here is hardly less

---

*It is bizarre that the validity of Beethoven's metronome marks, hitherto regarded
as of no more than academic interest, should have latterly risen to become such a
cause célèbre. Those of many composers—like Bartók for example—are no more realistic,
while even so rigid and pedantic a composer as Schoenberg always insisted that his
were not to be followed religiously but should be taken as a guide rather than an
inflexible instruction.

than outrageous and moreover cannot remotely be made to relate to the mark of ♩ = 116* when this same passage returns for the final Presto. Indeed, since Presto must surely be appreciably faster than Allegro molto, the thought might enter the mind that Beethoven had meant ♩ = 76, except that this is now absurdly too slow.

The opening of the finale can therefore be taken at a speed of no more than ± ♩ = 104, which can be satisfactorily maintained right through to bar 109 since it admirably suits both the grotesque bass with its own little collection of variations and the theme itself which sails in at bar 78. The only thing to change should be the conductor's posture which, powerful and dramatic in the first eleven bars, can become marionette-like in the bass theme with its half-comical, half-sinister gaps, echoes and fermatas. The little variations for strings alone acquire a more human face with light gracefulness and more than a touch of warmth in the melodic phrases of the cellos and 1st violins.

At bar 12 an admittedly cavalier step of changing the strings to arco can be logically argued by Beethoven's altered notation from quavers to crotchets as well as by the otherwise redundant 'pizz.' at bar 31. It also makes good artistic sense, but must remain a controversial issue to be decided by each conductor for himself.

The fermata in bar 57† appears variably on the 1st violins' E♭ or D in the different editions, but can also be found across both as over the rests in the silent instruments. This has a good operatic tradition behind it and makes for an excellent reading corresponding with a rubato across the whole cadence. Beethoven himself seems to have changed his mind in favour of the D, but it would be plainly unmusical on that account to move on to it in strict tempo before pausing.

Strong encouragement needs to be given to the 2nd violins in bar 55 in order that they should hammer out the three notes in imitation of the preceding *ff* tutti hammer-blows (the same naturally applies also to the 1st violins in bar 71), and the violas require a very clear lead for their up-beat entry in the third

---

*Not, of course, ♪ = 116 as given by Peters and some Breitkopf printings and, strange to say, taken seriously by Weingartner.

†A (two-bar) discrepancy in the counting between Breitkopf and the miniature scores is again occasioned by the first- and second-time bars.

repeated section; this can be a tricky passage for the best regulated orchestras in obtaining clean bow-control of the spiccato triplets after the up-beat semiquavers.

The geniality of the great theme needs the least widening of pulse as it enters in bar 78, in order to establish the change of character though not, as has been said, of tempo. It seems incredible that Beethoven should have already used this melody in no less than three other totally different earlier works,* and yet the impression still remains that it is presenting itself to the world for the first time.

Interestingly, Beethoven at this initial symphonic statement of his principal theme takes care that the bass, which has been the subject of the preceding variations, should remain prominently featured by having it sung in long notes on the horns and, shortly after, the trumpets. This is of great consequence since despite the long-awaited coming of the tune itself, this bass is by no means to be put aside as of no further intrinsic interest in its own right, but is to be developed fugally and in other ways throughout the movement. These horn and trumpet lines, therefore, presenting the bass not merely as a foundation to the melody but as a countersubject, should be brought well out in performance.

At letter A (bar 109) all expository variations and statements are now over and the movement starts to take wing. The nervous energy here becomes restless and the music tends to sound laboured unless it is allowed to move forward. If the pace is stepped up very gradually it is possible to arrive by imperceptible degrees to a new basic tempo of $\downarrow$ = 126 for the first fugal development beginning in bar 119.

In conducting this complicated section it is once again a greater aid to reliability to call on instinct rather than academic analysis in the shaping of the bar phrases wherever the one conflicts with the other. On this basis the contrapuntally overlapping sections can arguably be viewed as follows:

1. Bars 119–24: 6-bar phrase presenting the Subject and Countersubject.
2. Bars 125–7: 3-bar phrase consisting of the first motif only

---

*Many commentators overlook the Contretanz (Kinsky W-O 14) which was its true first appearance.

of the Answer. The reason for the truncated phrase is the strength of the 1st violins' modulating passage.

3. Bars 128–32: the priorities of the Answer take second place in the listener's awareness to the dominating 1st violins' F minor figure. The double statement of this must be placed on strong bars, here the first and third of what is to become a 5-bar phrase. The fifth bar is a codetta preparing for the viola's entry of the Subject in bar 133.

4. Bars 133–5:* 3-bar phrase, corresponding with Period 2, with the subject similarly truncated in preparation for

5. Bars 136–9: 4-bar phrase, at first balancing Period 3 but without the latter's extension of a fifth bar. The strong symmetry of the violins' figuration is here strengthened still further so that the cellos and basses appear to have jumped in a bar early, forcing the correctly-spaced woodwind entry in the following bar into the role of a stretto-like false entry. The lower strings accordingly need a particularly confident lead from the conductor before he turns to cue in the woodwind. The later piled-up woodwind false entries, however, should require no especial attention.

6. Bars 140–1: 2-bar modulating codetta (once more in F minor) despite the presence of both real and false entries.

7. Bars 142–7: 6-bar phrase corresponding as before with Periods 3 and 5, but extended still further in order to enable the forte entry of the Answer in the 1st violins to become the strong first bar of the next Period and not the crescendo entry of the Subject which occurs a bar earlier on flutes and clarinets.

8/9. Bars 148–50 and 151–4: 3- and 4-bar phrases corresponding with Periods 4 and 5. The general forte indication in all voices makes bar 148 the first major corner-stone of the fugue, with the power of the high-poised 1st violin statement of the Answer overriding all the related figures of the lower instruments. So jubilant is this entry with its natural emphasis restored, that the last overlapping false entry of this woodwind stretto in the oboes and bassoons is generally blotted out (bar 149); at the least their minim G's and the first of their crotchet C's can sensibly be marked up to *ff*.

---

*The Breitkopf 1st violin parts give an impossible page-turn here, requiring a few bars to be written out enabling them to turn at the following 7-bar rest.

Like the cellos and basses in Period 5, so here in bar 154 it is the 2nd violins who jump in with a vigorous *sf* before the end of the symmetrical phrases now played by all the rest of the orchestra.

10. Bars 155–7: 3-bar linking modulating codetta, with strettos both on (strings) and off (wind) the strong beats of the bars. Helpful as cues always are, it would be hard to work out any system of priorities; yet to give every one would be impossibly fussy and even confusing. The conductor might therefore be better advised to keep his own head clear for—

11. Bars 158–60: 3-bar phrase dominated by not only the re-entry (if only after a brief respite) of the 1st violins but by the entry of the horns which this heralds. These players have been counting a 39-bar rest and are always grateful for an unequivocal lead at this important juncture. It is in any case an extremely important entry pursuing more strongly still the preceding woodwind figures of Period 9, themselves significantly derived from the inverted Subject.

From this point the periods are regular 4-bar phrases, in which the melodic interest of the 1st violins is at first paramount. The stretto entries of in turn 2nd violins, 1st violins, and violas followed by similar but compressed woodwind entries in bars 165–71 all heighten the excitement as the *ff* of bars 173–6 brings the fugue to an end, allowing the development section of the movement to emerge from the mêlée.

One of the important consequences of the quicker tempo which will have been held firmly throughout the fugue is that the delicate semiquaver passage-work which succeeds the brief B minor/D major return of the principal melody will scurry easily and swiftly from 1st violins (bars 185–92) to solo flute (bars 193–200). With bar 200, however, we enter a different world.

This is not the only place in the symphony where despite Beethoven's predilection for subitos (whether piano or forte) a linking gradation of tone seems indispensable. (The other obvious instance in the present movement is bar 382 where it is surely unthinkable not to make the violins play crescendo *possibile*.) So also here in bar 200 it is idle for the conductor to attempt to restrain his string section as it plunges through bar 200 into the turbulence of the next passage. For what has been light and swift is now all dramatic fury and a tightening of the reins is ideal for the heroic episode of bars 213–52 as well as for the second fugue.

As for the episode itself, this undoubtedly gains from a majestic stance on the part of the conductor, while the cellos and basses always show delight if appreciation is shown for their splendid line whether in the striding of the bass motif (of which this is the central variation) or in the vigorous pursuit of the quaver triplets which are played in a heavy spiccato. Some viola sections try to protest that their ascending scales in bars 228 and 236 need two bows, but this is absolutely not the case and breaks the phrase to bad effect. A single up-bow over all seven notes after a strong, quick stroke for the single first note of each of these bars can be made to produce ample volume and a fine sweeping lead into the following bars.

Like so many instances in the codas of Tchaikovsky, who may well have taken his precedent from Beethoven, the repetitious closing bars of the episode can seem over-extended if held strictly in tempo. It is, however, not so much a question of making an affrettando as simply taking the brakes off, so to speak, and encouraging the orchestra to edge forward. This will also allow the music to return to the quicker central tempo which is once again important both for the return of the melodic main subject in its most genial guise and for the second fugue.

This fugue on the inverted bass is both more sheerly exciting and less complicated than its predecessor. The running semi-quaver countersubject comes easily and gently off the string without the angularity of a true spiccato. In order to start it with reliable ensemble, violin sections are prone to skimp, or even suppress altogether, the first note of bar 279, a safety measure to which it would be pedantic to object.

The chief events of this fugue are patently not the fugal entries so much as those of in turn the flutes and horns. A full rich tone is needed by the flutes, doubled woodwind being an obvious advantage to fulfil Weingartner's attractive suggestion that '... if four flute players are to be had, they might all play the passage in unison. This', he adds cautiously, 'produces a better effect.'

Where the horns are concerned, however, he oversteps the mark in advocating the co-opting of the 1st and 4th as well.

This is part of an area in which the 3rd horn has taken over the principalship in order to leave the 1st player free to change crook for the solo in bars 272–5. These lengthy periods of rest may seem unnecessary now that the practical necessity has passed, but they should still be observed faithfully, especially in view of the strenuous playing which lies ahead. In the meantime bars 305–9 provide a grand opportunity for flamboyant solo playing for horns 3 and 2.

In bars 311–15 the sforzandos in the 2nd violins and lower strings will require the strongest attack since Beethoven is holding the entire wind and brass in reserve for the mighty entry of the bass theme (now the right way up again together with the inversion in half-bar canon) in bar 316. This, with its need for a high trumpet Bb, has become another point of major controversy in view of today's pursuit of unswerving authenticity. For as at the culmination of the first movement, Beethoven felt it unwise to risk so high a note on his low-crooked instruments and thus sacrificed the very climax of his scheme, the trumpets and flutes alike having to dodge the apex of the phrase. Until the purist movement of recent years it had been taken for granted that not only must the trumpets play intact the *ff* crowning entry of the restored theme but the flutes also. That this supreme moment, in preparation for which we have been watching the skeleton bass going through not only a string of variations but two substantial fugal developments, should be robbed of its glory because of the limitations of the instruments available to Beethoven in 1803 is surely sad.

The build-up continues after the *ff* tutti of bar 316 and with it the tempo, which might even reach a pulse of ♩ = 132 by bar 330. In bars 336–9 it is the cellos who deserve especial attention and encouragement right through firstly their undulations and then, together with the basses, their frenzied scales leading to the pause. This great central fermata is sustained for several bars, the strings taking as many bows as they may need, before the orchestra is then cut off completely in preparation for an entirely new start.

It would be wrong, however, to make too long a hiatus before giving the solo oboe his up-beat, as this movement is like the finale of the Ninth Symphony in being unusually complex and episodic. Moreover it is most desirable to give the new variation, which initiates the enormous closing paragraph of the finale, a feeling more of a divided 2 in a bar for the first six bars, lest the adoption of a true quaver pulse imposes too much constriction on the natural melodic shaping of the oboe's 8-bar phrase. Nevertheless all preparatory beats will be given as quavers, and the up-beats of bars 352, 354, and 356 are real beats and not half-crotchet subdivisions. It is also a good idea to indicate the placing of the demisemiquavers, lest someone moves too soon.

Yet while bearing in mind the constant need to prevent the music from dragging, it is at the same time unrealistic to try to reconcile Beethoven's ♪ = 108 with his own 'Poco Andante'. In fact this is one of the more improbable of Beethoven's metronome marks and if any true feeling of *Innigkeit* is to be given to this contemplative and profound variant of the principal melody the tempo is unlikely to be faster than ♪ = 72, and in many halls may settle down to as steady a pace as ♪ = 60 without feeling unduly expansive.

In bar 356 an essential quaver beat is unavoidable and it is best to stay in a real 4-in-a-bar from here on. The entry of the horns in bar 359 tends to create a sforzando ahead of the true attack two bars later. If a weighty third beat is given in the one and a sharp stress in the other the differentiation can in fact be accomplished.

The tempo should not have been allowed to become too ruminative as a result of the thickening of texture in bars 359–66, but in any case it can legitimately be moved on again with the entry of the clarinet triplets which will be the monitoring influence in all that follows, ♪ = 66 proving to be a good compromise for this transition passage as well as for the mighty peroration of bars 383–8. The strings' triplets will be taken off the string until bar 382.

The violins' descending broken arpeggios are actually printed with a crescendo in the parts and I have only once heard it played without, that is to say with a *subito ff* at the end of bar 382; this was in a performance under Klemperer and may have been by way of experiment—I cannot say that I found it convincing. As for the peroration itself, this is always played by as many horns as can be called into service, but it should be admitted that this practice rides on the knife-edge of vulgarity.

Furthermore, the 3rd horn notes in bars 387–8 have every claim for inclusion (the same could theoretically be said for the 2nd horn except that these low G's will never be heard anyway) and should be retained even if the player is doubling the melody for the remainder of the passage. All conductors are united in having three (or more) horns on the melody, although it is crucial to be on the alert for any tendency to overblowing; but it would be fascinating to ask some star first horn to play it solo with his best ringing tone; it might well be a revelation.

With the great melodic enunciation over, the drama seems at an end; but this is by no means the case and the tempo must not be allowed to flag at this remarkable manifestation of Beethoven's genius. The three-part extension to the Poco Andante follows naturally and easily upon the end of the horn(s)' solo and leads to its own moments of drama. It is extraordinary how vivid the simple trumpets' octave minim at bar 420 can be made even after all the panoply of sound which has been ringing in one's ears (the bassoons' solo line in this bar is very hard to bring through); there is then a breathlessness of anticipation about bars 422–32, both in respect of the cellos' and basses' pedal point (the moment at which the basses double the frequency of their entries is a feature often missed) and the highly dramatic rises and falls which seem to portray glimmers of hope replaced by disappointment and ultimate resignation, upon which the exuberance of the triumphant Presto bursts with overwhelming jubilation.

It is the more necessary, therefore, to keep strict control over the tempo of the Presto. Steady though the indication $\rfloor$ = 116 appears to be, it can be faithfully observed as the texture is so busy and the fanfares follow so fast upon each other that it could well be considered to be in reality $\flat$ = 232 (though perforce beaten in 2) which would certainly be consistent with Presto. Bars 459–62 present a passage of glory for the timpanist, and the final bar must be a real brick-like crotchet, clearly differentiated from the preceding quavers by being held for its full length.

Symphony No. 4 in B flat, Op. 60

◀▶

THE disparity of style, content, and even scale over the span of Beethoven's symphonies is greater than with those of any other composer. It would be easy to say that no wider contrast can be imagined than between the Fifth and Sixth were it not equally so between the Seventh and Eighth, or indeed the Third and Fourth, and so on. Yet all are unmistakably stamped with the hallmark of Beethoven's personality. Just as we today cannot in any way envisage how Beethoven would have followed the 'Choral' Symphony with the Tenth, had he lived, so at the time no one could possibly have foreseen the shape of the work which was to come so close upon the heels of the monumental 'Eroica'.

I

No doubt Beethoven was well aware of the conundrum he had set his listeners, since the introduction of the first movement of his Fourth Symphony is by any standards quite extraordinary starting one of the most light-hearted of all his compositions enigmatically in tones of such gloom that his contemporaries even wondered if his sanity was crumbling.

There is a temptation on this account to start this mysterious and seemingly static music too slowly. In fact the autograph marks the time signature as   (unlike all modern editions) which although this in no way suggests that it should be beaten in 2, does show that the 'Adagio' refers to minims rather than crotchets. At the same time Beethoven's $\sqcup$ = 66 is quite out of character for any sort of Adagio, whereas at $\sqcup$ = 54 the music moves naturally and the ensemble falls easily into place; slower than this the pulse becomes mannered and self-conscious.

The opening unison B♭, five octaves deep, has to be both simply and decisively given. If the style of the beat is directed towards the pizzicato, the wind need find no great problem in choosing their moment of attack. Beethoven has ingeniously helped by thinning his wind group—the oboes (whose troubles Weber so signally ignored in the first bar of his *Freischütz* Overture) are silent, and the flutes are reduced, for the whole of this symphony alone among the nine, to a single player. The instrumentalist with the hardest task is actually the 2nd horn whose pedal C for the B♭ basso crook is a very low note indeed (in terms of the standard F horn of today it is actually a semitone below the official lowest note on the instrument, but is lipped down without difficulty in preference to taking the fundamental on the B♭ crook of the modern double horn, a fat and rumbly note hard to initiate gently), and requires a prodigious amount of air and lung control to sustain for four slow bars.

Although after the placing of the opening pizzicato the first bar is entirely uneventful, the conductor should not be so immobile as to suggest a fermata. Something in the manner of his behaviour should prepare wind and strings alike for the tempo of the passage to come even while refraining from actually beating time all through the bar. Hence, despite all appearances, both the first bar and its recurrence in bar 13 are in fact strictly measured.

Confidence needs to be given to the 1st violins as they prepare for bar 6 (as again bar 18) so that the spacing of the quavers will be established in their minds beyond any shadow of a doubt; the regular crotchet beat can then be given quietly and purposefully. The sinister entries of the cellos and basses (bars 9 and 21) can be acknowledged over one's shoulder, as it were. (Beethoven used the same effect in the Violin Concerto at bar 207 of the first movement.) On the other hand, the violas' variant in bar 21 deserves quite different treatment and is worth bringing out with expressive phrasing. The same warmth of expression should also infuse the whole string body briefly in bars 31–2 before draining away to a hushed pianissimo in bar 33, the conductor's gesture being one of total withdrawal.

A curious phenomenon of bars 26–9 is that the clarinets tend to sound a very little, yet uncomfortably, sharp; the fact that the A of the 2nd clarinet is on the 'break' may have something to do with this.

In bar 34 the conductor's regular pulse may profitably cease even though the tempo must continue to be firmly maintained. It is of the essence of this introduction that the impression be given of a winding down of the musical flow prior to the explosion which heralds the exuberant Allegro.

In bar 35 the crescendo starts with the first upper A quavers of the violins which may therefore be given by means of a new resolution in the style of beat. The duration of both fortissimos and silences in bar 36 are then again strictly counted out although the rests in bar 37 will feel inordinately long. Yet such elongated stillnesses are integral to Beethoven's dramatic language, as the even more exaggerated examples in the Overture *Leonora No.* 2 reveal. The violins' upward swoops should begin at precisely the half of the fourth beat, whereas the up-beat semiquavers of the tutti come unmeasured, more like acciaccaturas, and given with a flicker of the stick prior to the cut-off down-beats. This is, of course, the moment of truth in respect of whether in the winding down of the introduction the tempo has been allowed to droop—in which case strictness in the violins' demisemiquaver groups would cause them to lose their necessary impetus. Moreover, with this *élan* in mind it will be wise to adopt the custom of taking these swoops in a single bow; nor will the resultant panache sacrifice sharpness of attack at the barlines since this is strongly effected by the entire remainder of the orchestra.

I am at odds with Weingartner who recommends that the tempo of the Allegro should be exactly doppio mosso. On the contrary, the new pace should be vastly quicker and indeed as brilliant as Beethoven's semibreve metronome mark suggests although there can be no question of actually beating it 1-in-a-bar. Nor can the precipitation of $\mathbf{o} = 80$ (or $\mathsf{J} = 160$ as it would be) ever become a practical proposition; the movement need not however, be given at anything less than an enthusiastic $\mathsf{J} = 144$.

There is an element of ribaldry about the passage beginning at bar 81 which a degree of frenzy in the conductor's manner will do well to accentuate, especially when the brass and timpani crotchets turn to quavers; this change of notation can indeed be interpreted to signify an extra degree of rinforzando, of hammering the point home as it were. The violins' tied semibreves (as equally those in the lower strings four bars later) are often played with a bow-change at some point. But it is hard to disguise so ugly a contrivance in this specific context (resorted to in order to arrive at a necessary down-bow in bars 83 and 87) and it is better to sustain over the two bars and then retake with a new down-bow, even though this gives a brief gap in the continuity. The reiterated crotchets in bars 92–5 should certainly be on trumpets as well as horns, the trumpets dropping out after the first note of letter B.

A slight relaxation of pulse is called for in preparation for the woodwind solos of bars 107–12, the quavers of which will otherwise sound hurried and out of character. The return to full tempo will then naturally and imperceptibly evolve with the long rising string phrase of staccato minims.

Controversy has sometimes arisen with respect to the violins' B♯ in bar 119 since the analogous note in bar 393 is not E♯ but E♮; similarly the F♮ in bar 128 contrasts oddly with the corresponding B♮ (not B♭) in bar 402. Nevertheless, the autograph is clear on both counts and there is little purpose in altering the text in order to bring everything into line.

In the vigorous bridge passage of bars 135–40 one of the most important rhythmic features is oddly given only to the violas; these can therefore be encouraged to play with the sharpest and most incisive bow-style. The gentle canonic second subject then follows in which, unlike the transition section and despite so radical a change of mood, the full impetus must be maintained. Any relaxation of tempo here would be most frustrating at just the point where the exposition (and reprise in its turn) is plunging forward towards its closing section.

In bars 149–56 the oboes and bassoons need to play *ff* and staccato assai if they are to be heard in what is, after all, a most effective contribution to the overall sonority, and which is actually reinforced by horns and trumpets as well as timpani on its return in bars 423–30. On the other hand the upper strings' *p* in bars 159–60 and 163–4 (= 433 etc.) is rarely played softly enough. If bar 158 is taken down-bow by 1st violins and violas this can take them to the extreme upper half which can give the required delicacy, but it takes an unusually scrupulous and well-trained section to get back again each time after the *ff* interjections.

The cello/bass thump in bar 183 actually stems from the autograph but there seems no musical sense in keeping what must surely have been a slip of Beethoven's pen.

Weingartner states that the first-time bars 'are so important that they should not be omitted on any account' and this is the view that is again broadly accepted today after a long period during which the repeat was virtually never taken. While agreeing in principle to the arguments for playing the unusually long and eventful first-time period, I have to confess to an in-built resistance against so abruptly checking the excitement generated during the exposition and which, on the contrary, wants to boil over into the even more boisterous beginning of the development without first going through the formalities of conventional restatement.

At the 2ª Volta the conductor's demeanour can be demonstrably effervescent during what amounts to a 32-bar-long outburst of high spirits, the strings remaining very strong all the way to bar 202. In order to maintain this, some extra encouragement may be found necessary to prevent a slackening of intensity especially during the last four bars (199–202); the surprise hush of the next section will then be absolute, Beethoven requiring the tone to be dropped still further over the next few bars from whatever degree of piano has been achieved at bar 203.

The cellos' change of notation from staccato crotchets to quavers separated by rests in just bar 205 is sometimes thought to carry some significance, but there can be no detectable difference to the sound in practice even though the autograph shows that the change was originally intended by Beethoven to extend over the next few bars, for it is clear that the passage should be played throughout in a very light spiccato.

In bar 217 the strings should play one quick forte bow-stroke which will take them at once to the upper half, the quaver ostinato then being played on the string at the point. This background pattern can also be profitably marked *pp*, though the violins and cellos in bars 221–4 and 229–32 may sensibly be re-marked up to piano dolce for the purpose of the melodic line. An up-bow beginning for this will bring bar 224 on to another up-bow, conveniently for the 1st violins' and cellos' new *pf* at bar 225, which is taken off the string and in the middle of the bow.

The melody's shape in bars 223 and 227 is one of the principal bones of contention in the symphony, some conductors actually maintaining that the appoggiatura should be not merely long but played in even crotchets. Weingartner simply dismisses this view categorically as 'wrong', adding that 'the grace-note would have to be notated as a crotchet for this to be correct'. At first this might seem to weaken his argument, as some later printings of both Peters and Breitkopf do in fact present it in that way. But in the event this proves to be contrary to the autograph, the dispute being thereby reduced to whether the grace-note should be played on the beat—if perhaps a little elongated—or before the beat and short, which is surely preferable in being more true to Beethoven's idiom (cf. his use of appoggiaturas—similarly notated in the autograph as quavers—for the woodwind transition theme).

The third fortissimo in bar 257 with its timpani entry is patently the mightiest—by the time of the Eighth Symphony Beethoven was writing *fff* at such moments—and the *sempre f* in bar 261 should, as repeatedly in Beethoven, be read as *sempre rf* (rinforzando) still at a dynamic level of fortissimo.

There can be a slight delay in bringing in the *ppp* full body of strings at bar 281. If the 1st violins have correctly been playing the previous bars right at the tip of the bow this will present no danger of untidiness; two tiny down-bows are taken in bar 280 and the semibreves all begin up-bow.

Bar 288 provides one of the worst 1st violin page-turns in the repertoire. A good solution is to write out the next few bars at the bottom of the previous page.

In bar 290 some editions give B♮ to the violins which has even been thought preferable. Beethoven's own hand, however, clearly gives B♯ as shown in Breitkopf.

The corner at bars 304–5 once again needs sensitive handling and as at bar 280 the least hesitation is amply justified. This whole passage requires a certain skill on the part of the conductor if the continuity of line is to sound convincing, first driving its descent through three octaves, ever a danger area for intonation, and then as it rises from the cellos to the flute via the upper strings; the 2nd violins in particular always sound too

tentative and need some encouragement from the stick. There
is much to be said for beginning bars 302–3 down-bow (this
will also have the virtue of bringing bar 305 to the point of
the bow) and marking the 2nd violins up for just the start of
their entry.

Care will have been taken during the whole of this breathless
interlude to maintain tempo, with the exception only of the
two corners just suggested. The build-up to the *ff* outburst which
starts the reprise at letter G will then have the necessary onrush
of itself without the artificial aid of any unstylish accelerando.

The extra emphasis given by the timpani to the repeated
cadence bars which conclude the reprise in bars 454, 458, and—
leading to the coda—460 might suggest a solo treatment of these
pounding crotchets, which played no part in the corresponding
section of the exposition. Indeed so strikingly can they be
brought out that they might even fractionally hold up the pulse
at their second repetition in bar 460 in a kind of Mahlerian
Ausholen, so as to usher in the coda with the maximum weight
and jubilation.

In bar 467 the cellos and basses are the instruments which
need especial featuring, as their imitation can too easily merge
into the overall texture, the listener's ear being naturally focused
on the violins.

Another variant of some editions gives the sustaining of the
tutti chords with ties from bar 477–8 and 481–2 in what, it
must be admitted, is a very convincing way. Nevertheless the
autograph proves that the Breitkopf text is, after all, correct.

At bar 493 Eulenburg sets a hare running which derives from
no less distinguished figures than Czerny and Schumann. Their
proposal was that Beethoven himself, as well as Simrock—the
first publisher of this symphony—must have made an oversight
as a result of which there is a bar too many here for the 4-bar
structure; bar 493 should therefore be deleted. According to
Max Unger, the editor of the later Eulenburg printing (who,
to be fair, admits that he is not convinced by the evidence),
many conductors have been making this omission for years.
This is, however, simply not true; nor is there any substance
in the structural argument, since Beethoven would have had
no compunction in making an irregular period in order to add
emphasis, as amply proved by an outstanding instance in the

first movement of the Fifth Symphony. Fortunately in the event bar 493 appears in every edition and is always played as a matter of course.

Many string players take it upon themselves to scratch out one or even two of the last quavers in bar 494 in order to start the triplet semiquavers more incisively. Yet this is a bowdlerization which should be discouraged, for if the last two quavers are both taken up-bow the problem is solved without having to make any break in continuity.

II

Perhaps the Adagio's greatest interpretative problem lies in the ubiquitous little jerky motif which is, of course, the primary feature of the entire movement. If this figure is rendered militantly so that the demisemiquaver has to be the exact fourth part of a quaver, the music sounds still and ungainly and the players themselves become embarrassed. The solution is for them to relax and put to one side pedantic accuracy, so much a built-in discipline in the present-day orchestral fraternity. The demisemiquavers can then come a little nearer to their succeeding semiquavers, almost as if they were one of a quintuplet, as Britten actually wrote in his *War Requiem*; the music will then immediately flow and come to life. The figure is also best taken not bracketed but in a series of down-ups which give an easy and natural bowing style.

The problem is still further alleviated if not too slow a basic tempo is adopted, though the printed ♪ = 84 is so brisk that it turns the movement into more of an Andantino. Taking into account the many lyrical and rhythmic factors which constitute this beautiful piece, ♪ = 69 will not be found too steady; it is of course beaten in a real six.

The simple indication 'cantabile' in the 1st violins at bar 2 can be taken to imply not merely piano, which is admittedly the prevailing dynamic level, but a warm singing quality which especially in dry halls can necessitate a slightly stronger marking. The crescendo to *sf* in bar 6 can then rise to at least *mf* before dropping to a true piano in bar 7. Some sympathetic warmth of tone can also be drawn from the violas, the interest of whose line should not be underplayed. The *sf* itself in bar 5 is naturally one of duration similar to corresponding instances in the funeral march of the 'Eroica'. There are many such sforzandos in the present movement and the conductor's beat needs to be concentrated on this maintaining of tension to the brink of the piano subito at the barline in all such places (bars 13–14, 45–6, etc.), to counter the players' natural tendency to let the tone subside too soon after the notes actually carrying the *sf* indication.

Despite the plethora of sforzandos, bars 17 ff. should not be played violently. This whole movement represents Beethoven at his most genial so that the conductor's whole demeanour should reflect generosity of spirit. This applies equally to the 1st violins' richly spread chords in bar 18 and 20 as well as to the evoking of a singing beauty of sound in the oboe and flute solos of those same bars. There will be a temptation to allow the violins' tone to grow in the last group of demisemiquavers of bar 22 and this need not be resisted as long as sufficient moderation is exercised, so as not to rob the *fp* in bar 23 of its impact.

The repeated notes in bar 23–6 should be very short and the main string body's demisemiquavers can certainly come off the string. The lead into the second subject at letter B will then need the least Hindemithian *einleitend* to prepare for the new mood of tranquillity.

In view of the complexity of the strings' accompanying passage-work during the second subject it is all too possible to devote so much attention to them as to detract from the clarinet whose melody, much broken up with rests as it is, should never cease to carry the primary interest. The ascending arpeggios in bar 26 are in practice best taken down-bow but can nevertheless be as gentle as they must be smooth. The 1st violins in bar 27 can conveniently take a second down-bow on the minim which will not have the benefit of constricting them dynamically but will bring them to the upper half for the figures in the succeeding bars.

In bar 30 it would be logical to invite the cellos and basses to play their pizzicato Bb at a higher dynamic prior to the piano subito which they share with all other parts, even though Beethoven himself seems to have made no such provision.

The long demisemiquaver passages in bars 34–7 are often broken by players in pursuit of comfort but at too great a sacrifice of smoothness and purity of tone. They can in fact all be accomplished in a single bow with the exception of the cellos' phrase in bar 34 itself, which not only becomes unreasonably cramped but needs an up-bow (taken at the D on the fifth beat) to bring them to the right part of the bow for joining the basses with the jerky figure.

The recommendation concerning the shortening of this figure made earlier need not be jettisoned here on account of the need for the detached demisemiquavers to correspond with those of the legato phrases. If the groups are listening to each other and the conductor keeps the tempo ever flowing the ensemble can be made to sound perfectly natural, which is of particular value in view of the character of the following bridge passage.

For in bars 38–41 the movement suddenly acquires a forward momentum as it builds towards the first fortissimo outburst. This also carries with it a slight quickening of actual pulse before, after only a single bar, it subsides into the varied, but otherwise rondo-like restatement of the principal subject which, complete with its introductory bar of 2nd violin repeated figures, must have fully regained its poise and mood of serenity. Yet, even in such a dramatic boiling-over, it is not the actual pacing of the figure itself which is interfered with but rather the gaps between its repetitions. These will at first be contracted imperceptibly during bars 38–9, then held firm as the beat suddenly adopts a more vivid style at the *ff* entry of trumpets and drums, and then equally unnoticeably widened once again during the diminuendo as calm is restored. This will create an illusion that the overall pulse has also been strictly maintained, so subtly will the transitions be effected.

The variant of the 1st violins' melody adds grace to lyricism, the staccato notes all coming off the string (including the last note of bar 43, a particularly attractive touch often lost when an inappropriate bowing is adopted).

In bar 49 the 1st violins enter a note earlier than they did in the otherwise identical bar 9. The autograph shows this to be intentional and it should therefore be strongly emphasized.

Despite the forte at bar 49, the second fortissimo outburst should erupt suddenly and violently upon the scene. It could be likened to a tunnel leading to the development proper which begins equally unexpectedly, although a slight placing of the down-beat of letter D is called for, not only in line with the majority of such subito pianos but so as clearly to initiate the total change in atmosphere the new section brings to the movement.

As for the fortissimo bridge passage itself, two salient features need to be pin-pointed by the conductor's manner of presentation. The first is the band of sustained octaves held by the upper woodwind and horns. The *f* sempre is perhaps on the conservative side, bearing in mind that *ff* is the prevailing dynamic level; 'sempre ben sostenuto' might be a better mark to give the necessary suggestion of relentless penetration, which an upheld left hand might help the players to sustain in what is, after all, rather a long breath.

The second feature is the thickening of texture in bar 53 where the other strings join the violas and cellos in the repetitious demisemiquavers (there can be no thought of tremolo here, despite the difference in notation common to all scores). All these demisemiquavers are played closely on the string and the opacity of the sound can be the main concern of the beat in this last bar before the air suddenly clears.

Strangely, the duet between the violin groups, with which the short development begins, can easily sound thin and spidery. Beethoven's 'espressivo', not a common mark for him, is significant and can be invoked to ensure that all the demisemiquavers have equal importance and quality.

Bar 59 is a moment of particular poignancy and the strings' hairpins can be interpreted almost in line with the meaning Schubert was to make particularly his own, that is to say, with an expressive stress before the diminuendo. In this case the sequence of three such stresses (violas and cellos; 1st violins; 2nd violins on their Cb) creates a moment of tension which can dissolve magically into the bassoon solo.

It is impossible to overemphasize how softly the cellos and basses should play their bar 62, but on the contrary the clarinet and bassoon should not be allowed to underplay on account of the extreme stillness which has been created since bar 60. Their solos are marked *p* not *pp*, and the preparation for the 1st horn's *pp* entry on his high Bb (as it will be for the present-day horn in F) need not be made more nerve-wracking than necessary. For all the improvements to present-day instruments, the use of wider bores, higher crooks and so forth, this entry ever remains a cliff-hanger. The degree of concentration required is so great that it is probably best to avoid looking directly at the player, but merely to give an infinitely gentle but confidence-giving lead in his general area.

The suggestion made by the printed *pp*'s for the start of the reprise is misleading. In the autograph the flute solo bears no such mark and the atmosphere of lyricism should have been re-established with an overall richness of sound that will comfortably accommodate the oboes' piano entry in bar 67. The *sf* in bar 68 should also extend to the lower strings, which is not the case in all editions.

The slight dotted variant to the clarinet melody given by some editions in bar 82 does not come from Beethoven, even though it originates from as far back as the first printed full score; it can thus safely be ignored.

In bar 95 a slight coaxing with eye and stick can suggest a fractional rubato on the last four descending cello demisemiquavers leading into the coda without the need for anything so radical as a subdivision. Letter G itself should then be in strict tempo so that there will be no wavering of pulse to upset the 2nd horn as he approaches his little solo from the vantage-point of his long sustained pedal-note, an inspired touch of instrumental colour.

Except in some Breitkopf printings, which annoyingly iron out the difference by adding dots where they were carefully omitted by Beethoven, there is a most attractive change of style in the arch of demisemiquavers which rises and falls across the orchestra in bars 98–100. The staccato dots should start only as the flute reaches his top G; the descending scale then initiates a true staccato which is carried on by an equally light spiccato in the violins and, in their turn, the lower strings; the horn, 1st violins, clarinet, and flute will have previously played in a less short—though naturally never long—mode of execution.

There are many indications (more especially still in the next two symphonies) that Beethoven intended the lower bass notes, here only given in small notes by some editions in bar 100 and 101, as also already in bars 53–4.

The last quaver of bar 101, as well as those in the last two bars, should be given their full length and, accordingly, weight.

In the second last bar the horns clearly start their crescendo from *pp* like the timpani (the 2nd horn G as given by Breitkopf is correct according to the autograph, not D in unison with the first player as in Peters and others); it is also a moot point whether the *pp* crescendo should be added to the pizzicato strings as well since Beethoven omitted to mark this, possibly with intent.

III

This time the printed metronome mark is eminently suitable for what is an intensely energetic Scherzo. The vivacious 1-in-a-bar may at first profitably be given a slight jerkiness in order to emphasize the strongly syncopated character of the theme, which will then alternate with a conspicuously smooth beat for the sinuous contrasting altercation between woodwind and strings.

In bars 24–5, 27–8, etc. the 2nd violins and violas should be given a specifically clear beat if their interplay is to be both confident and rhythmically accurate; on arrival at bar 35 on the other hand, it is the bassoons and cellos whose stepping stones can be positively directed to the point of suggesting stresses at each new footstep, especially when they double in frequency during their long descent.

The 2nd horn needs encouragement during bars 67–75 (and similarly thereafter); although on paper this G does not look very deep it may be remembered that it is written for a horn in B♭ basso and thereby becomes a pedal-note with a good rumbling effect if brought to prominence.

A pronounced springiness of beat to spark the abruptly syncopated forte in bar 75 will prevent the rhythm from becoming sluggish. Then at the jubilant *ff* the intensity of the upper strings can be moderated during the bars (79, 80, 83, 84, etc.) in which the cellos and basses give the answering phrases.

The printed metronome mark only drops from ♩. = 100 to 88 for the Trio, which is hardly enough to allow for the latter's suave oboe melody and the graceful humour of the violins' response; ♩. = 72 would be more appropriate without losing the sense of momentum which so strongly characterizes the whole movement.

The violins' sforzandos in bar 94, 98, etc. should be marginally placed to gain extra pointing, though not so much as to disturb the rhythmic structure, whilst at bar 133 it is well to remember that the silent down-beat of the next bar must, however small, be sharply pointed so that there is no danger of insecure ensemble.

Uniquely amongst the editions, Eulenburg economizes in not printing out in full the double alternation of Scherzo and Trio, so much a feature of Beethoven's middle period, but merely indicating it by means of dal segnos. This not only plays havoc with the bar-count (224 instead of 397) let alone any attempt to insert the rehearsal letters C and D, but is also ambiguous over the question of repeats during the first return of the Scherzo proper.

In bar 312 the Breitkopf parts see fit to give an immediate crescendo (unlike bar 134) which is certainly wrong. There can be no question that this or any other discrepancies between the repeated sections can be traced back to Beethoven since he never wrote out any of the music more than once.

Unfortunately bars 353–6 are entirely lacking in the autograph but even without being able to consult Beethoven himself it is probable that the 2nd violins, who are in any case likely to be less strong than were the 1sts in bars 175 ff., should begin their crescendo immediately at the Tempo I.

A slight broadening in the penultimate bar will help the horns to give a sufficiently dramatic crescendo into the violent short final *ff* chord.

IV

Beethoven's near-Prestissimo whole-bar metronome mark of ♩ = 80 gives an entirely false guide to the tempo of this finale which he himself most sensibly marked as an 'Allegro ma non troppo', nor can it be beaten in 1, however much some sections might be so felt. Apart from the character of the movement, whose boisterous humour loses rather than gains by being taken at a hectic pace, certain passages have to be taken into consideration in deciding upon the tempo, such as not only the famous bassoon solo of bars 184–7, but the 1st violins' semiquaver pas-

sage-work during the first- and second-time bars (100–17), as
equally the corresponding period in the coda (bars 278 ff.). A
suitably lively pace can be $\rfloor$ = 138 which also allows plenty
of scope for Beethoven's paroxysms of mock fury as at letter
D (bars 161 ff.) or at the climax of the coda, bars 302–15.

A transparent texture in the strings is necessary in bars 337–40
if the clarinet triplets are to be heard. This may be even more
important at the return in bars 215–18 where the string background lies higher and the second subject becomes a duet for
the two clarinets.

The repeat in this finale is indispensable; the 1st horn bars
contain an important motivic contribution which is soon to
be developed at length, while the first-time bars also lead back
particularly happily to the opening bars of the movement.

In bar 114 the crescendo no longer persists and the *più
f: ff* mark is a dramatic subito needing very clear pointing from
the conductor. The *p subito* of bar 120 then follows equally
abruptly and without the accommodating comma sometimes
appropriate in such cases; here continuity is the overriding
priority.

It is particularly vital to check any tendency of the violins
to hurry during the breathless build-up from bar 149 to the
ff of letter D. Not only would the furore of D itself be weakened,
its effect lying not in speed but in multiple emphases, whereas
the energetic syncopation of the cellos and basses needs elbow-
room, so to speak, which any frenetic animando would restrict.
Moreover, the bassoon solo which lies in wait only a few bars
ahead could be jeopardized, and any artificial slackening of pace
to accommodate it would be shaming as well as deflating at
the very moment where the development's denouement is to
lead precipitantly into the reprise.

Bar 257 must to some extent remain an open question over
whether the little woodwind flips should be played by the oboe
as in Beethoven's autograph and followed by Breitkopf, or by
the flute as in the first printed score which is also the version
given in every other edition (i.e. Peters, Eulenburg, etc.). The
analogy with bar 79, which gives the whole passage to the flute,
is not conclusive as the phrases in this earlier bar would have
been in a most uncomfortable register for oboe. While there
is not the least room for doubt where the autograph is concerned,

the problem remains whether Beethoven might have changed his mind at proof stage. Certainly the conjecture posed by Eulenberg's editor that it must have been a slip of the pen seems presumptuous.

Once again at bar 278 the tempo has to be held carefully in check both for the clarity of the semiquaver figuration and for the second and parallel bassoon solo. Furthermore, as before, the power of the fortissimo outburst is the more electrifying if it is held rigorously under control with forceful impetus added each time to the fourfold descending scales of the middle strings. A sforzando on each of the G's which cap the phrases can even be suggested by an extra emphasis on every alternate up-beat by the conductor who otherwise will be holding the true furore in reserve for bars 312–15.

These tumultuous bars are of an entirely different order of fortissimo from the preceding passage, strong as this will have been. As we have seen already, Beethoven was still not using the dynamic *fff*, but this is certainly an area worthy of the mark. Moreover, the sudden burst of volume must occur not at the change of harmony in bar 311 but where it is marked, at the succeeding barline. This *coup de théâtre* is not always given sufficient explosiveness; nor is it static through its 4-bar duration. The cellos and basses should use so staccato a bow-style that their rise and fall will penetrate even against the thunder of the timpani, giving yet further forward thrust towards the fermata which can be held lunga. Then without any cut-off, the cellos and basses take their turn at the violins' semiquaver passage-work in a sotto voce subterranean growling.

The ending of the symphony consists of the kind of fun Haydn was fond of enjoying in the last movements of his string quartets. The main semiquaver theme is spelt out at half speed by different groups and with quizzical pauses *en route*. This is usually carried out at much slower tempo, but to make too great a difference is to labour a joke, and ♩ = 120 is probably steady enough with gentle pull-backs towards fermatas given more with the fingers than as subdivisions with the stick. The separated phrases should also lead on to one another without any break, each in turn only to be stopped in its tracks, holding on to its last note. That of the two bassoons could perhaps be held slightly less long than the strings', before giving the *ff* lead to the lower strings with the least warning possible but maximum violence. Neither the lack of some conventional preparatory gesture nor of the down-beat will cause the slightest misunderstanding, whilst both will contribute excellently to the exuberance with which this happiest of symphonies careers to its end.

Symphony No. 5 in C minor,
Op. 67

◄►

I

WITH the Fifth we arrive at one of the great watersheds of all music. It is hard to think of a better-known orchestral work, other than possibly the Schubert 'Unfinished'. After its appearance the very concept of Symphony was never the same again, while it was the universal familiarity of the opening bars which, since their rhythm coincided with the Morse code for the letter V (= the Roman figure 5), prompted their use as the V for Victory symbol during the 1939–45 war.

Yet Beethoven's Fifth is by no means an easy work to conduct. Even apart from the responsibility of presenting such well-known music, it may—perhaps more than any other—give the measure of a conductor's stature. Indeed it is ironic that of all symphonies the opening of this should present one of the greatest technical hazards to any but the most experienced artist. Tales abound of would-be adopters of the baton, prominent soloists among them, who have engaged a professional orchestra with a view to appearing in this dearly sought-after role, only to suffer the humiliation of being unable to start the first movement at all. Other equally authentic legends are handed down of world-famous conductors who have given a succession of silent preparatory beats in attempts to minimize the problem, or of over-rehearsing the orchestra in order to compensate for their lack of gestural expertise. Even so great a conductor as Mahler is documented as having kept his superb Viennese orchestra for hours at a stretch on just these bars until they were so infuriated that they were on the verge of rebellion. 'Keep your outrage until tonight', he is reported to have said, 'and then we shall have the right performance.'

The technical problem of launching that formidable first phrase is partially linked to the fact that it comes after a rest, so that the conductor's first gesture has to be a silent syncopated down-beat, clearly identifiable as a beat *after* which (as opposed to *on* which) the orchestra enters. Such down-beats which initiate a work or movement always contain an element of risk. The slightest extra sign or preparation produces the possibility of accident (a 'domino' as it is known in orchestral parlance) and confidence has not only to be felt but conveyed by the man on the 'box'. Similar instances can easily be found in the orchestral repertoire, prime amongst them, perhaps, being the Overture to Smetana's *The Bartered Bride*.

But the Fifth is the worst of all, partly because of its vehemence, but largely because the initial rest is so short that the syncopated beat, which has to be so forceful, cannot of itself prescribe the speed of the succeeding *ff* quavers. The safety device of beating any number of preliminary bars could be argued to be wrong *ipso facto*, in that to an even greater extent than in the Scherzo of the 'Eroica' this destroys the element of drama. But the crux of the problem continues to lie in deciding on that element of tempo which has to be suggested without the advantage of any kind of preparatory up-beat.

So much depends on this sheer question of speed. Certainly the quicker the quavers the easier they are to indicate; but whether the symphony—ferocious as it is at the beginning—should really start in a furious rage is very much a matter of opinion, even though none other than Toscanini used to conduct it in exactly this manner. After all, Beethoven's metronome mark is ♩ = 108 which is, as usual, certainly brisk but for once not fantastically fast, whereas a slightly easier pace of ♩ = 96 will allow just that extra margin both for the detailed interplay between the sections of the orchestra and for the dramatic events which are such a feature of this highly original conception.

But once the speed of the movement is established, this will not of itself take for granted that the pace of the declamatory opening phrases must necessarily be at full tempo, bearing in mind the significance with which they should be imbued.

It can in the first place be assumed that the movement must be conducted in 1-in-a-bar, so that in purely technical terms every bar is of course actually a down-beat. (I only once had the misfortune to play with a conductor who actually took it in two, which was with Malcolm Sargent in the First Orchestra at the RCM; he believed that we students needed that extra guidance; the result was a disaster.)

But thereafter it is fundamental to decide whether bar 1 is an 'up-beat' or a 'down-beat' bar. In this respect Weingartner was the first to reveal the bar-structure by rewriting the opening sentence as follows:

Ex. 3

This certainly goes a long way, and yet not far enough. To understand in full the structure so that one is never in two minds over which are weak (up-beat) and which strong (down-beat) bars, it is necessary to regroup the passage into still larger periods dominated by the primary, but not inflexibly regular, 4-bar format. Thus in applying Weingartner's thesis in the larger scheme it becomes at once, and for the first time, clear that there is an immediate and salient irregularity:

Ex. 4

This demonstrates not only Weingartner's point regarding the down-beat function of bar 1, but also that of the first two bars as a 2-bar period complete in itself, a fact which further increases its power and significance. Bars 3–5 then repeat the gesture in elongated form, with bar 3 still a *ff* down-beat bar but the fermata extended to bar 4,* this being the third bar of a 4-bar period.

---

*It has to be remembered that the original autograph lacks this elongation which would seem to have been an afterthought. Whatever one chooses to deduce from this, it is at least apparent that Beethoven himself gave careful consideration to the matter of bar structure since he subsequently took the trouble to have the extra bar added throughout the movement.

The fourth bar (bar 6 of the symphony) then starts the exposition proper with the *p* entry of the 2nd violins, an entry which may legitimately initiate the full tempo of the Allegro con brio.

If the concept of a strong first bar can be accepted (and there are notable opposing schools of thought, especially those based on the analysis of Heinrich Schenker), it will be self-evident that the conductor's evocation of that bar must be of the utmost vehemence, conveying as it should not only the syncopated point of rebound *off* which the orchestra works but the enunciation of the three quavers. It is useless to try to formulate the way this is done in terms of conventional stick technique. It is direction by pure force of gesture and depends entirely on the will-power and total conviction of the conductor.

The next question often raised is whether it is necessary or even desirable to take the orchestra off after each fermata. This is indeed sometimes done in the interests of simplicity and to avoid any possibility of misunderstanding. But to do so wrongly elongates the quaver rest, thereby unwarrantably breaking up the music. A better continuum is established if pairs of pauses are taken together, a cut-off only being made before the piano phrases which start the new and longer sections. In this event the stick rises during the first fermata so that the second syncopated *ff* down-beat can be given. Then after a quick demarcation of the extra barline, not to be omitted on any account, the stick rises again during the second fermata, though more slowly so as to prevent any lessening of intensity before the cut-off. The lead for the piano string entries can then be quietly given with the character of an up-beat, which will also facilitate the extra momentum necessary to establish the forward impetus of the Allegro con brio proper.

This principle governing which fermatas are taken off and which are not is perfectly regular, but nevertheless not always understood. While double fermatas carry only the one cut-off for the sake of continuity, single fermatas are always taken off (as, for example, at bar 128) since, like the second pause of each pair, they occur at points of structural demarcation characterized by complete change of dynamic and pace.

Bar 21 is no exception to the fermata principle and indeed, since the intensity of the 1st violins' sustained G is such that it can be held lunga (balancing, if naturally to a far less extent, the oboe cadenza at the equivalent place in the reprise), it serves a double purpose. The first is essentially practical, for it enables the violins to take two bows (down/up) which not only allows for maximum sustaining power but brings the bows back to the heel for the immediate continuation. The second consideration is the function of bar 21, for Beethoven saw no need to show that this bar corresponds with both the third and fourth of the 4-bar scheme, thus enabling bar 22 regularly to assume its down-beat status. The shape of the music thus emerges as:

Ex. 5

The Leipzig Breitkopf parts add slurs to the 1st violins in bars 34–7 not to be found in the score. No doubt this seemed to be justified by analogy with, for example, bars 15–18 as well as matching the ties in 2nd violins and violas. But it is not at all a clear-cut case, and later there will be even more important instances where the phrasing can be shown to start at the barline rather than merely maintaining a symmetrical pattern. Hence, if bars 34–5 are played as shown in the score:

Ex. 6

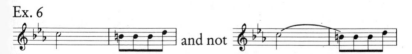

the crescendo of bars 34–7 gains enormously in intensity. Yet a further element in this build-up lies in the wind contributions and especially Beethoven's horn crescendo at bars 34–5, correctly restored in the Breitkopf parts though omitted from most scores.

Bars 38–43 naturally make an irregular 6-bar period: nor is this the only instance, for bars 88–93 make another, similarly introduced as further means of adding power as the transition approaches the horn-call which prefaces the second subject. (These two balancing 6-bar phrases recur identically in the reprise.)

The mighty fanfare of bars 59–63 calls for the utmost ring in the tone quality. But it easily becomes *cuivré* (or *schmetternd*) if overblown and this tips the balance from supreme exultation into vulgarity. Moreover it is better played by two horns rather than four, or even three (allowing for the support of the bumper): curiously, extra horns add weight but reduce vibrancy, and the effect here becomes gross instead of thrilling. If the 1st horn wishes to work with 4 or 5 horns for Beethoven's two parts in this symphony the additional players should be scrupulously held in reserve for the finale (i.e. not even the Scherzo). There is, however, patently no objection to the 3rd and 4th playing the Andante on their own in alternation to the first pair.

In phrasing the gentle second subject one should always bear in mind that the first bar is an up-beat, i.e. the fourth of a 4-bar period. Commentators have over the years been assiduous in stressing the importance of this, on the basis of which the whole section falls correctly into shape, including the entry of the oboe in bar 84.

Although for the first time in the symphonies there are no first- or second-time bars, the repeat in this movement is imperative. Apart from its function in balancing the relative proportions, the organization of the return is of the utmost significance where the bar-structure is concerned, as Beethoven makes the reappearance of bar 1 occur unequivocally as an up-beat, thus changing its initial function and thereby arguably influencing the way it should be performed. For it does not need quite the same exaggerated emphasis on the quavers as it had when, as one of the strongest first bars in the history of music, it inaugurated the whole furious 'Fate-knocking' drama.

Nor is this duality of the opening bars' design merely fortuitous, for their return at the recapitulation brings them once more into exactly the same relationship as at the beginning, whilst at their ultimate return in the coda the first bar arrives as an up-beat, corresponding to its positioning at the repeat of the exposition. That this difference is intentional and central to the construction of the whole movement can be illustrated by an adjacent comparison of the relevant passages rebarred as before.

Ex. 7a

Ex. 7b

The development at first presents no new problems. Standing as an isolated declamatory utterance, bars 125–8 need the kind of extra weight and intensity which will again broaden the actual speed of the quavers, while the fortissimo fermata is, of course, taken off before embarking on bar 129. But now the pattern is rearranged to include a contribution by the clarinets, and these need to be brought out a little. Bars 145 and 153 are two of Beethoven's typical subito pianos which can be exaggerated by giving the preceding crescendos ample scope. It is then surely legitimate to take the *pp* in trumpets and timpani as the cue to drop the dynamic in the rest of the orchestra excepting, perhaps, the principal woodwinds whose answering phrases need to be clearly audible.

Bars 162–8 patently produce a 6-bar period similar to the crescendo-orientated 6-bar groups of the exposition, but when we come to the next section the framework is less self-evident. There are many places in the repertoire where the phrasing of the music is at odds with the conventional barring notation. Brahms was particularly fond of writing passages where the phrases are set wholly against the regular system of barlines, as any conductor familiar with the First Symphony slow movement or the last movement of his No. 4 will readily recall; and in the following passage Beethoven plays his own characteristic game in throwing the natural inflexions of the music out of step with the strict formal pattern. Had he lived fifty years later he might even have laid out the movement in larger bar-units which would have made the ingenuity of his phrase-syncopation immediately apparent to the eye. But as it is, it requires no great knowledge of mathematics to discover that the whole of the remainder of the development continues to maintain the regular 4-bar structure right through until the arrival of the recapitulation at bar 248, even though this is not at all the way the music plays, or should be made to phrase.

This accounts for the savage *ff* string crunches at the first quaver of both bars 228 and 240 with which Beethoven brings the perceptible rhythm violently back into line. But inexcusably these were once actually ironed out in the Breitkopf orchestral material on the grounds that in this primarily monothematic movement it seemed to the editors axiomatic that all phrases must begin uniformly at the second quaver of the bar. The parts were accordingly bowdlerized by moving the *ff*'s a quaver forward in each of these bars, and Beethoven's splendid device to restore stability of bar-rhythm was utterly obliterated. (It may, however, be added gratefully that later printings of the Breitkopf material correct this editorial interference, although sets of the older parts are still in wide circulation.)

But it is one thing studiously to have analysed a structure and quite another to reveal its essence securely and confidently in performance. The need to be able to set aside consciousness of Beethoven's bar syncopation, so that the way it has practically to be presented can be clearly indicated, has already been shown in relation to the Trio of the 'Eroica', and will again arise later especially in both the Scherzo of the present symphony and in that of the Seventh. In all such instances the difference between theory and practice remains the primary consideration, with knowledge of the theoretical structure relegated to the background of the practical performer's thought processes.

On this basis the second part of the development may be felt and directed as follows:

1. *Bars* 180–7 *and* 188–95: each of these 8-bar phrases divided into two subsections of 2 + 6, the first bars of the 6-bar periods beginning with a strongly syncopated gesture to the lower strings in order to spark off their vigorous descending phrases. The wind are then brought as much as possible into prominence, whilst recognizing that their rhythmic groups do not in fact pass from one to another with the easily heard continuity suggested on the printed page. Indeed, the bassoon figures in bars 183–4, and especially 190–1 where they initiate the sequence of events, are almost impossible to bring through.

2. Two regular 4-bar phrases follow, *bars* 196–9 *and* 200–3, with no conflict between theory and practice; the principal consideration here is rather the question of how the strings' answering minims should be bowed. Although their forcefulness causes them often to be played with two down-bows, this makes them too separate, as well as unduly rugged. A better plan is to prescribe down/up while at the same time making a little gap between the bow-strokes. Now, however, the trouble begins.

3. *Bars* 204–14: clearly in the pattern of alternate wind/string chord sequences it is the wind who always take the lead, and it is they who accordingly initiate the harmonic changes (at bars 209, 211, 213, 215, and 221) which can only be perceived as occurring on strong rhythmic bars. But, to arrive at this, a hop has to be made in the bar-rhythm, and the subtlest as well as the most convincing way to do so is to convert bars 204–8 into a 5-bar phrase by reversing the bowing of bars 206–7 to up/down, thus instinctively transferring the implied stress to the modulating second chords of this and the following woodwind pair of minims. The audible musical shape then gives a 6-bar phrase (bars 209–14) during which the wind, having been brought into the lead, now direct the harmony into an entirely new key.

4. *Bars* 215–20: these bars are now plainly revealed as a threefold alternation in the new tonality of F♯ minor.

5. *Bars* 221–7: a similar but fourfold alternation then follows on the first inversion triad of yet a further tonality, that of D major. But this is rudely interrupted by the first of the savage *ff* initial quavers bowdlerized by Breitkopf, which in fact, as Beethoven wrote it, forces the music back into its basic 4-bar rhythm by its insistence that bar 228 is the first bar of a new period.

6. Even now this is not the end of the story: the phrase beginning at bar 228 (bars 228–32) dovetails with its successor (bars 233–9) in such a way that the 12 bars of these combined passages (= 3 × 4 bars) can only be felt and conveyed as 5 + 7, the 5 bars presenting the horn-call motif and the 7 bars being another fourfold wind/string alternation, interrupted and curtailed in its turn by the second savage *ff* initial quaver, as Beethoven again violently forces the pattern back to regularity. The effect, as we have seen in the music example above, is of initiating the last two 4-bar periods (bars 240–7) which are to lead to the arrival of the recapitulation, so that it corresponds with the opening bars of the symphony.

The recapitulation seems to start regularly enough but the deceptive simplicity of the oboe's long sustained notes is to lead to the cadenza of bar 268 which is essentially the continuation of his extended solo, and with this in mind it may be as well to mark the strings *pp* for their reprise of bars 6 ff. (i.e. the passage beginning at bar 253). The bassoon's line, also of some importance and interest, will thereby also make a stronger contribution. The cadenza itself is, of course, left entirely to the oboist, the conductor standing quite still once the fortissimo chords have been dismissed.

The dying away of the oboe leaves behind so awed an atmosphere that the tension should be maintained for some seconds before the recapitulation is resumed. Furthermore the strings can again begin extremely softly as if the orchestra has yet to recover from such a moment of drama. In neither of these suggested pianissimos should there, however, be any relaxation of tempo, for this is an extra expressive resource to be kept in reserve for a later and still more significant return of the same music in the coda. Only at bar 273 will the unison of the full string body allow for a swift return to forcefulness with its rapid crescendo from *pp* to *f* over just four bars.

The controversy with respect to the reprise of the horn fanfare at bars 303–5 continues unabated. In these days of overriding authenticity the pendulum of opinion has swung right away from the once automatic take-over by the horns of their heroic gesture from the bassoons, who indeed tend to be positively offended at being so unceremoniously supplanted. In the interests of purist adherence to Beethoven's text many conductors are today being persuaded (even by players of both departments) to restore the original instrumentation, but it is idle to maintain that with our present-day style of refined bassoon playing the outcome is anything but a grotesque caricature, even with the best instrumentalists in the land.

This is not, as is often believed, because the actual instruments are incapable of producing some semblance of the necessary quality or volume, especially if three bassoons are pressed into service (a simple expedient in the circumstances, since the contra player can be instructed to carry his regular bassoon for just this passage). But bassoonists refuse with outraged indignation to emulate the sound of the instruments of Beethoven's day by means of overblowing, except perhaps in mockery at rehearsal, even though the effect they are able to create by so doing approximates surprisingly nearly to what must have been the intention, and is not so dissimilar to the sound of natural horns as might be expected.

One somewhat artificial alternative is that of retaining the bassoons but adding one of the horns in support. At best no more than a compromise, it at least preserves the bassoon quality Beethoven actually prescribed together with the corresponding horn tone indigenous to the passage, which is in any case reinforced by the printed entry of the 2nd horn in bar 306. But it cannot be pretended that this is the ultimate solution and one thinks wistfully back to the days when every conductor used horns as a matter of course on the assumption that Beethoven's only possible reason for giving the passage to the bassoons had been his reluctance to spoil the effect of so grand a *ff* horn call by accepting the edged stopped tones of his natural horns for two notes out of the four, as there was no possibility of leaving sufficient time for crook changing as he had done in the 'Eroica'.

The overwhelming effect of the unique 5-bar period in Beethoven's own bar-structure which occurs early in the coda has been the enthusiastic subject of many a commentator. But with alternative views being held over exactly where the 5-bar phrase occurs, it is surprising how many analyses surely come down on the wrong side. Bars 391–4 correspond exactly with 382–5, as the lower strings' octave jumps in both bars 382 and 391 plainly show, so that it must be the silent bar 389 which supplies the extension and not one of those between 392–4. Lest, however, the concept of bar 390 as an up-beat bar might risk robbing the entry of its essential strength, all three quavers must be given maximum accentuation with every instrument marked *fff*.

If the approach to bar 478 is made without any broadening whatsoever, the result is unwarrantably brutal. The rage is so towering, the sense of manic hammering so superhuman, that time and space is necessary to summon up the tutta forza emphases. Bar 480 in particular wants some further separation of the quavers leading to a lunghissima corona to the limits of the winds' breath control.

Just as after the oboe cadenza, but to an even greater extent, bars 483–90 have the sense of a shocked reflective aftermath, and now Beethoven does indeed mark back this last version of the strings' imitative thematic entry to *pp*; but here a slightly reduced pace is additionally appropriate for the woodwinds' solo melodizing, as they sadly outline the contours of the strings' thematic passages. Full tempo primo then returns abruptly at the *ff* of bar 491, the last two bars being played pesante but in strict tempo.

II

The Andante is better taken at ♪ = 72, rather than the printed 92 which would give an Allegretto feeling to what is primarily a calm movement after the fury of the preceding music. The more leisurely pace will still allow for Beethoven's 'con moto' whilst preventing a feeling of hurrying, particularly later when the demisemiquavers become an essential feature. One of the movement's outstanding characteristics is the differentiation between short notes, such as the semiquaver at the end of bar 5 which was once commonly misplayed as a demi. But whilst this is now less of a hazard in any reputable orchestra, the wheel has gone full cycle and a school of thought has arisen which actually proposes that Beethoven would have assumed the double-dotting. Similarly the 4-against-3 of the 2nd clarinet and violas in bars 14 and 18 may no longer be an open-and-shut case and the possibility has to be considered that, as with composers of earlier centuries, the demi and the triplet semiquaver should perhaps be made to correspond. This is a problem which, already having raised its head in Haydn (cf. Symphony No. 93 in D, second movement), becomes quite acute in Schubert. It is, however, very doubtful whether this kind of baroque attitude to notation can be made to apply in blanket uniformity to Beethoven and especially to instances such as constantly recur during the present movement in which rhythmic figures like the prevalent ♪. ♬ | ♩ would be woefully softened if turned into triplets. At the same time the opposite extreme has also to be avoided whereby the little note is made to come so positively after the last of the triplet that it virtually turns into one of a sextuplet.

The Leipzig Breitkopf parts repeatedly give hairpin diminuendos between the strings' *f*'s and *p*'s, as in bars 9, 18, etc. There can be no doubt that these are wrong and that the pianos must be subito as is so typical of Beethoven's style. To avoid loss of intensity during the latter part of these forte bars however, the beat needs to show an unmistakable preserving of tension, remembering that the string players have to be encouraged to compensate for the fact that they are approaching the weaker end of the bow. A suddenly relaxed down-beat then naturally results in the soft resolution of these cadences. Moreover, the opposite kind of subito occurs for the fortissimo of letter A, the unexpected explosion of which being another of Beethoven's favourite devices.

On both practical and musical grounds the triplet figurations of the strings in bars 32 ff. should be played martellato, in which event those in the violas a few bars earlier will be taken in the same style since although soft they need the same firm quality rather than lightness.

It is disappointing to have to document that a favourite point of interpretation, the timpani sforzandos on the third beat of both bars 35 and 36 (and again, of course, 84 and 85) prove to be a misreading of Beethoven's autograph. The *sf*'s should come on the first beats of each bar together with the rest of the orchestra.

The interlude of bars 41–7 conveys an atmosphere of such stillness that the less beat one gives the better; indeed, after the 1st bassoon's change of note in the middle of bar 41 (which can be given by hardly more than a raised eyebrow) it is only the chord changing at each new barline which requires indication by some marginal movement of hand and stick. Nevertheless the tempo must be conscientiously maintained, a discipline which needs great concentration as well as awareness that when this whole passage returns with the addition of the cellos' figuration (bars 88–96) the tempos will have to be exactly matched. A true 3 in a bar is resumed for the crescendo and to prepare the accentuated octave-jumping E♭'s.

In bars 72 ff. the violas' demisemiquavers need attention and can be marked up to *mp*, though perhaps with a diminuendo in bar 75 as they hand over to the 1st violins. The little figure which now appears for the first time (and is to become the cellos' dominating motif at the return of the static interlude) is taken off the string.

Bar 80 brings into prominence a controversy which will have even greater relevance in the finale (see pp. 94–5), namely Beethoven's treatment of the lowest notes of the basses. We know that in German-speaking countries, as also in Russia, basses with the low C had been in existence already in Mozart's day and were often, if not regularly, to be counted upon. The evidence seems to suggest that Beethoven must surely have preferred the low C in bar 80 no less than in bar 31.

At bars 114 ff. (letter C) the lower strings need to use many more bows than Beethoven's phrasings indicate, even a change of bow every beat in order to bring their variation through against the reiterated semiquavers of the violins and woodwind. It may even be necessary to reduce the rhythmic accompaniment to *mf* until a general crescendo through the ascending scales leads to a glowing climax on the fermata. The pause itself is held on the down-beat lunga, but not more extended than can be accommodated by a single bow; the orchestra is then taken off with a preparatory second beat to allow for overhang before bringing in the *pp* strings with the third beat. A single down-bow for the fermata, sufficient if sustained no stronger than a single forte, will bring the strings to the upper half and the succeeding bars can be taken with a minimum amount of bow at the point.

In bars 145–6 (two before D) the repeated notes on the wind can be a little less short than the preceding staccato semiquavers for purposes of the crescendo; in particular the dramatic entry of the horns which in forte needs considerable weight, should be emphasized as if they were marked with lines and dots (‾·). As we have seen in the Andante of the Fourth Symphony, Beethoven was prone to omit the dots on repetitions of similar notes, but there are places, as here, where this can conveniently be taken to indicate a difference in style.

Timpani notation is such a grey area that in bars 150 and 153–5 it is hard to determine whether the single quavers should be specifically emphasized or merely taken to indicate the end of the rolls. Undoubtedly they add greatly to the drama of the passage if strongly accentuated, whether or not this had been Beethoven's intention.

Bar 164 can be magical if the 1st violins are asked to play even more softly (*ppp*); this will further contribute to the expectancy Beethoven arouses by continuing their broken chords for an extra bar before the entry of the woodwind.

It is an attractive piece of play-acting to pin-point the little 'peeps' on the oboe, possibly with the left hand forefinger: one can decide for oneself whether these notes are humorous or whimsical, but either way they cannot be allowed to pass unob served, relating as they do to the corresponding 'flips' in the più moto (bars 210–12) where, incidentally, the grace-notes come before the beat.

In bars 181–4 the cumulative effect created by the rising scale figures needs to be organized so that the dynamics of each starts where the last leaves off, i.e. the violas *p*, the 2nd violins *mp* and so on until the woodwind pick up the thread at not less than forte.

The movement's opening returning so powerfully, during bars 185–94, presents some difficulties of balance. If Beethoven's *ff* marking across the orchestra is observed strictly the woodwind imitation recedes into the background and one might well wonder what prompted Beethoven to use the oboes merely to fill in the harmony, when their penetrating tone would have made so much difference to the thematic counterpoint. It is, however, perfectly possible to deal with the matter without old-fashioned *Retuschen*, such as Malcolm Sargent was prone to adopt, but by organizing instead some staggered system of hairpins indicating alternate rises and falls between the phrasings of wind and strings which, if skilfully done, need not sound fussy or intrusive. The ascending scales of bars 191–4 must also stand out clearly, though this can be more easily effected by ensuring that they are played more sharply staccato than the supporting repeated demisemiquavers of 2nd violins and violas.

The thoughtful return of the recurring after-phrase in bars 199–205 can be very subdued and, uniquely, without any vestige of its customary accents and swells, especially as before long it is to be followed by its final statement (bars 223 ff.), which on the contrary carries the most poignant dynamics of all. However, the mood here is one of resignation which is the more profound for its undemonstrative reserve, although it seems to want the least suggestion of lingering as it merges into the più moto.

The variation of pulse for this short contrasted section is predominantly gentle, such as would be disturbed by too fundamental a gear-change, so to speak; ♪ = 100 gives ample difference and also allows the tempo primo to be restored effortlessly in bars 218–19 through the placing of the notes which build up the B♭ major chord. Even experienced wind players sometimes do not realize how this works and so their entries fail to match convincingly. There is a similar and extended chord-building operation both upwards and downwards in the Passacaglia of

Britten's *Peter Grimes* which presents this same exercise in acute form.

After the peak expressiveness of bars 223–7 the movement subsides to a trough of absolute tranquillity, more static even than the two interludes of earlier periods in the structure. As the music fades away during the cadence of bars 227–9 the increasingly soft string quaver chords may legitimately be spaced further and further apart and with no hint of pulse-beating between them. The last entry of the string group in bar 229 can never be hushed enough.

The final sentence can start below tempo (perhaps ♪ = 69) but the feeling of the original Andante con moto will gradually return once the calm of the held A♭ chord is disturbed by the measured woodwind pulsations in bars 237 ff. The initiation of the triplets in bar 239 needs to be indicated with positive rhythmic clarity or the boat can all too easily rock. By this point full tempo will have been reached and is then maintained to the end, excepting only in the penultimate bar where the *ff* unison wind E♭ may be a little sustained in an expressive tenuto. The conclusive string chords are not staccato but firmly placed and non divisi.

III

The need to consider bar-phrasings arises again with the Scherzo. In the first place, strict formal analysis reveals the fact that the first bars of both Scherzo and Trio function as up-beat bars; the whole movement then can be shown to fall, like the development of the first movement, into an unbroken succession of 4-bar phrases.

But here, too, analytical truth is not the main issue, for Beethoven is again playing a number of different games with the accentuations of his themes, and in the audible musical phrasings the bar-lengths seem accordingly to provide a variety of irregularities. For example, he gives clear wind entries indicating that bars such as 4, 48, 60, etc. are to be thought as first bars of their respective periods, while the extension of the passage leading to the *sfp* at bar 13 shifts the emphasis so that bar 15 is made to feel like the start of a phrase, unlike the phrase beginning at bar 5.

Furthermore, the great subsidiary motif begins so powerfully that despite the up-beat feeling generated by the delayed entry of the strings it too might suggest a first-bar beginning, a concept which Beethoven reinforces not only at the restatement on massed wind and strings in bar 27 but with even greater emphasis at the entry of trumpets and timpani in bar 71,* the *ff* of bar 113 even seeming to clinch the matter. Nevertheless, despite the seeming ambiguity, this gives a false view of the phrasing as is proved by the harmonies, which throw the accentuation forward on to the dotted minims, so confirming the structural purpose in the delayed entry of the pounding strings at bar 19, the very first entry of the motif.

When four horns are carried for performances of this work they are all too often used to thunder out the powerful annunciations of the rhythmic figure which, with its close relationship to that of the first movement, might be taken as the primary motif of the whole symphony. But, as in the first movement, the result becomes crude and, as has been said before, the extra players should not be introduced until much later.

Whichever way one decides to break down the bar-phrases for clarity of thought in conducting, some 6-bar periods must inevitably be allowed to disturb the regularity of the strictly 4-bar format of the movement as, for example, not only at bars 10–16, but at bars 32–7, 54–9, etc.

At the poco ritardandos a kind of semi-subdivision can mark the last crotchet before each of the pauses which might otherwise be reached too abruptly. On the other hand too wide a gap can turn the bars immediately preceding into seeming $\frac{4}{4}$ bars, a danger most commonly encountered at bars 253–4.

Conscientiously as one may reckon to play the Trio at the same basic tempo as the Scherzo proper, in practice this remains an unattainable ideal. The Scherzo itself can be made to work naturally at $\downarrow$. = 88, which allows for the forcefulness of the secondary theme as well as the delicacy of such passage-work as bars 116 ff., this being only a fraction steadier than the printed

---

*In some Breitkopf scores an erroneous letter A is given at bar 70 in addition to the one at the proper place of bar 96.

mark of ♩. = 96. But at the stormy entry of the Trio the weight
of the cellos and basses inevitably pulls the tempo back to about
♩. = 72, especially as the string entries are all so strong that
they require emphatic separation of each of their first two notes,
such as will be secured with the necessary weight and force
by two consecutive down-bows; the initial loss in momentum
can nevertheless be gradually restored as the fugatos pile up.

Where the rhythmical bar-patterns of this Trio are concerned
Beethoven is again deliberately confusing the issue. No matter
how much analytical study can prove that its first bar is technically an up-beat, this furious fugato is so planned that every
entry must actually give the effect of a strong bar, so that the
fugato subject inevitably comes across as a 6-bar phrase starting
immediately at the outset (bar 141). The violas' answer is then
another 6-bar period, and the two cumulative violin entries are
contained in a phrase of 5 bars plus a truncated 3-bar extension
for the first-time repeat, but with an extension to 4 full bars
for the second-time continuation. Indeed, the way in which
the completion of the period with the 2nd violins' and violas'
violent answer of bars 160–1 is withheld until after the repeat
is highly typical of the economy which is a particular characteristic of the Fifth above all Beethoven's symphonies.

It is more than apparent through Beethoven's dynamics that
this delayed extra bar had for him particular emphatic purpose
since the Trio, for all its tempestuous drive, is only designated
by a series of single fortes (albeit to be interpreted as rinforzandos) until just this point where he specifically introduces the
double forte, as again similarly at bar 196.

Moreover, as a result of this added bar, from bar 162 onwards
it will be found that the fugato really does start on a strong
bar, whether interrupted (as in bars 163 and 165) or with continua-
tions, so that once again Beethoven has deliberately imbued
a principal theme of this extraordinary movement with an ambiguity of accentuation.

The repeated down-bows of the fugato entries continue,
through the diminuendo of bars 199–200 and until the piano
of bar 201, by which time the passion has drained out of the
Trio and an up-bow can start the cellos and basses on the last
section leading back to the uniformly quiet return of the Scherzo
proper.

Here we arrive at the second major controversy of the symphony. As the text stands, the collapse of the Trio leads with dramatic purpose into the hushed restatement of the Scherzo material, which itself dies wholly away to the unprecedented calm of the link to the finale. The conciseness and logic of the form is one of the most masterly in the history of music. Yet it did not come easily to its creator who was at a period of his development during which he was experimenting repeatedly with a double scherzo-trio relationship, as can be seen in the Fourth, Sixth, and Seventh symphonies as well as numerous chamber works. For a time it is known to have been in his mind to pursue the same second appearance of the Trio here too, but he ultimately rejected it as unsuitable for the particular circumstances which prevailed in this unique work. The story of the two extra bars which survived in early materials despite Beethoven's letter to his publishers, stressing the need for their removal, has been told often enough. These bars, occurring between bars 239 and 240 in the score as we have it, were intended to have made provision for a return to the beginning of the movement, although they seem at one time foolishly to have been played not as alternative bars for the first- and second-time but together, the one pair after the other.

Until recently Beethoven's decision was accepted as indisputable, but a number of present-day scholars have latterly formulated the theory that the master may have had yet further thoughts on the matter. Performances have even been initiated and a miniature score published (edited by Gülke for Peters in East Germany) in which the bars are restored and the five-part format of the movement reinstated. But, despite the vehemence of the arguments, the final verdict has shown that however much 'es liess ihm keine Ruhe' (as Beethoven wrote at one stage) he ultimately left unchanged the terse format which is so strongly in keeping with the compact structural balance of the whole work, and that to alter his published text on no more than conjectural evidence must surely be an error of judgement.

It has also been said, nevertheless, that Beethoven's choice of bar 238 as the place for what was to be the abortive first-time bars confirms the view whereby the whole movement had begun

with an up-beat. There is undoubtedly justice in this but in
the transition bars Beethoven goes to great lengths to disguise
the fact; the change back to the Minore key signature and the
arco cellos and basses all point to an arrival situation on a down-
beat at the double-bar, thus requiring an extended 6-bar phrase
to restore the rhythmic equilibrium.

The violins' and violas' appoggiaturas in bars 255 ff. come
just before the beat, but they should be so close to their respective crotchets as to make the matter almost academic. In any
case throughout this whispering return the beat wants to be
as tiny, and the whole manner of conducting as restrained, as
clarity and the preservation of pulse will allow.

The end of the Scherzo and the beginning of the awesome
bridge to the finale are elided by means of another 6-bar phrase,
and letter C (bar 324) starts a new series of 4-bar periods which
are clearly characterized by the changes of pattern in the timpani;
the entry of the 2nd violins then occurs at the beginning of
one of these periods. But what happens subsequently is very
much a matter of personal choice.

Until bar 352 the 4-bar structure seems incontrovertibly to
continue, and the phrasing in Beethoven's autograph (unlike
the printed scores) takes it on for yet a further pair of regular
groupings to bar 360. Yet this is not necessarily the easiest way
either to think or to bow the passage. On the one hand a simplistic case can be made for thinking in 3-bar phrases since this
puts an upper note at the beginning of each group, i.e. in turn
E♭, E♮, G, B♮, D, and finally F, the latter also coinciding with
the entry of the oboes. (This is not to say, however, that the
bowing need conform, as too many bow-changes would result,
and since smoothness over the entire curve is the required end-
product these could occur at various less frequent intervals or
even be taken freely with staggered bowing.)

On the other hand if it is thought that Beethoven's own phrase
lengths should be retained for as long as possible, all that is
needed is yet another 6-bar period at bars 360–5. This will then
cause the last two 4-bar phrases to arrive at respectively the
strings' crescendo (plus the timpani change to quavers and the
entry of the bassoons), and the final cataclysmic upsurge of tone
with the entry of the brass and flutes, leading to the most significant double-bar in the history of Symphony.

IV

It is surely unimaginative to launch this finale without reflecting on the overwhelming impact the opening bars must have had upon its first audience. This is to some extent because of the unprecedented forces which are suddenly unleashed at this moment into Symphony—that is to say, Symphony as a form, not specifically this fifth symphony of Beethoven. Piccolo, con-trabassoon, above all trombones, these were hitherto instru-ments with religious or theatrical affiliations, and their intrusion on to the symphonic arena was a dramatic stroke only to be compared with the same composer's introduction of the human voice twenty years later; their effect upon an unprepared public can only have been galvanizing.

Nor was this all: possibly even more revolutionary was the quite new relative importance of this finale *vis-à-vis* the earlier movements. Previously a symphony's last movement was to be considered the lighter-weight rounding-off of the overall scheme, the deepest import of which lay essentially in the first and slow movements. Admittedly Beethoven had already in the 'Eroica' shown that a finale could introduce profundities and triumphs of its own. But after the finale of his Fifth no composer could ever again approach the composition of a sym-phony without considering, planning, determining how the question of the finale was to be tackled, a problem which, until now, had simply not existed. Henceforward the finale was to be a challenge: either it could again be a climactic movement as here initiated by Beethoven, or on the contrary it might be organized on some quite other basis; composers, in fact, could no longer continue as if the Fifth had never been written but were often driven to invent different solutions of all kinds, such as the use of cyclic restatements of material from earlier move-ments or by totally contrasted ground-plans, such as the Adagio lamentoso which usurps the place of a conventional finale in Tchaikovsky's *Symphonie Pathétique*, a measure imitated by Mahler in his Ninth, these giving obvious examples in the Special Pleading category.

It is tempting, therefore, to try and mark the arrival of Beetho-ven's great pioneering finale by some kind of demonstration.

One wishes that it could be possible to jump in the air, or perhaps hold up a flag. Certainly anything less than an atmosphere of *triomphale* would be a betrayal of the occasion and, in the creation of this, the first two bars may be poised at just one degree below tempo, the true pace of which is established in bar 3 by a hammering at full force and speed of the sharply detached quaver chords, all taken in the strings by a succession of non divisi down-bows for which the printed metronome mark of ♩ = 84 is admirably suited.

In bars 381, 383,* and similar places it is good to turn to the lower strings as, together with the contrabassoon, they continually descend to the bottom C, reaching it each time just after the upper strings and woodwind have risen to their upper C's, though together with these melodic instruments when at the third phase they ascend further to the top E. The fundamental C's, which can be made to resound wonderfully, raise the question—already posed in the earlier movements, as well as previously in the Fourth Symphony (and furthermore soon to recur in those which follow)—as to whether Beethoven actually wished for the basses to continue below E in all these instances.

The facts are these:†

'Beethoven writes a single cello/bass-line almost throughout, though he is punctilious at first about writing a separate bass-line whenever the cellos go below E♭—the autograph shows a clear E♭ for the basses soli in bars 9 and 56 of the Andante. But gradually more and more often he forgets, until by bar 607 of the finale he is writing 'coi violoncelli' even in whole passages for whose previous statement he had thought about a separate bass-line, as at bar 405. What seems odd, moreover, are the instances where he starts a 'coi violoncelli' instruction in a very bar where the cellos have a low C, as in bars 381 and 453. He clearly had no positive desire here for the basses to take the upper octave, but would perhaps only have written them so (had he remembered) because of his assumption that they would not necessarily possess the notes.

There is therefore a good case for leaving the part exactly as he wrote it and to revel in the results. Nor contrariwise is it a good plan to bring bar 405 into line with bar 611 (which possesses magnificent

---

*Unlike the miniature scores which restart the finale bar-count from 1, Breitkopf continues through so that the finale starts at bar 374.

†I am indebted to my son Jonathan for this clear exposé of what is a complicated situation.

panache of its own when not previously anticipated). To iron out all such inconsistencies would be dangerous; would one, for example, change the opening bars of the Symphony? (This also explains the curious contrabassoon part; all Beethoven wrote was 'Contrafagotto coi Bassi' and every now and then, 'senza Contrafagotto'.)'

Bar 390 (with the up-beat) is so strong and violent in its jagged rhythms that a change in conducting style from broad exaltation to one of ferocity may well be in order. Then after the succession of sharply syncopated beats in bars 395–8 letter A brings a return of the grandiose. Here, though the four horns can have been introduced from the beginning of the finale, is their first moment of surely legitimate glory in terms of the present-day orchestra, their delayed resolution in bar 405 being particularly worthy of especial featuring.

But both horns and trumpets can be marked back to a single *f* for bars 407–13, partly because the *ff* in 414 will then be strikingly subito, but also to allow the upper strings to be heard clearly, the violas especially needing to be brought out, lying so low. Curiously, Beethoven's autograph shows the violins to be in unison—not octaves as in all printed scores; whether or not this was Beethoven's final intention and should therefore be adopted must again remain a matter of opinion. Musically it is not a straightforward issue leaving, as it would, so uncharacteristically wide a gap between the violins and violas.

The short interjections of reaffirmation in bars 416–17 of the last phrase of bar 415 should be hurled with the utmost vehemence, especially by the cellos and basses who can thunder in, but thereafter the second subject itself (bars 418 ff.) need only be played at a single forte, such as Beethoven himself prescribes in bars 421, 3, 5, and 7. It is all too easy to play the greater part of this tremendous finale at a relentless fortissimo, but its stature as well as its inner and formal logic loses instead of gains by so doing. Also whereas precedent shows that many of Beethoven's single fortes can be interpreted as *rf*'s, their significance here as true *f*'s makes excellent sense. It may be additionally observed that at the actual *ff* in bar 431, which comes after a huge 2-bar crescendo from pianissimo, the trombones are still uniquely held back to the single *f*, only reaching their own *ff* twenty bars later when the 1st player, designated as an alto trombone, is graced with a top F in alt.

In fact is at the same pitch as none other than high C for the standard F horn, normally regarded as its top note (even if Haydn, and in latter years Strauss, both take the instrument higher) and actually above anything Beethoven ever gives the horn in F, although he does write top C for horns in the lower crooks.

Now, although this very high note can certainly be reached today by good principal trombonists on the tenor instrument, the return of the once obsolete alto trombone is much to be welcomed, giving not only greater assurance at this extreme upper register but also a fine quality of sound. None the less all players appreciate the help of some high-placed gesture from the conductor which has the additional virtue of drawing attention to this spectacular piece of orchestral virtuosity.

In bars 433, 452, and 642 the use by Breitkopf of abbreviations such as or in place of and as given in other editions, obscures the surely intentional crotchet-by-crotchet emphasis which is assuredly as much within the strings' province, despite their tremolo of semiquavers, as in that of the wind and timpani.

Two crashing chords—the second beaten in isolation, not as part of a continuous tempo—and the last theme of the exposition is presented. Piano as is its first statement, the repeated *fp*'s show that the tension is not to be relaxed through the brief lull. At the forte repeat of the passage the 1st violins' turns are given to the piccolo alone, the first time this new colour is given a solo line. It is therefore doubly unfortunate that these motivic ornaments are so seldom audible against even the single forte of the tutti. The fact that the printed slurs do not appear in the autograph is significant in this respect since if played staccato the semiquavers are undoubtedly far more penetrating.

Until very recently the repeat in this movement was never taken. However, there has come into being a blanket belief that all repeats should invariably be observed across the entire repertoire, a curious piece of pedagogic dogma which, as part of the latter-day 'authentic' movement, has increasingly been given credence. In consequence, this finale too has been subjected to such gratuitous extension in some performances. There is, of course, no doubt that Beethoven took the trouble to write a repeat, complete with first- and second-time bars, as part of his invariable practice in sonata form until only in the first movement of the Ninth Symphony, when he at last allowed himself avowedly to break with so pedantic a tradition. But one need not assume thereby that he always insisted, or even expected, that these repeats were inviolate; and in the present instance, of the many structural arguments against the practice which might be invoked, the most important is that the abrupt return (the first-time bars being disconcertingly terse and conventional) presents the opening bars of the finale in circumstances dictated merely by convention when the whole point had been the innovatory effect of their climactic entry.

Indeed it was this very need so carefully to prepare for their arrival that caused Beethoven to pioneer yet other departures from tradition in leading from Scherzo to finale without a break and then actually to return to the Scherzo during the development in order to come back to these opening finale bars for the reprise in the same way as before.

It is therefore not only inadvisable to take this repeat but there is a strong case for considering it a positive fault in interpretative thinking to do so (*pace* Dr Robert Simpson who, in an article in *The Score* (No. 26, Jan. 1960), somewhat scurrilously ascribes the omission of the repeat to nothing short of sheer laziness, or alternatively lack of interest in music, on the part of conductors).

Unless the 2nd violins are seated on the conductor's right (a very desirable but not always practical plan) their all-important take-over of the arpeggiando figuration at bar 461 may well be totally imperceptible. A good device, should the violins have all to be seated together, is to write this passage into some of the 1st violin parts as well. There will be no danger of this little piece of sharp practice being aurally detected and the marginal reduction of power in the 1st violins' sustained tremolo will further benefit the woodwind in their own subsequent take-over of the passage from the 2nd violins.

The development brings the first and only moment of quiet amiability in the whole movement and it is well to make the most of it, the strings and woodwind both being encouraged to play dolce or cantabile according to the nature of their double counterpoint or imitative passage-work.

But with the crescendo into letter C (bar 480) the sense of drama is quickly restored, the cellos and basses taking the lead in the cumulative build-up of the minim motif, for which they should certainly be marked to play with separation as the trombones will instinctively do six bars later. (These latter must not blaze away but give a noble quality to their magnificent entry.) The violins six bars later again are actually written with dots over the notes, as are the lower strings in bars 493–4 for a canonic entry which is often lost in the growing mass of concerted sound. It is thus only common sense that all the entries must be executed in the same marcato style.

Similarly there is much to be said for slurring the violins' and violas' imitative triplet ejaculations in bars 481 ff., in line both with the cellos' previous passages of the kind and with the woodwinds' identical outbursts in bars 493–4. Beethoven undoubtedly omitted the slurs in question, but there is no way of knowing whether he merely took them for granted or intended to make the difference and thus sharpen the jagged nature of these particular interjections.

The fury quickly intensifies during the vivid alternations between upper and lower strings and after another high note pealed out by the alto trombone a whirlwind is set in motion, initiated by the 2nd violins and violas who can be launched with a vehement upbeat.

The thuds of the brass and timpani at 2-bar intervals can be given weight suggestive of sledge-hammer blows leading into the paroxysm of bar 515, where *sempre ff* seems hardly to meet the situation and I mark everyone *fff* (and would gladly emulate Tchaikovsky with his *ffff* if it would make any difference). It is hard to give adequate force to the 1st violins' arpeggio work here, and again some extra desks can conveniently be borrowed from the 2nds, whereas the poor piccolo has been having a wretched time already since bars 507 and 509, there being not the smallest chance that his little turns will ever be heard, lying so ineffectually low in the compass. It is surprising how many composers overestimate the piccolo's power of penetration in any but the higher notes, including such masters as Smetana (*Vltava*) and Borodin (Second Symphony). To put the figures up an octave would certainly enable them to be heard but at the cost of producing a colour alien to the orchestra of the period, while to add a second piccolo makes curiously little extra effect. It has to be recognized that this is a problem which is insoluble outside the radio or recording studios with their artificial aid through extra microphones.

The custom of taking the three mighty string semibreves of bars 523–5 all with down-bows is not technically necessary and, as in earlier instances, creates too much separation. Here it has the further disadvantage of anticipating Beethoven's own isolated bow-strokes in the succeeding bars. One retake in bar 524 is inescapable, but this can then be followed by an up-bow, after which the six repeated 1st violin crotchet G's can certainly begin by being taken with a series of down-bows.

The bar phrasing of the Scherzo reminiscence presents no problem as long as it is recognized that there must be a 6-bar period at bars 542–7. The woodwind solos are of course syncopated, both the oboe solo lead at bar 557 and that of the flute, oboe and bassoon in bar 565 coming at the second bars of their respective periods.

Since no truly great moment can ever be recaptured or made to recur with the same dramatic force as before, there is little purpose in attempting a parallel *coup d'état*; the lead into the recapitulation therefore no longer requires a corresponding broadening at the restart of the Allegro. On the other hand it must not be overlooked that whether or not Beethoven's metronome marks are observed precisely they make it plain that he reckoned the minim of the finale to be a degree steadier than the whole bar of the Scherzo. Strictly, therefore, at the return of Tempo I (as Beethoven now designates the Scherzo tempo), the pulse should be a little quicker than in the climactic bars preceding the change. At the reinstatement of the finale, then, there will automatically be some broadening of pace, even if not to the extent of the first time.

The grandeur of the opening bars' reprise can accordingly be taken if not for granted, at least with the awareness of precognition until new events start to occur, beginning with the cello, bass, and contra's deepest C of bar 611 already discussed. This leads to a figure which previously had been the exclusive property of these low instruments but is this time subsequently taken over by the piccolo. It is thus even more unfortunate that the piccolo is again too low and accordingly too weak to give the imitation its proper significance. Here, however, a second piccolo does make a perceptible difference and is well worth co-opting if possible. At the same time the upper strings, brass and other woodwind can profitably be reduced a little, concentration being rather on the continuation of the violins' melodic line now transferred to the lower strings.

The entry of the timpani in a thunderous roll at bar 665, after a strategic 3-bar rest, is one of the main events as the coda is approached and can be exaggerated by under-conducting the preceding bars before giving a strong direction to the timpanist. This is also another place for a *fff* subito for the whole orchestra, being again a tumultuous moment balancing to some extent that of bar 515 in the development.

The coda then surges forward and must acquire great momentum. The working out of the material corresponds at first with many details from the development section such as the hammer blows of brass and timpani at two-bar intervals as well as the frenzied passage-work of the strings, all surrounding the great marcato theme which, rising from the cellos, via the 1st violins to the assembled wind and brass, culminates in the heroically affirmative pile-up of bars 681–4. The upper strings always have difficulty here in sufficiently accenting the sforzandos and accordingly need extra emphasis from the conductor through strongly syncopated half-beats; and the detached alternations of dominant and tonic chords in bars 685–90 will obviously be most effectively given by a succession of isolated beats placed and delivered with powerful downward force.

Over a hundred years later Sibelius concluded his Fifth Symphony with a row of similarly hammered chords, and may have consciously or otherwise done so after the example of the present passage. But whereas in Sibelius's plan the chords are more widely spaced and presage total finality, Beethoven is far from the end of his scheme; hence the last hammer blow is of a dominant chord from whose echoes the bassoons and horns, phoenix-like, raise up the argument to a further section of this huge coda. It is therefore of primary importance that the forward thrust of tempo and tension be not relaxed in the slightest degree through the repeated silences.

The accelerando of bars 726–34 into the concluding Presto is by no means easy to effect smoothly, as it is so steep. Again, like the tempos for both Scherzo and finale, the printed mark of o = 112 is excellent so that in fact the speed more than doubles itself in only nine bars. Nor can there be any alleviating of the difficulty by a spread of the acceleration over a wider span, as the tempo must only be stepped up where Beethoven decrees, that is to say, once the three bars of chattering quavers are past. It is one of those familiar cases in which a conductor may work harder to force the pace but to no avail, since the increasing whirling of baton and gesture become self-defeating. Accordingly a useful device, here as in similar situations, is to change into a semibreve beat ahead of the double-bar—a couple of bars, say, before the Presto actually begins.

This hectic section of the coda starts surprisingly soft and tense, though with its regularly spaced jabs on which the conductor's style is well advised to concentrate, using restraint in all other respects until the flamboyant entry of the trombones sparks the ultimate paean of triumph. At the second bar of this fanfare (bar 764) there is a notorious point of dispute with respect to the timpani. The printed score gives what could be a discrepancy in the rhythm of the drums. This might have had the purpose of pin-pointing the canonic imitation in the bass instruments, a feature often missed in performance; in the event, however, the many players who ask to be allowed to play in rhythm with the wind and brass have the right of it on their side, for the autograph proves the present-day editions to be at fault.

The alto trombone is once more the hero of the hour in the final page with its high E in bars 803–4, although the rise and fall of the C major arpeggio in the lower strings must not pass unnoticed. Needless to say, there is no question of actually beating the silent bars of the last page. The conductor's gestures will show purely the architectural shape of the chords with a suggestion of what Mahler graphically terms *Ausholen* for the last bar of all, a bar containing its own enigma in the strange notation for the timpani.

Ex. 8

Since tremolo and trill are no more than alternative notations for the identical effect, Beethoven's intention must remain conjectural, especially as he made three distinct attempts to find the way to write it which satisfied him best. One answer can be effectively contrived in the form of a crescendo on the tremolo leading to *fff* on the trill held by the fermata. This is at least a dramatic solution, even if there is no guarantee that it is what Beethoven had in mind; it preserves moreover to the very last an element of surprise in what is one of the very greatest, as well as the most familiar, symphonies in the orchestral repertoire.

Symphony No. 6 in F major, Op. 68 ('Pastoral')

◀▶

No greater contrast than with the preceding symphony can be imagined; it seems hardly credible that the two works should have been planned simultaneously and that their joint premières took place at the same concert, in which their very numbers were reversed. It is indeed this extraordinary variety of utterance which is one of the most remarkable facets of Beethoven's genius, and which needs a corresponding flexibility of style from his interpreter. Each symphony, in particular, calls for an entirely different manner on the part the conductor, whose first consideration when approaching the 'Pastoral' should be the sheer beauty of orchestral sound. Above all the tonal quality wants to be warm and gentle to a degree, even in the fortes and fortissimos, excepting only during the storm which is of course a law unto itself. Otherwise there should be no rough edges, no sharp dynamic gestures; the whole approach to the music from conductor and orchestra alike needs to reflect geniality and affection.

As with the Fifth Symphony, in which extra instruments appear only in the finale, the 'Pastoral' profits from being rehearsed back to front. A conductor who at the start of these symphonies confronts the complete complement of players and plunges directly into the first movement is unlikely to be viewed sympathetically by the piccolo, brass, and timpani who, even in the unlikely event of a non-stop run of the earlier movements, will have to sit for over twenty minutes before playing a note. For there are neither trumpets nor drums in either of the first two movements, let alone trombones—an extraordinary example of Beethoven's imagination in the variety of his orchestral colouring—while the piccolo and timpani only take part briefly for the storm itself.

In both the Fifth and Sixth symphonies, therefore, when confronted with a restricted schedule, the conductor may very properly begin the rehearsal with the Scherzo; in fact, in the case of the 'Pastoral' this is of particular psychological importance in view of the close rapport required between the conductor and his players, whose co-operation can by no means be taken for granted; since, if the brass and drums may find themselves idle over long stretches, the strings on the contrary play almost incessantly so that—unexpectedly to anyone who loves the music but is unacquainted with the players' point of view—this is the symphony after the Schubert Great C Major the very prospect of which can cause an orchestra's spirits to droop.

I

The opening bars look deceptively straightforward; on the contrary, the bare fifth on violas and cellos can be curiously hard to place firmly yet gently before the 1st violins begin the dancing principal theme on the half-beat. Also the correct basic tempo has to be established easily yet unequivocally in those very first bars even though it is so soon to be interrupted. The printed $\downarrow$ = 66, while only a very little too hasty, has had the unfortunate effect of misleading some of the more determinedly strict devotees to Beethoven's metronome marks into actually racing through this lovely movement 1-in-a-bar. A good *gemütlich* gait might rather be $\downarrow$ = 112, which preserves both Beethoven's *heiterer Empfindungen* and his cautionary Allegro ma non troppo.

Especially in view of its singing character, bar 3 warrants a slight lead into the pause, and there is then naturally no take-off, and since the violas and cellos have arrived on an up-bow the music can simply proceed without interruption.

The new *f* in bar 13 occurring so close to an uncontradicted *f* in bar 11 suggests a missing dynamic between them, and indeed bar 12 does not need to continue at the same intensity. Beethoven's penchant for using the single forte sign as a symbol equally for rinforzando suggests that this could legitimately apply specifically to bar 11, upon which, after a drop in the next bar to *mf*, bar 13 could mark a renewed outburst of glowing forte tone.

An outstanding feature of this quite unusual movement is

the device of reiterating a single bar identically many times. Initiated already at bar 16 in a manner which is highly intriguing, there are nine such bars: four rising in dynamic, one at the top with added bassoons, and four subsiding. This is a heart-warmingly typical example of one of Beethoven's most attract-ive characteristics when in a good humour, a half jocular by-play with the simplest musical germs—scales, repeated notes (or, as here, bars), extremes of compass, and so on. The piano sonatas are full of such things, the symphonies less so—Beethoven usually being more earnest; but in this work he is patently enjoy-ing himself. It is also fascinating to watch how he incorporates a varied version of the fun into the recapitulation.

In bar 42 the basses should have a minim corresponding with the C in bar 46 (the same misprint occurs at bar 317). These are joyful bars and the whole forte statement of the main theme should be effervescent and exuberant with the flutes' grace-notes coming on the beat.

The last quavers of each of the 1st violins' ascending groups (bars 54 ff., and later 329 ff.) continue to be controversial and can easily be the cause of time-consuming argument in rehearsal. When this happens it becomes very hard to obtain a reading from a violin section which does not sound self-conscious. The point at issue is that these last quavers are not printed staccato like all the others; the phrases should simply come gently to rest on their last notes with a grace that is spoilt if they are either clipped or on the other hand unduly elongated, as players are prone to make them when deliberately avoiding a staccato. The situation is moreover further confused by the crotchet in bar 63 which is often featured as a notable exception and, let us admit, an enjoyable one. Yet this may not at all have been Beethoven's intention; in the autograph the A in bar 61 is also clearly a crotchet coinciding with the change of note-lengths also of the pizzicatos, a matter in which Beethoven was notor-iously careless. In the parallel place at the reprise all the last 1st violins' notes are quavers and all the pizzicatos notated as crotchets, so nothing can be proved by analogy and the prob-ability is that a correct interpretation would be for all the phrases to end alike on a somewhat tenuto quaver.

Again the gentlest 'einleitend' will lead affectionately into the new section at bar 67. Even while coaxing the 1st violins to play bars 67–70 (followed by the 2nds in bars 71–4) cantando possibile it has to be remembered that it is actually the long notes in the cellos which introduce the true second subject and whose melodic intensity needs to be immediately and specifically emphasized. Later canonic entries (1st violins, flute, horns) come more readily to the forefront of the texture, when conversely it will become a primary preoccupation to evoke the cantando quality of the arpeggiando *Nebenstimme*. In particular, when the upper strings change to undulating figurations in bar 83 it is necessary to make an artificial drop to piano with a re-start of the crescendo four bars later, lest the clarinet and bassoon continuation of this secondary motif disappear altogether.

Like the Fourth Symphony, this is a work in which, in company with most conductors, I do not take the repeat although there is no doubt that a strong case can be made for doing so. Somewhat in the manner of the Dvořák 'New World', also a long symphony whose repeat is rarely taken, the first movement seems disproportionately short compared with the second. The 'Scene am Bach' is a quite unusually discursive movement lasting all of a quarter of an hour, longer even than the Marcia funebre of the 'Eroica', and it could be argued that the opening Allegro needs to have enough weight to balance and prepare such an important central movement. Yet much of the charm of the Allegro lies in its conciseness, despite its deceptively easy-going air. For all its use of bar and phrase repetitions (and the development in particular is full of both) it is notably economical and direct in structure.

Furthermore, the return is made by a bald double-bar repeat sign with no amelioration of the harmonic juxtaposition of the bare fifth in the home key of F major, which in consequence comes with disconcerting abruptness (indeed one might wonder why Beethoven did not choose to put the repeat sign four bars later which would have worked so much more smoothly) and without the formal motivation which had necessitated the equally direct return in the Fifth Symphony.

The development which relies so much on a carefully graded series of crescendos is greatly harmed if each of the 4-bar sustained row of minims which alternate in the 1st and 2nd violins is broken with a change of bow. Yet this can easily be avoided if, against all the principles of practicality, a seemingly clumsy bowing is adopted each time at the last repeated bar of the motivic figure:

Ex. 9

(pt.)

which enables the long note to be taken in a single 4-bar up-bow. This mode of execution does actually work perfectly and can be made to sound indistinguishable from the other bars of the identical figure whose quavers are taken in the natural manner down/up off the string. A similar bowing device will be seen in the development of the Seventh Symphony, first movement (see below, pp. 133–4).

The crescendos from bars 151–74 and 197–220 are so extended, and the harmonic switches to D and E major respectively at bars 163 and 209 so magical, that a sudden drop to *pp* is irresistible for all instruments with the exception of the 1st oboe, whose entries thereby become the centre of attraction. The crescendos then resume, of course, culminating in the *ff*'s of bars 175 and 221.

A logical *Retusche* might seem for the chromatic horns of today to play a corresponding row of F♯'s in bars 221–7 by analogy with Beethoven's E's of bars 175–81. At the same time it is hard to condone the erstwhile tradition whereby the horns were given these F♯'s in octaves when Beethoven had previously avoided the perfectly practicable lower E of the 2nd horn, both players on the contrary pitching the upper E in unison. In the final analysis there is really no case for adding these F♯'s which at the higher pitch are obtrusive while in octaves give a wrong stylistic effect.

Bars 243–6 mark a corner-stone in the development and require a margin of spaciousness before the new section begins in bar 247. The isolated quaver D for the bassoons in bar 255 is a curiosity; it was at one time thought to have been a survival from an old tradition whereby such a note would mark the end of a passage in which the bassoons had been expected to double the cello line, similar perhaps to bar 97 of the 'Eroica' first movement. As it happens, however, this does not appear to be borne out by the autograph, which shows a messy fusion of three versions of the passage over a page-turn. The likelihood, therefore, is that the note should be quietly suppressed.

In the Leipzig Breitkopf & Härtel orchestral parts the semi-quavers of the 2nd violins in bars 255–8, and the violas in bars 259–62, are slurred, a bow to a bar. This unwarrantable piece of editing must certainly be removed.

So subtly does Beethoven dovetail the emerging of the recapitulation out of the end of the development that it is not at all readily apparent during the onward flow of the music that the former has actually begun at bar 278. Accordingly, just as a slight relaxation of pulse in bar 3 led into the fermata, so there needs to be a corresponding phrase-cornering in bar 281. The 1st violins then fill what had previously been a pause with a kind of cadenza in tempo which is, however, not without its hazards.

In the first place, the violins' trill cannot continue right through to the end of bar 284, but at the same time the Breitkopf score is careless in suggesting that the trill comes to rest already on an unadorned tied dotted-quaver G. Indeed the trill itself is best interrupted by a gap in the sound and not with a plain G of whatever length, so that it only remains to determine exactly where the violins should prepare for the semiquaver by stopping the trill. This may best be after rather than on the second beat, as in the following suggested notation:

Bar 288 has come to present an interpretative problem due to a faulty reading in the Leipzig Breitkopf 1st violin parts where the last three quavers are indicated with a slur over the staccato marks; as a result they have come to be played with longer, almost portato bow-strokes, even though this may not have been the editor's intention. If instead the quavers are kept fully staccato off the string it will be easier to avoid an over-exaggeration of what is in principle a perfectly legitimate rubato.

In the following passage it is always the triplets to which primary consideration must be given, however much they merely provide ornamentation for a varied restatement of bars 5–28. It is particularly important that in bars 300 ff. the other instruments relate to this triplet figuration even if they are playing the principal motif, or the ensemble can be seriously endangered.

The 1st violins need to be particularly adaptable in this respect because of their change of role at bar 304, where after previously having the primary voice it is they who are suddenly required to relate to the violas as these now take over their triplets.

The beginning of the coda presents another delicate area where rigid adherence to a metronome pulse simply sounds insensitive. At the end of bar 421, which tails away unlike the corresponding bar 150, the strong syncopated down-beat should be marginally delayed so that the boisterously staccato strings do not enter too precipitantly and the universal quaver rest lose its value and significance. The very brief codetta of bars 426–7 can then be played quietly and thoughtfully, the flute and clarinet taking plenty of time over their semiquavers.

The magical section beginning at bar 428 will thus be introduced with all the preparation proper for so poetic a passage. Nor need the sudden change to a glowing forte at bar 440 upset the serenity of the evening song, while the equally sudden increase of tone to *ff* at bar 458 has the breathtaking beauty of a splendid sunset over the peaceful countryside. However much Beethoven may have cautioned against seeing too great a pictorial imagery in this work it is hard not to believe that some such vision was at the back of his mind when creating this music.

All the fortes from bar 469 to the end of the movement should be indicated gently, but especially those which accompany the long clarinet solo; there must be no necessity for the player to overblow in the least degree.

The last quavers of the 1st violin and woodwind passages in bars 498, 502, and 504 respectively will be seen to lack the staccato dots of the preceding notes and this difference should be observed if the delicacy of the section is to be fully realized. There can then be the least gap before the *p subito* of the last two bars, which are themselves slightly broadened.

II

For long the tempo and mood of the 'Scene am Bach' was considered to be, above all, one of thoroughly relaxed tranquillity. Mahler even argued that the Andante molto moto (as corrected by Breitkopf from the slight adaptation 'mosso' of other editions) was meaningless and therefore had to be a misreading for 'modᵒ' (= moderato). How wrong he was is proved by the autograph which reveals that Beethoven had at one time added 'quasi Allegretto', although he later struck this out. Nevertheless, it was not until the 1930s, when Toscanini shook tradition by actually adopting Beethoven's swift-moving ♩. = 50, that the custom changed until it has become accepted that the movement must be played without the heavy sluggish pacing of older interpretations.

However, with this change of approach the question of stick technique arises, for it must be admitted that this is by no means an easy piece to control taken, as it should be, in four forward-moving dotted-crotchet beats while still constantly retaining the ability to shape the curves of the melodic lines. A compromise has occasionally been tried of beating in

8: ♩ ♪ ♩ ♪ ♩ ♪ ♩ ♪ but, apart from making very heavy

weather of the already dangerously thick texture, this method can only be an impediment to the natural phrasing of the music.

Yet however much the flow of the brook has to be kept on the move, the printed metronome mark could be considered too restless for the cantabile quality of the 1st violins' melodic semiquavers if maintained inexorably, and a slightly easier ♩. = 44–6 will accommodate more comfortably their elaborate contours. On the other hand a more leisurely tempo inevitably increases the restriction a conductor may feel through accepting the proper style of giving only the four slow beats, with subdivision into quavers kept in reserve for a few brief moments. Where salvation lies is in the never-ceasing array of heart-warming events which occur between the wide dotted crotchet pulses which will surely suggest many and varied means of communication through an overtly evocative, however economical, use of gesture.

An important omission in all editions is that both 1st and 2nd violins should be muted throughout the movement in addition to the two solo cellos, as shown unmistakably in Beethoven's hand. This makes it the more essential when starting the first bar to place the beat in such a way as to indicate clearly that the melody begins with the 1st violins' very first note The style of the beat should also have the effect of differentiating the quality of tone between the warm singing melody and the shadowy brook-depicting background of undulating quavers or, later, semiquavers.

The grace-notes in bar 3, unlike those in the flutes during the first movement (bars 42 ff. and 316 ff.), are placed before the beat, and so similarly throughout the movement. There can, nevertheless, be no distortion of rhythm to allow for these ornaments even whilst the need for some flexibility has to be recognized by all the instruments, melodic and accompanying alike. This is especially relevant when in the preceding up-beat the theme contains semiquavers right to the barline, as in bars 2–3 or 27–8.

Cadential bars or changes in the pattern are obviously danger points in maintaining control: bars 17–18 need particular alertness in preventing the pulse from sagging, in which case the succeeding bars can easily run amok, the strings' groups of six semiquavers being taken off the string.

The lack of any expression marks or changes of dynamic before the crescendo in bar 29 must not be taken to inhibit any pursuance of the natural demands of the music which is too poetic to permit of a dead-pan interpretation. The violins' sudden higher and more sustained phrase in bars 22–3 suggests a heightening of tension which can perhaps be relaxed with a conciliatory answering group in bars 24–5. The solo entry of the 2nd bassoon (which gains from a friendly glance to the player) then starts a gathering of wind tone which contributes to the establishment of a general feeling of contentment already in bars 27–8. The whole ensemble can be encouraged to play more fervently here, even though there are still two bars before Beethoven actually calls for a crescendo.

With bar 30 the 1st violins' staccato semiquavers begin which, taken again off the string, call for the most precise orchestral discipline. There is not a great deal the conductor can do to help, other than to focus his concentration upon the section, especially at the end of bar 32 where a slight rubato is justifiable in order to nurse the bassoon as he turns the corner into the second subject. Nevertheless a subdivided beat would still be undesirable; nor is one necessary with a skilful and alert violin section, although it must always remain a tricky corner.

The slur over the first sextuplet in this bar (32) seems to have been an afterthought on Beethoven's part, albeit an important one. He nevertheless omitted to bring the corresponding bar in the reprise (104) into line and Breitkopf dutifully omits the slur in the later context, replacing it with staccato dots. Other editions match up the phrasing, however, which is at least logical.

The trills for the 2nd violins in bar 33 ff. present the difficulty that the last notes of the turns tend to land together with the quavers which follow instead of just before them. This is even more prevalent in the reprise (bars 105 ff.) where inexplicably the ornamented notes are quavers instead of crotchets.

All the different wind entries in bars 36–7 need featuring if they are to make their proper cumulative effect (so again of course in 108–9). The chief point to stress is that some of the imitations are entrusted to the 2nd players who may not instinctively play like soloists to balance with their principals, especially where—as in bar 36—two players of the same instrument follow one another.

The temptation of beating bar 39 in six needs to be firmly resisted. The alternate groups have to sound gently syncopated and only the last one, with the entry of the flute, can be allowed guidance from the conductor's hand or wrist. Bars 40 and 112 are inconsistent in that the cellos and basses have 'pizz.' on their second note only in the latter. Peters and the miniature scores make both contexts arco but this turns out to be the wrong 'correction', as the first edition shows that there should be a corresponding pizz. in bar 40.

Bar 46 (= 118) is the one type of corner where there is a real need to use subdivision with the stick in order to control the entry of the tutti on the last two quavers, whereas entries such as those during the next three bars (and there will be many more like these in the course of the movement) certainly need coaxing but no extra subdivided beats.

The beginning of the development at letter C (bar 54) is another awkward corner, relying again upon an alert violin section if unanimity of ensemble is to be accomplished. The problem is that a strictly rhythmical initiation of bar 54 betrays the meaning of the music, which must clearly be heard and understood to start a new paragraph. Yet there can be no ritenuto at the end of bar 53: the musical solution lies rather in a slight delay in placing the down-beat, which the 1st violins have to catch and rethink as a new point of departure in starting their spiccato.

The oboe's dotted-crotchet G in bar 56 makes it apparent that his melody begins with this note, as in the case of the violins at the start of the movement, even though the solo clarinet does not follow his example in bar 59.

The flute meanwhile takes over Beethoven's arpeggiando yellowhammer* which is too important to be reduced to a true piano, especially at the lower end of the compass. The 1st violins and violas, on the other hand, should be very unobtrusive, playing perhaps sul tasto. Then all is tranquillity for the duet in bars 62–5, the end of which is another place which requires a briefly subdivided beat for the entry of the strings on the last two quavers.

Bar 68 is hardly less than a purple passage in the glowing modulation from G to Eb, bringing us to the clarinet's interlude. The violas now take the yellowhammer, which they can handle more delicately if they take a new up-bow for the top crotchets of their calls. At bar 73 the tranquillity is even deeper than before and if the background can be made soft enough, and the conductor's beat barely perceptible to the audience, the effect can be breathtaking.

The cellos' and basses' two quavers at the end of bar 76 are subdivided as before, and with the slightly less purple bars 77–8 the dynamic marking returns to a more normal piano. But the 1st violins' development of the principal melody contains a series of almost conversational utterances which cry out for imaginative treatment: the first phrase of bar 79, for example, can be played with great tenderness, with the answer in the following bar infinitely withdrawn.

If, as may easily happen, some loss of momentum has been suffered during these events, the 5-bar return in bars 86–90 provides the opportunity to allow the brook to flow smoothly once more at its true pace. This is particularly important for the interplay between flute and oboe which begins in bar 88 and which can be brought forward against the very quiet accom-

*As Sir George Grove aptly remarks in his *Beethoven and his Nine Symphonies* (Novello, London, 1896), this bird's actual call is entirely different. Perhaps Beethoven was pulling Schindler's leg; if the composer was notoriously irascible, his sycophantic acolyte must have tried his patience sorely.

paniment. The 1st violins' repeated semiquavers in bar 90 can then be played on the string at the point of the bow, which will facilitate the crescendo to a piano subito at bar 91 for the reprise which follows without any hold-up or rubato. There is now a considerable complexity of background atmosphere, but the flute solo should have no trouble in dominating, its first long note (now longer than ever) being again the start of the melody.

In the reprise most of the events correspond closely with the exposition but there are a few features to be mentioned. In bar 94, the 1st violins change quickly from their 'yellowhammer' off-the-string figuration to a melodic legato, and this cannot be done sensitively without a slight adjustment of the pulse, which will also allow the flutes to enjoy their re-entry; in bar 99 it is only the second solo cello who plays the quaver undulations, which thus become an unexpected soloistic element for this player; so too the horns have a brief moment of glory in bar 110 which, in a movement where they are largely relegated to a sustaining or accompanying role can happily be brought into prominence; and in bar 119 the three 1st violin trills are played without *Nachschlag*, as shown in the autograph, i.e. like bar 40 but unlike bar 47, and the sudden rise of the octave is a dramatic stroke which can be made the more poignant if Beethoven's crescendo is brought forward.

The beginning of the coda has a heartfelt quality which, starting from a moment of great repose burgeons into two widely rhapsodic sentences; the swells can accordingly be played effusively, the phrases rising and falling both times from *pp tranquillo* to *mf appassionata*. The whimsy of what follows will then evoke a pleasurable element of surprise instead of embarrassment. The device, which in the hands of a lesser artist might have been uncomfortably arch, owes its success not only to its own intrinsic beauty and sincerity but to the touching way in which it is introduced during these five prefatory bars.

The bird-calls themselves can be quietly directed with the minimum of fuss, and virtually no rubato where the nightingale's first appearance is concerned; its second and longer call, however, will seem stilted if too strict a devotion is paid to the printed note-values and dynamics. Most flautists have their own way of playing the passage which will be respected by a wise conductor, but it is worth suggesting an interruption of the crescendo with a pianissimo subito at bar 134 followed by a new crescendo and perhaps a hint of accelerando so that the increased number of semiquaver groups can seem to merge into the trill. Imaginatively carried out this prevents the charming stylization of bird-song from becoming too mannered.

Where the cuckoo is concerned it often proves necessary to insist upon the services of the 2nd clarinet who may protest that he has never before been required to play the cuckoo in unison with the first. Yet the sound of two soft clarinets playing together has a pronounced and unmistakable timbre as, for example, Dvořák and Tchaikovsky regularly exploited.

Of the after-phrases to the bird-calls, the first is presented in strict time but the second is too wistful in its *pp* to be treated in the same way. Its entry can be slightly delayed with the hand, which also directs each new woodwind imitation so that these last three and a half-bars leave one with a feeling of reflective contemplation. Nevertheless within this relaxed pulse the last chords need make no further rallentando, but bring this ravishing movement to an end in a mood of total serenity.

III

The dance of the country folk, for a dance it undoubtedly is although Beethoven carefully avoids the use of the word, is a Ländler and therefore requires a degree of galumphing steadiness in the choice of speed. The printed ♩. = 108 is a margin too quick from that point of view, bearing in mind what is to come, such as the horn solo of bars 133 ff., and in any case lacks the easy-going gait of a country hop. A less frantic ♩. = 88 is better, though it is not at all a simple pace to set and a cautionary up-beat followed by undue control of the first bars can all too easily produce a dangerously stilted tempo; undemonstrative as this opening is, it must above all sound carefree.

Despite my usual prejudice against such artificialities I confess to enjoying an echo *ppp* at bar 107; only the 2nd bassoon remains obstinately and oafishly set in his ways, making no effort to conform. The return to a good unrefined, almost rough-sounding wind-band *p* for the clarinets and bassoons at bar 123 then produces a splendid contrast, which a *mp* entry for the violas and cellos can underline.

The *sempre più stretto* is hard to spark off to a sufficient degree. One expedient is to mark all the low instruments *ff* and to conduct abruptly very fast indeed. There is a considerable accelerando to be accomplished in a very short period, and it should all sound fairly hectic. Beethoven's ♩ = 132 is exactly right for the a tempo Allegro $\frac{2}{4}$ of the Trio section.

The violins might be asked to play all of bars 165–80 sul G. This adds to the gusto and will not interfere in the slightest with the flute solo which, on the contrary, needs the chords of the wind to be reduced from the level of forte in between the sforzandos if it is to stand out sufficiently. Sometimes the flute is doubled in the mistaken belief that this will make all the difference but, strange to say, a second flute adds very little in sheer volume and actually detracts from the clarity of articulation which a good 1st player with a sharp tongue can bring off in style.

The two pauses of bars 203–4 are essentially the solo spot for the trumpet, who has only entered for the very first time in the symphony during the last few bars. The pauses can be quite long, each worth at least three of the Allegro bars, after which the double-bar repeat sign indicates that the entire Scherzo/Trio format is taken again from the beginning. This is in line with Beethoven's custom for the majority of his symphonic and chamber works from the Fourth Symphony onwards and is therefore mandatory. It is in fact commonly observed but performances have been known, and indeed by Viennese conductors such as Joseph Krips and even Karajan, in which it was cut.

There must be a considerable element of surprise about bars 215–21, after which the piece continues as if nothing had happened—it was all a false alarm—so that the greater surprise of the Presto can come without warning, bursting in with a tempo jump to at least ♩. = 120. This headlong pace underlines the necessity of the grace-notes in bars 242–3 and 250–1 to fall on the beat and carry the accentuation, as accordingly they will also in bars 60–1 and 68–9. The horns can ring out boisterously in bars 257 ff. but it is vulgar to have them doubled: as already discussed with respect to the corresponding places in the Fifth

Symphony, four horns sound merely fatter and with less, not more, of the true ring of the open horn tones of Beethoven's day.

IV

Strictly speaking, the ominous rumblings of the approaching thunder follow without a break; certainly it would be wrong to stop the pulse as if there were a fermata sign over the double-bar. At the same time the last down-beat for the whirling dancers can be so organized that it falls a little late for the next bar which marks the beginning of the new movement with the start of the cello/bass tremolo. This has both a practical value for these players and an illustrative purpose in conjuring up the alarm of the merry-makers as they suddenly see the approaching storm-clouds.

There would in any case have been no need for an up-beat in the new tempo, for which the printed metronome mark of $\downarrow$ = 80 is again exactly right; nor can there be any doubt that the music is alla breve despite the signature of common time. It is, however, important to mark the four minim beats of the first two bars, as the 2nd violins need every assistance to be together in bar 3, an entry which never loses its element of risk.

In bar 11 the piano is certainly subito, the crescendo during the two previous bars rising to nearly *mf*. The repeat a tone higher of bars 3–8 must then be noticeably less distant (*p* instead of *pp*) making manifestly apparent the approach of the storm.

If the conductor has been deliberately restrained throughout the symphony so far, the unleashing of the storm at letter C (bar 21) provides the moment for a first more extravagant gesture. The entry of the timpani, reserved throughout the work exclusively for its illustrative quality (it is silent again in the finale), must have the effect of a thunderclap, not just a simple roll, albeit in *ff*. The use of hard sticks, though not wooden, would be in order here since, according to Berlioz, the use of leather—far harder than our conventional felt—was the normal alternative to wood at that time.

This is also the place for the appearance of doubling horns, if four are to be used. (As in the Fifth Symphony, however,

the 3rd and 4th players are commonly allocated the slow movement, in alternation to the first pair.)

The upward leaps in the strings are rarely emphasized enough:
the 2nd violins and violas in bar 21, the 2nd violins in bar 26,
all three groups in bar 29, these can all add a positive extra
intensity to the dense, drenching cloudburst. Strong syncopated
beats directed to the relevant players get enthusiastic response
since these tiring passages, which seem on the surface to be
the merest hackwork, can be made unexpectedly rewarding.

Although there should be no actual variations of tempo
throughout the storm, some freedom of style in the beat will
add to the movement's electrifying effect as well as making the
players sit on the edge of their chairs. Hence in bars 33 and
34 a sharply subdivided first beat followed by no second beat
at all will emulate the graphic description of lightning flashes.
Again, at letter D (bar 41) there is occasion for some exaggeration
of *pp subito*, since it is not easy for the 1st violins to accomplish
this without additionally playing the crotchet D staccato, which
they really ought not to do. (A useful trick is to insist on this
D being played with a new up-bow.)

Bars 41 and 42 are then hardly beaten at all other than by
encouraging the cellos and basses, which latter specifically need
the low notes down to C, as they will to even greater purpose
later in the movement. Between this point and bar 56 it is really
only the flashes (which should be startling) and the crescendo
of bars 49 and 50 (especially in the timpani) that the conductor
need portray.

The precise rhythm called for by the delicate staccato passage
of the 1st violins in bars 56–61 is ingeniously prepared by Beethoven's double lightning flash in the previous bar. The hush
in bars 62 and 65 is then absolute, the conductor standing as
still as he dares, only bringing in the basses in bar 64 by, as
it might be, a slight lift of the head in their direction.

The violins' figuration in bars 66 ff. can be imaginatively handled by beginning all the quavers up-bow and gradually introducing separate spiccato bowing as the crescendo takes effect. (Note
especially the D♮ in bar 70 followed by D♭ in bar 71.) The
crescendo itself should start by being somewhat restrained in
the 2nd violins and violas to enable the rising woodwind solos
to soar through to maximum advantage. It is as well additionally

to mark all of these wind entries *f crescendo*, except of course for the flute whose three doublings of the 1st violins can be marked respectively *mp, mf*, and *f*.

One cannot be dogmatic over the correct bar-phrasings for the eleven bars of torrential rain from bars 78–88. Probably the best solution is 3 + 4 + 4 although the timpani strokes seem almost indiscriminately placed and the all-important (and often unnoticed) piccolo entry comes curiously at the second of a 4-bar period. (For economic reasons the symphony is occasionally played with only two flutes, the 2nd doubling piccolo, but although it might be protested that in emergency the compromise is not totally catastrophic it is obviously undesirable.)

The trumpets' entry at the end of bar 84 must ring out like a fanfare, the crotchet C being a little shortened. The piccolo in bar 88 is also to be played strongly marcato, while bars 93–5, where he is at last in his most favourable register, should be earsplitting.

Hopefully it is not too fanciful for the conductor to indicate the howling gale of bars 95–102 with broadly lateral beating, and to give quite a histrionic leap for the work's first entry of the trombones at the peak of the storm, occurring as it does at a half-beat which adds immeasurably to its cataclysmic effect.

This outburst then persists for its span of concentrated fury without further demonstration; the 4-bar period is simply marked while the concentration is on maintaining full intensity. There have been many subsequent tempests in music from Verdi to Richard Strauss of far greater elaboration and complexity of orchestral virtuosity, but none creates a greater impact than Beethoven's of 1808.

With the long-delayed entry of the trombones it transpires that Beethoven is using only two of the conventional three, and moreover, a different two from those he elected to employ in *Fidelio*. Unlike the timpani, however, they remain to participate in the beautiful *Hirtengesang*.

With the eye of the storm past, it is the alternating sforzando bars which alone need emphatic gestures, bars 111, 113, etc. being demonstrably underplayed. At bar 119, on the other hand, although the 1st violins share in the general 'sempre diminuendo', they carry the force of the driving rain and should start with a renewed *ff*, their double strokes played close to the string. The power of their bow-arms is then lessened as gradually as possible through the 11 bars which carry them little by little to their piano. The bassoons, clarinets and oboe in turn also start their sustaining octaves each with pronounced intensity, but slackening the tone as they hand over from instrument to instrument.

In all that has happened so far during the movement, the notation of the basses in the different editions has followed Beethoven's autograph, not by any means always consistent in this respect as we have seen in the Fourth and Fifth symphonies, taking them with impunity down to the low C, whatever he may have expected to have been the practical reality of the instruments of his day. It is the more strange, therefore, to find so many variants in perhaps the most important place of all, the descending passage leading to bar 136. Peters jumps the octave for the last two notes, Eulenburg only for the final C itself, while Breitkopf retains the lower octave for the whole of the descent in the score—as shown unequivocally by Beethoven's own hand—but omits this essential reading in toto in the orchestral parts.*

It can be gratefully documented that the *p* preceding the timpani diminuendo in bar 141 given by Peters and other editions (but not Breitkopf) is apocryphal. This penultimate burst of thunder certainly needs a more pictorial treatment, with even the suggestion of a rumble about it. The reappearance of blue sky marked by the oboe is a magical moment well characterized by Beethoven's mark of 'dolce', which can be taken to indicate a dynamic slightly above the prevailing *pp*, especially as Beethoven himself added 'SOLO' to the oboe line. The flute solo then leads with only the very least rubato into the finale, whose Allegretto ♩. = 60 is yet again just right.

V

With this movement the style returns to one of gentleness in beat and gesture, the conjuring of warmth and sheer beauty

*There are similar editorial emendations to the bass-line in the last movement, such as bars 43–9.

of sound again being the constant preoccupation of all concerned.

The fourth bar of the horn-call (bar 8 of the movement) is
sometimes thought to be wrongly printed in the editions, mainly
on the evidence of Grove who, in his *Beethoven and his Nine
Symphonies*, when discussing the harmonization of the passage,
quotes the call with a D instead of an E at the sforzando. He
was, however, led astray by taking his text from the first Breitkopf edition of 1826 which contains this crucial misprint amongst
numerous others.

Nothing in the bald printed dynamics or expression marks
indicates the radiance of tone quality called for by this sublime
melody, whether when played by the 1st violins at bar 9 or,
perhaps even more so, by the 2nds at bar 17. Significantly there
is no change from a general fortissimo when its glowing third
statement, characterized by the horns (now possibly doubled)
passes on to the modulating motif which combines the roles
of transition passage and second subject. This accordingly
plunges forward as if in continuation of a single magnificently
extended sentence. These 25 bars of generous outpouring inevitably acquire a momentum of their own which need not be
checked for yet a further four bars until the declamatory statement—reinforced by high trombones—at bars 54-5, and correspondingly during the reprise (at bars 162-3) where the pile-up
gives the illusion of being even stronger and more extended,
although in actual fact it is exactly the same number of bars
in length.

The natural broadening which brings the music back to the
basic tempo for the return needs only the least hesitation in
pulse to allow for the piano subito at the top of the 1st violins'
semiquaver run.

All the wind solos in bars 57-63 need to stand well out from
the background string texture even (or perhaps especially) when
they are in unison with the 1st violins who should therefore
not play warmly until the resumption of their great melody
in its original *cantando* guise at bar 64. It may be added that
the little trill in bar 66 (surely a stroke of genius) is played
as a double mordent without *Nachschlag*.

The 2nd violins again take up their most beautiful singing
quality as before, but this time there is a heightening of tension

as the movement takes a new departure. For this purpose a slight quickening of pulse will prevent a feeling that the music is tending to plod, a danger which is all too prevalent in the following episode unless the meandering clarinet/bassoon line is allowed to flow. This is a problem one is apt to meet elsewhere in Beethoven as, for example, at several places in the Seventh Symphony. Here it is between bars 75–9 that the forward pressure needs to be exerted, and it is helpful in this context that the cellos' and basses' arco turns out to be wrongly printed a bar too early in the printed copies; Beethoven's placing of it at the end of bar 76 provides an admirably fresh support for the 2nd violins' sweeping imitation after a fourfold repetition of the rhythmic pizzicatos, as well as assisting in the impetus of the surging crescendo leading to the movement's central section.

This beautiful episode swings amiably along until it reaches the purple harmony of bar 93, which is so highly coloured that it warrants some appropriately generous response from the conductor. An imperceptible calando is then made to the original basic pulse during the tender pianissimo bars 95–8 in order that the new figuration of bar 99 may not be unduly hurried.

The semiquaver pattern was for long played incorrectly with the first two notes of each sextuplet group slurred symmetrically, on account of editorial changes made in the Breitkopf parts, which pandered unnecessarily to the convenience of a simplistic bowing but which has the effect of distorting Beethoven's subtlety of phrasing. Moreover, through its extra accentuation, it tends to obscure the important viola part with its references to the principal subject.

The music then surges into a fine solo for the first flute (not two flutes plus two oboes as in the current scores) in bars 109 ff., the conductor pointedly demonstrating how the interest passes to corresponding solos for, in turn, the clarinet and horn, the latter coming to rest on an E (not C) at bar 117 for the start of the decorated reprise.

The pizzicato chord for the 2nd violins in bar 115 is not often noticed and may reasonably be marked up to f since it lies in a weak register. It is also often skimped as in the editions the players are wrongly given only half a bar to prepare for it, Beethoven having in fact rested them for an additional half-beat in the previous bar.

Many commentators have over the years failed to appreciate the seraphic quality of what they see only as the conventional manner in which Beethoven ornaments his melodies, a procedure which finds its apotheosis in the 'Choral' Symphony's Adagio. Here is an outstanding example, and it is incumbent upon the conductor to delineate its contours by an imaginative use of eyes and stick so as to infuse the line with the utmost expressiveness over the whole length of the travelling phrase, lest for any single moment the flow of notes may be mistaken for some kind of superior Kreutzer Étude. Where the 1st violins are concerned, the printed phrasing over two bars at a time can also be taken to equate with the bowing, but with the 2nds this will not be enough, and as the crescendo develops two bows to a bar will soon become necessary. Even with this bowing, however, the violas and cellos can easily be obscured at the fortissimo of bars 133 ff. by the weight of passionate orchestral detail they support (much as in a similar passage in the Fifth Symphony Andante). Yet in the event it all works better than one might expect; the staccato horns can outline the motivic element without thickening the texture, and even though the violins and upper woodwind are marked to be played strongly the colour should always be rich rather than sheerly powerful.

Bars 169–76 provide another instance where, unless the pulse is allowed to quicken with the rising animation there is a feeling of constriction; and after the first fortissimo outpouring of bars 190–5 has unexpectedly drained away, the resumption of the excited surging of bars 196–204 once more needs an urgency which sweeps all before it. Even so, it again needs careful judgement to avoid inadvertently reaching a più mosso either at the mighty cello statement at bar 177, or at its ornamented version at bar 206, which latter must not seem more agitated than at its first appearance at the start of the reprise. Furthermore, should any difficulty of ensemble arise during either of these passages, which are shared alike between cellos and bassoons, the onus of responsibility will always be on the cellos for, whereas they cannot ever be heard by the bassoons, they themselves can hear the wind without difficulty.

The bassoons' continuation of the condensed theme in bar

213 is hard to bring through adequately after the clarity of the preceding horn and flute solos. At the least they can be upgraded to *mf*, but the strings' crescendo may also reasonably be restrained until bar 215, after which the whole movement boils over.

This second fortissimo blossoming is one of the greatest glories of the whole work and if handled sympathetically should bring a lump to the throat. The span of sound is extraordinarily wide and cries out for the deep C's and D's of the basses which are indeed present in all scores, as they have already been in the anticipatory *ff*'s at bars 175–6 and 192.

Yet even now it is not just the beginning of this heart-stirring passage which offers the experience of such great poignancy but above all bar 227, which accordingly needs a general expansion of tone during the two bars leading to it; in this, furthermore, it is the trumpets and trombones who can take priority. A corresponding relaxation of the tension then follows two bars ahead of the printed diminuendo, which however must not itself start to descend from less than forte; at such a dynamic the flute can then take over the melodic line, handing it across to oboe at bar 234, who in turn hands it back to flute for the cadence in bar 236.

There is surely no way in which the basic tempo can be retained for the sotto voce strings at bar 237. The very idea is deeply alien to the profound *Innigkeit* of which this perhaps is the first example, and at the same time one of the greatest, in the romantic era. Clearly, while the *Stimmung* must never descend into mere sentimentality, yet the reflective calm should be all pervasive. At first any pulse faster than ♩. = 40 will run the risk of breaking the spell; nor can there be room for rubato other than the obvious gap to allow for what is certainly a piano subito at bar 242. Nevertheless the beat must, for all its inwardness of manner, suggest enough momentum to give the players the sheer confidence to play one note after another—or, come the performance, that awful creeping paralysis will infect the orchestra in which all sense of tempo is lost because everybody is waiting for someone else. The little turns of 1st violins and oboe in bars 243 and 247 need particularly affectionate guidance from the point of the stick.

By the forte of bar 245 the tempo will have tautened a little.

but not beyond ♩. = 46, which pulse will maintain until bars
254–7, during which four bars an appreciable degree of movement can briefly interrupt the calm. Bar 255 is a moment of
glory for the trombones who deserve an appreciative glance
for that splendid entry.

But with the two bars of placed dotted minims the relaxed
tempo returns, although it is above all important not to let
these bars spread into quasi fermatas despite the separation
between them and the feeling that the whole structure has at
last come to rest.

The last five bars provide one of the rare instances of Beethoven using a muted horn. This makes its closing solo the harder
for the strings to hear and accompany unless the tempo is
allowed to move forward a fraction, in which case the semiquaver figures will then unfold naturally as they descend through
the string groups and so lead into the last two chords. These
must both be indicated, of course, but in such a way that despite
their purpose of finality they are not too widely spaced, nor
the concluding crotchet held beyond its proper value; for the
fermata is significantly placed over the rest, not the chord, and
if the symphony has been played with the right sentiment the
applause will not begin until that silence too has played its part.

Symphony No. 7 in A major, Op. 92

◀▶

HOWEVER much Beethoven's Fifth continues to maintain its reputation as the most famous symphony ever written, the Seventh bids fair to challenge it in terms of sheer popularity. There is more than one contributory factor here: in the first place the purely practical element in the relative orchestration of the two symphonies is bound to weigh with concert promoters when planning and budgeting a sure-fire programme. For although both are large-scale and powerfully mature examples of their creator's art, the Fifth calls for no less than five extra players, whereas the Seventh can be included in a concert requiring no more than will be engaged for any standard classical programme with double wind, horns, trumpets, and timpani. In addition, for all the tremendous triumph which ends the Fifth, it is the Seventh which, when played at its full potential, can be guaranteed to bring the house down at the end, a privilege which it shares with one other symphony in particular: Tchaikovsky's Fourth.

A third element can also be taken into account: although the Seventh plays substantially longer than the Fifth, even without the conventional repeats in the first and last movements, it is considerably less difficult technically and thus need not eat up too much rehearsal time. It is overall very much a tutti symphony, in contrast to its predecessor No. 6 and to a greater extent even than the first three movements of No. 5. As for the question of doubling the horns, this hardly comes into consideration since if such a procedure is thought to be desirable this would apply equally to the two earlier symphonies with the only difference that the doubling would not be kept in reserve for the last movement but to some extent adopted throughout. At the same time, with the goodwill of the players, a strong case can be made for preserving the purer ring of only the two horns, especially when balanced against a smaller string group.

I

The question of style with respect to the mighty chords with which Beethoven so characteristically opens the work has already been discussed in connection with the first bars of the 'Eroica'. In the initiation of the Seventh the very first chord might be considered harder to enunciate, partly because of its particular stylistic quality—it has a totally different resonance from any of its predecessors—but also because the 1st trumpet's note (G for the D trumpet, which becomes a top B for the standard B♭ instrument) is really quite high to pitch into the expectant silence which attends the beginning of so great a work. In fact all four of the forte tutti pillars of sound, which punctuate the opening sentence of the symphony in the alternate bars 1, 3, 5, and 7, are indicated with confidence-giving and emphatic deliberation, with down-beats which are 'bedded in' at the bottom, as it were, the orchestra habitually responding a fraction of a second later.

Nevertheless, the firm placing of these chords must not reflect adversely on the tempo of the melodic lines which, in Beethoven's interestingly conservative indication 'Poco sostenuto', is not at all slow. If in the event the printed metronome mark ♩ = 69 is admitted to be somewhat too hasty, ♩ = 56 (but no slower) will better allow for the clarity of the semiquaver scale passages which are soon to follow, while keeping the pace and vivacity which are so strong a feature of this symphony as a whole.

In bar 6 a corruption appears in the text of many editions of the score giving the flute a C♯ instead of the A correctly shown by Breitkopf. This has been known to cause embarrassing incidents, as when one child prodigy on the rostrum, having learnt his score from the Philharmonia miniature, tried in vain to insist that the 1st flute of a major London orchestra was playing a wrong note.

The string semiquavers are none too easily set in motion with immaculate ensemble. As soon as the horns have been helped down to their lower octaves (it is a considerable leap for the 2nd horn), a complete change of style has to be adopted in bar 9 away from the smooth outlining of the cantabile passages between the chords to a clearly rhythmic demarcation of pulse. An effective contrivance is to play the repeated notes of bar 9 marcato on the string changing to spiccato for the pianissimo scales of bars 11 and 13. This is not only in line with similar passages in, for example, the Fourth Symphony Andante but also corresponds with the autograph where the sharp staccato indications clearly begin with the scales themselves.

A sudden heightening of tension should be apparent at the very outset of bar 14, the crescendo perhaps starting already at piano rather than pianissimo. However, in the *ff* section which follows it is dangerous to be over-demonstrative towards the wind and brass. The important element must always be the scales with their jagged articulation, especially as they are handed over from lower to upper strings, and the constant minim sforzandos of which the fourth in each group (F♯ of the 2nd violins, top E of the 1sts and so on) can be further reinforced.

In bar 22 the last four semiquavers will lead into the succeeding melodic section with the least suggestion of rubato (as again of course in the parallel bar 41). During these quiet wind-orientated passages—bars 23–8 and 42–7—it is the violins who need particular nursing so that their entries do not disturb the wind figures and yet have a positive quality of expressive beauty. This can conveniently be conveyed by the fingers of the left hand, which will also control the descending phrase in bar 28 (= 47). This group will again need some small degree of rubato and perhaps diminuendo into the hushed string melodic takeover. There is, however, an added risk in these rubatos since the violins must be very precisely paced with respect to the resumption of tempo as they have to fit exactly with the alternating repeated semiquavers in lower strings and woodwind. Moreover these have themselves to dovetail impeccably, for which purpose a particularly clear beat is required especially for the wind, who can barely—if at all—hear the cello/bass definition while they are themselves sustaining minims.

The crescendo in bars 32–3 is short and very steep, so that a vehement encouragement is not too extravagant as soon as it takes effect half-way through bar 32. In the second fortissimo section, on the other hand, economy of gesture is valuable since the preponderance of sforzandos is of a different order from the parallel preceding passage. Furthermore the tonal structure of this second outburst leads towards an inbuilt climax at bar 40 with the appearance of the chord of C major, which represents the central high point of the whole long introduction (the most extensive and fully worked out example of its kind up to this time) and which justifies a renewed intensification of tone from the whole orchestra. There will be a similar place in the last movement where the highlighting of a moment in one of Beethoven's extended *ff* passages might be suggested (see pp. 149–50).

At bar 49 the crescendo is both sooner and more extended than the corresponding one at bar 33. It is indeed to be felt as the beginning of a new 4-bar phrase which has interrupted the previous period after this has run for only a single bar. The contrary motion on the violas, already in evidence in bars 32–3, can now be brought to the fore, beginning not less than piano, as can also the entry of the 2nd woodwind players.

Letter B has obvious shock value, the *ff* quavers in bars 53 and 55 being as brusque as possible. The same applies to the violins' jabs in the same bars which must be no less startling. But the linking passage which follows gains by being conducted in a mock-serious dead-pan style, befitting one of Beethoven's best musical leg-pulls. Attempts have been made to invest these bars with some deep psychological significance, but this over-looks Beethoven's penchant for finding sheer fun in music-making. The points to be made are only the change of pattern at bar 60 (the wind taking over the lead in the alternation with the violins) and the placing of the up-beat semiquavers thereafter. The quavers in bar 58 are not to be played staccato; nor is there to be the slightest deviation of metronomic pulse right up to the double-bar, the Vivace beginning abruptly at the new $\frac{6}{8}$ section.

The printed mark of ♩. = 104 is somewhat too hectic for the grace as well as accuracy in the 'Amsterdam' rhythmic figure which predominates in this exciting movement, though some such tempo will certainly be approached during the dramatic build-ups in development and coda. A pulse of ♩. = 96, although only a little more relaxed, gives just the necessary elbow-room for delicacy of phrasing especially at the beginning of the dance.

The wind's *p subito* at the fifth bar of the Vivace needs a hair's breadth of comma not merely as is usual with such subitos but in order for the up-beat semiquaver of the strings' first entry to be clearly perceptible; thereafter these string punctuations fit easily against the wind.

There is a school of thought which insists that a fermata ($\curvearrowright$) should be held for a duration equal to a strict number of beats in the prevailing tempo. Hans Swarowsky, for example, used to preach this gospel in his widely acclaimed class for young conductors, and Malcolm Sargent was not alone in sustaining bar 88 for three precisely measured beats, continuing the upward surge of the strings on the fourth.

A diametrically opposite view has, however, much reason on its side when it maintains that the whole point of a fermata is for it to be held for any other length of time than will exactly correspond with the basic pulse. The pause should thus provide a brief but dramatic interruption to the rhythmic continuum of the structure. In the present instance, occurring so early in the movement, the hold-up may be relatively short, as compared with the equivalent pause—or pauses—which will come in the reprise after so extended a series of crescendos and fortissimos which have been a major element in the development. A little more than three, but less than four dotted crotchets' worth may be thought about the warrantable length; in particular there should be no occasion for the strings to need a change of bow. The chord is then taken off before the *ff* up-beat, this giving the horns time to prepare for the high top B and G♯ respectively with which they embark upon the first of their many ringing solo passages in the symphony.*

It is very questionable whether this passage benefits by being played by four horns, as is so often heard; like corresponding places already discussed with respect to earlier symphonies, the extra doubling robs the instruments of their bright resonance in favour of undue weight and thickening of the quality. It

*The Philharmonia miniature score, having put rehearsal letter A at bar 34, now marks B here and has in fact its own system of rehearsal lettering throughout the symphony. It is hard to imagine what purpose the publishers had in so doing, as these letters relate neither to any other edition nor to the orchestral parts.

is on the contrary particularly exhilarating when the two horns elect to play this whole symphony on their own although it has to be conceded that a 'bumper' can be of great value to the 1st horn in a heavy programme.

There is much to be said for delaying the strings' crescendo in bar 101 until perhaps 4 bars before letter C. If the cellos and basses can then lead the ascent by exaggerating their printed staccato, the redoubled frequency of the principal motif will then contribute to the heightening excitement.

Bar 110 and similar places raise another issue concerning the horn parts of this, even above the other symphonies: Beethoven repeatedly exploits the brilliance of two unison horns in their upper register without taking into account the many hazardous leaps for the 2nd player. Weingartner spends many pages of his book in detailing the numerous places where he advocates recourse to the lower octave, as equally in the 2nd trumpet, wherever he considers that Beethoven would have written the lower notes had they been available on the instruments of his day. Yet, on the other hand, it should be remembered that Beethoven often turned such limitations to colouristic advantage, and was moreover prone to use a pair of high unison horns or trumpets even in places where the lower notes would have been perfectly feasible. Bars 124–5 and 132–3 are instances where the high notes (F♯'s for F horns) are of outstanding importance in creating the atmosphere of almost feverish excitement. At the same time, the conductor would be well advised to be aware that orchestral musicians are inclined to keep out of trouble by surreptitiously transposing the dangerous notes down the octave, or by simply leaving them out, hoping that these safety measures will pass unobserved.

Another custom relating again to the lack of appropriate harmonics on Beethoven's natural instruments is that of writing extra notes into the horn and trumpet lines where he left rests. An outstanding instance will arise in the last movement, but here in bars 125 and 127 the erstwhile custom of restoring the gaps in the trumpet parts with notes composed *ad hoc* is fortunately less prevalent today.

In bars 120 and 122 the downward sweeps on 2nd violins and violas are so important and stirring that it is worth adopting a special bowing to bring them into prominence, such as:

Ex. 10

in preference to the more usual bow per half-bar. And at the return the extravagant, if perhaps inconvenient, bowing:

Ex. 11

at bars 332 and 334 is also very effective.

After some energetic beating at letter D (the strings' C major descending phrase could reasonably be marked *ff*), the diminuendo in bars 138–40 will naturally be created by no more than a series of progressively smaller down-beats in order to conjure an atmosphere of expectation, the strings re-entering as softly as possible. If their crescendo is also delayed the little woodwind bird-calls may just be heard during bars 147–50.

In bar 157 the 1st violins can be encouraged to enjoy one of Beethoven's characteristic leaps. Since the corresponding figure in bar 369 is so much less striking it is the more important to feature the one here.

Only unswerving obedience to the printed page can provide justification for taking the repeat in this movement, as the abrupt return is musically ineffective and unmotivated. But when the cliff-hanger of bar 174 is reached it transpires that the strings' page-turns come at this very point. Here therefore is another place where it is an idea to write in some bars of the continuation at the foot of the page; alternatively the inside players might be instructed to turn during bars 172–4 in order to preserve the drama of Beethoven's link into the development.

Neither of the pairs of G.P. bars (175–6, 179–80) are to be beaten out although both are counted strictly. The violence of the re-entry at bar 177 as well as the mysterious *pp* of bar 181 will be the more significantly demonstrated after moments of frozen immobility on the part of the conductor and orchestra alike.

A slight break before bar 185 will give the correct feeling of a new start to the rhythm after a drop to *ppp* on the upper strings as the cellos and basses initiate the series of 2-bar imitations rising through the orchestra in a meticulously held pianissimo. At the same time considerable danger lies in having allowed the tempo to have become sympathetically relaxed, as the crescendo in bars 195–200 is the outstanding place in the movement where the AMsterdam-AMsterdam $\frac{6}{8}$ rhythm tends

to degenerate into: *etc.* (exactly as

invariably occurs throughout the Scherzo of Schumann's *Overture, Scherzo and Finale*, Op. 52). This can be avoided however if the momentum is kept well up and thereafter actually driven forward.

Another bad old custom, again fortunately no longer prevalent, used to be of omitting the 2nd violins altogether in bars 205–6 in favour of an added lower Bb on the 2nd horn by analogy with the corresponding bars 211–12. On the contrary, the unison horns against the background of violins in the first pair of bars, followed by the naked wind with the horns in octaves supporting the group in the second pair, make an electrifying effect in varied and contrasted colouring. The whole section between letters F and G gains in strength if in the tutti groups of bars the conductor's beat delineates and encourages the lower strings rather than the violins and violas, whose passages always come over splendidly without the need for additional whipping up.

Then in bars 217–19 only the strings' first beats need to be conducted at all, the wind automatically supplying their echoing answers of their own accord. This gives the conductor the possibility to address a specific and new beat to the wind in bar 220, placed with greatest clarity a fraction late, thus creating a slight *Luftpause* after their group in the previous bar, so necessary for the subito piano and the quiet section to follow.

In this balancing 'grazioso' section of the development the strings need at once to make overt the alternation between

and , a differentiation

rarely made sufficiently audible but which becomes increasingly the main point at issue all the way from bar 222 to 273–4 where the woodwind and horns suddenly change from the one style to the other with powerful cumulative effect. Tchaikovsky must have loved this passage for he makes jubilant play with the identical device in the parallel development section of his own Fifth Symphony.

The long crescendo dotted minims in the strings between bars

238 and 249 present an analogous problem to the violin crescendo long notes in the first movement development of the 'Pastoral' Symphony. Again, as suggested in that context, an unconventional bowing does in fact work admirably and avoids clumsy and always audible bow-changes half-way through the long notes. But by working gradually towards the upper half of the bow during the staccato groups the sustained crescendos can be accomplished in a series of single up-bows by upper and lower strings alike.

When the four bars before H are reached (bars 250–3) the extended gradual crescendo will have arrived at a single forte and there must be no further crescendo during these bars, the *ff* at H itself being one of Beethoven's most typical and spectacular subitos. It is a mark of the conductor's mastery in the art of presentation demonstrably to exercise an element of restraint in the approach to letter H before letting the fury break suddenly loose at the *subito ff* itself.

In the third and fourth of each succeeding 4-bar phrase it can be quite difficult to enable either the woodwind lines or the string imitative phrases adequately to penetrate the sustained *ff* of horns, trumpets, and timpani. Yet the subito pianos so often applied to these instruments sound mannered and artificial. Moreover the high point of the build-up, which must patently stand at the arrival of the recapitulation at letter I (bar 278), still lies ahead and if Beethoven's *più f* of bar 274 after no less than twenty bars of fortissimo is not to be meaningless, some adjustment of dynamics is inescapable. The following may be taken as suggested solutions:

1. In bars 254–5, 258–9, and 262–3 the woodwind need only play a single *f*, reserving their strength for the in-between bars 256–7 and 260–1 where, as well as in bars 264–7, their line is the *Hauptstimme*.

2. In these same alternate pairs of bars the horns, trumpets, and timpani should not resolutely maintain their full power, but neither should they drop suddenly. A tapered reduction of tone across each of the two bars to a poco forte will give sufficient transparency to the texture without a noticeable sacrifice of dramatic intensity.

3. Again in these bars the strings, who have the *Nebenstimme*, must certainly initiate each entry with the utmost power, but

may phrase away their concluding notes to allow each new voice to tell equally effectively. With this in mind, they too can preserve their strength in bars 258–9 so as to be able to redouble their efforts thereafter. But whereas the woodwind are advised to do the same in bars 262–3 the strings should continue their *ff* until the second half of bar 267, or bar 264 will seem to start a new phrase, whereas on the contrary the violent altercation between wind and strings should arise out of the dynamism of bars 262–3.

4. The string entry in bar 267 and that of the wind four bars later will accordingly start the final crescendo of the development at a level of *f*, passing logically through Beethoven's *più f*, and with the abrupt eleventh-hour stepping up of dynamics in trumpets and timpani (which is well worth exaggerating) arrive with the utmost aplomb at the jubilant return of the main theme, this to be accomplished without any perceptible broadening of pulse.

It is strange to have to place on record that Eulenburg, generally so reliable an edition, has actually bowdlerized the string parts in bar 285. The arguments which once raged over the surely intentional harmonic divergence between wind and strings are now all but a hundred years old; Grove, in his *Beethoven and his Nine Symphonies* refers to letters on the subject in the *Daily Telegraph* of July 1893 from which he unfortunately came to too hasty a conclusion. Today no one seriously believes that the passage should be altered any more than the analogous places in the 'Choral' Symphony. Fortunately the Breitkopf material is correctly printed and all that is necessary is to incite the lower strings to ever greater efforts as they maintain the tonic A major figuration, the cellos and basses climbing through their upper octave, against the wind's anticipatory change to D, with which they are then reunited in the following bar.

Of the two fermatas in bars 299 and 300 the first should be held the longer, indeed it may be more markedly sustained than the corresponding pause in the exposition at bar 88, since it is now the culmination of so extended a build-up. The orchestra is then sharply taken off with the same gesture which gives the preparation for the down-beat for the wind's surprised piano reply-fermata. This is, however, a more complicated situation due to the wind's semiquaver, and orchestras are prone to challenge the conductor over how he intends them to react to his stick. One standard and simple method is, unusually, not to indicate the barline but the semiquaver itself, the strings' pizzicato being placed as a kind of reflex action with a bounced sub-beat. The second fermata is then, like the first, firmly taken off although with the left hand, upon which the oboe solo follows directly with an up-beat given by the stick, not in the main tempo but giving the player enough space for the scale to rise melodiously in Beethoven's mark of 'dolce'.

Four bars later there is so sudden a change to the minor mode that it must surely be played in pianissimo to make its full impact. As the oboe's line leads into the repeat of the phrase it is better perhaps to make a general diminuendo during bar 304 rather than making a subito drop in dynamic which, had he wanted it, Beethoven would certainly have prescribed.

The following passage is then so reflective in character that to forge ahead in strict tempo is to be guilty of sheer insensitivity. Furthermore bar 308, which introduces the woodwind's gentle conversation, will benefit from an expressive rise and fall on the strings as the pace is gently relaxed.

The next six bars (309–14) can be played 'un poco esitando' with a 'poco a poco ravvivando' taken at the entry of the timpani who, despite the prevailing *pp sempre*, can take the initiative in pressing forward to reach tempo primo already at bar 319, the crescendo in the following bars then being at full driving speed.

As before, the two G.P. bars 387–8 are not beaten, though counted out scrupulously, and are followed this time by the isolated *p* bar (389) which is a very real gasp of dismay. A shorter freeze, the single G.P. bar, then leads to the subdued entry of the cellos and basses which can begin once more at a slackened pace which is, however, taken subito. In view of the freedom in conducting style in this area, the wind entries—and especially that of the horns, always an accident-prone phrase—should be given careful pointing.

Strange to say, the deepest sonorities are missing from the crawling low string ostinato. One might even have relished a contrabassoon here, yet in the event even the basses are not written at their deepest octave even though it is only a bottom

D♯ which comes into question, where already in the three previous symphonies, as well as several times in the present movement, Beethoven has taken his basses down as far as the low
C. Moreover in the coda of the finale the similar cello/bass
ostinato continually dips to the D♯ (although Eulenburg curiously takes it upon itself to transcribe the basses up the octave
there too). This sinister passage is accordingly one of the few
places where a *Retusche* to Beethoven's text may be condoned
as being dramatically effective in the highest degree.

With the fourteen-bar crescendo between bars 409 and 422
the pace tightens once again to a vivace assai at the fortissimo.
There would indeed seem to be virtually no limits to the energy
and exultation that might be generated in this coda, and yet
it would be unwise not to cast a shrewd mental eye ahead to
the finale. Even the virtuosity which the horns have to display
in bars 442 ff. is matched by similar exhibitions during the closing pages of the symphony. The best method of restraint, as
so often in unusually strenuous works, is to concentrate on
essentials: the last minute più crescendo in bars 421–2 with heightened featuring of the timpani; the rhythmic imitation in the
lower strings during bars 427–9 to be given the utmost power
at the expense of the violins who need no such specific attention;
the high trumpets in bars 430–1; the string punctuations in bars
432–7 (here it is the wind who can look after themselves without
even the aid of the second beats in each bar, which would only
impede the plunging momentum); and the eventual ascent to
the pealing horn fanfare which must on no account be lost
as it descends through the texture in bars 446–7. The last two
chords are delivered as with a cleaver.

II

As we have already seen in the 'Scene am Bach' of the 'Pastoral',
Toscanini startled the musical world in his famous cycles of
the Beethoven Symphonies during the 1930s with several seemingly revolutionary tempi, two of which occurred in this
Seventh Symphony. The first concerned the present Allegretto,
until that time generally considered—despite the tempo marking—to be essentially a slow movement and therefore to be played

somewhat ponderously. Yet as in the 'Pastoral' what Toscanini did was to obey Beethoven's indications, metronome mark and all, to the letter in the same way that today, half a century later, the authentic movement is once again advocating as part of a blanket policy. Yet Sir George Grove quotes Nottebohm (in his *Beethoveniana*) as having documented Beethoven's anxiety in latter years that the movement should not be taken too fast and that he even wished that the marking could be changed to 'Andante quasi Allegretto'.

In actual fact, already in 1906 Weingartner had written the following on the subject of this tempo: 'the time-signature tells us that this movement is not be be taken like the customary adagio or andante. The metronome mark $\downarrow$ = 76, however, nearly gives us a quick-march, which cannot have been the composer's intention here. I have therefore adopted $\downarrow$ = 66.' There is much wisdom in this, and it soon transpired that Toscanini had few followers, as the sprightly pace was thought to give the music a character more appropriate to Donizetti than to Beethoven. Yet the shock the Italian maestro had delivered did produce some lasting effect and the movement has indeed since been recognized as the quasi-Allegretto it is, even though Weingartner himself failed in practice to live up to his intentions. For, when all is said and done, $\downarrow$ = 66 is still a shade too jaunty although the pace should not be slower than $\downarrow$ = 60, while the bowing style can also prevent the quality of sound from becoming glutinous if the semi-staccato quavers are taken off the string.

The cellos are best divided at the desk until letter A (bar 27), but thereafter by desks, those at the rear playing in unison with the basses as shown in the score layout.

The echo effect of bars 19–26, and again 43–50, can never be soft enough even though the latter passage carries the melodic line. Both sections can actually be played effectively senza vibrato in contrast to the rich tone required when the violas and 1st cellos first state the melody, and for which the plain mark of 'piano' is altogether too bland. In this connection it is surprising how often the grace-notes give trouble, less with regard to their positioning—they must certainly come on the beat—as to their speed of execution, which should be neither strict semiquavers nor demisemiquavers but something in

between, as might be notated thus:

Again at letter B the second violins, who handle the melody by themselves, need specific encouragement to begin their crescendo not from the previous hushed *pp* like the rest of the lower strings, but from some dynamic in advance of the 1st violins' piano.

When at last the great tune streams out on the 1st violins themselves at letter C Beethoven twice uses the perhaps odd device of dropping an octave in mid-flight. There will be other even more curious instances of this in the Ninth Symphony, but here it enables him to make expressive capital when each time he allows the violins to soar back up again to their proper octave.

With the ending of the first section and the approach of the secondary material, as equally of course at the return, the pulse should be allowed to edge imperceptibly forwards, to the undoubted satisfaction of the cellos and basses whose ostinato will otherwise feel laboured.

It is helpful to the 2nd horn to suggest that he exchanges octaves with the 1st horn in the bars immediately preceding his solo so as to avoid the awkward leap just as he needs to project his tone in answer to the clarinet.

Bars 131–4 echo the phrase played eight bars earlier so precisely that it may be thought musically desirable to restart the crescendo from a characteristic piano subito rather than continuing the expressive crescendo of bar 130. This will have the further advantage of preventing too great an increase of tone by the flute entry in bar 135, which should hardly be stronger than a mezzopiano.

The sforzandos in woodwind and strings in bars 144–5 are quite hard to stress sufficiently and will need to be exaggerated if the hearer is to be at all conscious of their existence; with this in mind the violins can with advantage begin on a down-bow, bringing their *sf* also on to a down-bow, whereas the wood-wind can perhaps keep their true forte in reserve for the single accented note since their possibility of dynamic contrast is proportionately so much less. The *ff* chords in bars 148–9 then require positive quaver emphases, although without a true subdivision with the stick which would result in too great a hold-up of the pulse. Even the *p subito* of letter E (bar 150) can be achieved without the slightest trace of a comma. By now, too, the original tempo will have automatically reinstated itself for the reprise.

A particularly curious textual conundrum is posed by the *ff* quavers here. In all scores until the most recent Breitkopf reprint, the horns were shown to play G's: which for horns crooked in E sound B's. The Breitkopf parts however have always changed these to C's sounding E: so putting them into unison with the trumpets and drums; this accordingly is the version to which all ears are accustomed. Yet there is logic, however strange-sounding, in the earlier scores' reading whereby the strings give the complete first inversion chord, the brass and timpani only the bare fifth, and finally the woodwind the simple unison, which reading appears moreover to be corroborated by the autograph. Nevertheless the matter is still not settled once and for all, as these particular bars are clearly the result of a change of mind on Beethoven's part, the two bars being crowded into a space wide enough for only a single bar of those on either side, and written in what could well not be Beethoven's hand.

The woodwind return of the opening melody should make no attempt to emulate the warm outpouring of the strings in the earlier context, despite Beethoven's *p dolce*. The mood is now tranquil and will soon be more so after the short interlude with its background of trumpets and drums, the rise and fall hardly reaching a mezzoforte.

The conductor's manner can be altogether withdrawn during the fugato with the merest leans towards the relevant sections for their various entries. The change comes in bar 208 with the violas whose statement prompts the woodwind entry in the following bar, a point often obscured in performance and thus worth marking up to piano. There was a day when conductors habitually made a pull-up when leading into letter G, but it is now universally recognized that the fortissimo bursts full tilt upon the scene.

In bar 223 there is a curious anomaly between the quaver of the wind as against the crotchet of the strings especially when compared with the parallel bar 92 when the same passage first occurred, where both wind and strings have crotchets. Such inconsistencies are not unusual in Beethoven and, as has been seen in earlier symphonies (and has especial relevance in the Violin Concerto), it can be dangerous to read too much into them. There seems little musical point to be made here, and yet further comparison needs to be drawn with bars 248 and 252 where the strings should surely play a full crotchet.

This, however, raises yet another argument with respect to note-lengths since the answering quaver in bar 250 should itself not be played staccato, in contrast to those which are specifically marked with dots in bars 249 and 253. Such questions, which constantly recur in Beethoven (Third and Fourth Piano Concertos, Eighth Symphony Allegretto, etc.) are especially worrying where, as so often, the Breitkopf parts add dots with prodigal abundance, presumably on the principle of bringing all phrasings into uniformity. It can then become very difficult for the players, in making the notes less short, not to make them too long—to get back into neutral as it were.

The pizzicato chords in bars 255 ff. are better marked *pp*, matching the woodwind drop at the beginning of this period. Here is another place of such an atmospheric hush that the less movement from the conductor the better. Nevertheless a careful focusing of attention on certain players brings grateful appreciation: the 2nd oboe in bars 257–8 and 265–6, and the 2nd horn for his entry in bar 260, especially perhaps for his octave leap in bars 271–2. The last rising fourfold string imitation can then be slightly brought out, the violas' and violins' entries justifying a return to a single piano.

It is believed to have been Erich Kleiber who started the hare running of a possible reading of sempre pizzicato in the 1st and 2nd violins in this closing passage. The argument is based on the suggestion that the mark 'arco' against the violin lines in the autograph does not look too much like Beethoven's handwriting. He was in the event mistaken, the hand being indeed that of Beethoven, but in any case it would have proved nothing as the composer could have given the direction to a copyist. Certainly musically speaking the arco is far more satisfactory, the more sustained quality of the crotchets, especially of the 1st violins' entry at the half-bar, giving a feeling of finality as it dies away leaving behind the same woodwind chord which opened the movement. In this respect it is important that both these chords should be exact in duration without any suspicion of fermata; at the end the music must seem to hang in the air.

III

Even allowing for Beethoven's Presto, the metronome mark is predictably a little too frenzied. Instead of 132, $\downarrow$. = 126 is a more practical proposition, although in a dry hall a slightly livelier tempo could be hazarded. At all events the pace should be perceptibly faster than the corresponding movements in the Third and Ninth Symphonies which, both at $\downarrow$. = 116, Beethoven merely designated Allegro and Molto Vivace respectively.

After an introductory pair of bars, the 4-bar phrases continue regularly enough (apart from a further 2-bar extension in bars 15–16) although, as Tovey pointed out in one of his famous 'Essays', Beethoven plays one of his typical tricks with the principal theme when it returns coyly a bar too early in bar 63, the stress being thrown as a result on to the last crotchet of each descending phrase. It is nevertheless virtually impossible to hear the passage in this way, especially as Beethoven has hidden the false accentuation with both the 1st violins' change to arco and the start of the crescendo at bar 74, as well as with the cello/bass initiation of the imitative pile-up in bar 82. Far better therefore for the conductor to recognize the hiccup in the phrasing and balance a 5-bar period at bars 61–5 with a corrective 3-bar phrase leading into the forte of letter A.

The beginning of the second section in bar 25 calls for considerable vehemence, being one of Beethoven's best humorously dramatic gestures. It would hardly come amiss to mark the timpani as well as the strings up to *ff*—the single forte seems somewhat tame, to say the least. This is one of many places in the symphony where the modern seating with the cellos and basses placed together on the conductor's right works to the music's clear advantage, visually as well as aurally. In view of the excitement generated by this passage it is a pity that the second repeat in the movement is so rarely observed; for great play can be made with the *sempre ff* of the first-time bars, leading to an even more thunderous restatement by timpani and basses, coming as it does so soon after the parallel passage in bars 137–40.

As always with woodwind, a true change of dynamic from *p* to *pp* in bars 33 and 49 is difficult to achieve to any marked degree, and it is not a bad plan to encourage them to start the phrases at bars 29 and 44 not less than *mp*. Conversely the characteristic furore of Beethoven's *subito ff* at bar 91 loses its effect if the previous forte is allowed to have become too strong after so extended a preparation.

The sudden cessation of trumpets and drums in bar 94, their momentary reappearance in bar 98, as well as the seemingly inconsequential appearances of 1st horn and timpani in bars 101 and 106, are of course all dictated by the fact that these are the only places where harmonies fit the available notes of the instruments. Since the effect is splendidly comical, this must be cited as an outstanding instance of Beethoven ingeniously exploiting the instruments of his day.

Bars 149–53 constitute the second-time bars* which, supplying the bridging diminuendo, will also relax the pace of the four marking down-beats as the 'Assai meno presto' of the Trio is approached.

There is evidence to show that Beethoven generally used 'assai' in the sense of 'somewhat' rather than 'very'. Either could be correct in the dictionary meaning of the word, but whereas for Verdi it was virtually synonymous with 'molto', in Beethoven's day it was more usually taken as corresponding with the French 'assez'. This has, however, only been recognized comparatively recently and the Trio is the second of the tempos with which Toscanini revolutionized musical opinion through observing Beethoven's metronome mark in defiance of the prevailing tradition of a very heavy and stodgy tempo.

Yet once again the printed ♩. = 84 is so fast that it is hard

---

*As in the 'Eroica', Breitkopf's bar-count oddly continues through both first- and second-time bars in the whole of this symphony. In the Scherzo therefore the bar numbering is now ahead of the miniature scores by four bars.

to believe that it was really Beethoven's true intention, being moreover wholly out of character especially with the Austrian pilgrim's hymn on which—as Thayer reported on the authority of the Abbé Stadler—the theme is based. Indeed, as Weingartner reasonably says, at that tempo the Trio would resemble a gallop. The speed of the movement has therefore come to be moderated at least to some extent, until a tempo of c. ♩. = 66 is widely accepted as a sensible compromise.

Some broadening of tempo to usher in the *ff* of bar 211 is unavoidable and is accomplished with a suggestion of separation within the beat for the crotchet in the previous bar. Care needs to be taken, however, to re-establish the tempo immediately afterwards lest the strong return of the theme becomes inadvertently too stately. The trumpet and timpani reiterations in bars 217–18 should be immensely dramatic if pointed with appropriate panache from the stick.

The descending crotchets on the trumpets call for sympathetic attention from the conductor as, lying very high for the 1st player, they are somewhat hazardous. For this very reason the players sometimes take a breath before the written E's, but this—apart from the musical distortion of such a measure—tends to heighten rather than lessen the danger of accident. Furthermore, despite the flamboyance of the preceding bars, the trumpets should not have held the high notes so strongly that they are compelled to make an uncalled-for diminuendo as they come down.

The bars linking the Trio back to the return of the Scherzo will be primarily concerned with keeping a really hushed quality in the ever softer string chords through which the 2nd horn's little dipping figures must penetrate without difficulty. Then as the last of these figures is transferred to the cellos the conductor will automatically turn in their direction with eyes opened wide for the *ppp*, as the last dip cannot come in strict tempo and will need to be indicated before giving the sharp twitch, made clearly visible to the tutti, which is all that is needed to restart the Scherzo on its way.

There is a strong case for taking the repeat in the Trio on the first, but not the second occasion. This, together with a decision to take both the first two repeats of the Scherzo, makes a convincingly symmetrical and well-graded structure:

I	Scherzo	1st repeat
		2nd repeat
I	Trio	1st repeat (written out with variant)
		2nd repeat
II	Scherzo	1st repeat (written out with piano variant)
		No 2nd repeat (none written)
II	Trio	1st repeat (as before)
		No 2nd repeat (!)
III	Scherzo	No 1st repeat (none written)
		No 2nd repeat (none written)
III	Trio	Fragment
	Coda	

The quiet written-out repeat at bar 265 needs to be played even softer than marked if it is to achieve its effect of contrast. A general level of *pp* is highly desirable with *ppp* in the strings where they are already marked pianissimo. Whilst this section should be directed with the least possible movement it is so full of humour that it cannot pass without some reflection in the conductor's gestures, however minuscule these may be. In particular the first bars of the second section, once so startlingly vivid, are now hilariously tiny and can be delineated with a touch of whimsy as group after group tickles the wee figures. The one-time explosion of bars 43-4 is also no more than a gentle puff in this return which can be happily triggered by the least lift of the stick.

The reprinted Breitkopf material has a disastrous page turn for the 2nd violins at bar 400, which has sometimes caused the sections of even the most experienced orchestras to falter if attention is not drawn to it in advance, especially since it occurs during a repeated section which is not normally rehearsed at all.

The fragment of a third time round of the trio should suggest hesitant uncertainty at the repeat of the phrase, both pace and dynamic perhaps being affected. It is then peremptorily blown away by the concluding Presto, which can reasonably be played very fast, with maybe even a hint of accelerando.

IV

The spectacular finale can follow almost segue, two opening thunderbolts being hurled at the orchestra with strong syncopated gestures separated by slightly elongated G.P. freeze-bars. Theatrical as such a procedure undoubtedly is, this movement is so violent in itself that it may surely be thought permissible for the method of its presentation to be as electrifying as possible.

An important feature throughout is that each statement of the opening figure should always be indicated by a single composite gesture, the second beat of the relevant bars being eliminated as much as possible but not actually going into 1 (although at three specific points during the movement this will actually happen), despite Beethoven's minim metronome mark, as the pulse is basically one of crotchets.

As for the printed ♩ = 72, this in terms of its equivalent ♩ = 144 is excellent once the emphatically repetitious sforzandos of the principal subject have ceased, but if these are to be given their true weight of accentuation the music can hardly be driven faster than ♩ = 132. This will also allow for the powerful evocation of the chromatically descending phrase in bar 17 (16).*

But at the second-time bar, bar 22 (20), the slight brake on the tempo may be withdrawn and the pulse allowed to gather pace until by letter A the headlong precipitation of Beethoven's printed direction can be given full rein.

In so doing certain features should come into prominence: firstly the horns' fanfare in bars 26 ff. (24 ff.), which lying so high dominates the woodwind; then at letter A the order of the semiquaver figure entries on the different instrumental groups demands particular attention, as it becomes more and more interesting during the course of the movement.

In bars 54–63 (52–61) the normal method of execution for the strings' rhythmic figure is  etc.

But objection is sometimes taken to this on the grounds that the style presupposes an off-the-string technique which by curtailing the dotted quavers gives a faulty reading:

etc.

Undeniable as this is, the alternative bracketed bowing (⊓⊔⊓⊔

*Extra bar numbers in brackets are now added because here again, when referenc is made to the miniature scores, it becomes necessary to remember that Breitkopf's bar-count continues through all the first- and second-time bars, becoming no less than eleven bars ahead by the reprise.

etc.) is so tame by comparison that the sacrifice of the dotted quavers may well be considered the lesser evil.

In bars 65 and 69 (63 and 67) extra care needs to be taken to ensure that the flutes can be heard distinctly as they provide the essential link in the six-octave descending phrases via the bassoon to the cellos and basses. Staccato flutes are gentle creatures at the best of times and are here easily obscured by the overhang of the violent chords which begin the passages.

The twelve-bar crescendo leading to the *ff* of letter C sounds curiously laboured, even pedestrian, unless the pace is moved forward yet again by encouraging the strings to take over the groups from each other with ever more impatient urgency, until by letter C itself there will certainly be a feeling of one pulse per bar. The tempo will have attained to not less than ♩ = 76, although at bar 116 (114) the shift of the sforzandos to the half-bars as well as the perfect frenzy of the 2nd violins and violas restores the necessity for crotchet pulsations.

Bar 115 (113) is the place referred to above (p. 131) where Beethoven, faced with a shift of harmony which would require impossible notes, made dramatic capital out of the limitations of his natural horns, trumpets, and timpani, by momentarily dropping them out of the texture, only to bring them back with renewed emphasis a bar later. It will additionally be noticed that on this re-entry the two horns are in passionate unison on what is by any standards a high note (top G♯ in terms of the standard F horn of our day) whereas the lower octave would have been perfectly practical for Beethoven's 2nd horn. To fill in the missing bar is a quite unwarrantable *Retusche* and destroys one of Beethoven's most imaginative pieces of instrumentation.

If the exposition repeat is taken, the two short repeats at the beginning of the finale should undoubtedly be taken also as in the case of, for example, the Mozart G Minor Symphony, K 550. In the event, however, the issue is largely academic as the long repeat is hardly ever taken, since it robs the movement of too much of the headlong impetuosity which must be its primary characteristic. The super-human ferocity here presents no occasion for the niceties of formal convention which would only weaken the argument as the music careers headlong into the arresting declamatory question marks posed by the fortissimo strings before letter D. These can at first be sustained a fraction beyond their exact length, both by the high, and then in turn the low string sections. The two bars which make the modulation into C major then abruptly pick up the tempo, the movement plunging once more into a full restatement of the first subject with, of course, both repeats duly observed.

This time, however, both the raising of the tonality by a full minor third and the energy generated by the driving force of the exposition give a heightened excitement making it desirable to maintain full tempo, not—as at the beginning of the movement—held back in order to give extra weight to the repeated sforzandos. Indeed the accumulation of *sf*'s as the first subject plunges onwards into the reactivated development causes the tempo to acquire even greater momentum, for in the ensuing section from bar 171 (161) through to letter E there are no fewer than thirty-seven consecutive bars in which the conductor's upbeats have to be strongly emphasized at the expense of the downbeats, these latter degenerating into merest preparations.

For clarity of thought, and thereby direction, it is as well consciously to have broken down this extraordinary passage of repeated hammer-blows into its constituent periods, which thought process will also prevent any danger of a purely machine-like series of reiterations on the lines of, say, Mossolov's notorious 'Steel Foundry'. The first three of these periods are, of course, self-evident being the alternations of violins, woodwind, and back to violins. With the reinforcement of the wind by the cellos and basses, however, the phrases are a great deal less obvious. The descending groups are here extended to five before the chromatically ascending build-up begins in the middle of bar 188 (178). From this point there will need to be a steady and inexorable gain in intensity through six steps to the entry of the horns and timpani in bar 194 (184), and then through seven further steps to the climactic point when the rising figure attains for the first time the narrow semitone interval D♯/E in bar 202 (192). This is then delivered twice with maximum force, followed by three times more in rapid retreat from the terrifying menace and, with a half-bar turn of the corner, relief comes at long last in the form of a little light-hearted interlude.

This is an oasis to be enjoyed before the pounding starts again with the reprise. The strings' *pp* echoes of the once forceful opening figure can even be played ricochet, and the flute's gam bolling should be completely carefree in manner.

But the crescendo which brings the interlude to an end is even more brusque than the diminuendo had been before, and to launch headlong into the reprise after the *ff* enunciations of letter F would therefore be too precipitous and insensitive to the movement's architectural design. Furthermore, the last abbreviated reappearance of the mighty first subject must reflect the manner of the finale's opening bars, which is effected by first making a momentary but riveting hesitation before setting it in motion after the two breathless silences, and then by allowing its emphatic sforzandos to pull the tempo back as at the beginning of the movement.

Beethoven's masterly cut of the second stanza at bar 242 (231) allows the tempo to spring back to its true thrusting vivacity after what has in the event been so short an interruption that the reprise seems to have even greater momentum than the exposition had had before. The excitement is further intensified by the ringing trumpets in bars 267–74 (256–63) which are very high and exposed being thus not only highly effective in themselves but enabling Beethoven to sustain his A's in horns and trumpets four octaves deep, a *coup de théâtre* the conductor can enjoy encouraging with some upward sustaining gesture, both to assist the 1st trumpet to proclaim these high notes and to indicate the continuing penetration of tone needed by all four players over these bars.

In bars 289–90 (278–9) most editions, including the older Breitkopf score and parts, oddly lack the 2nd horn quaver motif. It has, however, been correctly restored in the later Breitkopf printings.

As at bar 94 (92), bars 318 (307) ff. initiate the crescendo with the necessary feeling of forward surging leading into, once again, the sense of a single pulse per bar at letter H, this time over an extended period of fourteen bars. There is an important difference, however, apart from that of sheer length. At bar 336 (325) Beethoven repeats his *ff* for another 23-bar burst before resuming the bar-by-bar sforzandos: so formidable is this moment that one need have no compunction in anticipating Beethoven's first use in the symphonies* of a higher dynamic mark—occurring

---

*Beethoven's first orchestral use of *fff* had actually been seven years earlier in the Overtures *Leonora No.* 2 and *No.* 3.

at bar 438 (427)—and calling for *fff* already here in all the instruments including timpani. In the harmonic resolution of this outburst in bars 342–3 (331–2) high horns are featured again, and in anticipation of their soloistic function during the closing pages their jubilant tones can already here be allowed to soar over the whole orchestra.

By now the tempo will have accelerated once again to at least ♩ = 152 and this is maintained to the end. The whole coda is histrionically a golden occasion for the conductor and orchestra alike, and there are in the entire repertoire few passages so rewarding.

First, after the last return of the separated enunciations with which the whole movement began, come the four positively insistent down-beat slashes of bars 356–9 (345–8) (only one beat per bar here) followed by the string imitations descending through the sections, but followed again by, in reverse, the string imitations now ascending back from basses to violins indicated by driving crotchet beats.

As repeatedly in the Scherzo, the modern string seating with the cellos on the conductor's right again serves the visual aspect of the performance as the theme wheels across the orchestra from right to left, culminating in the 1st violins' two great bars 376–7 (365–6). This whole sequence may surely legitimately be raised to a vehement fortissimo, after which it is necessary to allow the dynamic to drop a little for the long, curious passage which precedes the *sempre più f* of the last surging climb.

This 22-bar transition section is very elusive and irregular, with its juggling of the first-subject figure to and fro between the three violin and viola groups, as well as the isolated trumpet and timpani punctuations. The latter always come on weak bars as well as ceasing altogether for a brief spell when the woodwind harmony arrives at the far distant tonality of B♭ minor, whither their limited resources can no longer follow. With the woodwind chord changes occurring always on weak beats the feeling of being on shifting sands becomes absolute, as Beethoven intended.

And yet, after the 2-bar 1st violin phrase which had initiated it, the passage falls regularly enough into 4-bar periods until a 6-bar extended phrase carries the quagmire over into firm ground with the re-entry of the horns and regular sequences which feature the sempre più forte from bar 400 (389) onwards.

From the conducting point of view, too many leads to the different groups become bewildering to players and audience alike and are actually counterproductive, especially in the wandering atmosphere which Beethoven is aiming to create. It might almost be said that the fewer indications the better, enabling the conductor to concentrate on the essentials, such as the woodwind chord changes and the endlessly restless heaving and growling of the cellos and basses. At the same time a nod to the timpani at bar 389 (378) never comes amiss, partly because after a 13-bar rest there is a certain shock-element in its sudden seemingly inconsequential reappearance, and partly to give confidence to the player in what is not, for the same reason, the easiest of entries. Considerable drama may also be derived from the two viola phrases in bars 384 and 386 (373 and 375) since starting on their open bottom C strings these can legitimately be given maximum evocative strength.

With the entry of the horns' dominant pedal the irregularity of the modulating meanderings give way to orderly patterns for the 16-bar crescendo, dominated by the interplay between the 1st and 2nd violins, and the direction of beating needs to highlight this antiphonal by-play, occurring initially four bars at a time but, with the heightening fever of excitement, changing to every other bar. Here it has to be admitted that there was considerable gain in the classical seating, with the violins on either side of the conductor, and Beethoven may well have had this in mind when orchestrating the passage.

According to all expectation the climax of the crescendo might have been the fortissimo of letter K, but Beethoven allows no such feeling of arrival, driving the music relentlessly forward, the pressure being additionally intensified by the cellos and basses who, having been grinding away for all of 38 bars, now persist right through the A major resolution to pursue their ostinato on or around E for a further 22 bars. This is so powerful an extension of the dominant pedal that the conductor's concentration should be focused on this lower area of the orchestra during both of the 4-bar phrases 416–19 (405–8) and 424–7 (413–16), the beat style describing the continuing crotchet figuration rather than the thrusts of the principal motif in the upper instruments.

In between, during bars 420–3 (409–12), there are some small changes in notation from the previous statements of these same bars earlier in the movement. However seemingly insignificant, and indeed scarcely perceptible unless brought strongly to the hearer's attention, these were palpably intended by Beethoven to make this last reappearance so much the more exciting. The changes concern flutes and horns who jump up sooner to their higher notes, and in the case of the horns this further emphasizes the row of ringing high B's (as they become for our F horns) by adding to their insistence. The horns are again prominent during bars 428–32 (417–21) where the rising pattern of their quavers should also be made prominent, a feature of Beethoven's orchestral setting often missed.

If, for these purposes, the beat has hitherto remained clearly in crotchets during the following six bars, economy can be exercised so as only to mark stresses once in each 2-bar phrase and to indicate the ever-increasing cumulative power of the violins' and violas' scales in contrary motion leading to the first of Beethoven's avowed *fff*'s.

Such use of economy in beating becomes ever more important in the closing bars of this frenetic coda, partly to prevent an undue exhibition of balletic activity from the rostrum, but in particular to allow for maximum clarity in indicating the wide variety of pulse and movement over what is a considerable span of such hecticity. For example, the four cadential bars 442–5 (431–4) are patently evoked by jubilant single beats per bar, whereas the *subito p* and the 8-bar build-up which follows it require a resumption of crotchet motor energy. Bars 463–9 (452–8) are characterized by a flowing style for the wind phrases—a lift for the 2nd horn pays dividends in the first of each 4-bar period—after which the vehement accents return, 2 per bar for two bars, and then forcibly on every quaver in bars 470–1 (459–60): two concluding thunderbolts to counterbalance those which opened the movement, and the symphony ends in an éclat of the highest possible exhilaration.

Symphony No. 8 in F major,
Op. 93

◀▶

THE fact of the Eighth being the shortest of all the Beethoven Symphonies makes it particularly valuable for programme building, especially since it is also one of its creator's greatest and most high-spirited masterpieces. Hence it is equally successful as the culmination of a classical programme for a smaller orchestra or as the prelude to the 'Choral' Symphony when it is thought desirable to preface that mighty work with a brief first half.

When it originally appeared within months of the première of the Seventh it was thought to be disappointing by comparison, and was accordingly so much less popular that the slow movement of the former symphony was even sometimes inserted as a kind of make-weight-cum-audience-bringer. On being confronted with this absurd state of affairs Beethoven is said to have growled caustically, 'that's because it's so much better than the other'. But however typically cynical such a retort may have been, there can obviously be no sensible yardstick of excellence for two such different and yet equally fine works of Beethoven's full maturity, and the composer had clear right on his side in regarding the more obvious *tour-de-force* of No. 7 as in no way better or more important than what he had to say in the brilliantly fashioned workmanship of its superficially slenderer sister-work.

I

The exuberance of the Eighth Symphony is from the very outset exceptional even for Beethoven. The metronome mark in whole-bar units is again misleading, as in the first movements of the

'Eroica' and the 'Pastoral'. To attempt to beat 1-in-a-bar at the beginning of this movement is to belie the very character of the opening theme which is given by the essential precipitation of the crotchet pulse. Beethoven prescribed ♩. = 69, as compared with ♩. = 60 for the 'Eroica', which is no great difference although the two are worlds apart. Yet the extra impetus does mean that there are many more places in the Eighth where the second and third beats of the bar should be sufficiently under-stressed to enable the movement to get off the ground.

In the event Beethoven's metronome mark is, as usual, uncomfortably fast and ♩ = 152 will provide a practical speed, both where the vivacity of a crotchet beat is desirable and for those places where the extra thrust will cause the rhythmic impulse to verge towards a single dotted-minim beat per bar.

There was a day when conductors used to ease the tempo in the quiet bars 5–8, but fortunately this is no longer a living tradition. On the contrary, the pulse must be kept pressing resolutely forward so that when the transition passage beginning at bar 12 is reached, economy of gesture can be exercised by giving hardly more than a sharply syncopated down-beat directed to the cellos and basses in the alternate bars 13, 15, etc., followed by a firm address to the wind and timpani for their enunciations in the bars between. The violins, meantime, simply need such attention as will prevent them from dropping the tone during their long notes. Here is just such an instance where a lapse into dotted-minim units might risk suggesting the lilt of a Ländler which would be totally out of style.

Letter A (bar 32) creates the illusion of a sudden hiatus but nevertheless this is not produced by means of freezes like the G.P.s in the Seventh Symphony. However much the conductor may refrain from beating out the silences he must be consciously aware of the movement's continuity for which the strings' staccato crotchets in bars 34–5 simply provide audible confirmation. A clear crotchet up-beat, a simple matter when the movement is conducted in 3, will mark this delicate but sharply pointed entry which is taken off the string.

This leads naturally into the graceful second subject which has to be felt and beaten in a real 3 for its flowing lyricism to find its proper expression in so fast a tempo. The first little ritardando can then also be handled with subtlety since there will be no change of pulse-unit.

On the other hand the 'a tempo' which follows the second, and surely greater, ritardando of bar 51 instantly restores the full exuberance of the primary tempo and is, with its return in the reprise, the single instance where the movement can really be beaten, however briefly, in dotted minims. Yet, even now, this can be communicated to the cellos and basses by no more than a lightening of style which is sufficiently similar in character to allow for the gradual reintroduction of the crotchet pulse by bar 62 without the need for any significant change.

Although logically the crescendo of bars 58–65 would seem to lead into the *ff*, this comes in such a strange and arresting place—four bars earlier than might be expected—that it is probable as well as characteristic for Beethoven to have intended a *ff subito*, in which case the carefully graduated ascent will have reached no more than a single forte by bar 65.

After the mock anger of letter B a conciliatory tone should infuse the answering phrases which can even be played with the very slightest relaxation of pace, the original fervour being abruptly restored at the 2-bar crescendo of bars 90–1.

The sforzandos of bars 92–5 are followed by a fortissimo outburst in which there should be no barline consciousness at all, the continuity of crotchet beating being aimed at a rhythmically opaque section of 24 or even 48 equal units, as the upper strings press out their semiquaver arpeggiandos with maximum precipitation. The octave motto-theme, for it is hardly less than that, of bars 100–2 should not be over-conducted, the full force being reserved for the first- and second-time bars, every note of which can be emphasized. This is a symphony in which, like the Fifth, the repeat is obligatory for, apart from the requirements of length and form, the return itself is immensely exciting and dramatic.

After the elation of the repeat, the second-time bars lead to a period of relative calm, the conductor's attention being focused on the threefold contrast between the first subject's quiet answering phrases passing upwards through the woodwind, the staccato repetitions of the motto figure and the joyful outbursts of arpeggiando string scrubbing. With the third time round, however, a vivid sense of suddenly mounting excitement should infuse the seemingly innocent crescendos of bars 132–5. This is not quite easy to achieve since the strings' upsurge, while needing to start perceptibly at the very beginning of bar 132, must be prevented from overwhelming the woodwind entries; for curiously these are all still marked a uniform *p dolce*, as on the two previous occasions. Hence, if the *ff* of bar 136 is to be as sudden as those in bars 112 and 124, electrifying as the abrupt growth of intensity in the strings must be, this should in reality barely reach more than *mf* by the end of bar 135.

Since bar 136 begins a period of continuous fortissimo lasting no less than fifty-two bars, it is clear that some restraint is a *sine qua non* for the conductor. Bars 140–3 naturally need to be as vivacious as possible with a strong beat suggesting maximum sharpness of articulation, especially from the cellos and basses who often tend to sound more woolly than the higher pitched instruments. Thereafter, however, it is the fugato entries which need the greater emphasis apart from the sforzandos which, coming so regularly on the second crotchet of each bar, will be the predominant factor in the beating style. For much of the time indeed, the down-beats will be minimized, the main gestures being repeated sideways stresses.

The points of especial attention, then, will be firstly the initial cello/bass entry of the motivic fugato theme at the up-beat to letter C (bar 144) followed by the two jagged sforzandos of the 1st violins in bars 144 and 146. The wind entries beginning at bar 147 next need pointing although without undue fuss; quite small prods in their direction will convey the necessary message. The fugato entry of the 2nd violins (the clarinets are mere reinforcements here) is followed by the sforzando entries of the horns. Their splitting dissonance in bar 155 in particular can be highlighted, recalling as it does the similar effect in the first movement introduction of the Second Symphony (bar 22).

The 1st violins' take-over in bar 159 is engineered with such flamboyance that a correspondingly dramatic evocation by the conductor may not be considered inappropriate. Both horns leap to their upper G (for the 2nd horn it is a two-octave jump) whereas the violins, being previously fully occupied, find that their acrobatics to start the entry bring them on to the scene a quaver too late. One might well ask oneself which other composer would not cautiously have relegated the previous scrubbing semiquavers to the otherwise unoccupied violas, leaving the 1st violins free to enter punctually together with the flutes and oboes. But the strength of Beethoven's device lies specifically in the hectic last-minute plunge, which the conductor can intensify with a similar about-turn in their direction immediately after encouraging the horns. The subsequent figuration of the middle strings in bars 161 and 163 also adds enormously to the excitement.

Now counterpoint gives way to architecture so that the shaping of the periods is the prime consideration even while the beat must continuously stress the second crotchet of each bar. Although the tension has to be constantly maintained over so long a span there must be no suggestion of hurrying, as can easily occur with less than well-*routiné* orchestras.

With bar 180 the excitement is positively stepped up, at first by spacing out the sforzandos from every bar to every two bars, and then transferring them to the down-beats of the succeeding four bars. Even now, however, there is no need for an over-demonstrative approach to interpretation; if the pattern changes are clearly and sharply marked the music plays itself. Nevertheless, the conductor's orientation will need to be once more towards the cellos and basses, whose line becomes ever more important over the next ten bars. The point is worth stressing, because if Beethoven's dynamic marks are observed to the letter the return of the theme in the lower regions of the orchestra for the start of the reprise is bound to be swamped. Furthermore, the orchestra is already playing so enthusiastically that a further swell in tone to this rare example of *fff* in Beethoven will add to an already difficult area of orchestral balance.

Various solutions have been mooted over the years, all with a greater or lesser degree of artificiality or sacrifice. Ideally it is clear that the two bars before D represent the ultimate accumulation of tone leading to a climactic outburst in which the return in full of the symphony's opening bars are restated at maximum volume. With ingenious use of microphone and modern recording techniques it is possible that such an interpretation might be contrived. In a live performance, however, it is customary to drop the level of tone during bar 189 in order to make a real crescendo in the next bar, only the cellos, basses, and bassoons aiming for a full 2-bar crescendo starting from a single forte, so as to concentrate on a consistent level of increase through to the *fff* which they then aim to maintain for the next 8 bars. The remainder of the orchestra, strings and wind alike, will on the contrary reduce their level during bar 190, returning to *ff* at the beginning of bar 194 (where the half-way point of the theme occurs) and then withdrawing again to a single *f* for the conclusion of the passage. If this is thought too far from Beethoven's intentions, the best alternative is to forget the problems and play the text as it stands, leaving the listener's inner ear to supply direct to the brain what he may not actually be hearing. There is no system of *Retuschen* – which can be applied here, such as the concept of doubling the theme on tuned timpani, said to have been contrived by Bülow, but which is today frankly unacceptable.

The return of amiability is welcome after so prolonged a period of frenetic activity and this is ingeniously built into the reprise in such a way that even some slight reduction of pace can be allowed, although the brief interruption at bar 201 is of course played full tilt. A gentler tempo will then also favour a cantabile treatment of the strings' imitative re-entries in bars 206–8.

The 1st violin line which ornaments the once purely rhythmic transition passage is often misphrased as the result of a bad bowing given in the Leipzig Breitkopf material. The following gives an alternative which, while eminently practical, is also more faithful to Beethoven's text:

Ex. 12

The horns' alternation with the cellos and basses in bars 217 ff., forceful as it has always been, is now made more so by the way Beethoven suddenly reverses their position at bar 223. Attention can be drawn to this by marking *sf* the repeated dotted minim which effects the change, and by accenting still further the quavers which in the next bar now come together with those of the strings.

The handling of the recapitulation then presents no new issues other than two very attractive solos for the 1st horn which, placed irregularly, arise due to the reorganization of the wind entries in the conciliatory passages (bars 270–6 and 280–6) and can be beautifully brought out.

But with the long coda some striking points of interest arise once more. In the first place the strings' drop to *pp* in bar 305 should create a real and sudden hush, interrupting the progress of what had at first seemed to be a continuum on the same lines as the development. The clarinet solo occasioning this drop will then lead instead to the softest moment in the movement, the conductor seeming hardly to be beating, although in fact clarity can never be jeopardized for the sake of the strings' staccato (especially enjoined by Beethoven) which can never be too light.

Much should be made of the rapid 6-bar surge of tone which heralds the first of two jubilant exposés of the principal subject. Nevertheless for all the fortissimo markings the conductor has to ensure that the strings keep some force in reserve, especially as the clarinets and bassoons have an interesting contribution to make when in bar 328 they suddenly find themselves all playing in unison. This is a happy rather than a frenzied outburst, and in the pause bar with which it culminates the block entries can be a little spaced out, so that the trumpets and timpani will add something of a festive note.

The fermata is then held for really quite a long time, before the whole orchestra is taken off with a warmly generous preparatory gesture aimed at encouraging the 1st and 2nd violins to re-enter immediately with their melodic continuance in a glowing cantabile, perhaps somewhat richer than the rather neutral printed '*p*'. The same quality is naturally taken over by the lower strings two bars later.

The sforzandos are excitedly transferred to the third beats during the 8-bar gathering of power which follows; yet economy of gesture should still be exercised, until at last the horns suddenly trigger off an explosion into another of Beethoven's triple fortes. The extravagance of such a marking in this context again reveals the composer's own exuberance when writing this work, and can be the excuse for a dramatic jettisoning of restraint from conductor and orchestra alike; letter I can be a splendidly hilarious affair.

The G.P. bars 359 and 361 are of course strictly counted out though not beaten, and bars 362–9 are portrayed as frankly humorous in Beethoven's best 'unbuttoned' style. (It is additionally fascinating to see the young Brahms imitating what must have been a favourite passage at the end of the first movement of his own first orchestral work, the D major Serenade, Op. 11.)

The single dotted crotchets of the 3rd and 4th bars from the end may perhaps be held a fraction more tenuto than their strict value, but the last two bars must surely be played in tempo and without any exaggeration of cadential phrasing. The fun lies in making the final pianissimo statement as simple and unsophisticated as possible, although with the last note clearly a crotchet and not a staccato quaver as is sometimes heard.

II

In view of the primary purpose of the Allegretto in representing Beethoven's caricature of Maelzel's newly invented metronome, it might seem that the printed indication for this of all movements should be scrupulously observed. Here, after all, would seem to be the fountainhead of the whole controversy over Beethoven's metronome marks.

But such is not the way of things: anyone who has tried to time a work, say for a carefully planned broadcast or recording, let alone checked a tempo away from the living sound, knows that in the reality of bringing a score to performance these hypothetical measurements almost always change radically in the process. Sadly, the speeds and durations which Bartók misguidedly documented for many of his works, section by section, and each carefully timed to the nearest second no less, bear witness to this harsh but inescapable truth.

Where the present movement is concerned, the printed ♪ = 88 is not so far from the widely accepted reading. A semiquaver unit of 160 (rather than 176), to correspond with the illustrative tick-tock of the woodwind is, broadly speaking, the tempo which the wind section of an experienced orchestra will instinctively strike with perfect ensemble. This may often be a valuable criterion; if a good band has problems in following the conductor's choice of pulse in a repertoire work it may very well mean that there is an unnatural feel about that tempo, regardless of the documentary evidence or intellectual rationale which prompted its adoption. It goes without saying that the actual beat is a bouncy 4 in a bar.

The chief difficulty of this movement, which once successfully initiated mostly plays itself, concerns the lengths of notes in the string writing. In particular it should be observed that the quavers which end the phrases of the principal theme bear no staccato dot (although the Breitkopf material is by no means reliable in this respect). This is not to say that these are pronouncedly long notes; there are many such quavers (one has only to look at bars 14–17 to find a whole succession) and if they are not played correctly as a matter of course—if, for example, the conductor has been forced into making an issue of them—the movement can become uncomfortably self-conscious and mannered. The only quaver which is conventionally played with ostentatious full length is the very last note of the whole movement. Perhaps Beethoven did not really mean or expect even this point to be exaggerated, but it makes a good effect and moreover emphasizes the B♭ as both the final and the home-note of the movement's over-all tonality, which after a curiously long last-minute excursion into the subdominant key of E♭ does need some extra underlining.

In bar 29 and correspondingly the G♭ in bar 62, the staccato is often mishandled because of a clumsy bowing indication in the Leipzig Breitkopf material. Conversely the last cello/bass notes in these same bars are generally played too short because the F in bar 62 is given as a semiquaver, instead of a quaver like the C in bar 29.

The corner of bars 39/40 is the centre-point of the movement and hence justifies a slight hesitation and restart for the reprise. Similarly in bar 73 a marginally tenuto tied dotted quaver has much to commend it before giving the cellos and basses a nod for them to lead the music into the coda, followed by similar directives to the wind. The little 1st violin twiddles in bars 75 and 76 also want a touch of humour in their delivery—too much would at once be arch; but the passage—as indeed the whole

movement—cannot be played quite poker-faced without seeming heavy-handed, however well executed.

This movement is the *locus classicus* of ultimate refinement
in conducting technique, combining good humour and clarity
within the smallest scale of rhythmic beating, yet allowing for
the occasional explosions, which incidentally all occur in the
middle of bars. In fact, as often in Mendelssohn (e.g. the second
movement of the 'Italian' Symphony), the conductor has constantly to keep his head clear (especially when conducting from
memory) in respect of just where the barlines do occur. It can
be surprisingly easy, if one is momentarily distracted from awareness of this, to fall erroneously into a 4 in a bar across the
printed layout to the consternation of the players, however
much the cross accentuation of the passage-work was deliberately planned by Beethoven.

III

The beginning of the Tempo di Menuetto is marked with no
less than five sforzandos in a row, although significantly these
do not include the very first forte up-beat. If they are to have
weight rather than mere sharpness, as demanded by the character
of the music, such accents will inevitably put a brake on the
tempo proper which is only fully established in the third bar.
The printed $\downarrow$ = 126 is somewhat too hurried for this part majestic, part broadly lyrical movement and $\downarrow$ = 112 gives a more
sympathetic, yet not too sluggish pacing. The Trio, on the other
hand, needs to be appreciably steadier still—say $\downarrow$ = 96, as dictated both by the clarinet's and horns' solo passages and by
the quietly graceful staccato cello triplets.

The handing down of the melodic phrases through the string
groups during bars 11–14 can be spotlighted by addressing the
relevant sections in turn, the violas and cellos being coupled
together but the basses given individual attention. The two-beat
units, and then single beats of the phrases which follow alternately on wind and strings, want characterful shaping before the
bassoon reintroduces the long singing cantilenas once again, the
style of beat changing accordingly.

The woodwind imitation of the brass fanfare in bar 38 must
seem as if it is trying to throw the rhythmic structure off balance,

especially when on the third beat tonic and dominant sound together in a manner one day to be exploited so significantly by Stravinsky, and an illusion of irregularity is created. The second timpani entry accordingly needs extra pointing in order, as it were, to restore stability. The toing and froing between wind and strings then culminates in a particularly heavy *ff sforzando* on the strings at the end of bar 42 which, however, must drop to *mf* at the barline for the bassoons' part in the subsequent pile-up to make its necessary contribution.

The conclusiveness of the first- and second-time bars after so much throwing around of strong pulses is of such great importance that it should not be hurried over. The cadence needs time for completion even when, in taking the repeat, the tempo has once more to be picked up by the strings' quaver phrases, almost as though the necessity to go back was in the nature of an afterthought.

On the second time round, however, a corresponding breadth of cadential phrasing will allow the 1st horn to lead gently into the easier flow of the soloistic Trio without any interruption of pulse. It is the recurring *p subito*s which require particular skill in securing a convincing rendering of the solo horn parts; such constant checking of natural phrasing generally presupposes a slight hiatus in the pulse, but here it is precluded by the unceasing cello triplets. The continuity of these must in no way be disturbed until the closing *pp*, when their pace can yield a little in sympathy with the clarinet's approach to his final top G. The da capo is taken only when this high note has been allowed time to make its point.

Where this cello passage is concerned, the question is sometimes raised whether it is really correct or desirable that it should be played by all the cellos. Perhaps, it is mooted, it is really for a solo cello (as in Haydn's Symphony No. 95) or only for 1st cellos, the 2nds playing with the basses (as in Schumann's Fourth), and the orchestral material does in fact render such expedients possible, for the cellos and basses share a composite part. Sir George Grove does indeed quote the passage headed by the words 'cello solo' stating that this is 'as played' and '... points to some circumstance in the orchestra', a somewhat enigmatic phrase. He gives, however, no authentication for the practice and Beethoven left no evidence that any such was his

intention. Today it is more customary for the triplet figure
to be played by the cello section as a whole, which in a good
orchestra should present no problems either of lightness or in
the many abrupt variations of dynamics.

The clarinet and both horns are equal soloists in this magical
Trio and, if they acquit themselves with distinction, deserve
to be raised for special credits at the end of the performance.

IV

It would hardly be overstating the case to say that the printed
mark $\mathbf{o}$ = 84 is not merely absurdly precipitate but frankly
impossible, so that it might even be considered as primary evidence on which to discredit the whole current concept of obey-
ing Beethoven's metronome marks to the letter. Moreover, so
far from being designated as a Presto or Prestissimo, the tempo
is merely headed 'Allegro vivace', and $\downarrow$ = 144 is quite fast
enough for this, which at least brings the 2nd violin and viola
lines into the realms of practicability as well as allowing the
humour and violent contrasts, in which the movement abounds,
to make their full effect—the movement being, of course, conducted in 2. There will then be no question of having to hold
up the momentum anywhere, with possibly one single exception
in the coda as will be suggested in due course.

As with *fff*, so triple pianos are rare in Beethoven, and those
which occur in bars 15–18 (and at the returns of this passage
later in the movement) can be reduced to the barest threshold
of audibility; it is tempting to suggest that the conductor might
well emulate the famous Hoffnung drawings of 'The Maestro'
as he starts to crouch under the podium to get the most exaggerated pianissimo, before leaping up for the startling C♯ outburst.

In this fortissimo restatement of the previously whispered
rondo theme the octave cello/bass-line should surely be brought
to the audience's attention since it is to be so prominent a feature
of the movement, the very timpani being tuned unconvention-
ally in just such octave F's.

At bar 28, which initiates the transition section, the lead is
given to the lower strings, who thus again merit the conductor's
primary attention, although without the need for any flam-

boyance. Despite its strength of dynamic, this is a relatively easy-going section. In particular the conductor should be aware of its terseness as compared with its return at bar 189, where the whole escapade is enormously extended. It is only with the sforzandos in bars 42–3, which should be continued into the following bars, that emphases are reintroduced into the beating, with the universal octave G's occurring immediately before the surprise entry of the second subject, both hammered out.

The rise in tone as letter B is approached (as again before letter F) must not be allowed to have the effect of a crescendo but is carefully tiered, the ultimate step to *ff* having the character of an explosion. The entries of the violas and violins can then be planted into the expectant silences just above piano in order to emphasize the *pp* echoes at the repeats of the little figures. This will be particularly important the second time the passage occurs (at bar 267) where the comic by-play will lead to the violent interruptions of the cellos and basses, resulting in the headlong career of the movement being stopped dead in its tracks.

The development can seem hard to shape, with Beethoven throwing entries around the orchestra with all the skill of a master juggler. The regular pianissimo return of the rondo theme is roughly interrupted by a forte restatement of its last theme which can be delivered with a certain brusqueness of manner, after which the beating must equally abruptly return to minimum gesturing for the repeat of the phrase in its original pianissimo. But thereafter it keeps restarting from its 'Not Smetana' phrase (to quote from that composer's well-known *bon mot* about the accentuation of his name) with some tricky imitative entries which need cueing until Beethoven takes the bull by the horns and, after a curtailed 3-bar period, embarks on an odd little fugue the start of which, coming unexpectedly as it does, can be launched with a kind of plunge towards the 1st violins. The order of the strings' entries, with the 2-note fugal motif occurring at in turn 2-bar, 1-bar, and half-bar spacings, are regular with the violas coming last. As a result these warrant especial pointing, as do the echoing wind which, like the crazily irregular timpani entries (making comic play with the fact that he has only F's to work with), can lack the appropriate humorous conviction unless brought in firmly.

Beethoven's unusual specification of the open E string in bars 148–51 is naturally always obeyed even though the wire string of today will tend to give a certain extra twang; the effect was clearly intended to be part of the fun and the slight exaggeration does no harm.

The return of the transition section at bar 189, now nearly twice as long as its original statement, is best controlled quite undemonstratively until the sforzandos of letter E which, however, introduce changes that are both witty and dramatic. Whereas the wind had taken the lead in bar 42, here the strings begin the alternation but are furiously rebuked by the wind. The strings refuse to give way, however, and for an extra four bars both groups go at it hammer and tongs. The conductor can bring out the humour of this contretemps splendidly by first continuing to mark the sforzandos on the alternate notes (exactly as suggested above for bars 42–3) but, at the winds' bid for leadership, changing the accentuation to all the notes equally, in which furious insistence the strings then also join, the dynamic being given as a new *ff* to both groups in turn.

The cello/bass outbursts in bars 279 and 281 will obviously want to be played with great violence; Beethoven's single *f* can legitimately be construed as one of his characteristic uses of *f* to signify rinforzando. The first fermata is not too protracted, but when the cellos and basses ferociously interrupt a second time the break in the proceedings must be long enough to suggest bewildered consternation.

The pick-ups after these G.P.s can be accident-prone, but if the conductor's leads are given as distinct up-beats there should be no need for uncertainty. It is only important to be aware that the violins' re-entries after the second fermata need indications of especial clarity, while the horns absolutely rely on a well-designated down-beat in their direction for their entry in bar 286, the process being repeated with equal care in bars 290–1 and 294 respectively.

The legato beat which then pursues the phrases on their journey changes style perceptibly at bar 306 as the minims change their manner from gliding to striding with the onset of the crescendo. (The trumpets appreciate a glance for their entries in bars 306 and 310; those E's and especially the unison D's for both trumpets, harmless as they look on paper, are unexpectedly high notes since they are written for instruments crooked in F.)

The forte at letter G can be misleading; it is no more than a stepping-stone on the path of a climb which occupies no less than forty bars. The appearance of the timpani alone, especially with its thunderous triplets in bar 322, can make so strong an impact as to risk overshadowing the true climax which is by no means due yet. But as the modulations steer the music towards the key of D, the timpani—anchored on a couple of octave F♮s—are increasingly unable to take part in the final approach to the *ff* of bar 345, and it devolves upon the rising scale of the cellos and basses during bars 342–5 which, after the sudden breaking of the pattern into crotchets, sixes in the wind and then fours in the strings, should be so emphasized as to produce an eleventh-hour *coup de théâtre*.

Beethoven's mock furious unison C♯, now notated as D♭ because of its changing harmonic function, and then reiterated (again as C♯) four times, as if to make sure it has not missed its mark, will of necessity be delivered with as much thrust as can be put into up-beats without their looking even remotely like down-beats. The three adjacent ones in bars 377–8 should be slightly separated for greater emphasis and are taken by the strings as three consecutive down-bows.

Thereafter the conductor's manner must reflect the purest good humour as the rondo theme is played full tilt in the absurdly distant key of F♯ minor (how strange that Beethoven should have elected to change the key signature to two, and not three sharps, the G♯'s being given as accidentals) until forcibly, even brutally, pushed back into F by the onslaught of brass and timpani—whose mark of a single *f* is another of Beethoven's use of that dynamic to indicate rinforzando, and in no way to be taken as a lesser degree than the prevailing *ff*. It is also of particular importance not to be misled into taking bar 393 as the first of five ferociously accented identical bars. The sforzandos, of which there are specifically four when occurring at the rate of one per bar, only begin a bar later. The way in which they press home their point with such insistence (with no less then twenty further sforzandos delivered at the rate of two per bar) reminds one of nothing less than Shostakovitch's adoption of the idea a century and a half later, grimly to hammer home his determination to assert his identity with the musical letters of his name DSCH in the Tenth Symphony and other works, albeit alas without Beethoven's infectious fun and high spirits.

The growly entrance of the second subject in the cellos and basses in bars 420–7 is another humorous touch to which the attention of the listener should be drawn, although the beautifully curving phrases of the 1st violins can be attractively delineated by the conductor's left hand. The formidable *ff subito* of bar 432 is undoubtedly yet another leg-pull, with the horns and trumpets blaring their out-of-tune seventh harmonic with what in Beethoven's day must have been so formidable an effect that it is hardly surprising that it puts another abrupt and disconcerting halt to the proceedings.

After a substantial pause the movement is restarted, again with a clear up-beat (there can be no hint of a down-beat for the fermata) to the horns and bassoons as the first subject puts out a couple of tentative feelers, which can be played rather below tempo, the only place in the whole movement where there may be even the slightest variation of pulse. It is also worth marking the strings down (even to *pp*) and the flute up a degree; full tempo is then brusquely reinitiated for the lead up to the final fantasia on the F major chord. When the thirds go up and down the wind groups it is patently unnecessary, even fussy, to give every entry, yet part of the purpose of the exercise is for conductor and orchestra alike to demonstrate the fun which can be derived from music making.

The timpani octave tuning has its heyday here especially in the bravura displays in bars 480–1 and again eight bars later where the passage is repeated *ff*. Indeed the single forte for the full orchestra at bar 480 should not be allowed to pre-empt the later climax but can on this occasion be taken at true face value. As for the timpani passages, these are virtuoso exhibitions which no player worth his salt will tamely play with double taps by each hand alternately when the over-arm technique both looks and sounds so spectacular.

Symphony No. 9 in D minor, Op. 125 ('Choral')

◀▶

I⊤ would be a conductor of no more than superficial artistry who embarked on a performance of the Ninth without a feeling of profound responsibility. Not only the sheer size of the work, but the range and depth of musical thought are on an entirely different scale from anything that had gone before. There have even been conductors of the younger generation who have ventured to say that they would be loath to tackle the 'Choral' Symphony until they had reached the age of at least 45.

Yet from this point of view the paradoxical argument can be advanced that no one should conduct any important work unless he has already performed it numerous times before. This obvious contradiction in terms contains within itself the clear counter-recommendation that the sooner some first immature performances can be put behind one the better; for not even the wisdom of maturity can altogether take the place of familiarity with the abounding problems of such a conception, and—as in opera—no matter how well established a conductor may be, if he is not *routiné* in the particular work in hand he can easily find himself at a disadvantage when faced with the background and expertise of the artists who will be looking to him for guidance and inspiration.

Amongst the many purely practical details the conductor has at an early stage to take into account is the complexity of the rehearsal schedule. A particularly acute problem is presented by the fact that the most elaborate section of the symphony and involving the largest forces—that is to say, of course, the vocal section of the finale—amounts to only some 15 minutes out of the total duration of 65, and that orchestrally speaking these are by no means the most difficult. Admittedly, assembling and co-ordinating the soloists and chorus can be time-consuming, but even so one has to be careful not to overestimate the proportion of the available rehearsal time that can be allowed for the preparation of their part in the proceedings. Other considerations when planning the rehearsal schedule include the fact that the trombones only appear briefly in the Scherzo and then not again until the latter part of the finale; it can thus be a wise plan not to call them until later and to begin with the first and third movements. A preliminary string rehearsal also pays valuable dividends in breaking the back of both the Adagio and the cello/bass recitative of the finale's opening—which, like the 1st violins' arabesques in the Adagio's variation sections, always requires especial and painstaking attention.

Much of the often scanty orchestral time will be saved if practical matters which concern only the chorus have all been taken care of at a previous piano rehearsal. It is, needless to say, of primary importance that a preliminary meeting with the conductor should be included in the singers' schedule at which the chorus master is also present. This will give the opportunity not only for the music itself but for elements of presentation to have been both established and practised such as, for example, the exact bars in which the chorus should stand and reseat. Points of pronunciation, placing of final consonants, and so on cannot be attended to when the chorus is at a distance behind an impatiently waiting orchestra, the clock ticking away the valuable minutes. But at a piano rehearsal it can be surprising how many highly relevant details can be sorted out, especially with an energetic and efficient chorus master in attendance.

Turning to the soloists, they too should if possible have been allowed to sing their passages with piano, if only in the green room during the interval of a rehearsal. All too often they will only have been called on the day of the performance, but there are vital points which should not be left undiscussed until the full forces are assembled. One of these is indeed the crucial question of whether they will be present on the platform already at the start of the symphony. There was a day, incredible as it may seem in this more enlightened age, when the very chorus used to assemble on the platform after the performance of the first three movements. But although the horror of this is mercifully a thing of the past, many soloists still try to avoid the gruelling ordeal of having to sit for nearly an hour before opening their mouths, and beg to be allowed to enter at least at the end of the Scherzo. One distinguished Russian baritone pre-empted the situation only a few years ago by disappearing at the start of a Festival performance and thus forcing the opening movements to take place without him and his fellow soloists present.

But some discomfiture, even embarrassment, can be mitigated if the platform arrangement is adopted whereby the four soloists are placed behind the orchestra and immediately in front of the chorus, with whom they are then correctly identified. In most halls this provides an admirable solution from every point of view including that of balance, strange to say, and the soloists can then be tactfully persuaded to accept the supremely desirable requirement that they enter the hall with the conductor at the start, albeit at different levels and sometimes even from opposite directions.

Unlike the earlier large-scale symphonies, a real case can be made in the Ninth for using doubled woodwind, excluding however piccolo and contra; nor should the horns and trumpets need reinforcing. Nevertheless, despite the precedent established by so many star conductors, this is actually less necessary than is generally supposed, and with careful balancing, the deaf Beethoven's often maligned orchestration can be made to tell entirely convincingly. If, however, doubled wind should be decided upon, this cannot be left to the players merely to join in at their discretion for the tutti, or fortissimo passages. For it is a far more intricate matter which needs careful and precise thought on the part of the conductor who should perhaps never condone it at all without adequate rehearsal. Even then ideally a duplicate set of wind copies should be provided, clearly edited to indicate exactly where the extra players should or should not play.

The 'Choral' can obviously stand alone in a programme, and for special occasions is frequently allowed to do so. It makes, however, for a shortish evening by most concert standards and on that account a first half is not infrequently added. In this event the most commonly played introductory works are generally either the First or Eighth Symphonies without further preamble.

I

More than usually does this greatest of all symphonies require the establishment of a rapt atmosphere before a note is heard, which should be communicated in the conductor's demeanour from the moment he appears on the platform; and the performance itself should not start until there has been a marked period of absolute silence in the hall. The initiation of sound can then be motivated by the smallest possible up-beat, directed not to the strings but to the horns; the strings can to a large extent look after themselves. An excellent story is told of Furtwängler fulminating against what he regarded as a heinous misunderstanding of the opening bars when a young conductor, anxious to prove himself, wasted twenty valuable minutes of rehearsal time in order to achieve perfect ensemble in the 2nd violins' and cellos' sextuplets. 'But', spluttered Furtwängler in a historic overstatement, 'the whole *point* is that they must not be together!'

Beethoven's ♩ = 88 is predictably a little too fast for both the inwardness and by contrast the towering declamation of this music. If the conductor has totally involved himself in its presentation, so that the preparation for the first mighty *ff* unison D minor statement has been properly spaced, it will turn out that ♩ = 69 will be nearer to what the orchestra and the hall's acoustics will enable him to attain. Quicker, the introductory 16-bar period will seem too terse; any slower and the carefully planned build-up will lack that all-important sense of direction.

Nor should the unleashing of the fortissimo itself happen too abruptly, as it will if taken in resolutely strict tempo. The key to the passage lies in the demisemiquaver rest in the strings which must be given that extra fraction of a second before the full orchestra bursts in with the primary theme. For this purpose a divided beat in the second half of bar 16 is indispensable.

Such a subdivision of the beat serves both to mark the last string semiquaver before their rest and to hold the wind momentarily before indicating their own cut-off. For whilst the unison declamation presupposes a clean new entry from strings and wind alike, it would be wrong to ignore the wind overhang present in their tied double-dotted quaver. To achieve all Beethoven's requirements therefore, a slight broadening of bar 16 will be in no way inconsistent with the significance of so great a moment.

As for the conductor's evocation of that giant amongst themes, this can hardly be other than a sternly dictatorial delineation of its contours, devoid of actual time-beating and yet rigidly within its rhythmic framework. In bar 24 it is helpful to mark both the syncopated extra *ff* in the lower strings and the 2nd beat *ff* entry on flutes and horns, as these significant points of emphasis are easily submerged. The portato quavers of bar 26 will then need weighty indications, but the martial trumpets and drums of bars 27 and 29 need no encouragement from the stick as they can tend to be overplayed. It is the three sforzandos of bars 31–3 which are next designated with full power, after which the whole awesome pageantry collapses in the manner of the huge genie vanishing as smoke back into its tiny bottle, in the *Arabian Nights*. The flutes and trumpets, which mark the completion of this grotesque accomplishment with a unison low D, need for the purpose a clear indication from the stick.

Beethoven's dovetailing of the opening bars' restatement brings the 1st violins' sotto voce entry a bar earlier than might have been expected, a subtlety of which the conductor should be more than subconsciously aware, for his own comfort.

The majestic first subject's restatement is presented as before, bar 50 being given the same quaver subdivision and broadening as at bar 16, even though it cannot recapture the galvanizing surprise element of its first appearance. In bars 56 and 58 the suggestion of a query in the winds' repetitions can be evoked by deliberately not giving the second beats at all but sparking the entries by facial expression alone. After what will have seemed like hiatuses (though again there can be no interference with continuity of pulse) each succeeding sforzando on the tutti unison E♮ and F in the following bars will gain immensely in power.

In bars 63–73 the syncopated pairs of slurred semiquavers can afford to be exaggeratedly phrased, just as all the sforzandos in this entire tutti section need maximum weight rather than sharpness of attack. The forcefulness then drains away with a more lateral beat during bar 73 to merge into the gentler lyricism of the second subject.

A mystery surrounds one of the phrases of this melodic section. In bar 81 the flute and oboe are given a quaver D instead of Bb in both the autograph and first edition, and indeed none of the early sources give the Bb which appears in all current editions; even Grove in his *Beethoven and his Nine Symphonies* (p. 342) quotes the passage in this seemingly distorted version no doubt because, writing in 1896, he will have been working from the original Schott score, as indeed he advocates in his Preface. There might seem to be an analogy here with the notorious and equally curious F in the first statement of the melody in the Andantino of Tchaikovsky's Bb minor Piano Concerto. As there, so here too, no recurrence of the oddity can be found in any of the theme's numerous restatements. Indeed, Beethoven's variant of bar 81 four bars later would seem to substantiate the Bb, which is moreover so familiar to our ears that a return to the D would raise every eyebrow in the hall, an undesirable reaction even if it could be proved that the D's were no slip of Beethoven's pen. Perhaps they were a first thought which, like Tchaikovsky after him, he neglected to revise.

Bar 95 presents a problem of balance, as Beethoven's bassoons will have had less difficulty than those of today in making their proper effect against the prevailing rinforzatos, especially as the horns should be playing with the upper instead of the lower strings as wrongly shown in the editions. Nevertheless if the tutti quavers are really played staccato as marked it should be possible to hear these bassoons' semiquavers, especially if ostentatious encouragement is directed towards them by the conductor.

The feverish syncopated scale-like episodes in bars 92–101 require a corresponding restlessness in the style of beating. This will then come to an abrupt end with the peremptory commands of bars 102–3 which recall the parallel passages in the Overture *Egmont*, these also alternating with quiet responses.

If a suitably dramatic conducting technique has portrayed these events, the extreme reticence which should follow will be the more effective. The hush of bars 110–13 turns to weirdness for the uncanny undulations of the strings during the following six bars, and even in the next gradual gathering of the clouds there is an unearthly atmosphere as new to Beethoven's own style as it was to the whole of symphonic music at that time.

The renewed turbulence to which this leads is a confused

mêlée largely dominated by the rushing strings which need most of the conductor's attention, though there is no occasion for an over-demonstrative style of beating, the main concern being control of ensemble. Curiously the oboes seem (except uniquely in bar 135) to be trying to protest some thematic allusion, but this can never be heard and it may be significant that in the reprise (bars 401–6) Beethoven will be seen to have himself abandoned it, so that there is no case for any attempt to force it through the surrounding textures by means of artificial *Retuschen*.

In bars 146–9 there may be some doubt over whether the repeated fortes are simply rinforzandos within a general dynamic of piano as so often in Beethoven. Yet the extra *f* indication at the strings' entry in bar 147 might well be taken to show that, rinforzandos as the rows of *f*'s undoubtedly are, they should also be in a general dynamic level of forte representing an intermediate stage between the curious *p* wind conversations and the fortissimo subitos of bars 147 and 149 shortly to burst in on wind and strings respectively.

Letter E is self-evidently the point of arrival of all that has gone before and the conductor can draw himself up to his full height to deliver, with all the majesty he can command, the exposition's closing assertions of B♭ major. So conclusive must this be made to seem that the collapse of the final spaced-out unisons must have something awesome about it, even the last unison B♭ being in a shocked diminuendo.

The semitone drop to A could well have made provision for the conventional repeat at this point, especially as bars 162 ff. correspond exactly with the first bars of the movement. For the first time in the symphonies, however, Beethoven rules this out by marking neither repeat signs nor first- and second-time bars, and the music merges imperceptibly into the development. (It is not without interest to recall that Brahms followed Beethoven's example in proscribing any question of the first-movement exposition repeat in just the last of his own four symphonies.)

In conducting this passage the main difference from the symphony's opening lies in the absence of the previous atmosphere of expectation. All is now calmness for the unfolding of the development which, as in the 'Eroica', is an unusually long and discursive section so that an intuitive grasp of its architectural proportions is a primary prerequisite. For example bars 188–91, and again 206–9, are obviously first cousins to the closing exposition statement of letter E and yet must not attempt to emulate its air of finality. The very fact of there being two such extended periods, each with its seemingly full-sized coda passage, is in itself an indication of the enormous scale of Beethoven's edifice. Moreover the ends of these codas, bars 191 and 209, require subdivisions similar to those in bars 16 and 50, though handled in such a way as to minimize the resultant pull-up.

These passages with which the development begins, with conversations on and around the first descending phrase of the first subject, are again not without their problems of balance. The aim will be towards transparency of texture, in which elements such as the bassoon solos and the basses' interjections will emerge without having to be artificially brought into undue prominence. The oboe phrase in bars 200–1 can, however, reasonably be marked 'espressivo', a term Beethoven had already introduced for the flute at bar 186, but curiously not elsewhere in these contexts.

In a different way the appending variation on the first subject's second figure, given to a woodwind chamber-group, also needs sensitive handling, even if without loss of pace. There is an air of resignation about these interlude-like passages which at one time led to the custom of playing them at a markedly relaxed tempo and with the first two a tempo bars after each ritardando included as part of the hold-up. Certainly all four of the hesitant semiquavers in bars 195 and 213 need to be carefully guided— perhaps best with left hand articulations—but the printed 'a tempo's need to be re-established immediately, the succeeding pairs of bars given, on the contrary, a forward-looking function.

Bar 217 is another of those curious occasions where Beethoven writes totally conflicting harmonies in wind and strings (cf. the Seventh Symphony, first movement bar 285). Yet, strange as this looks on paper, in performance the logic of each harmonic progression is perfectly convincing and should not be 'corrected' in the overhasty assumption that Beethoven has committed an oversight. (A further instance will be seen in the finale—see below p. 212.) Furthermore the clash heightens the tension as these bars press the development forward into its next and stormy fugato episode.

Here it is not so much the entries of the subject itself which should be the conductor's primary concern as those of the semi-quaver countersubject on the 2nd violins and violas in bars 218 and 224 respectively. Staccato as they are and taken off the string, these restless passages need great weight in bowing style. Further entries on the clarinets in bar 232 and lower strings at letter H should receive no less attention even though they are now more an element in the progress of the symphonic structure, which continues to get more and more agitated as letter I is approached. A striking contribution is the 2nd violins' breaking into semiquaver sextuplets which then jump up an octave in violent protestation, details easily submerged if not positively brought into prominence.

Beethoven left few dynamic marks in this section to help the interpreter make the most of his spectacular ideas. The dou-ble-octave leaps in bars 220–1 and 226–7 are certainly well be-sprinkled with sforzandos, but the clarinets at bar 242 could profit by a new mark of forte, and the bassoons perhaps of *ff* at bar 246. The 2nd oboe undoubtedly needs to know how important his moment of solo is in bar 249, and the 1st and 2nd horns might also be marked '*f* soli' for their pealing E♭'s in bars 246–9. These incidentally should all be tied, Beethoven's purpose in writing them as tied quavers rather than crotchets being to ensure that they will be sustained for the full length of the notes. This is an example of an important facet of Beetho-ven's notation which will be discussed again in connection with the second movement's Trio section (see below p. 186). (It is ironic that the intention here, as later, should have been so misunderstood that successive copyists, and hence editions, omitted the ties.) Finally, the woodwind answering phrases in bars 250 and 252 should be isolated and brought well out, the bar in between being less in need of emphasis as it is a repetition of the last utterance of the 1st violins, flutes and bassoons.

The next quiet section of the development has no outstanding problems for the conductor except that the wind are prone to ask how far the crescendo in bars 265–70 should rise before the sudden collapse to *pp*. A good answer might be to *mf* so that in the passage which follows the solo fragments of melody can legitimately be played *p* even after the drop in dynamic, against a background of *pp*.

In bars 287 ff. Beethoven gives no new indication of tone quality, but there is an intense radiance in these bars which calls for a new and most affecting beauty of tone in wind and violins alike, making the abrupt plunge back to the fury of the return the more terrifying.

There should be not the slightest pull-up in the approach to the *ff* of letter K. This becomes the more apparent when it is discovered that in the autograph* the trumpets and timpani also have unrelenting semiquavers, and that the quavers in all scores, from the original Schott to those of the present day, owe their origin to an early copyist's error. The broadening to be heard in so many performances actually weakens this riveting moment of drama.

As it stands, the outburst which marks the beginning of the reprise creates virtually insoluble problems, and every conductor is inescapably driven to make changes of dynamics—sometimes in the past even of notation—to try and realize as nearly as possible what Beethoven had intended. Weingartner devotes no less than four and a half pages of his book—including three of particell—to a revision of the score which, even if his measures are too radical for present-day thinking, amply repay detailed study.

The main principles which can guide the conductor through this formidable passage may be reduced to the following:

1. Since none of the thematic work will be audible if the wind, brass, and, above all, timpani sustain an unrelieved *ff*, some reduction of tone in these instruments cannot be avoided.

2. A return to maximum effort must clearly be made at the pivot points of the passage which are set out by Beethoven with reiterated *ff*'s.

3. If the reduced dynamics are made subito or to any degree within the range of a *p* they will sound exaggerated and must therefore be controlled with great sensitivity, especially by the timpanist.

4. All the string parts are of primary importance, not merely the upper groups who have the thematic work. In fact the cellos

*Originally published half a century ago in an edition by Kistner & Siegel, this ha recently been reissued by Peters with some of the previously missing pages restored.

and basses can be encouraged to make maximum crescendos as they rear upwards precisely as the wind are phrasing in the opposite direction.

5. At bar 315 it may seem as if the troubles are over, but this is by no means the case. In particular the cellos and basses will continue to need the greatest attention as the storm continues unabated and in full driving tempo during the monumental first subject, which had originally been handled in declamatory style. It is in these lowest string groups that the directional flow of the passage essentially lies, even as the fury begins to reduce in intensity. The cellos will need more encouragement still, as Beethoven recognized in his indication 'ben marcato', when they lose the support of the basses during bars 329–38.

6. Finally, where the reiterations of emphasis change from repeated *ff*'s to *f*'s and thence to *sf*'s, these can be taken as lesser degrees so that the outburst passes by imperceptible stages to the return of lyricism at letter L.

The change to the minor in the reprise of the second subject could be thought to warrant a drop in dynamic like other such examples in Beethoven. In this instance a mark of *pp* to the strings in bar 351 would undoubtedly have the added benefit of allowing the darker-toned clarinet and bassoon to emerge more readily though these, like the other wind, being specifically marked 'espress.' by Beethoven, should not take any part in the reduction of tone.

The problem of the bassoons in bar 95 is transferred to the violas where this passage recurs at bar 362, and it is these who will now need to play fortissimo, as well as strongly off the string.

Bars 405, 412–13, possibly 416–18, but especially 501, all exhibit the same strange characteristic that the 1st violins seem to be written an octave too low. Until recently these bars were widely subject to emendation according to current tradition or the opinions of international conductors: Weingartner altered some but not others, Toscanini and Walter all of them and so on. On the face of it, the lower octave in bars 412–13 does seem tame (though possibly deliberately so) and out of line with the parallel bars 143–4. Bars 501–2 cannot be compared with any corresponding passage since bars 92–4 are so very different in register as well as instrumental layout. It is rather Beethoven's adjustments to avoid the, at that time, uncomfortable and ugly top flute notes which come to mind. But whilst the analogy is possibly inexact, performances with all the upper octaves restored—whether of flutes or violins—can sound oddly anachronistic and un-Beethovenian. Hence one is apt to seek, and perhaps find, musical arguments for playing the original text without *Retuschen*. It is nevertheless important to mark the flute in bar 501 with a 'solo *f*' as this entry can otherwise also sound disappointing with the violins left at the lower octave.

Bar 426 again requires a subdivided second beat, this time to prepare for the long and profoundly thoughtful coda, whose melodic line begins with the bassoon which Beethoven marked 'Solo' (not *p* as in all scores). This often unjustly maligned instrument seems to have been in the forefront of Beethoven's mind, so important a role does it play throughout the symphony. Doubled by the 1st violins though it is here, it requires a margin of time to establish itself in the listener's mind as a primary colour, and, since it continues to occupy that function consistently throughout the whole section with its 14-bar crescendo, care should be taken to prevent the busy sextuplet figuration of the middle strings from becoming too opaque.

Unlike similar previous places, and despite the *subito p*, letter Q (bar 469) needs no preparation of up-beat subdivision. Here continuity is of the essence, the poetry of the horn solo emerging in strict tempo from the previous period of protest. Beethoven's *p*'s and *sempre p*'s should now be read as *pp*'s, except for the solo horn and other wind solos, until bar 477 when they too can join in the pervading atmosphere of tense withdrawal in anticipation of the massive crescendos which lie ahead. Even the strings, motivic as they are, should fall within the conductor's restraining gestures. Only the 2nd horn can perhaps be brought up a degree since his low register dips, as in the Scherzo of the Seventh Symphony, tend to be obscured.

The caution cannot be relaxed where the string crescendo is concerned at bar 481, lest the increasing strength of the alternating woodwind solos led again by the bassoon become comparatively ineffectual. Above all, the strings' intensity should at first only rise to a single *f*, the *ff* in bars 489–90 being sudden and violent as well as unexpectedly brief, reducing instantly at the end of bar 490 where the diminuendo begins, and dropping once again to a sinister *pp* before the storm-clouds gather. Since the tempo is unyielding and ensemble no problem here, it is this drama of dynamics which is the conductor's main preoccupation.

Bar 504 is the last of those bars where a subdivision is necessary. Moreover, this time the extra beat will have the effect of putting the brake firmly on the tidal wave of surging scales during the preceding bars. There can even be a slight gap before the *subito p* at bar 505, which is best changed to *subito pp* in the strings so that the limelight will at once fall on the woodwind.

This last statement of the hesitant development episode may be more reflective than those of the development itself. Even the 'a tempo's, which had then been resolutely forward-looking, are now less determined especially in bars 511–12 where allowance has to be made for the flute's demisemiquavers.

A more tentative pick-up of the a tempo in these bars will also lead naturally into the final eerie dead-march which cannot begin its curious spectral gait any faster than ♩ = 60. This more measured tempo will make provision for the reality of the strings' demisemiquavers (there is naturally no suggestion of tremolo), with their dramatic upward octave leaps requiring clear and awesome gesturing from the stick, as well as accommodating the final unison of the principal theme. There will then also be no case for any broadening in the last two bars, but only the summoning of full power for the cadential *A D* punctuated meaningfully by brass and timpani.

II

Although taken in strict tempo, the Scherzo's opening bars are naturally not all beaten out, the G.P. bars being simply gaps between forcefully delivered enunciations, so as to emphasize the declamatory dramatic character of this introductory sentence as well as highlighting the timpani solo of the fifth bar.

The printed ♩. = 116 is a hair's breadth precipitate for this greatest and mightiest of Beethoven's Scherzos. Moreover, when the 'Amsterdam' motif takes over at bar 77 it can, like the corresponding figure in the Seventh Symphony first movement, too easily degenerate into a $\frac{2}{4}$ rhythm unless sufficient time is allowed for both the first and third notes of each bar to be given their correct valuation. A pulse of ♩. = 108–12 is only slightly steadier and yet makes the necessary provision for this as well as allowing for the magisterial second subject at letter C (bars 93 ff.).

The 2nd violins are often understandably uneasy about starting the fugato main section of the Scherzo, but if the 2-bar G.P. preceding their entry is correctly measured they should have no problem. A clear beat is more relevant here than an undue concern for pianissimo until all five groups have been brought in. The slightly unusual order of events makes it wise to give pointedly placed indications, but once the basses are established the sharp clarity of stickwork can give way to a restraining manner so as to prevent any anticipation of the crescendo which is still so very far off.

The fortissimo of letter A is controlled by a continuous series of strong down-beats of unvarying intensity, the only changes of style being called for by the extra note in bar 68 and the two extra in bar 72, additional emphases being directed towards the timpani and lower strings. But at B the relentless succession of down-beats can for the first time be softened to suggest phrasing within the consistent 4-bar structure. In particular the placing of the rise and fall between bars 78 and 84 requires direction as the apex is not at the obvious place.

The days are unfortunately still not past when it was thought acceptable and necessary for horns to be added to the woodwind for the second subject at letter C. In truth, so far from correcting any miscalculation on Beethoven's part, this contrivance changes the sonority of the passage with disagreeable and uncharacteristic effect. Naturally, if anywhere in the symphony, doubled woodwind solves this problem at a stroke, yet if the upper strings are kept firmly in check at a dynamic of *poco f* and the wind induced to play a true *ff* it may be surprising how well Beethoven's unedited orchestration can be made to work in most halls. The horns (who should also play the parts Beethoven wrote for them but at a reduced dynamic) and trumpets should return to their printed *ff* in bar 109, the strings and timpani two bars later, the latter being an entry of considerable dramatic effect.

At bar 127 Beethoven again adopts his typical notation of successive *f*'s to indicate rinforzandos. What this can fail to indicate is the general dynamic level, which here really is of a single *f* unlike bars 61 ff. where it was patently fortissimo.

The pianissimo 4-bar phrase in bars 139–42 is only soft enough if the violins are persuaded to play it in a single up-bow. This in the nature of things cannot apply to the violas and cellos, but given the lead from the upper strings they will balance their dynamic as a matter of course. (So also naturally in the reprise at bar 376.)

The canonic form of the figurations between bars 143 and 155 can trap the unwary conductor into counting the silent bars as 1, 2, and 3 instead of as bars 2, 3, and 4 of their respective 4-bar periods. The possibility of momentary fallibility should not be discounted, especially during the corresponding passage at the end of the reprise where the long first-time bars—both repeats in the Scherzo should always be taken—have a curiously wispy character making them particularly confusing. The players depend on absolute reliability in all these places and the silent bars are accordingly beaten out, however unostentatiously.

The link to the development, beginning at the crescendo, must be thought of as four 3-bar phrases (for all that the regular alternation between strings and wind during the stepwise ascent of the melodic line means that the 3-bar phrases also have their own such alternation) followed by three increasingly assertive 2-bar statements. The third of these culminates on a fermata at the woodwind's last crotchet which the conductor catches and sustains with intensity. He then takes the wind right off before giving the bassoon the lead to start the new section.

In view of these 3-bar phrases at bars 159 ff. it is of some interest that Beethoven elected to use, surely for the first time ever, the formula 'Ritmo di tre battute'—contradicted later by 'Ritmo di quattro battute'—at bar 177, although admittedly the pattern continues uninterrupted for a very considerable period. (This, translated into the German 'drei-' or 'vier-taktig' was to be a favourite mark of Richard Strauss and also for quite short spans.)

The timpani solos of bars 195 ff. are marked with only a single '*f*', and yet it should be taken at face value—i.e. not as a euphemism for *rf* in *ff*, unexpectedly restrained as this might seem. If the player will really make the drums 'speak' these solo entries will have the required electrifying quality without anticipating the true *ff* of letter G, and especially bar 272, where Beethoven repeats the triplets' convulsive effect he had created with such success in the Overture *Egmont*.

In bar 208 the timpani's diminuendo does not stem from Beethoven, who simply repeated the long-styled hairpin accents he had given to each previous entry. Nevertheless it is a matter for personal judgement whether he would not have welcomed some reduction of intensity in sympathy with the woodwind diminuendo such as is the normal practice in present-day performances. (Six bars before H the repetitious *f*'s are certainly once again *rf*'s in *ff*.)

A serious misreading robs the timpani of one of his most arresting contributions. In bars 352–3 he should have the whole phrase and not just two isolated crotchets, to some extent corresponding with bar 111 in the exposition. But the altered placing to immediately before the piano subito gives it an increased element of ferocity which, when carrying out its restoration, is worth marking with an extra *ff* in Solo.

It has already been said that there is an especial element of potential confusion for the conductor in the first-time bars at bar 388. This is largely due to Beethoven's subtle handling of the modulatory progression in relation to the bar-structure, so that the arrival on a chord of E♭ occurs a bar earlier than would be expected: it comes in fact, on the last bar of a period. There is thus the sensation, hard to overcome, of having wrongly started to count the crucial silent bars on a weak bar.

An element of uncertainty can also intrude in the analogous, yet by no means identical, second-time bars leading to the next fermata in which the wind is caught in mid-air just as before. On the face of it this is now a simple 8-bar phrase and yet it is curiously hard to feel it as two conventional periods of four bars each. Here there is no cast-iron solution other than thinking of the passage in such a way that bar 394 is an up-beat; for the fermata bar is one of the chief corner-stones of the movement and must be delivered with the utmost conviction.

The fermata itself is held lunga, and then taken off as on the earlier occasion before starting the transition passage containing the 8-bar stringendo to the Presto which is one of the most notorious controversies in orchestral literature.

I have written elsewhere at length on this subject and the possible origin of the patently incorrect metronome marks with which the Presto at bar 412 is graced,* whether the '116' relates to a minim or semibreve. Here it suffices to say that it cannot have been Beethoven's intention either on the one hand that each half-bar of the Trio should be at the same tempo as the Scherzo, which is much too slow and could in any case only be achieved by means of an abrupt 'Tempo 1° subito' at just the point where, on the contrary, Beethoven marks 'Presto'; or on the other hand that each whole bar should equate with one bar of the Scherzo as a result of a feverish accelerando possibile aimed at reaching a preposterously fast tempo in the vain attempt at making two incompatible movements relate exactly.

Instead it is only necessary to set in motion an exciting but not exorbitant degree of stringendo in order to accomplish a smooth transition to the Trio whereby the new half-bar of the Presto alla breve will exactly correspond with the last and most accelerated bar of $\frac{3}{4}$. This relationship has to be kept very clearly in the conductor's consciousness as the alla breve is actually best beaten in a quick 2, both on account of the violent rinforzandos in bars 412–13 and to establish the pulse beyond any shadow of doubt. For this new tempo ♩ = 160 is a good target, and one which will serve well when it becomes necessary to synchronize the strings' staccato passage-work with the horn solo of bars 438 ff.

The entry of the bass trombone at the third bar of the Presto is a touch of colour often submerged although the isolated note—his first in the entire symphony—is a real solo, there being nowhere else a D at that octave. This particular trombonist also has a more interesting part from letter M onwards than is generally realized, unlike the other two who make only a very slender, however important, contribution shortly before the end of the Trio. There is strategic purpose in focusing attention on these majestic instruments so that their brief appearance

---

Orchestral Variations: Confusion and Error in the Orchestral Repertoire (Eulenburg, London, 1981), 40–1. Much chapter and verse is cited there.

does not go for nothing, especially as they fall silent once more thereafter until the 'Seid umschlungen, Millionen' section of the finale, a mere eight minutes before the end of the whole symphony.

There is no occasion at any point throughout the Trio to change into whole-bar beating; the beginning of the second repeated section (both Trio repeats are again beyond question obligatory) benefits from a suavely flowing—although admittedly hasty—minim beat, while in the long oboe solo all the phrases both in the solo itself and in the gentle accompaniment start on the second minim of their respective bars. These phrasings, being always from half-bar to half-bar, need to be felt as true rhythmic impulses and not as a series of syncopations as they would if the whole passage were conducted in 1.

This is especially relevant to the subito piano of bar 471 in particular—which, as the conductor needs to be fully aware, occurs after an extra crescendo group at bars 470-1, making a 5-bar period momentarily disturbing the otherwise regular 4-bar symmetry.

The *fp* at the second-time bar which initiates the extensive coda demands more shock treatment than, for example, the not dissimilar one at letter M. This should suggest at once that something new and important is going to happen, as is indeed the case. There should be an almost ceremonial air about the upward striding of the minims towards the two climaxes which dominate this impressive section, the one only brief and quickly falling back in order that new strength may be gathered to attain the second and greater peak. Both summits are characerized by the bar-long alternations of tonic and dominant so that it is the weight of these which the conductor's beat should indicate with pesante down-beats, four in the first instance, eight in the second, the up-beats being temporarily understressed.

Beethoven intended that the length and importance of these alternations should be dominated by the violins, who should fill each bar to the maximum. For this purpose he used a favourite notation consisting of tied pairs of notes, a method which has been much misunderstood in the past but has been the subject of considerable reappraisal in recent years. An outstanding later instance is the first statement of the Grosse Fuge's main theme, but there are countless others, one of which has already appeared in this symphony (see above p. 177). It is thus the more regrettable that the early copyists already mistook Beethoven's meaning, and in the current editions of the score and orchestral material these ties are lacking.

It is apparent that in between and after the climactic periods (bars 507–14 and 523 ff.) normal minim beating is resumed, although the last eight bars will introduce a new character of retrospection. Here for the first and only time the pace can be relaxed a fraction albeit with great subtlety, by means of careful manipulation of again the second beats in each bar, but using these now to describe a gentle cantando quality to the 1st violins and cellos. While this will in itself moderate the speed, only the crotchets of the 2nd violins in bar 529 can seriously reduce the tempo, slightly anticipating Beethoven's poco ritardando. This will then start at quite a new and steady pace, and the second half of the bar is subdivided to indicate how the 1st violins come to rest on the fermata. There should be no take-off before the Scherzo da capo roughly interrupts the brief moment of calm.

In both the autograph and the first edition the return of the Scherzo is not written out at all, and many have wondered how it came about that in all current editions it is not only printed in full but with the first, though not the second, repeat retained. In the event this owes its origin to a separate 'Anzeige' slip issued by the publishers in April 1827,* in which, together with numerous corrections to the E♭ Quartet, Op. 127, the instruction is indeed given for the Scherzo da capo of the Ninth Symphony but stating no more than that the second section is to be played only once.

The inference may be thought to be clear, but is not quite explicit, and one's doubts are not dispelled by the further knowledge that Beethoven had had a number of thoughts on the matter of how to print the da capo instruction (in the autograph he actually specified 'ohne Wiederholung'). In practice this last exposition repeat is never observed (except in 'authentic' performances); certainly, whether Beethoven could ever seriously have considered it or not, the prospect of restarting the Scherzo

---

*It is reproduced in full after letter No. 1548 of Emily Anderson's complete edition of Beethoven's Correspondence (Macmillan, London, 1961) Vol III. 1330–1.

for the fourth time is too discouraging to contemplate.

At the end of the movement the abortive return of the Trio stops in mid-air and, after a moment's hesitation, is brusquely waved aside by the last two bars which should be declaimed decisively and in strict tempo.

If the conductor should be so unfortunate as to be forced to agree to the late appearance on the platform of the solo singers, it is now that they would have to enter. But there is no escaping the fact that the atmosphere of what is to come, as well as the overall structure of the work, is fundamentally disturbed by the sight of four soloists making their uncomfortable way towards the guiltily vacant chairs awaiting them, with the risk— all too often realized—of tentative applause. In any case there should be a fairly extended period of repose before embarking on the long, deeply spiritual Adagio, which will run virtually without a break into the finale, as will be discussed in due course.

III

The first bar of the Adagio is beaten in 8; only in this way can the woodwind entries be confidently brought in one after another in correct rhythmic spacing. But immediately at the second bar this subdivision becomes unnecessary and moreover disturbs the stillness and devotional poise this sublime piece demands at the opening statement of its great melody. Despite the enormous difference in the number of participants on the platform there must be the same intimate feeling in the hall as during the 'Heilige Dankgesang' of the A minor String Quartet, Op. 132.

The printed $\textbf{J} = 60$ makes no kind of sense, being almost exactly twice too fast. The first bar can be quietly guided at $\textbf{♪} = 66$ after which the subsequent slow crotchet beats will stabilize themselves at a totally rapt continuum of $\textbf{J} = 40$ after an imperceptible tempo adjustment during the second bar of which no one, if it is handled skilfully, need be the least aware. So too the quavers when they become essential, with occasional subdivision necessary, will move with measured step at $\textbf{♪} = 80$.

The secret of obtaining the desired hushed mezza voce from

the strings lies in starving them of bow, a recourse generally resisted ('out of pure laziness' as one highly experienced leader of great integrity once put it) but which can be successfully insisted upon. In fact Beethoven's printed slurs may to a very large extent be interpreted also as bowing marks.

At bar 17 it is the 4th horn who for the first time demands attention. Remarkably enough, although Beethoven used four horns frequently elsewhere (the *Leonora* overtures, *Egmont*, etc.) they do not appear in the symphonies until the Ninth where, however, they are employed as an integral part of the wind section throughout, not merely kept in reserve like the trombones for key points in the scheme. But it is even more noteworthy in this Adagio that although the 1st and 2nd horns in Bb (basso) are handled normally, of the second pair in Eb the 3rd horn has practically nothing to play (he enters, literally for the first time, at bar 120 and has only a handful of notes thereafter) whereas the 4th horn is treated as a soloist in his own right. He is also given a great many chromatic notes, which has led to much scholastic research over how Beethoven expected the passages to be played, especially at bars 90–7. The most detailed explanation is given by the veteran specialist of the French horn R. Morley Pegge in his outstanding treatise on the instrument,* in which he conjectures that 'according to tradition it was Edward Constantin Lewy (one of two brothers) who played 4th horn in the first performance of Beethoven's Ninth Symphony, in which case the part was probably played on a two-valve horn in conjunction with some degree of hand-horn technique, switching into E for the famous Ab scale. 'This', he adds, 'does not mean that Beethoven actually wrote the part with the valve horn in mind,' although since the recently invented instrument had just appeared in Vienna and was being exploited by the two Lewy brothers it does seem probable.

Apart from the chromatic nature of the writing, however, it was not unusual for Beethoven to write soloistically for the second player of a pair, or even for the second of two pairs when both are crooked in the same key. The *Fidelio* and *Leonora No. 3* overtures give examples of both practices respectively, whilst the Overture *Leonora No. 1* gives a splendid further

**The French Horn (Ernest Benn, London, 1960), 108–9.

instance of quite free writing for a 4th horn solo, if less chromatic than in the present example. The interest here lies not only in this respect—Brahms was to write even more daring chromaticisms (still resolutely for the natural instrument) in his Horn Trio, Op. 40—but also in the extremes of range he knew he could count upon in his 4th horn: since the Lewy brothers were, after all, considerable virtuosi. Yet in the years which followed such a compass was regarded as quite unrealistic, especially for a player specializing in the lower horn parts, and conductors would regard some form of wholesale redistribution as indispensable. The 1st horn, for example, would take over the 4th horn solos with the aid of the 2nd player for the really low notes, the 3rd horn would take the part Beethoven had intended for the 1st horn, while the poor 4th horn—by definition assumed to be the weakest member of the quartet—would have to rest content with the barren 3rd horn part. Today such a reshuffle is far less common, for a 4th horn has his pride too, and shows extreme reluctance, if not outright offence, at a conductor's temerity in suggesting that he should relinquish his moment of glory, and, apart from an occasional brief supporting note from his neighbouring colleague, will insist on himself executing his solo line unaided.

Foolishly, one might think, the slurs over the upper strings' grace-notes in bars 21–4 (and correspondingly 61–4), given in some editions and in the earlier Breitkopf parts, were carefully removed in the later printing. There is no question of playing them with separate bows, and it is known that Beethoven never bothered to mark grace-note slurs, taking them for granted. They should, it may be noted, be played before the beat.

Whilst the printed ♩ = 63 for the Andante moderato can no more be observed literally than the ♩ = 60 which preceded it, the narrow margin between them is indicative and should prevent the conductor from making too diametric a change of pulse. Yet as in Bruckner's Seventh, whose Adagio is directly influenced by Beethoven's, the contrasted section must be given a new and real character of its own, the outstanding quality of which is that whereas in the Adagio proper the quavers do at certain points acquire reality of pulse, in the Andante they do not. The rhythm is now controlled by the crotchet undulations of the basses which can flow at about ♩ = 56.

The heart-searching melody in the 2nd violins and violas should be played with real depth, while at the same time the fragments of counter-melody in the woodwind and, later, 1st violins should contain an element of pathos which can be infused with momentary flashes of great tenderness if each entry is gently enticed with the stick.

Then during the last three bars before the return to tempo primo the conductor's manner will show that the vision is fading, and with the melting of the harmonies during bar 41 the tempo is already losing much of its impetus. The fermata bar is thus appreciably slower and will need to be organized by means of a subdivided beat as well as an extra indication to help the 1st violins to give the right amount of hesitation before placing the held E♭.

It is possible to view Weingartner's proposal to conduct the tempo primo of bars 43 ff. in 8 with as many qualms as he exhibits in his disdain of other conductors' 'dilettante' adoption of 12 beats at bars 99 ff. Certainly one must feel the half beats with the horns and pizzicato strings, but this can be simply reflected in the style of beating wherever it will not interfere with the delineation of the 1st violins' melodic variant. The manner of direction used in shaping this, especially in the use of the left hand, with the utmost flexibility of wrist and fingers, needs to be constantly concerned with guiding, coaxing and phrasing so that the ornamentation comes across as an outpouring of continuous melisma. Such restless melodizing round and about the great theme naturally robs it of the stillness which had originally been its primary characteristic and the source of its beauty. Consequently the tempo can afford to be a little more flowing—say, ♩ = 46.

The transition to the return of the Andante will be smoother than on the first occasion since the difference between the tempos is less, for the speed of this contrasting section must be the same as before. Now three octaves deep in the woodwind, the wonderful melody is disturbed only by the need again to entice the fragments of counter-melody which, all now on the upper strings, lead this time to a strangely jaunty little tune on the 1st violins which has a dance-like character. Moreover it is characterized by the kind of 'trompe l'oreille' such as Brahms and Tchaikovsky were to be fond of, whereby the ear is deceived over the true placing of the barlines. The present example ought, as the result of a syncopated style of beating, to come across as if each phrase were to begin at the barline instead of after a quaver rest:

Ex. 13

from which it can suddenly be seen to be half-way towards a tune from, say, *Die Fledermaus* (which only goes to show what a fine composer Johann Strauss was. Perhaps the conductor may be allowed to lilt slightly in these bars).

Bars 81–2 again bring a fade-away, and the second of these two bars has, like bar 42, to be subdivided with six quaver beats although this time there is no fermata and no extra semi-quaver to be re-subdivided and controlled. Indeed Beethoven has not even marked any kind of 'rit.' for the ensuing return to Adagio, although some sympathetic *einleitend* is self-evident.

In the score the quaver groups of the upper strings in bar 82 give the visual impression that the 2nd violins and violas should be playing arco like the 1sts. That this was not Beetho-ven's final intention is proved by the actual erasure of the slurs in the autograph, perhaps to ensure that the entry of the solo 4th horn will not be obscured by too thick a blanket of string tone.

The central Adagio is, of course, this player's most notorious hunting ground. The texture is now thinned out to a degree almost suggestive of a wind chamber group and, although the mood of calm has descended once more, the conductor should show that there is no longer the earlier rapt or devout feeling. Hence, while there must be no suggestion of impatience or hurry, the tempo can again be a little less sustained than at first.

The string pizzicato punctuations all need careful leads, section by section, full of rhythmic implication such that the duplets will turn accurately into triplets in bar 87, or back again in bar 92. None of this inner pulsation should be overemphasized such as would be the tendency if subdivision of any kind were introduced. Even the separated triplet groups of bar 95 which prepare for the solo horn's arched cadenza need no extra beats, however much the end of the bar contains a feeling of phrase-ending. If the conductor conveys to the players a strong thought-process in which the last triplet quavers (in the 2nd violins) are carefully placed, and the down-beat of bar 96 slightly delayed for the purpose, there should be no risk of insecure ensemble.

The horn is then left uninhibited by any further beating during that bar, the conductor maintaining absolute stillness, until the moment comes to show his expectation for the wind re-entry with the up-beat quaver.

One still occasionally hears the incorrect slur at the rising fourth (E♭ to A♭) at the centre of the horn's bridge passage, although this is mere tradition, no slur being printed in any edition or material.

With bar 97 beating is quietly resumed, the main growth in intensity being reserved for the following bar where, with the sense of arrival imminent, the last three—but only three—triplet quavers are indeed beaten out. A wide stick movement is appropriate now, shaping the strong crescendo which leads into the $\frac{12}{8}$ in which all the pizzicato string groups except the 1sts are assembled; some pull-back of tempo will happen naturally at this culminating moment.

With the piano subito start of the $\frac{12}{8}$ the tempo is immediately resumed, and if the right degree of quiet movement has been established during the preceding Adagio section it should be able to correspond correctly with Beethoven's 'Lo stesso tempo'. This should then also provide just the amount of flow which will prevent the unornamented wind from dragging and yet allow all the semiquavers of the 1st violins' embroidery to be played cantabile.

From the point of view of sheer conducting technique this is a particularly demanding section since, as in the 'Scene am Bach' from the 'Pastoral', so much has to be communicated between the reliably maintained slow 4 beats to the bar. Extra pointing is called for by the accents in bar 105, these often being understressed if the conductor's command of subtle gesture is inadequate, while the call upon his resourcefulness and flexibility becomes even more pressing when in bar 109 the violins for a few beats acquire a jerky rhythm in their melodizing.

In bar 108 the flute should be gently nursed back to the texture with his expressive turn of phrase just after the barline, and the violins also pointedly reinitiated as they resume their ornamentation now at the increased speed of triplet semiquavers, whose extra liquidity needs encouragement lest it should sound in the least degree laboured. The solo horn's arpeggio in bar 111 will need sympathetic indulgence, allowing it space to complete its descent before giving the violins the down-beat with which to start upon their concluding ornamental phrase.

The end of the violins' variation must not appear to take place in the middle of bar 114 any more than the earlier versions of the melody reached their conclusions in bars 18 and 58 respectively. It is the extra elaboration and the complexity of the events which have made this variant seem more substantial. On the contrary, the continuity in bars 114 ff. presupposes an especial degree of forward pursuit with very clear attention to the 1st and 2nd horns and the timpani to ensure correct synchronization. The solo 4th horn on the other hand no longer needs any more room for manœuvre than will be afforded by the conductor's alert orientation towards his line, not only in bar 117 with its arpeggio twists but through his heavings all the way to the end of the section four bars later.

This magical and deeply moving second variation has been another subject of controversy over the years. Indeed it was one of the blind spots of our own dear Ralph Vaughan Williams, who regarded the violins' semiquaver meanderings of this particular movement as mere mechanical decorations typical of an era in which such contrivances were the dreary stock-in-trade of every composer who found himself short of new ideas. It is not difficult to imagine a performance under an unimaginative interpreter which might well give such an impression, and hence there is no exaggerating the importance of the rapport the conductor has to have with his players to do proper justice to this most fervent of all Beethoven's adagios.

The fanfares of two bars before letter A (how bizarre that this should be placed only at bar 123) and again two before B announce the enormous coda, and for the first time provide the necessity for 12 real beats together with the 3 subdivided up-beats in each case. Both fanfares are marked forte rather than fortissimo until the last enunciations of the horns and trumpets, whose *ff* marks are subito and must create as arresting an effect as possible.

In bar 121 (and 131) the players are sometimes in doubt and ask for guidance from the conductor over the length of the staccato crotchets. If they really find this to be a problem it can be a difficult question to answer precisely, since there should be no resemblance between a crotchet and a quaver marked with a dot and a line respectively, even though the two will actually be very similar in the sheer matter of length.

Letters A and B themselves both return to a slow dotted-crotchet beat although with different subsequent requirements. Letter A is characterized by its sudden extreme stillness, which is so spell-binding after all that has gone before. Into this hush, and if possible without disturbing it, the wind entries have to be placed firmly and confidently. The tension is then relieved by the cello/bass quavers at the end of bar 124 which have to be indicated with a clearly subdivided beat broadening the pulse a little. These pizzicato notes are of course played meaningfully but piano, though Beethoven seems to have considered it unnecessary to add new marks anywhere to contradict the forte of bars 120–2. Similarly the hairpins over the wind parts at letter A are heavy, what we today would call Schubertian, accents rather than diminuendos, and where two such accents are adjacent they are not cumulative, but return to the basic dynamic in order to take a second stress of the same intensity as before.

With bar 125 a return is made to the flowing manner of the $\frac{12}{8}$ variation which must seem to be trying to reinstate itself for a further period. The conducting style, however, very soon changes again for, after beginning to urge the 1st violins to a warm cantando playing in which every quaver, every semi-quaver, wants full melodic fervour, from bar 127 a smoother bowing style should be the aim, the beat even infusing the slow pulsation with a lilting rhythm into which the spaced-out crescendo quavers of the lower strings can be implanted by some suggestive series of gestures from the point of the elbow, the neck, the head, or any other medium than hand or stick.

Similar to A as it may superficially seem at first, letter B has quite different connotations as it plunges into the deep purple of D♭ major. Up to a point there is a comparable stillness, though this is now ruffled by the regular echoes of the fanfare on the 2nd violins, all of which need indicating with little elaborations of the stick and wrist movements at each respective first and third beats. Beethoven marked these '*pp*' but this may be thought too reticent, soft as they should be. The strings' deep Db (the lower bass octave is certainly *de rigueur* here) will have been initiated with some considerable intensity, for which Beethoven made provision by this time marking the 'piano' although only at the end of the following bar. At bar 135 moreover, the 1st violins' Gb is so expressive a note that a greater dynamic than hitherto in these passages seems called for as a matter of urgency. This will then be echoed to some extent by the deep Eb of the lower strings, despite their hairpin—with which it need not conflict if warmth of tone is substituted for increased power.

In bar 136 the sound of the whole orchestra drains away in order to crescendo anew, up to what must certainly be a piano subito. This fourth beat crescendo is again a place which has to be controlled with three subdivided quaver beats; nor is this by any means the last such instance, as after barely two bars in which the melodic flow tries to reassert itself it takes a sudden turnabout to a new and deeply *innig* section. Since it is of primary importance that this last be experienced as a new train of thought and not as a mere continuation, it must be properly initiated even though it is only two bars since a similar preparation had been organized for the return of the violins' and woodwind's melodizing. This further hold-up is accordingly of an entirely different calibre and the subdivision has to serve not only for control in rubato, but in order to negotiate a real corner in the meaning of the music.

Beethoven here marks the violins both dolce and cantabile, so that an extra degree of tenderness will enter the quality of their sound. In addition the fertility of melodic inspiration is so self-renewing as bar follows bar that even while the pulse is constantly maintained by the rhythmic ostinato of timpani and pizzicato strings there should nevertheless be an ever alert awareness of the need for spaciousness, of enough time within the beats for the succession of ideas to project their full range of expression.

This includes passages as in bar 144 where the 1st violins' triplet to-and-froing might once more be considered by the unconverted to be mere passage-work; like the melodic events of the surrounding bars the violins should never be allowed simply to look after themselves within the wide dotted crotchet beats. On the contrary, every nuance, every hand-over to the wind and back, every rise and fall of the seemingly endless melody, should be tended with the utmost care and affection.

Nevertheless, despite the obvious difficulty of keeping control without resorting to a subdivided beat, the temptation must be resisted until the middle of bar 150. As long as the music is soft the problem is not so great, but it naturally becomes more acute in *f* or *ff* and bar 147 will thus need considerable skill and authority. The three and a half bars of diminuendo and crescendo which succeed Beethoven's momentary *ff* will then only be achieved with its proper gentle momentum if the players can be relied upon to keep to a strict pulse at so slow a tempo, the chords on the third quaver of each beat coming with unquestioning precision while the conductor concerns himself with the quality and phrasing of the 1st violins.

This acquires an even greater intensity of glowing beauty in bars 149 and 150, at the third beat of which latter bar the melodic evocation reaches such a pitch that, while there should still be no change of speed, the conductor has no choice but to take control with a quaver beat which guides both the ascent up to the 12th beat climax and the solo descending 1st violins.

The twelve beats are now retained virtually until the end of the movement since the quaver has become the essential unit; each of the triplet semiquaver groups in the 2nd violins and violas are to be felt as self-contained entities punctuated by the timpani/cello/bass ostinato which here returns as a motif in its own right, no longer merely as a background.

The effect of the thoughtfully descending violins followed by the throbbing pulsations which are all conducted in a real 12 will have inevitably pulled back the tempo to $\flat$ = 88, and this is maintained until the close. It goes without saying, however, that the empty beats between the events during the last three bars are counted (as quaver pulses) rather than overtly given with the stick. There is a sense of pausing in expectancy, especially in bar 155 which would be ruined by the sight of a conductor solemnly marking the silent beats.

Here it is the art of 'looking like the music' which comes

into prominence so that the conductor can communicate the inwardness of thought without the need for superfluous beats and still remain perfectly clear: the stresses in bar 154 which mark the cello/bass arco notes at the end of each dotted crotchet period; the sustaining of the winds' forte in the following bar after the two strong enunciations of the strings, brass, and timpani (the *fp* on the second of these is particularly noteworthy and difficult to portray), with the quaver lead for flute and oboe at the end of the bar which really does need to be most clearly shown to these players; the placing of the three *p* chords with quaver rests between; the control of the moving phrase in the penultimate bar in such a way that the woodwind (other than the flute) cannot misunderstand where their semiquavers should begin; the startling last forte chord, held—perhaps a margin longer than its exact value—and dismissed; and after a moment's hiatus the thoughtful spacing of the final notes, with a little click of the stick for the pizzicato (which must surely be no stronger than piano) and a slightly delayed positioning for the last chord of all, but which is held for no longer than its true value before establishing a silence of awed tension.

IV

And then all hell breaks loose. The concept that the finale should follow attacca is inherent in Beethoven's ultimate scheme for the symphony and especially in the unprecedented dramatic events of the finale's introduction. It is therefore the more disquieting to realize that at the time of its composition and first performance an apparently insuperable objection seems to have lain in the necessity both for the horns and trumpets to change crooks and for the timpanist to retune his drums, once laborious and time-consuming processes. It is supremely fortunate that in these days of chromatic valved brass and pedal timpani no such primitive considerations need be taken into account and the cataclysm so aptly described by Wagner as the *Schreckensfanfare* can suddenly and devastatingly shatter the still rapt beauty of the Adagio's end as Beethoven must, beyond all doubt, have contemplated.

The *Fanfaren* themselves have regularly been rescored over the years, with substantial doctoring of the horn and trumpet parts and even the woodwind to some extent. It is not hard to understand how this should have come about, although these are again obvious places where double woodwind could well solve the problems of balance at a stroke. But however much one may reinforce the woodwind, the fragmentation of Beethoven's original horn and trumpet parts can easily sound gauche.

But there are two ways which in conjunction can minimize the limitations of Beethoven's notation for the natural instruments of his day without in any way interfering with his text, given—that is to say—sympathetic hall acoustics. In the first place the trumpets must, from the middle of each second bar, drop their tone to match as nearly as possible the stridency of the woodwind, who in their turn must play with as much force as they can muster, the oboes and clarinets raising their bells in Mahlerian style. A return to *ff* can then be made during the last of the repeated quavers in bar 6 (and later 24).

Secondly the tempo must not be so swift as to prevent the woodwind from projecting their quavers with this extravagant degree of force. Weingartner unwisely stated that the printed ♩. = 96 is not too fast for the *Fanfare* but would be for the succeeding recitatives. In the event he was wrong, not merely because such a tempo really is crazily precipitate, but in that it turns out to be the result of a copyist's blunder in reading 96 for the 66 which Beethoven actually wrote, and which latter is very nearly a possibility. The qualification lies in the need for the outbursts to be conveyed with crotchet beating, which at ♩. = 66 would emerge at a barely practicable ♩ = 198. To beat the passages in 1 would be to give a lightness to the pulse which is altogether remote from their purpose as well as sacrificing the savagery of the woodwind's quaver-work. If, therefore, an athletic 3-in-a-bar of ♩ = 184 is substituted, starting both bars 1 and 16 with abrupt and vehement up-beats, this will be found to be quite frantic enough to give the impression of chaotic fury without the risk of it degenerating into disorganized confusion. And what is more significant is that even with undoubled woodwind the effect can then be remarkably successful exactly as Beethoven planned and scored it.

Bar 7 should be so emphatic that the two crotchets will have to be a little spaced in preparation for the ensuing recitative.

Correspondingly there must also be some broadening in bar 24 but this is manœuvred differently. Here it is the rests which are elongated so that the tutti quaver/crotchet figure, though still quick in itself, will enter a little late. For this purpose the wind, brass, and timpani must be carefully trained and clearly directed beyond any danger of mishap. The brief cello/bass interruption will then be able to make its point without being either lost or cut short prematurely.

As for the recitatives themselves, Beethoven's marking is to some extent self-contradictory. The lines cannot have both the character of a recitative and be in tempo since it is precisely the freedom from tempo which is the primary characteristic of recitative. The sensible compromise is to establish an initial basic pulse which will allow for the vehemence of the pseudo-verbal patterns, say ♩ = *c.*112, after which the cello/bass recitations will ebb and flow with considerable freedom:

Ex. 14

Of these six excerpts in which the cellos and basses come to the verge of articulate speech, (*a*) begins as straight declamation, corresponding most closely to the actual sung recitative 'O Freunde' of bar 216 ff. From the middle of the fourth bar, however, the expression becomes more agitated; the actual words must necessarily remain conjectural—perhaps Beethoven never managed to formulate them very clearly in his mind.

(*b*) is more indignant and leads by way of the two peremptory chords, which should still be in the slower tempo of the recitative, into the postulating of the first movement. (*c*) dismisses this outright in tones which are positively angry,* while the 'Nicht doch' of (*d*) is patently ben trovato, although it was in fact another of Wagner's interpretations recalling his own use of these very words for Fricka in her scene with Wotan in *Die Walküre*, Act 2.

---

*The bracketed and dotted slurs in the illustration of (c) given above appear in the Leipzig Breitkopf and Härtel material, but are editorial and should not be observed.

There should be an element of tenderness and regret about the Adagio's rejection expressed in (*e*), which seems to belie the mark of 'Allegro'. Beethoven's purpose in adding it, nevertheless, is clearly to prevent the mood from over-affecting the actual pace, so that the more expostulating part of this recitative can emerge naturally.

It is (*f*), of course, which for the first time exhibits real enthusiasm and once more parallels the subsequent vocal recitative with its 'freudenvollere'. The pull-up suggested in the fifth bar is fairly considerable in order to allow for the triumphant reiteration of D's in the trumpets and drums.

The concluding bar of all these recitatives, bar 91 of the movement, should—as Tovey was the first to point out—continue without any break whatsoever into the cello/bass initial statement of the great Schiller theme. The traditional gap at the double-bar negates Beethoven's notation of the introduction's

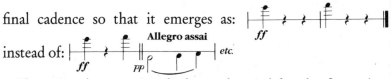

The printed ♩ = 80 is a little too hurried for the first sober enunciation of one of the world's most celebrated melodies, which may at least start with a margin more repose after the rough-and-tumble of all that has gone before, i.e. at about ♩ = 69. As in the quotations from the first three movements, which should correspond as nearly as possible to the tempos of those movements, bars 77–80 will also be mooted at the tempo to be adopted for the parallel passage, bars 237–40, which introduces the main vocal variations of the melody and for which Beethoven's metronome mark will then prove to be ideal, as will transpire in due course.

The conductor's manner in addressing the cellos and basses should be as reserved, even impassive, as possible. There is no occasion for the use of the left hand or arm, and only the gentlest of stick movements is required quietly to mark the pulse except for the momentary crescendos to *p subito*, which require some slight recognition from the rostrum; but even here the amount of extra movement should be kept to a minimum.

At bar 116, however, there must come a total change. Sempre

piano as the violas and cellos are marked, a degree of warmth should infuse their quality of expression whereas the basses now enjoy a truly independent line. The latest printing of the Leipzig Breitkopf material has at last recognized Beethoven's clear instruction in the autograph that the 2nd bassoon should play with the basses, printing the line in the part albeit in small notes. It was the conductor Walter Goehr who first drew my attention to the improbability of Beethoven having written two-part counterpoint in such a way that at one moment the lines would be two octaves and a sixth apart, and that the doubling with the 2nd bassoon was so bound up with long-standing tradition that it was the obvious answer. Weingartner had similarly been told by Stanford of the manuscript evidence but had rejected it on the grounds that the one bassoon's presence would adversely effect the other's soloistic individuality.

Solo bassoonists are often of the same opinion but none the less this is not really true at any distance from the bassoonists' stands, the tone of the 2nd player merging into that of the basses while that of the 1st always stands out clearly both by virtue of being in the high register and on account of the pronounced character of the line. At the same time it could be thought an elementary precaution to mark the 1st part *mp* and the 2nd *pp*. Moreover, once the middle strings are firmly entrenched in the melody the conductor can occupy himself wholly with the bassoon solo, encouraging and shaping the phrases and entries. In particular the separate quavers in bars such as 128–9 are to be taken quite staccato so as to accentuate the instrument's puckish individuality.

A show of even greater affection should greet the entry of the violins at letter A and it should be apparent that everyone is relishing the heart-warming glow of this lovely variation. From bar 156 the growth in joy and beauty is steady and all-pervasive until a total air of jubilation is attained at letter B. At the same time care has to be taken not to be over-demonstrative here; indeed it can be necessary to remind the horns and trumpets to keep to a single forte for the whole of the great paean. There need be no change of tempo either here or during the foregoing variations, and $\downarrow$ = 69 will still serve admirably for the poise and stateliness of this hymn-like section.

Much as it has been rightly stressed that there is now no

further crescendo for the whole of this section, it cannot but be fascinating to note that here is the famous place where Mahler is reputed to have used eight horns, four playing the melody forte, as marked, while the other four entered *pp* and rose gradually to fortissimo over the entire 24-bar period to letter C. While obviously impossible of adoption or imitation—like Stokowski's cymbals and tam-tam in the 'New World' Symphony—there is possibly occasion for regret that such imaginative strokes of creative ingenuity can no longer be countenanced.

At letter C all restrictions should be seen to be lifted and the music felt to be surging forward like a torrent in full spate. The exhilaration reaches its zenith at bars 201–2 after which the abrupt change to a brief period of lyricism requires very skilful handling. It is best not to go into crotchet beating until the poco adagio lest this is anticipated by too great a pull-up at the poco ritenente, but it needs graphic gesturing to flute and violins if they are to stay together in unsubdivided minim beating.

After only a single bar in 4 the return to alla breve is made with something of a leap as soon as the conductor has indicated to oboe and violins their resolution from Gb to F. Two stormy bars in 2 and the drums are back in *ff* for the return of the *Schreckensfanfare* in its original 3 quick beats. Here the conductor's quickness of thought and resourcefulness of gesture are stretched to the utmost, since not only have all these changes of mood and tempo to be conveyed to the orchestra but this is the moment for all the singers, soloists and chorus alike, to be brought to their feet. In respect of the four solo singers all should rise and not just the baritone, even though the other three do not actually sing until a little later.

There will be virtually no time for any very large-scale indication such as a chorus normally depends upon, and this, as much as the music itself, will be one of the prime elements to be thoroughly organized at the previous piano rehearsal, especially as with quite remarkable lack of foresight the Novello chorus score only begins at the entry of the baritone in bar 216 itself. The chorus members will have therefore to be fully familiarized with what comes before—perhaps from as far back as bar 201—so that when the timpani *ff* roll at bar 208 suddenly breaks in they will be ready and able to react to a mere glance and hand-sign from the conductor in order to spring up like one man.

With respect to the chorus formation, there is little purpose in this symphony for changing from the well-established traditional placing (with the men in the centre—tenors to the fore, basses to the rear—and framed by the sopranos and altos to the left and right respectively) to the newer and sometimes very successful style of grouping in simple block formation SATB. Naturally, however, the chorus layout will always depend to some extent on the stage or platform.

As in bar 7, the two crotchets of bar 215 should be a little spaced, after which the conductor will now simply mark the empty barlines, as again while the strings sustain during bars 224–8 and for the three bars 231–3.*

Where his recitative is concerned, no baritone ever uses the ossia C♯, which is in any case not in the autograph. At the same time it has to be conceded that the important expressive appoggiatura G on the word 'Töne' is not to be found written or printed anywhere, even though it would obviously match up with bar 16. Yet there is surely no doubt that Beethoven would have taken it for granted in a vocal line as stemming from traditional performance practice in, for example, Handel and Mozart, just as in the 'Dona Nobis Pacem' of the *Missa Solemnis*, and in Agathe's aria from Act 2 of Weber's *Der Freischütz*.

Strangely, authenticity cuts both ways in present-day performances where it conflicts with faithfulness to the letter of the printed text so that the two F's are still sometimes heard, when they sound bald and ungracious. Finally, the last phrase at the word 'freudenvollere' is certainly very long but by no means beyond the lung-power of any reputable soloist, unless he lingers with undue exhibitionism over his upper notes in bar 231. None of the word-repeating devices which make new breaths possible can be considered here, but a cleverly masked snatch-breath before an emphatic '-vollere' in the last bar may be conceded in extremis.

There is a certain danger that this whole first vocal passage may sound too stern, even angry, and that in his desire to make a great impression the baritone will be tempted to over-protest. He should be urged rather to introduce a quality of smiling reproachfulness, above all at the words 'nicht diese Töne', rather than

---

*The bar-count is as usual given here corresponding to Breitkopf. Eulenburg oddly and inconveniently restarts again from bar 1 not only at the return of the Presto in bar 208 but no less than six times during the course of the finale.

delivering some admonition of disapproval, as is so often the case.

A short gap can follow the chord at the end of bar 236 after which the Allegro assai is resumed in the same manner as before but with a little more buoyancy in the rhythm which will actually bring the tempo up to Beethoven's ♩ = 80. The chorus basses can thunder out their 'Freude' with full voice in answer to the baritone's challenging statements and the pizzicato strings must clearly still be forte before their *p* in bar 241.

The anticipatory 'Ja' for the baritone in bar 276, strong and fervent as it should already be, turns into a positive burst of enthusiasm when the chorus basses take it over in bar 284, and should be sparked by a very pronounced and invigorating up-beat.

Beethoven's *sf* emphasis on the word 'nie' is followed by a marked diminuendo to 'weinend' which has a poignancy rarely sufficiently brought out either by soloists or chorus, and can be made into something very special by the conductor, especially in the general collapse of tone from all the executants, orchestral and vocal alike, to a *pp* in bar 291.

The orchestral background to the florid vocal writing in the next variation is featherweight and can be allowed a confident delivery in all parts or it will vanish away altogether. The beat can really bounce here which will help not only the all-important 2nd horn but the string trills, as well as suggesting the exaggerated phrasing which should characterize the solo voice lines.

The changes of dynamic at 'Cherub', *f* in the solo section, *ff* at the choral repeat, are another of Beethoven's demands rarely observed. The staccato minims in bars 321–5 are also hard to get short enough from any chorus, each syllable needing to be completed and well separated from the next, there being no difference when two syllables make a single word. The chorus altos' mid-bar lead at 324 will then produce its true effect as the first of many such splendid moments Beethoven gives them.

An *Ausholen* before the monumental fermata on 'Gott' in bar 330 is clearly a *sine qua non* and the pause itself held for a period of some 4–5 bars, the strings changing bow as necessary and finishing on an up-bow. A conundrum is posed here by the diminuendo to *p* marked uniquely in the timpani part. Weingartner makes a great point of this describing it as 'death-shudders at the approach of the Almighty', but this is fanciful in the extreme. It is actually in neither the autograph nor the

Schott first edition and is certainly a weird idea for just the timpani to fade away while the entire assembled forces are holding a sustained *ff*.

There is a mass of conflicting evidence here which suggests that at some point, possibly at the time of the first performance, pressure was brought to bear on Beethoven to reduce the *ff* not only in the timpani but in other instrumental parts as well, in order to bring out the final 'Gott' the more clearly. But such a watering down of the huge outcry was certainly not part of his original intention, nor was it carried out comprehensively or authentically enough to merit its adoption today. An appreciable gap should then intervene before the extraordinary beginning of the next section.

Anything more grotesque than the first bars leading into the march it would be hard to imagine, especially as the contrabassoon, given an octave too high in all editions, should according to Beethoven's specific instructions be playing his very bottom Bb's, making an unforgettable effect.

The printed tempo mark is for once far too slow, and here again theories have been postulated in an attempt to validate the 84—even to the point of proposing that dotted crotchet is a mistake for dotted minim based on Beethoven's initial uncertainty over how best the section should be notated. But if ♩. = 84 is too laboured and dreary for so jaunty a movement, let alone the tornado of a double fugue into which it leads, ♩. = 84 is frenetic to a hair-raising degree. Further fuel has been added to the controversy by the fact that conductors have been prone to take a new and quicker tempo at letter K, and there is no doubt that if too steady a tempo has been set at the start there will be an irrepressible desire to forge strongly ahead for the orchestral fugue. Yet if on the contrary the crippling attempt to rationalize a patently incorrect metronome mark is abandoned, and a sensible tempo instigated on the basis of purely musical considerations guided by Beethoven's explicit 'Alla marcia', it is no great problem to find a speed such as ♩. = 116 which will in addition serve admirably not only for the furious orchestral section which follows the march, but for the re-entry of the chorus with its equally jaunty version of the Schiller theme, so that the entire $\frac{6}{8}$ section between bars 331 and 591 emerges as a single cumulative unit.

The stick-work is at first as economical as possible, marking only those beats on which the wind and percussion (the latter entering for the first time) actually play. The down-beats from bar 335 to 342, therefore, are little more than preparatory gestures.

Once the movement is in full swing, at for example bar 345, the ladies of the chorus should quietly and silently take their seats together with the three unoccupied solo singers, isolating to excellent advantage the male contingent, who together with the solo tenor, are so heroically featured in this variation. Here is another place where Mahler's theatrical sense is said to have led him to experiment, this time with an off-stage wind band.

The tenor soloist can be invited to sing with the utmost gusto, and to punctuate his dotted crotchets so that although these will differ to some extent from the crotchet/quaver-rest style there will still be some relationship in the swinging rhythmic punch of their delivery.

As the chorus joins in, and the orchestra grows steadily in dynamic up to fortissimo, there will inevitably be a point at which the soloist will have to struggle to surmount the surrounding forces. This is a fact of life, however, and one from which there is no escape, and one recalls with glee the tale of the distinguished tenor who complained to an international star conductor of the overwhelming power of the orchestra in the first movement of *Das Lied von der Erde*, only to receive the answer: 'My dear, if you can't make yourself heard don't sing the bloody piece.' It goes without saying that the precautionary ossias between bars 426 and 431 are always ignored; no tenor would consider for a moment leaving out these bars or of dodging any of the top B♭'s.

Following the example of the chorus ladies, the men will also take their seats once the fugue is thoroughly launched, at bar 435 one might say. To have them standing uneasily for so protracted an orchestral interlude is a distraction, and moreover there is a magnificent opportunity for dramatic effect in arranging for the whole chorus to spring to its feet in a single up-beat in full tempo before almost simultaneously bursting into song at letter M. If well rehearsed and organized this can be a galvanizing moment. As has already been said, there should be no increase or slackening of tempo in the least degree or at any juncture through the whole of this composite $\frac{6}{8}$ movement.

There is a breathless silence and the Andante maestoso brings the long-delayed re-entry of the trombones who must accordingly be highlighted. All the statements which one or more of them share with the chorus basses are characterized by pronounced declamation, each note of which has to be planted with energetic projection. This will naturally apply with especial force to the first chorus entry following the up-beat fortissimo lead, after which Beethoven's staccato marks over so many of the minims show how he intended each syllable to be again detached from its neighbour on either side—an effect difficult to obtain from a chorus when several syllables make up a single word, such as 'um-schlun-gen' and 'Mill-i-o-nen' (Beethoven showed himself to be particularly sensitive to the way the words were to be broken up where a vowel occurs) but which if insisted upon from voices and instruments alike produce an effect of unparalleled significance. In the pursuit of this the metronome mark of $\downarrow$ = 72, theoretically acceptable as it may seem, is in practice unattainable and $\downarrow$ = 66 will generally be the end product with any sizeable chorus and in most halls.

If a hammered, declamatory style of delivery is appropriate for the men's enunciations, when the ladies join in there should be the contrary suggestion of devoutness even though they too, and the wind with them, must follow the men's example in respect of the staccato minims.

At the men's 'Brüder' at letter N the beat should suggest the crotchet for the syllable '-der', without subdivision but followed by a clearance gesture, after which the down-beat of the next bar is abrogated altogether in favour of a majestic second beat lead for 'über', thus giving a style different from the next break in the chorus phrases, where a passionate *sf* from trombones and basses once more precedes the new entry on 'muss'.

As before, the up-beat lead to the upper instruments and voices in bar 618 should be soft-grained, bar 620 in particular having an ecstatic quality in the half-beat lead of the altos, tenors, and basses. In both these fervent sections the powerfully syncopated subsidiary line of the violas must not be overlooked and if suitably encouraged can, against all expectations, make an excitingly audible contribution.

The threefold sforzandos on 'muss' in bars 622–3 can never be emphatic enough, especially starting with the basses who are so easily covered unless pressed to redouble their efforts for this desperate affirmation of faith.

There should be only a slight reduction of actual pace at the Adagio ma non troppo for which the printed ♩ = 60 is completely valid, the difference from the preceding section being largely one of mood and sound quality. The sense of awe must already be felt in the instrumental bars, and both here and when the chorus takes over the phrase expressive marks such as the single-note swells, which were to become so striking an element of Schumann's style, are to be unmistakably indicated lest this so-called 'push-stroke', normally regarded as the acme of bad style, be understressed here where it constitutes a moving effect in its own right.

The conductor will need to give the chorus every possible help with a word such as 'stürzt' which is so hard to enunciate complete with its conglomerate of 's', 'z', and 't's', but the dynamic, unlike the tone quality, should not be too soft so that the *subito pp* of bar 634 can prepare a truly apprehensive expression for the word 'Ahnest'. There can then hardly be too great a contrast between the soft and loud dynamics, or too much evocation of the dramatic element of Beethoven's vision in this extraordinary episode. The 'Welt' of bar 638 is a veritable shout followed by the softest possible re-entry on 'Such' ihn'. On a larger scale the same applies to the two phrases beginning after their respective silent beats in bars 643 and 647, the magnificent rising sixth in the altos in bar 643 deserving a particular gesture with the left arm, while the silences themselves will be made as pregnant as the conductor can create.

The build-up, note by note, of the *pp* chord during bars 647–50 should be carefully and pointedly structured with indications to each group or instrument in turn. An entry to the sopranos and altos is then given as high up as the conductor may find convenient in order that they may produce as ethereal a sound as possible, conjuring up the whole wide starry heavens on a clear night. It only takes one soprano with a pronounced and penetrating vibrato to destroy the effect utterly. In the case of the men the demands are less, but they still will need to be given their entry followed by a clear enunciation of their words since the rhythm of their phrase is at variance with that of the women.

In the effort to attain the maximum atmosphere of rapt attention the conductor can never afford to lose sight of the rhythmic
co-ordination of woodwind triplet crotchets with the semiquavers of strings and timpani. The fermata on the last of these
comes suddenly without the least anticipatory rubato; the beat
simply freezes and the conductor, having kept his awareness
directed to the orchestral sections until they are all safely on
their respective pauses, holds an attitude of expectancy, even
as he continues to fix his look at the sopranos and altos, who
most of all need his Svengali-like influence if they are unswerv-
ingly to sustain the pitch of this high pianissimo chord. After
holding it as long as he dares, the conductor then gives the
altos their mighty up-beat which sets whirling the next swinging
double fugue.

The printed $\downarrow$. = 84 is again surprisingly steady; apart from
lacking the essential *Schwung*, so ponderous a tempo would place
an intolerable strain on the sopranos in what is for them the
most exacting section of the work. At the same time the 'sempre
ben marcato' does indicate that the tempo is not to be taken
too quickly.

The answer lies, as so often, in a moderate increase—perhaps
$\downarrow$. = 104—which will allow for the constant emphases on every
beat but still gives the suggestion of surging which will inspire
rather than discourage the hard-pressed singers. Nor is this too
fast a tempo for the strings to make some attempt to play the
quavers of the hectic accompaniment figures instead of just
sketching in the outline of their parts as they are so often forced
to do.

The horn and trumpet parts of this fugue seem to cry out
for completion with the notes missing from Beethoven's natural
instruments restored as advocated by Weingartner. Yet memories of such emendations in performances of the *Missa Solemnis*
as well as of this symphony by Toscanini and others have shown
how crude and unstylish even such obvious *Retuschen* can sound.

After giving the basses their towering lead at letter O, it is
the altos again who need particular attention for their percussive
'Freude's in bars 672 and 674, entries which can be made tremen-
dously arresting in the other voices but which lie in the middle
of their range as well as of the texture as a whole, and are
therefore very hard to bring through. Their next phrase in bars

675–6 is perhaps even harder to the point of being a lost cause, but they and the conductor can enjoy a moment of comradeship in the attempt.

The famous top A's of bar 717 ff. both of sopranos and of tenors are undoubtedly helped by the sight of the conductor raising a fully extended left arm and hand as if to lift them bodily to these exalted regions. Once securely poised, the basses and altos can be triumphantly set in motion on their last fortissimo double entry, the altos enjoying the glory of the rising end-phrase.

At letter R the clarity of the woodwind staccato crotchets is crucial as much for ensemble as for atmosphere. Where the chorus is concerned a similar clarity is all-important in the sharp enunciation of the words, neither 'stürzt' nor 'such' being at all easy to project.

The challenging shouts of 'Brüder' can surely be hurled out *ff* as also the string bar between (746) which must be played down and up, not with two down-bows, after which the subito piano of bar 749 can have a soft radiance over which the woodwind will clearly float peacefully upwards. It is also a beautiful effect to bring the altos out with real warmth at this further example of the special nature of Beethoven's writing for them, their descending third from C♯ to A in bars 753–4 being most affecting.

Bar 758 shows Beethoven again writing conflicting harmonies between the top and bottom of his score, as in the first movement (see above p. 176). The clash between the C♮ on the woodwind and the C♯ on the violas and chorus altos seems here again improbable on paper, yet in performance the logic of each in its own context is so convincing that there can be no case for trying to correct Beethoven's text by bringing either into line with the other.

The final upward drift of the oboes and clarinets presupposes some tempo relaxation; but the fermata should not be held too long, nor should there be any extended gap before starting the Allegro ma non tanto. One of the most dangerous characteristics of this finale can be its apparent diffuseness; any interpretation which allows the many contrasted sections to break away from one another weakens the complicated structure.*

The printed ♩ = 120 is, in the event, rather 'tanto'. For a clean and clear articulation of *pp* quavers ♩ = 100 is amply fast enough, although by the time the chorus enters at letter S the momentum of the canonic writing is bound to have carried the tempo forward to about ♩ = 112—and this is no bad thing for the jubilant nature of these sections. The four soloists will have stood some two bars after the section has begun and must remain up until the very last note of the symphony even though they have no more to sing after their solo quartet in bars 830–42.

There seems no doubt that, strange as it may seem, Beethoven positively wanted the two men to start with the word 'Tochter' in bar 767, unlike the women and against the apparent logic on the grounds of which, no doubt, the bar was changed in all later editions.

The chorus depends on a clear lead for their entry in bar 795 after which it is the soprano soloist who hangs on the conductor's beat until bar 801. In the next ten bars, however, it is all too possible to overconduct, so many and precipitous are the kaleidoscopic events which call for direction: the sudden *ff* of the orchestra when the chorus abruptly ceases in bar 803; the equally sudden drop to *p* with an immediate return to *ff* for the chorus's re-entry at the half-beat of bar 806 with repeated rinforzandos on the reiterations of 'Menschen'; all need to be communicated with clear projection and enthusiasm and yet with gestures as economical as the conductor's technique and his self-possession can command. Then from one moment to another we are in a slow tempo with chorus and wind holding a diminuendo crotchet and looking expectantly for the conductor's next indication.

This Poco Adagio will need to be a little more spacious than the exact ♩ = ♩ which is often advocated in principle. Nor should any concept of a relationship between the slow and quick elements of this section be taken to imply that a quaver beat could yet be desirable. A wide 4 in a bar at about ♩ = 48–50 will allow

---

*Even so minor a consideration as the 7-fold bar-count in Eulenburg could add untoward weight to the argument, sometimes postulated, that this last symphonic movement by the greatest symphonist of all time lacks unified cohesion.

for real tenderness in the violins' interjections and for an expressive manipulation of the sopranos' grace-notes in bar 812, which are best given with the fingers of the left hand rather than with the stick.

The resumption of the Allegro in bar 814 will be at its full tempo of $\downarrow$ = 112; there is no longer occasion for the steadier start called for by the quaver figuration of the introductory bars, after which the procedure is the same as before until the entry of the soloists.

Bar 832 is another of those controversial places of which this supreme masterpiece is so disconcertingly full. The printed scores suggest that the chorus's 'Menschen' in this bar would be enunciated weightily in the tempo of the Poco adagio, and under many conductors it has in the past often been interpreted in this way despite Weingartner's verdict that, on the contrary, the two syllables should be delivered in the previous quick tempo. As a matter of fact, the double-bar given in modern editions at this juncture is not present either in the autograph or the Schott first edition, and moreover Beethoven only wrote the words 'Poco adagio' above the strings and solo voices, which would certainly seem to indicate that he did not intend it to apply to the chorus. But if a ponderous 'Men-schen' is thus clearly out of order, there is still something to be said for giving some weight to these two crotchets, ideally by marking both with the left arm, however quickly, rather than leaving them to be peremptorily dismissed as they would be in the full precipitous tempo.

The stick is now concerned with sustaining and supporting the solo voices, whose phrases it should shape with careful clarity, including breath indications. These bars are so much the singers' territory that it is easy to neglect the woodwind and strings, who can be quite unsure where to place their notes unless given every entry and chord change. It is convenient in this respect to keep well apart the two elements under control, the face and stick always identifying themselves with the singers while the left hand gives the orchestral players the placing of their background phrases and chord changes.

It is a matter of urgency for the sake of the singers to keep the tempo as flowing as their elaborate embroideries will allow even though the illusion of some correlation with the previous choral Poco adagio should be created. At a flexible speed of ♩ = ± 56 these strictures should reasonably be met.

In bar 834 the soloists need guidance at the second beat with a twist of the stick and a suggestion of subdivision, while simultaneously the clarinets and bassoons will be brought in. This composite operation tends to confuse the strings who have to be warned against misunderstanding with the danger of some players creeping in too soon. In the following bar the soprano, tenor, and bass should take their breath at the comma before 'wo dein', unlike the alto who continues to the end of the bar, so bringing her line into prominence.

From here on it is above all important that each bar be phrased as an entity in itself, the singers taking the down-beats as new points of ensemble and departure, but especially those voices with solo figurations: bar 836, soprano; 837, alto and tenor in duet; 838, tenor (who must not simply go on but must clearly be launched on a new solo phrase or he will be bound to jeopardize the ensemble); 839–40, bass who—unlike the tenor—should indeed be encouraged to continue over the 2-bar arch so that the tempo will even be moving forward a fraction, this being of major benefit to the soprano who is entering one of the cruellest tests of endurance and breath control in the repertoire.

In bar 841 only the tenor breathes at the barline, the other three all at the third beat, including the soprano even if she has been forced to cheat earlier. This is the only way to last out bar 842, the fermata of which can only begin after the strings have been taken off with the fourth beat, and is thus inescapably a very long bar. The chord is pointedly brought to an end by means of a clear indication for the 't' of 'weilt'.

The Poco allegro is again a passage demanding an exceptionally clear beat, starting very steadily but changing to a considerable accelerando, which takes effect almost immediately and so is able to career forward right up to the Prestissimo with its accumulation of wind and percussion. For this ♩ = 132 is an astonishingly tame mark; a more suitable air of universal jubilation would be given by a tempo of at least ♩ = 156. There must be a whirlwind quality to this closing section which should again, however, not mislead the conductor into an over-extravagant manner. Once the strings are brought in, followed on their very heels by the chorus, his gestures will be orientated less by time-beating than by evocation of the outstanding events; indeed there could well be bars in which no actual conventional beating is necessary at all, such as 878 (where the orchestra can hardly be said to need any direction between the chorus's outbursts of 'Seid umschlungen') or 897 and 901 where the impetus given to the chorus in the previous bars more than carries the situation until it becomes sensible to place the sopranos' minims.

On the other hand bars needing especial accentuation or encouragement are: the 'Brüder' in bar 864 after the three and a half bars of sustained 'Welt!' (this is in no sense the end of a phrase even though it comes as the last bar of a 4-bar period, but must be prepared with all the necessary breath for a renewed attack on both syllables); bars 872–3, where the rising alto crotchets on 'wohnen' can be brought out in a surging crescendo; the chorus minims between bars 880–94, to be punctuated as shown by the staccato wind minim and indicated for this purpose by an inexorably pounding beat (provision must nevertheless be made for extra emphasis on the two fortissimo 'Welt's in bars 887 and 893, the former being additionally capped by the powerful half-beat lead for the sforzando 'Dies(en)').

From bar 903 the bar-count becomes less obvious and it is of primary concern for the conductor to be aware of the irregularities in his innermost subconscious if he is not to share in the listener's surprise when the precipitation is abruptly halted for the last Maestoso paean of praise to joy. The actual period changes, after what has been a consistently 4-bar structure, consist of one 3-bar phrase at bars 903–5 followed by an isolated 4-bar unit starting at Beethoven's first reiteration of *ff*, which leaves two more 3-bar phrases before the arrival of the $\frac{3}{4}$ Maestoso. The isolated 4-bar period of bars 906–9 is characterized by the winds' echo of the chorus's 'Götterfunken' as are the two 3-bar periods where again the wind re-enact the chorus's outburst, only to be interrupted by the culminating 'Tochter' which puts the brake on the whole frenzied outpouring, the conductor being left holding what for a moment will seem like a huge fortissimo fermata.

The illusion is real and should not be avoided. The next beats the conductor gives are at first only those which will control the wind and chorus on the syllables '-ter aus', two quaver beats projected with as much exultation as is consistent with clarity and dignity. Nevertheless, the timing of the upheld dotted crotchet must in reality be strictly measured in quaver units (not, of course, crotchets as indicated by the metronome mark, which at ♩ = 60 is once again inappropriately fast for this supreme moment of glory). A dramatic gesture has then to succeed these two quaver indications which will cut off the grandeur of the massed vocal and instrumental chord in order to prepare the new and ecstatic *p subito* of 'Elysium'. The strings will require especial attention not merely at their entry, in anticipation of which they will be looking up expectantly, but at the fifth beat of bar 917 (where the chorus are again taken off) for their demisemiquaver pattern, taken martellato on the string. This has to sound strongly rhythmic and thus depends on a positive quaver pulse by way of preparation as well as for the syncopated beat which initiates it. A pulsation of ♪ = 72 gives scope for just such control as well as allowing all the necessary breadth for the fervent outpouring of the chorus's last declamation.

The final Prestissimo can go even faster than its predecessor, perhaps as rapidly as ♩ = 176, but it only turns into a real semibreve unit of beating at bar 932 where Beethoven unleashes a veritable tornado emphasized by the renewed *ff* of both the timpani and the trumpets who, together with the wind, are shown in the autograph as changing from two rinforzandos per bar to a continuing and all-pervasive intensity of volume, this also giving the pretext for the conductor's change to a single beat per bar; at the end the woodwind soars upwards in strict time and the symphony ends quite suddenly in a blaze of light. There may still be many who will remember Furtwängler's performances of the 1930s where, if the opening of the first movement was the softest, the symphony's conclusion was the most exalted and tumultuous that had ever been heard.

It is now firmly believed that Schiller had at one time planned his poem as an Ode to Freedom 'An die Freiheit', but was constrained to adapt it for political reasons. It will have been an experience of almost unbearable poignancy when a Berlin performance of this hymn to the unquenchable spirit of man by one of the greatest creators of all time was recently given, substituting 'Freiheit' for 'Freude', in celebration of the sudden and unforeseeable dismantling of the dreaded Wall.

Index

CW01021436

Voyage of Prosilios
Newhaven to Corfu

YUGOSLAVIA

A D R I A T I C

UMBRIA

Dubrovnik

ABRUZZI

S E A

ROME

T Y R R H E N I A N   S E A

ALBANIA

Bari

Naples

PUGLIA

Monopoli

Brindisi

LUCANIA

Taranto

Otranto

Fano

CORFU

CALABRIA

Turn Right for Corfu

To Gwen & sic

with very much love

Matt & Maureen

Christmas 1977

Turn Right for Corfu

CECIL LEWIS

Illustrated by David Knight

THE TRAVEL BOOK CLUB
121 CHARING CROSS ROAD,
LONDON WC2H OEB

HUTCHINSON & CO (Publishers) LTD
3 Fitzroy Square, London W1

London Melbourne Sydney Auckland
Wellington Johannesburg Cape Town
and agencies throughout the world

First published 1972

© Cecil Lewis 1972

© Illustrations Hutchinson & Co. (Publishers) Ltd. 1972

Printed in Great Britain
by The Anchor Press Ltd,
Tiptree, Essex

ISBN 0 09 110550 1

Contents

By the same author

Autobiographical

Sagittarius Rising
The Trumpet is Mine
Farewell to Wings

Novels

Pathfinders
Challenge to the Night
Yesterday's Evening

The Unknown Warrior
(translation of *Le Tombeau Sous
l'Arc de Triomphe* by Paul Raynal)

TO HER
WITHOUT WHOM...

'To Begin With'

'BEGIN at the beginning, go on to the end. Then stop!' This Royal Command, given by the King of Hearts to the White Rabbit, has a sort of nutty logic about it. It sounds obvious, simple. If you're going to tell a story, what else can you do? But when you sit with pen poised, thinking 'Now where shall I start?', then it turns out to be practically impossible to pinpoint the real beginning. It recedes and dissolves into all the wishes and longings that created it. To follow these up is simply to plunge deeper into the labyrinth. It's like chasing rainbows to discover the point at which 'it all began'.

So at least I found when I started to delve back into the beginnings of our trip from Newhaven to Corfu. Soon I was rummaging about into things that happened over thirty years ago. In 1937, after six months on luxury pay in a Hollywood studio, I set out for Panama and boarded a tramp steamer for Tahiti. As the old boat nodded her way through the Trades, I spent many hours browsing through the writings of great South Sea pioneers—Roggwein, Wallace, Bougainville, Cook. It was then perhaps that the desire arose, almost subconsciously, to emulate them and discover the Pacific, as they had done, in my own boat under sail. The idea, fed by my imagination, grew underground. By the time war began it had surfaced and I had started to teach myself to design yachts. For by then the original plan had escalated. It was no longer merely to sail the Pacific, but to sail my own boat across the Pacific. And not even just my own boat, but one I had designed myself. Soon it grew even larger. Why stop at the Pacific? Why not sail right round the world?

I began to acquire a library on ocean sailing from Slocum onwards. There was practically nothing written on the subject that I hadn't read. I bought books on design. I pored over the volumes of Uffa Fox. I joined the Little Ship Club. I acquired drawing boards and ship's curves and splines and lead pigs. Soon I was deep in the mysteries of midsections, entries, runs, diagonals, centres of displacement, buoyancy and pressure, heeled areas, the metacentric shelf. As the bombs rained down on London in 1940, in the basement of the Air Ministry, I kept my mind off direct hits by working, sometimes right through the night, on my design for an ocean cruiser. This dream for 'after the war' helped, more than I realised at the time, to keep me going during that tragic year.

This passion for yacht design lasted all through the war. I became quite proficient. My designs were published in the *Yachting World*. I won competitions. I made the acquaintance of Robert Clark and his exceptional skill and experience gave me a target of excellence to aim for. Even today I still think that yacht design is one of the most desirable and interesting of careers. It requires a balance between a certain amount of technical know-how and an aesthetic appreciation of form. It requires craftsmanship and an 'eye'. When these are matched the result is a special rare kind of beauty. Nothing is more beautiful than a sailing ship and, unquestionably, a boat that is not beautiful will not sail well.

Anyhow, by the end of the war I had become an almost unique phenomenon—a designer of yachts who had never been to sea! A theoretical sailor! Ridiculous as it sounds, I don't think the effort was entirely wasted. I have a sharper appreciation of everything connected with the sea because of it. To give some idea of how far theory can take you, I will give an instance.

I had been posted to command the R.A.F. staging post in Athens when we reoccupied Greece in 1944. My drawing board had been left behind in the U.K., but my mind was full of boats. We had a pretty tough time that winter when the Greek partisans turned on us and it was touch and go whether we should not be driven out of Greece altogether. But when the affair was over, one spring afternoon my adjutant and I took a jeep and pottered along the dirt road to the Bay of Salamis where the indomitable Greeks were already beginning to build replacements to the 10,000 caiques they had lost during the German occupation. The fascination of seeing wooden hulls take shape along the seashore in the open air, the smell of newly sawn wood, the primitive tools handled with such skill, all this, coupled with the fact that it was the first day of relaxation after an anxious time, sharpened all the senses and made everything imprint itself clearly on the mind. Suddenly I saw, moored about 100 yards offshore, the bare hull of a large yacht. She was stripped right down. Nothing but the hull remained and yet there was something about her lines, the way she sat on the water, the perfect proportion of her overhangs and, above all, the lilt of her sheer, that set my blood tingling as if I were listening to fine music. For to those who have not been caught by this particular form of beauty I should explain that, of all the lines in the design of a yacht, the most subtle, elusive and difficult to bring into harmony with the rest is the one than runs from the bow to the stern, the 'top' line of the boat—the sheer, as it is called. It is the line by which you can unfailingly recognise a designer when he has reached any eminence. Rhodes, Stevens, Fife, Clark: they all sign themselves by the sheer.

So there lay that lovely hull in the calm sunny waters of the Bay of Salamis, looking terribly forlorn and forgotten in the aftermath of war and I couldn't take my eyes off her. 'I'll bet my boots,' I said to my adjutant, who knew nothing about boats whatever, 'that boat's by Fife. It must be by Fife. Nobody else could draw that sheer. But what on earth is she doing here in Greece? How did she get here?' I stood rooted to the spot. She was very large. They didn't build them so big any more. There was only one hull by Fife that I knew, so large, so perfect—but it seemed impossible. And yet she must be, she was, *Suzanne*.

The picture (taken by Beken of Cowes) of *Suzanne* under full sail is one of the finest marine photos ever taken. I had first seen it in one of Uffa's books and I see it still. It is the epitome of the pre-1st-war days of big sailing schooners, large crews and all the opulence and ease of an England now irrevocably gone. She is coming bustling down the Solent with the wind on her starboard quarter and everything she can carry set alow and aloft. She is all a-rustle with wind and foam and sunshine. 'Who wants to go to heaven,' I remember thinking, 'when they can have this here?'

I rushed down to the shore where a sailor was mending his nets and overwhelmed the poor man with questions that tumbled out of me in my excitement. What was that boat doing here? Who did she belong to? Was she for sale? What had happened to her masts, her sails, her gear? Was she British? What was her name?

In his few words of English he managed to answer. 'Yes, British. She is *Suzanne.*'

It was, I think, my best reward for those years of study. I was elated to have recognised her and yet deeply concerned to see her there, no more than a derelict hulk. I wanted to see her closer, to stand on her decks, to feel her under me. Would the sailor row us out? Certainly. When we clambered aboard it was dreadful. The varnish had peeled off. The perfect teak decks were lifting and rotting. There was absolutely nothing left—except the bare bones of a masterpiece.

'She is to be broken up next week,' said the Greek.

'Broken up! For God's sake! No!'

He smiled and shrugged. 'There are sixteen tons of lead in her keel. And lead, you understand—now. It is worth a fortune.'

I went to the Navy. They could stop it. They must. Such a ship must be saved. They were very sympathetic. But—there was nothing to be done. When I went along that coast a fortnight later *Suzanne* had gone.

So there it is. All that is twenty-five years ago now. After the war life intervened. I never built the dream cruiser. I never even set out on a circumnavigation. But the desire to make some sort of a long cruise must have smouldered on, for when at seventy the opportunity to buy a boat and make the trip out to Corfu came up, I leapt at it. The days when I could afford to design and build were gone. Only the interior layout was possible and on this I lavished all those wartime years of study. Everything began to revive. It was a happy time.

But the hard fact remained—I was a theoretical sailor. And if you struggle on through these pages you will see it in practically every paragraph. I knew quite a lot about how things should be done, but I knew nothing about doing them. I still don't know much. All the incidents which would be molehills to a real sailing man were mountains to us—for my wife didn't know a cleat from a halliard and had even a built-in resistance to knowing. But she struggled on with the indomitable devotion of a good wife.

So because today many people, amateurs like ourselves, are taking to the sea, the practical details of our trip, our route, our experiences, our mishaps and mistakes, and, above all, our enjoyment, may be of interest to others who set out in a small boat in search of adventure. Anyone who obeys fairly simple rules of caution and common sense can sail quite well enough to get from A to B without mishap. The fun would be less if it all went smoothly. To do it you don't need the theory of yacht design, but you do need determination to get there and a respect for and love of the sea.

I

The Canals

I

The Canals

AT 1100 HOURS the swing bridge opened, the gates of the Port de Plaisance swung wide and a gaggle of yachts streamed through into Calais outer harbour. An irritated queue of motorists held up on either side of the bridge cursed the delay and our 7 m.p.h. gait, but for the moment we had the priority and waved graciously to them as we passed. It was July 15th, 1969. Our little company of cruisers was bound on holiday to various Channel ports. Charles and Susie, who ought never to have been out of the Thames, were bound for Ramsgate. Barry Paton had an unlikely assignment to pick up his wife on the end of Southend Pier. Another couple were heading up to Bruges, another down to Cherbourg. As we streamed out, a wag on a nearby sloop, who had heard of our destination in the marina bar the night before, hailed us. 'Turn right for Corfu!' he shouted.

Although that magical island was some 2,000 miles away, you have to make a beginning and we did indeed turn right—or as the *aficionados* would say, put the helm hard a' starboard—and cruised slowly into the Bassin Carnot. It was a desolation of grey walls, black barges and a row of praying-mantis cranes immobilised in threatening attitudes. No sign of the sea lock which was open only for one hour either side of high water. The whole place seemed deserted, save for one lonely bargee. We hailed him anxiously and he thumbed us further in. At last, tucked away in a corner, we caught sight of a black shadow in a black wall. It looked minute, but this must be it. It didn't seem much of a front door to the canal system which was to be our route for the next month and lead us to the romance of the Côte d'Azur and the glories of Greece. We approached it cautiously. For, in spite of the coaching of the 'old hands', the prospect of the locks, frankly, intimidated us.

'Just come alongside,' they said. 'Fanny can hang on with the boathook while you climb the ladder. Then she just heaves up the lines, you put them round the bollards and stand between them holding the tails. As the boat comes up, gather them in. When she's up, cast off, jump aboard and there you are! Nothing to it. It's a piece of cake.'

Now at seventy-one (my advanced age) climbing slimy iron ladders is not an ideal form of recreation and Fanny (my wife) has no more idea of heaving lines than she has of turning cartwheels. It would be a 'challenge', of course; but repeated 200 times over—as it would have to be before we reached the Med—it might conceivably pall. However, here we were, for it. I hooted twice on the Swiss railway horn I had purchased from the marine store of Mr. Ffoulkes and nosed into the narrow entrance. It looked, at that moment, suspiciously like a coffin. A man in blue overalls slouched to the edge of the wall and regarded us with a sad, disdainful air. Then he signed for us to throw up our lines. The relief on our faces must have been obvious. I wouldn't have to climb that wet rusty ladder—and we had overshot it anyhow.

'*Quel est le profondeur de cet écluse?*' I asked in my best French, hoping to modify his pitying glance.

'I shall drop you about a metre,' he announced and disappeared.

Drop us! We should be going *down!* Below sea level! Somehow the idea of being three feet below the entire English Channel horrified me. As the lock gates swung to behind us, I imagined the whole weight of the oceans bursting in. I eyed those gates, hypnotised, but surprisingly they seemed to hold and a few moments later there was a clatter as our cast-off lines were thrown back on deck. The man accepted some cigarettes as if he didn't really want them and we chugged out into the Canal de Calais. We had made it. We were in.

It was a glorious day and we celebrated this first step by tying up between two filthy barges to lunch. Before we were through the watchmaker arrived. Only three hours before he had taken my wristwatch, soaked with sea water, and promised to clean it, dry it and return it to wherever he should find us along the canal. This he did, adding a six months' guarantee and confirming our opinion that Calais was a very affable little town and its marina a gem. When he had toasted success to the trip in our best brandy and left us, we cast off and set out towards St. Omer, navigating gingerly past a string of barges parked along a strip of water which seemed inconveniently narrow. The dilapidated outskirts of Calais lined the roads that ran either side. Before we had gone a kilometre we met our first obstacle—a bridge across the canal. Cars, bicycles and pedestrians streamed over it. How were we going to get past that?

'It is called the Pont de Vic,' said Fanny with her nose in our bible, *The Inland Waterways of France*. 'Shouldn't you hoot?'

I blew a long imperious blast on Mr. Ffoulkes and a minute later, to my amazement, barriers descended, cars halted, the bridge swung up and we swept through waving thanks to the operator in his cabin and feeling somewhat ashamed of disrupting the Calais traffic. Would a mere toot always produce such an immediate effect?

It would not. The next lift bridge did not respond to the treatment. Repeated hoots produced no effect whatever. The operator's cabin was empty. The whole place seemed asleep. Now what should we do? Rather gingerly we came alongside the iron railing that divided the canal from the road. I tied up and stepped ashore. The proprietor of the estaminet on the corner indicated that the bridge-keeper lived in the house across the road with a green door. I knocked. A young man with his mouth full opened it.

'And your bridge?' I asked him. 'Doesn't it open?'

' '*Faut quandmême manger*,' he grumbled and put on his cap.

We proceeded with growing confidence through and under other bridges for almost an hour before coming to our first real 'inland' lock. It was on a bend. Now we were in the country and a sudden plague of horseflies had set us slapping and swearing. The canal seemed narrower than ever. As we approached, the gates opened and, to our consternation, out came a barge! A barge! What was it doing in 'our' canal? The huge black empty monster charged us like a rhino and—I am still convinced—never saw us or knew we were there.

In a panic I turned abruptly into the bank. Then I reversed

to pull the stern in; but I had the wheel over the wrong way. So out we shot right under his foaming bow. I leapt on to the coachroof, seized the boathook to fend us off, crash went our stern against his iron sides, bashing us away, torrents of bad language poured down on us. Then he was gone, leaving us shaken and speechless at the encounter.

We took very good care after that never to come close up to a lock with closed gates, always to stand back two to three hundred yards to see what was coming out. We learned to approach any kind of hazard very slowly, so as not to get into a panic if we made mistakes—and we made plenty.

By evening we had passed through the narrow canals of Calais and the River Aa. The flat country of northern France means that locks are widely separated and on that first after-noon we had covered more than sixty kilometres. As we had worked out our daily average as forty-five kilometres, this was good going in half a day. We had bypassed St. Omer and emerged on to the Canal de Neufossé, a splendid waterway, sixty metres wide, recently modernised to carry heavy traffic to Belgium. It had been very hot and the sun had already begun to lobster our arms and legs. To save my aged brains from boiling, Fanny had fitted me with a paper plate on an elastic band, which, if it wasn't exactly elegant, at least lowered the temperature.

Then the sun went down and we tasted one of the greatest pleasures of the canals. At 7.30 the locks close and do not open till 6.30 the following morning. No traffic moves. A wonderful peace falls over the ribbons of still water—and you can stop anywhere you like. So we shut off the engine, tied up to the bank and began to think about supper. In the distance a tractor was making hay. A boy passed along the towpath with a rake. There wasn't a house in sight. So what with the crisp French bread, the delicate cheese and the light vin du pays, we turned in with a sigh of content. This was the life.

*   *   *

As every prospective traveller through the canals of Europe knows, there is a book called *The Inland Waterways of France* which gives, in meticulous detail, every lock, bridge and port in the entire system and to open the map of the continental canals is to be filled with astonishment. A complex net of green ribbons stretches from Le Havre to the Rhine, from Calais to Marseille, joins Bordeaux to Avignon, Paris to Amsterdam, Holland to Switzerland and the North Sea to the Danube and the Black Sea.

This web of canals, navigable rivers, tunnels and lake reservoirs is a viable commercial transport system. Comparatively unknown and unseen, tens of thousands of barges carry millions of tons of bulk cargoes, coal, sand, timber, grain, fuel, cement, all over Europe. Thousands of families, dedicated to life on the canals, operate these barges, for life on the canals is, or was, strictly a family affair. The canal people are born, marry, bring up their families and die without ever leaving the canals. Children and old women are to be seen at the wheel, cars and playpens stand on the hatches, flowers and pot plants decorate the wheelhouses, washing hangs on the lines. Travelling at 5 m.p.h. and covering perhaps twenty-five miles a day, they are relaxed and friendly people and accept the growing intrusion of yachtsmen good humouredly—provided their visitors keep to the etiquette of the water. This is the courtesy of the canals—never to pass a barge without being waved on by its helmsman, never to jump the queue at a lock, always to remember that these are people working an all-the-year-round eleven-hour day, that you are a guest and sometimes a delay and irritation to them. If you appreciate this and take an interest in their craft, often kept so clean and smart they could be sent straight to a stand at the Boat Show, they will reciprocate in many small ways, helping you with your lines, giving advice about the locks and tunnels ahead, inviting you to moor alongside them at places where it is difficult to get ashore. The elderly are often illiterate. They can neither read nor write, for their entire lives have been lived on the water, but they can place a 350-ton barge to an inch and know every lock in Europe. But now things are changing. Children must go ashore for compulsory education, leaving their slow-moving home for weeks at a time. With TV, radio and the craze for speed, many do not come back. The simple and wholesome way of life is being undermined (like everything else) by so-called progress. The entire system is in jeopardy. Will there be enough crews to man the barges in fifty years' time?

Every boat going south has finally to join up with the River Saône and follow it to Lyons, the Rhône and the sea. Our route from Calais was the most direct we could find and it now led us through the industrial north-east of France, an uninspiring area of coal mines, derricks and slag heaps, through towns with familiar names to the troops of World War I—Bethune, Douai, Lens, Cambrai, Peronne. The canals joining these towns form the main artery linking Paris with Belgium and Holland and the traffic is heavy. Barge after barge with their great bow waves thundered past us, their big deep-throated diesels raising a foamy wake. Some towed others behind them, some were hooked up to tractors on the towpath. But the new canals are wide and, in spite of their bulk, barges raise surprisingly little wash. Here we found our copy of the invaluable *Inland*

Waterways out of date. Deep, twenty-five-foot locks have replaced the older smaller ones, the 'staircase' locks have disappeared. All are electrically operated and some even have that boon to the yachtsman, the 'rising bollard' which floats up with the boat. All the same, the huge guillotine gates, lifting straight up out of the water, have quite a claustrophobic effect when you get inside and twenty-five feet, though it doesn't sound much, looks a very high wall indeed when seen from the bottom. The whole business has become efficient and impersonal. The operator, with his buttons, sitting high up in his cabin overlooking the gates, has no contact with the men on board the boats he puts through. Green or red lights tell the waterman what to do. Occasionally loudspeakers crack out instructions to hold back, come on or to climb up to his cabin to present papers. Modernisation and officialdom may speed the traffic, but they produce no improvement in personal relations. The only short-tempered lock-keepers we met were those who never went out among the boats.

On the second day out of Calais we made a surprising and pleasant discovery. Our Sharp Automatic Pilot was so accurate we could set it to steer us right down the centre of the long straight reaches. This freed us from the tedium of the wheel and at first we watched it, fascinated at its quick, delicate corrections. Then we left it to its own devices and both went up to sit on the front of the coachroof. Here the engine noise was reduced to a mere purr and the wind cooled us. Then, as we passed a bridge, the boat suddenly sheered wildly to port. I leapt for the cockpit. Before I got there it had sheered back, as wildly, to starboard. Then it straightened up again. What had happened? I sat and kept a close watch on it from then on; but it was not until the third bridge, I tumbled to the reason. The magnetic field from the iron in the bridge disturbed the compass and the wheel blindly followed it! After that we took care to cut out the automatic going under bridges.

But, alas, on the third day our wonderful third hand mutinied. The rudder no longer answered the instructions of the compass. It had packed up. We didn't get it working for the next 400 miles and I fumed at having £300 worth of new, worthless equipment on board. At Marseille the proverbial 'expert' appeared, tightened two screws left loose at the works and we were back in business.

* * *

If we made good time through the canals—and, in fact, we covered the 450 miles, 220 locks and six tunnels in twenty travelling days—it was due more than anything else to that boon to all canal-going yachtsmen, the Russell Hook.

At Newhaven we had been fortunate enough to meet Dr. Russell, an elderly mariner with an equally elderly twenty-four-foot cruiser in which he has made a good many trips through the continental canals, most of them singlehanded. When he heard we were soon to be off he offered us the benefit of his experience. 'Go to the farrier,' he said, 'and get yourself a hook.'

So next day we wandered inland through the quiet Sussex lanes, past Piddinghoe in the direction of Lewes, till we found a blacksmith. In the gloom of the forge, with the acrid smell of hammered iron and damp cinders, we drew out a hook on the back of an envelope. Two days later we went back, and the farrier, after giving us a long and informative disquisition on the shoeing of racehorses (which was his bread and butter), presented us with two fine wrought-iron hooks at a price, since he said he had enjoyed doing it, of five shillings.

I have already said that, to me at any rate, the nightmare of the locks was climbing those narrow slippery ladders, wondering how, with my stiff old knees, I should ever get up—since the ladders end below the top of the wall. The Russell Hook put an end to all that. Only once did I have to negotiate a ladder.

This is the technique. You simply drive into the lock, make for the ladder (there is usually one on each side) and affix the hook to the nearest convenient rung. As the water comes in and the boat rises, you move the hook up from rung to rung and so arrive painlessly and triumphantly at the top. As we gained experience we found that hooking on from the cockpit, aft, still allowed the bows to swing out across the lock when, as it sometimes happens, the water boils in fiercely. So we evolved a modification. We middled the hook into a line and made fast one end to the cleat forward. The hook itself was actually placed a little forward of amidships and the other end led back over the rear cleat and I held the tail in my hand. Sitting on the coachroof, the mate slipped on the hook as we passed and when I pulled on my end of the line we were snugly moored. Being forward of amidships, the hook held in the bow and checked the tendency to an outward swing. The same technique could be used either going up or down in a lock and our main preoccupation as we approached was confined to locating the position of the ladder. Set into the wall, it is sometimes quite difficult to see. We only met one lock with no ladders at all, but as it was only a five-foot drop, that didn't matter. The Russell Hook is the greatest labour-saving device ever invented for the peace of mind of a lock-nervous yachtsman and I heartily recommend it to all those braving the month's hard labour the canals imply. I can still hear the clank of ours as it fell reassuringly on to over 200 iron ladders!

*   *   *

Back in Newhaven before setting out, the 'old hands', friends with years of experience, pronounced our boat *Prosilios* (the Greek equivalent of 'Sunbound') 'just right for the canals', so I might as well give some idea of the sort of boat in which we made our 2,000-mile trip.

She has a fibreglass hull, twenty-six feet in length, and is a motor cruiser with an accommodation plan to my own design. This consists of a thwartship galley forward, with oven stove, Electrolux gas refrigerator and a three-foot sink and draining board. Stove and sink are fitted with removable tops and so are out of sight when not in use, providing a very large working surface and chart table. The galley is not divided from the main cabin, which has settee bunks either side, seven feet long, between which we can put up a 'caravan-type' four-foot folding table for meals. Deep shelves for books, cameras, torches, bottles and all the miscellaneous gear that seems to accumulate are tucked in behind the backs of the settees. There are sealed windows all round, fluorescent lighting and a hatchway in the roof. So the entire interior of the boat is on the open plan and is big and airy for the size of the boat. Aft of the bunks come the wardrobe on one side and the loo (which houses the dining table when folded away and the bathing ladder) on the other. A step up leads to an open cockpit, seven feet in length and six feet in width. Here on the port side is the wheel, the engine controls, the automatic pilot, the folding helmsman's seat. To starboard are lockers to hold two gas bottles with outboard drains. All this lies under a fibreglass hood. The rear half of the cockpit is a deep (three-foot) seat which is also an 'occasional' bed. Under it is the engine—a Perkins 4/107 diesel—with storage lockers on either side. Fuel and water are housed under the cockpit floor. The whole cockpit can be totally enclosed by a nylon hood. When the side curtains are zipped into place it makes a cool roomy extra cabin.

Right up forward is another hatchway giving access to the chain locker and a big spool on which to wind twenty fathoms of nylon anchor line. It also houses a water hose, spare warps, buckets, brushes and so on. The hatch itself is hinged aft so that, when we hook it open, it makes a fine airscoop and blows a current of air right through the boat. In the canals it was often ninety degrees in the cabin and that air flow just about saved us from heat prostration.

Prosilios is no greyhound. She has a cruising speed of about seven knots and will do nine knots all out. She uses about a gallon of fuel an hour and has a range of 300 miles on her main tank. In addition, we carried emergency supplies of fuel and water. Months of careful planning resulted in her being fitted out to meet every contingency we could think of. We carried extra filters and engine spares, Beaufort life-jackets, safety harness, distress flares, lifebuoys, first-aid kits, tools and stores for three months. We were equipped with two anchors, 100 fathoms of warps in twenty-fathom lengths and eight large fenders, besides thirty charts, two folding deck-chairs and two pairs of gumboots. Through the canals our sides were festooned with ten scooter tyres—half of which we wiped off en route.

But all this, plus a big outfit of winter and summer clothes, stowed away so neatly that the cabin always seemed un-cluttered and airy and welcoming to visitors coming aboard. The two of us lived happily in Prosilios for three months and apart from a few scratches she looks as smart today as when she left the yard. Fibreglass is a wonderful material.

Although the same old hands were somewhat reticent about the sea-keeping qualities of the hull and various acquaintances along the route looked at us goggle-eyed saying: 'Have you come all the way from England in that!', it is fair to say she never gave us the least anxiety at sea. She was buoyant and dry, if a bit skittish in a seaway. For basically there are two types of hulls—those that float on the water and those that float in it. Ours fell into the former category. The hull drew little more than a foot of water, so she was like a cork, bobbing about, often with far too much movement for comfort. But she rose to twelve-foot swells like a seagull and, although we met nothing worse than a Force 5 sea, she never shipped a pint of green water.

*   *   *

By the time we reached Peronne we were through the industrial belt. We had negotiated two neon-lit, well-ventilated tunnels and been soaked to the skin in two thunderstorms, so we decided on a half-day halt to clean up, do the washing and go into Peronne to shop.

A co-operative lock-keeper produced a pretty young greengroceress, who in her big Citroën whirled us into town to buy bread, cheese and mouth-watering peaches. By lunchtime we were shipshape and moved off. Now we were in the broad undulating Somme country I remembered from the First World War. Cornfields swept upwards from the canal, ploughs had already been busy in the rich earth, huge white groups of silos dwarfed the Norman churches, barges were being loaded with waterfalls of golden wheat. Sometimes, on the curves, the barge ahead seemed to be sliding through the fields. It was a wonderful afternoon, but though the thunder had cleared the air, the heat had returned and we were glad to stop at nightfall, with only one more lock to go before we turned off these tiring main waterways with their heavy traffic. Then we should be on the lateral canals that connect the Oise and the Aisne to the Marne where a mere 114 locks would separate us from the Saône, the Rhône and the sea. So we tied up above Noyon for the night.

Next morning a thick mist lay over everything. Absolute stillness. Nothing stirred. As we were a bit low in water, I walked along to the lock-keeper's cabin, offered him an English cigarette and asked if we could move into the lock and fill up with water from its hose. 'Help yourself!' He opened the gates and we moved in. The locks on the Canal du Nord are twenty-five to thirty feet deep and take two barges, which means they are over 250 feet long. As we were descending, we entered the full lock and floated above the top of the wall. We moored lightly to bollards at the back of the lock. As the hose and tap were at the front near the control cabin, I walked along and began to lay out the hose. To put out 250 feet of hose takes quite some time. Fanny had the filler cap off, we stuck in the end and I began to walk back to the tap. I had just turned it on when an agonised wail came from behind me:

'The boat's going down!'

I turned to see the cabin roof disappearing below the wall.

What the hell was happening? Had the man gone mad? I rushed up into the cabin. With the lock-keeper stood two bargees, who, unnoticed by me, had brought their barges in through the mist and were evidently complaining. Why should they be held up for a mere yacht to fill her water tanks? I expostulated violently and was met by a glassy stare.

'Ces gens travaillent,' said the button-presser.

To say that I was angry would be to put it mildly.

'You can't do this! You have absolutely no right to let a boat go down with nobody aboard. If you're in a hurry, say so. We don't want your bloody water, we can get it anywhere.

Why did you say we could have water and then do a thing like this? I shall report it to Paris.'

All this I told him and a good deal more. The three men just stood there, po-faced, looking at me. They knew perfectly well they had played a dirty trick and were enjoying the situation in that peculiar way which is essentially French.

'Bring the water up again!' I shouted. 'How am I to get on board?'

'Use the ladder.'

The water was still running out and by the time I got back to the boat it lay about fifteen feet below. Fanny had somehow managed to slack off the lines.

'What are we going to do? What are we going to do?' She was in quite a state—and so was I.

'I'm going down the ladder.'

'But you can't—it's dangerous . . .'

'Let go the lines.'

We led the boat along the lock by its lines till it was under the ladder. By now the lock-keeper had stopped the outflow of water and she lay there when I peered over, looking a very long way below. Telling Fanny to keep the lines taut to hold her well in, I gingerly took to that slimy ladder and went carefully down. At last I stepped on board. Already the fool had started dropping the water again. I looked up. Fanny, out of sight, was still gamely hanging on to both lines. At last we were down.

'All right. Let go. Throw 'em down.' They clattered on the coachroof and I started coiling them. 'Walk down and meet me below the lock.'

The gates opened. I motored out. Fanny walked down the towpath and I picked her up.

I fumed about this for days. I was going to lodge a complaint. I was going to see the man got the sack. I was going to complain to the Canal Authority, etc., etc. But, funnily enough, though I enquired, I never met a single lock-keeper who knew who the Authority was! All they knew was their local engineer. In the end, of course, I did nothing.

This was the only nasty incident we had on the whole trip. Although yachts are guests on the canals and the barges have a rightful preference, we had done nothing whatever to be subjected to what was, at its least, a quite unnecessary discourtesy. All I can say to any who come that way is 'Look out for the man on the Canal du Nord at Lock 10.'

*   *   *

Once we had turned on to the Canal Lateral de l'Oise the pressure was off. We found ourselves on a secret pastoral stretch of water. Not a ripple disturbed the green, not a barge hove in sight. Water lilies swayed in our wake. Filipendula, lythrum and pseudacorus fringed the banks. An occasional coot bobbed out of the reeds. A solitary angler brooded over his float. (There seem to be a few million of this breed in France.) We slid along between walls of high trees which screened us from the rest of the world.

To me perhaps the most surprising thing about the canals is their isolation from the whirl of modern life, their strange and beautiful loneliness. You might think that over the years villages would have sprung up along their banks, loading and unloading centres would have developed small townships; but although there are, of course, villages, towns and even cities along the canals, for miles and miles they lie in the depths of the country and not a roof is to be seen. Compared with diminutive and overcrowded England, France is a vast country and her canals, carefully engineered to avoid hills and gradients, meander along far from the direct lines of roads and railways. A screen of trees or woods shields them from the winter gales—cross-winds can be a hazard to barges in winter—and at the same time shuts them in, so that for the most part one's view is limited to the waterway itself and the landscape beyond is hidden. But this waterway with its gentle curves and peaceful vistas is a continual delight. It is the world of Manet, Debussy, Delius, where the droop of a willow, the plop of a rising fish, are the only accents, and the locks, with the keeper's cottage, his dog and his garden, a smiling punctuation in a journey that seems timeless. Although we knew that at the end of this tenuous green ribbon lay the sea and, many miles over that, the island that called us, the goal seemed so far away and the strength of its magnet so weak that only very occasionally did we remember, by some sudden association, the spell of that magic. Seeing the dawn wading through the river mists or filtered through the poplar copses would sometimes, by contrast, vividly recall the radiant translucence of daybreak in Corfu.

*   *   *

There a spectrum of light precedes the sunrise and a band of deep orange outlines the mountains of the Epirus, fading out to violet where it washes the morning star. A light easterly breeze darkens the waters of the Inland Sea. The last fisherman's light winks out. Soon the mother hen caique and her train of chicks will be clucking back to port. The sky pales and glows with a powerful crescendo of light. A molten sun pours out of its crucible of mountains, gilding the sinews of the olives that were bearing fruit when Christ was born. Soon in a cloudless sky there is nothing but light, a marvellous clarity of crystal light, so clear, so clean, it seems a man might reach up through it to touch the very source of Truth . . . It is in that light we wish to stand again, a light that dances on the water, etches the tendons of the rocks, blackens the shadows of the cypresses; a light that breeds a volatile, voluble people, sharp as diamonds, shrewd, humorous, warm, brave, fickle and proud as the sun itself, whose children they are.

*　　*　　*

The great heat continued day after day. By eight in the morning it was up to eighty and soon after that ninety in the cabin. We were usually breakfasting at 5.30 to be ready at our first lock when the gates opened at 6.30. If we were lucky we might get through five or six locks without delays, but sooner or later we would catch up with a peniche (barge) and remain in her wake for the rest of the day.

Although you have the right to overtake a vessel ahead, if the captain waves you on, you need a good stretch of water to do it in. Overtaking is perhaps the only mild nautical excitement on the canals. The width of the smaller waterways is not much more than fifteen metres and a barge is five metres wide, so what with reeds and shallowing banks the passing channel is narrow. A laden peniche raises a huge mound of water before her blunt bows and a corresponding deep trough amidships which ends in a fine foaming wake astern. As we hadn't much more than eight knots and the average barge speed is five, the overtaking margin was none too great. Barge captains, waving us on, would grin broadly when they saw us enter the sucking trough along their sides. Battling our way forward between this and the bank, we would start to mount the bow wave and then they would laugh outright at our attempts to climb over it. We seemed to get stuck on the crest. Then at last, full throttle, we would fight our way clear to shoot ahead as soon as we were in smooth water.

But such overtakings were rare and usually we had to stay in the queue. Barges enter a lock very slowly. Often they have less than a foot either side and only a yard and a half gate clearance for both bow and stern. So, weighing a good 350 tons, it's a close fit and they judge it to a nicety—they have to. It takes at least twenty minutes to empty and fill the lock again for the next customer—which automatically spaces out the traffic. This is why, way behind the barge ahead, you rarely have time to catch her up and pass her unless there is a good distance between locks.

After a while we began to find a certain rhythm. We ceased to hurry along, since it is pleasanter and cooler to keep going slowly than to arrive below a lock and have to wait. It was, we found, almost impossible to be strong-minded enough to opt out, stop altogether and lose our precious place in the queue. The distances ahead were so great we could not bear to waste the time. So we kept going for eleven hours a day, averaging about a lock an hour. In retrospect it seems that a canal holiday should not aim at a schedule of more than five locks a day to be leisurely and enjoyable. By the end of an eleven-hour day at ninety degrees in the shade we were usually exhausted.

Our slow progress continued, but now, as I write, all those days have run into one another and I can only remember random incidents, here and there. How we bathed in icy water at the summit level waiting to enter the tunnel at Bray-en-Lannois; how the engine stopped suddenly and we found a large green plastic sheet wrapped round the propeller which the Mate removed, plunging in with her best carving knife; how we followed the moon-shot on the radio—never has it cost so much to send so few, so far for so little; how the boat was nearly bashed to bits when some children out for a Sunday afternoon's fun opened the sluices wide to watch the water boiling into the lock; how one very Gallic lock-keeper invited Fanny into the woods to see the bluebells . . .

But one picture is firmly fixed in my mind—because it recurred so often—waiting below a lock for the gates to open. Lying back, 100 yards below, I watch the barge ahead creep through the gates and see the lock-keeper labouring at the big handles to close them. An age seems to elapse before the super-structure of the barge rises slowly above the walls and another before the further gates open. Then a roar and a boil of foam as—only a yard from the gates—the engine opens up sending a waterfall of water over the top towards us. Another wait, the front gates have to be closed again. Another wait, the water has to be let out. Here it comes. Eddies and whirlpools appear in the pool. At last a crack of light shows between the gates— they are opening? Is there a barge inside? No. All clear. I open up a bit and slide in, looking for the ladder to make fast . . .

So it went, day after day. We had already run out of English cigarettes and all we could offer to the hard-working lock-keepers was a few Gaulloises or Smarties for the children. It is no joke to open and close those heavy gates twenty or more times a day, especially for the women who seemed to manage most of them. But they were usually cheerful.

'Where have you come from, M'sieur?'

'Calais.'

'And you are going to Marseille?'

'Yes—and on to Greece.'

'To Greece! My, that's a long way!'

'It is.'

'Well, if you put one foot before the other, you are bound to get there.'

'Yes indeed. Well, au revoir, Madame.'

'Au revoir, M'sieu et Madame, et bon voyage!'

*　　*　　*

In ten days we reached Vitry-le-François. After leaving the Canal du Nord we had passed along the Canal de l'Oise à l'Aisne, the Canal Lateral de l'Aisne, the Canal de l'Aisne à la Marne and the Canal Lateral de la Marne. We had nosed in and out of seventy-five locks and four tunnels. Now we had reached the last great divide, the Canal de la Marne à la Saône. This is the most northerly of the three main arteries which connect Paris with Lyons and the south It is quite an engineering feat: a waterway 224 kilometres long with 114 locks, of which seventy-one rise to the summit, over 1,000 feet above sea level. Here there is a tunnel five kilometres long, after which another forty-three locks set you down at Heuilley on the Saône.

In spite of the distance we had already covered, this seemed a formidable prospect and only the thought that at the end of it we should be liberated from the constriction of the canals on to the broad reaches of the river urged us on. Already we longed for the sea.

Our start was not propitious. We moved out of Vitry to the first lock on the outskirts of the town. The gates were closed. After waiting an hour in the sultry heat I went ashore to find out the cause of the interminable delay. I found the young lock-keeper in a flap. Because of the drought and the summer heat the other two big south-bound canals had had to be closed. All the traffic had diverted to this canal. Now there were twenty barges ahead of us and the water had fallen so low the locks were closed till it had time to build up again.

If you pause to work it out you can see that an immense bulk of water is needed to empty and fill 114 locks an average of twenty times a day. My rough calculation brings it out at over three-quarters of a million tons. Huge lake reservoirs are necessary at the top. We could see the banks were a foot below normal. So, as a fully laden barge only clears the bottom of the canal by about eighteen inches, it was plain they would have to keep to the centre of the channel if they weren't going to scrape the mud. Evidently we were going to have a slow journey.

However, the young man started telephoning and at last obtained permission to let us through. There were five barges waiting below the next lock, so we took our place and tried to find a bit of shade along the bank. All morning we waited in the sweltering heat. At lunchtime we heard engines behind us. Two German motor yachts had also been let into this stretch. Their engines were noisy, their bearing aggressive. They explained to us that they had come from Hamburg, had only a limited holiday and must get to the South of France before it ran out. The barge captains were unimpressed. We explained that we too were eager to reach the sea. But there it was. There were five barges ahead. They couldn't jump the queue.

Up to this point we had met very few yachts on the canals and none going in our direction. The peace and quiet were now shattered by these newcomers, who never stopped their engines and filled the air with black smoke and diesel fumes. So, what with the delays and the heat, the tension began to build up. Two days later it exploded.

* * *

We had let them get well ahead and hoped we had seen the last of them when to our dismay we came upon their two boats moored below the lock at Froncles. A French *peniche* was just entering the lock. The Germans were moored to the bank, the three couples talking and gesticulating, evidently in some excitement. We tied up some way behind them and I walked along the towpath to be met by one of the group who spoke a little English.

'The wife of that dirty French bargee spat in Greta's face and called her a "*sal boche*".'

'No! Why? Had you upset her?'

'Last night his barge across the canal' and he made a gesture with his hands. 'So we cannot get through. We are very angry. We shall report him.'

On the face of it such an insult did seem a bit much.

'Please. You speak French. Tell the man we must pass. We are faster. We are in great delay here.'

I walked up to the lock. The gates were closed and the French *peniche* was rising. Below, on deck, I saw the elderly wife of the Captain. She was a large heavy woman. Her brawny arms were gored with two six-inch scratches, daubed with iodine.

'Ah, *Madame*,' I called, sympathetically, 'your arms. Have you had an accident? What has happened?'

She shrugged and did not answer, but the Captain, hearing my voice, burst out of the deckhouse.

'Ah, M'sieu, vous êtes anglais. Vous comprendrez. Venez. Venez.' And he rushed me down into his saloon. He was a gutsy little man, bristling with fury.

'These *boches* they are always the same, always were, always will be. You were in the war, M'sieu? Then you remember. You understand. You have seen my wife? You have seen those

wounds?' He shook his fists. 'Those *boche* bastards, let them
try to pass me. By God, I'll sink them.'

He then explained that when the locks closed at 7.30 the
night before, he was about to moor, when the yachts had
tried to push past him to get first into the lock the next
morning. He had seen their German colours and he certainly
wasn't going to let them jump the queue. So he had simply
turned his barge broadside across the canal.

'That German whore, the blonde one, she flew at my wife
with her dirty claws. You have seen what she did, M'sieu? You
have seen—*and* she threw a rock at her! Hit her on the back,
here. She suffers. She is in pain. I am calling the doctor to the
next lock. Ah, *merde* on all *boche*, *merde*, *merde* . . .' He was almost
speechless.

'What can I do, M'sieu? What can I do? I am a working man.
I have a load. Can I stop here and go to court and waste two,
three, days while the authorities come to take evidence? I
cannot. You see that I cannot.' He paused for breath. 'And
suppose I let them pass? Suppose I did. What's the good?
There are five, six, seven barges ahead. They will gain nothing.
Nothing. They have insulted me, a Frenchman, here, on a
French canal. Ah, the *boche* are hogs and their women whores.
They are all the same, always were, always will be.'

The water was up, the gates were opening, we returned to
the deckhouse. '*Au revoir*, M'sieu. I wished you to understand
this matter. You are English. You will remember.' Then a
smile of cunning came over his face.

'They will have a slow journey, M'sieu, a slow journey. I
promise you! *Au revoir*, M'sieu, *au revoir*.'

The lock at Froncles is No. 36. There were seventy-eight to
go before reaching the Saône. We were to find out when, four
days later, we came to the last lock, what had happened. Had

there been two German yachts through? Yesterday? The day before?

'They passed an hour ago, M'*sieu*,' said the lock-keeper.

'An hour ago!' We were astonished.

'Not very good people, I hear.' He smiled.

The Frenchman had been as good as his word. Every lock-keeper had heard the story. The Germans had had a slow journey. It never pays to jump the queue.

*   *   *

Froncles is a delightful little town, gay with flower beds and very clean, with a charming eighteenth-century bridge over its river. We stopped to shop and take on water—an intentional delay to let the angry parties get well ahead. The best part of canal travel is the wonderful peace and quiet. If this is disturbed it is nothing but a tedious chore.

Now we seemed to be at the tail of the queue. There was nothing behind us, nothing, north-bound, passed us. We thoroughly enjoyed these days, climbing steadily upwards, meeting a lock pretty well every mile. The Canal de la Marne must be one of the most beautiful in France. Lined with long avenues of poplars, sycamore and even cypresses, it often takes to the sides of the valleys, giving exquisite vistas through the columns of the trunks, curling and swinging round the hillsides. As we rose higher, the character of the country changed. Lush valleys merged into limestone cliffs. Averaging seventeen locks a day, we must have climbed almost 1,000 feet by the time we reached Langres.

Some nights before we had moored alongside a friendly peniche, and the captain, a young man, with only his mother on the boat, warned us about the big tunnel—Les Batailles—ahead.

'You know? It has no light.'

'No light?' It was disturbing news.

'This is France,' he laughed. 'It is the fourteenth century!'

Boats are like houses—you never stop spending money on them. But you have to call a halt somewhere. A searchlight, I thought, was a luxury we could do without. We did not intend to travel at night. Now we were going to be in trouble.

'It is a bad tunnel. Long. Difficult. There used to be a wooden edge to the towpath. Now this has rotted away. The bolts stick out. Dangerous. Yes. We used to light fires on the bows of the barges when I was a boy.'

'Fires!'

'Yes. With branches. How else could we see to get through? You see it is long and hardly five metres wide.'

To understand why we had some cause for anxiety, I should perhaps explain that Prosilios has a Z-drive. For those who have no idea what this is, a Z-drive is a sort of swivel outside the boat with the propeller on the bottom of it. There is no rudder and the boat is turned by swinging the whole drive from side to side. The system is in common use and has certain advantages which do not, in my opinion, outweigh its disadvantages. The chief of these is that, unless the propeller is turning and actually driving the boat, you cannot steer it. You cannot 'coast' with engine off as you can in a normal ruddered boat. Besides this, the slower you go, the less steering control you have. Even at full speed the boat never stops swinging from side to side. It never runs quite straight—and this adds greatly to the fatigue of the wheel. If ever I have another boat, the one thing I am certain of is that it will not be fitted with a Z-drive.

Now canal tunnels are always tricky, they are so narrow. For us, with our eight-foot beam, there is about three-foot clearance on either side. To keep *Prosilios* straight at walking pace, or less, through such an alleyway would be very tricky anyway. To do it in the dark, pretty well impossible. Without a good light we should certainly bash the walls and those dreadful protruding bolts.

So at Langres we must get a light. The picturesque old town does not stand on the canal but on an eminence above it, reached by a funicular. All the morning, short-tempered in the great heat, I searched high and low for some sort of spotlight. There was nothing to be had. Then, when I had almost given up, I found a big Japanese torch in a radio shop. It wasn't ideal, but it would have to do.

'What we really need,' said Fanny, 'is a Corfu fisherman's light.'

*   *   *

Off Cavos the two big lights on the stern of the boat throw a brilliant glare on the water. The October moon is still high. You can see the mountain outline of Corfu four miles to the west. You can see the silhouettes of other boats. But the sea itself is black. Black and absolutely still. So still that the drop from the oar blades etch growing circles on the water. The fisherman is holding his lights in the centre of a golden necklace that is slowly closing around him. It is a circlet of plastic balls holding up the top of the net, into the heart of which his lights throw thrilling shafts of emerald, driving them deep into the water where, far below, the fish glitter like points of silver, flashes of diamond, flukes of steel.

For hours (while the fisherman slept) the light has been calling the fish up from the deeps and now they circle round hypnotised by the two great eyes above them.

There is a cry from the mother boat—the drawstring at the

bottom of the net has been closed. Now it is no longer a tube but a huge goblet of sea water. The fishermen begin to haul on the meshes, heaving the net inboard. In the glare of the light, side by side, bending and straining, they look like a frieze of heroes. Slowly they haul, calling to each other in deep ringing voices. Now it is almost up. They can feel the weight of the catch. They shout with excitement as they heave it clear.

And then comes that extraordinary sound, the death agony of a ton of small fish. It builds in a crescendo, a flutter of terror, like the flurry of a thundershower, like a sudden gust of wind rustles the olives and dies away in a million sighs . . .

We move homeward in the warm darkness, spellbound by the glory of the night. Nodules of phosphorescence swirl in our wake. The old crone in the Kafenion is already up and we sip our metreos, half asleep . . .

*   *   *

The rules governing the passage of barges through the tunnel of Les Batailles are simple. It is one-way traffic. Boats going north may enter from four o'clock in the morning till eight; boats going south between midday and four in the afternoon. There are no guards on the tunnel and no telephone from one end to the other, the time lapse between the north- and south-bound traffic is supposed to be sufficient to avoid that obvious disaster—two barges meeting head on in the dark!

It was about half an hour after midday when we reached the summit level. Ahead of us was a barge, a yacht (on which four cadets, paddling their canoes from Calais to the Med, had cadged a lift through the tunnel. They did very well—in fact they got to the sea before we did.) Astern of the yacht came another barge. We, as usual, brought up the rear.

As we knew there was no ventilation in the tunnel and a concentration of diesel fumes can be very unpleasant, we hung back to let the last barge get ahead—it turned out to have been a mistake.

Some way before you reach the mouth of the tunnel the canal narrows to half its usual width and runs straight towards the entrance. On either side is an avenue of tall cypresses, sombre and funereal. Above the tunnel is a bleak hillside. In the silence the whole place seems absolutely lonely and forgotten. Nothing stirs, and there, at the bottom, is that black semicircle of ebony like the entrance to the Underworld. We badly felt the need of Orpheus to twang us a cheerful tune, but, as he didn't turn up, there was nothing for it but to chug on into the mountain . . .

Curious how, although a boat's speed is so slow, things seem to happen so quickly. We never seem to be ready. Now we rigged the new torch on the coachroof in a hurry and Fanny fished out our second torch and crouched behind me.

Coming out of the sunlight, the blackness as we went in was absolute. I thought the inside of the Beehive Tombs at Mycenae was the darkest place on earth—Les Batailles was darker. It was an absolute nothing of light. For a few moments I had that old feeling I knew so well—flying in cloud with no horizon, no top, bottom or sides to anything. It is a frightening feeling of being somehow outside life, like a soul after death. The new torch on the roof threw a long sword of light straight down the tunnel which stabbed the darkness and illuminated nothing at all. Only the torch that Fanny held threw a dim glow on the wall far too close at our side.

How to steer in this? I had no idea how the boat was lying,

couldn't feel the wheel. There was a bash as we hit the side and cannoned off to bash the other. I threw her into neutral, this would never do. In something approaching a panic, I jumped up to the coachroof and tried to adjust the torch, stuck a book under the back end of it to deflect the beam downward and swung it to one side so that it made a circle on the tunnel wall, about fifty yards ahead.

Gradually we steadied up, put her in gear at tickover revs and, as our eyes became more night adapted, slowly edged our way along at about one mile an hour. It was like driving in a thick fog when all you can see is the kerb and you feel completely lost on a road you know like the palm of your hand.

Fanny was terrific. Crouching behind me, getting cramp from holding the torch over the side, she kept up a running commentary, 'You're doing fine, darling. Just fine. A bit to the left. That's it. No, too close, too close . . .' And I spun the wheel, as usual overcorrecting that damned Z-drive. 'That's better . . . Now, we're too far . . . back a bit . . . that's it. Well, we're moving, darling, moving along. We must get to the end sometime . . .'

I devoutly hoped so, though at that moment I couldn't imagine it, and so it went, both of us tensed to the hilt, for half an hour. And then—bless the straightness of that tunnel! I saw, miles away, a tiny golden glow-worm, the tail-light of the barge ahead! At first I thought my eyes were playing tricks; but no, there it was, a murky orange candleflame in the absolute black—and, believe me, a life-saver.

What it is to have an aim! Immediately I was able to steady the wheel and, though it continued to demand the greatest possible attention, the lost feeling had gone. As long as I could keep my eyes on that light, all would be well. The boat felt good under me. We should get through.

So it continued at this snail's pace for a whole hour. It was one of the longest I remember. Then, beyond my guiding star, I saw a small golden half-moon, deep orange as it is at rising. What on earth could that be? Slowly, very slowly, it grew in size. It seemed to have a black block in the centre.

'It's the end of the tunnel!' I almost shouted. 'Look!! That black blob's the silhouette of the barge!'

It was certainly a moment of relief. The moon enlarged, paler now as the density of the diesel fumes grew less, and at last we came out into the sun! Never had the light of day seemed so marvellous! It had taken us one and three-quarter hours to cover a distance of two and a half miles. Never again!

But if, in fact, I had to do it again, failing a fisherman's light, I would put a Tilley lamp up in the bows to give good general close illumination and have two searchlights, one playing on each wall; but more than all this, I would carefully arrange to follow the tail-light of the man ahead—and hope he was well lit too.

How ridiculous it is! Hundreds of barges ply through that tunnel. Many belong to rich combines to whom the cost of a hundred neon tubes, spaced at 100-yard intervals, would be nothing. But nobody bothers. Truly France is, as the young man said, still in the fourteenth century.

So we pottered on for a mile and moored at the canal side where an enterprising chap had set up a depot of fuel and water. We gave the boat a drink and had a stiff double whisky ourselves. Believe me, we needed it.

*　　*　　*

But now our spirits rose, we were in the home stretch, so to speak, only forty-three locks to go before reaching the Saône! We slid down them easily and pleasantly, seventeen one day, twenty-two the next and just before we dropped into the river, where there was a 'staircase' of two locks, I stood watching a barge coming up, and enter the lock below.

It fitted the lock exactly—or did the lock fit the barge exactly? Which had come first, the chicken or the egg? Who had decided, over a century ago, to standardise the lock length at thirty-eight metres and fifty centimetres? Or a barge at thirty-six metres? All these locks and barges, thousands of them, they were all exactly the same length, give or take a few centimetres! Whether they were French, Belgian, Dutch or German, somewhere around 1850 they had got together and agreed. To this the whole system of European inland navigation owed its success. A man would load a barge anywhere from Marseille to Hamburg and know that the cargo could be delivered to any destination. Imagine the chaos that would have resulted if some places were inaccessible because the barges were too big or the locks too small!

In the locks themselves there were local differences and improvements. The new locks on the Canal du Nord had a sort of side basin that saved half the water lost in lowering the level. The Vee-lock gates themselves, which are sealed by the weight of the water above them, we owe to the genius of Leonardo, but the 'paddles', or sluices, are of various types. Those called '*jalousies*' are like shutters that slide over each other, admitting more or less water by the width of the slots. Into such locks the water boils violently, making it very troublesome for those moored up near the front end. The Canal de la Marne à la Saône, the one we were now on, had a much better system. The water was funnelled down large pipes which came up all along the bottom of the lock, so the level rose smoothly and evenly without turbulence—and this was dated 1865.

The Canals

Now on the main arteries of canal traffic the locks are being lengthened and widened, some taking two, four, eight or even twelve barges, in preparation perhaps for bigger units; but in general the whole intricate and beautifully balanced system was standardised over a century ago and is still working efficiently.

So, at last, blowing Mr. Ffoulkes like mad (the canal bystanders thought we were crazy), we celebrated our exit from the last lock and came out on to the wide stretches of the river. It was a marvellous relief. Eighteen days ago we had left Calais. We had passed through 201 locks and six tunnels! It was enough and we were heartily glad to reach the end of it. Now there were only nineteen locks to the sea!

Just like a cow too long confined to the byre kicks up her heels and cavorts about in the ecstasy of being put out in a meadow, so we opened up the engine and rushed here and there over the open water. It was a wonderful feeling. Gone was the need for meticulous steering, the day-long attention to every yard of the way, the constant waiting, the stopping and starting, the endless succession of black gates. It was over. We could relax.

Surely the Saône is the queen of rivers! There is a nobility and graciousness about her upper reaches which fills the eye with pleasure. The majestic sweep of the water, the willow-fringed islands, the poplar-lined banks, the families of swans and cygnets, the tireless anglers—never, among all the thousands we had seen along the banks of the canals, did we ever see one hook a fish!

So we came that first evening to a broad backwater below a lock called Les Athés and moored there to an overhanging branch. It was, I think, the most idyllic spot we found on our whole journey. The backwater curled away in a dreamlike vista, trees crinolined over the water. A file of huge poplars were marshalled along the further bank. The river was utterly smooth and still. Two men were fishing in a green boat. A flight of small birds fled low over the water, swift and light as a passing thought. We ate out in the cockpit, a celebration feast of omelettes, cheese, glorious peaches, country bread and some *vin ordinaire*, which seemed that evening quite *extraordinaire*. But the best part of the meal was our feeling of content. We had made it. We had come through.

*   *   *

So thick was the mist next morning we couldn't even see the poplars on the further bank, but as we ghosted out into the river it cleared and the rest of the day was perfect. We covered seventy miles and moored above Chalons. The day after, the weather broke. A brisk south wind blew upstream, braiding the muddy water with white caps and sending lashings of spray over the cockpit windows. After a few hours of this we got fed up and sidled into a little dinghy port to rest and pick up provisions at a caravan site. When the wind abated the rain came, a thunderstorm, which found us, as usual, unprepared. We could see nothing in the downpour, so we edged the nose on to a sandy bank where two young mermaids were disporting themselves in the water with a ball. They took our line and tied it to a hawthorn tree. We gave them peaches and their efforts to eat them up to their necks in water in the pouring rain sent them into peals of laughter.

The rain abated and we put off again, but it was a circular storm and came back, drenching us through our oilskins. We held on for another couple of hours, and then, seeing a pretty yacht port, whose guardian kept flashing a green light at us, put in to its landing stage, thick with yellow water-lilies. It was a perfectly equipped little mooring and turned out to be a private club where rich Lyonnais kept their speedboats. They were very hospitable and full of local knowledge about the river. When I spoke of going down the Rhône without a pilot one of them looked at me sideways, 'C'est assez delicat'—a very subtle way of saying 'Don't be a bloody fool!' They were perfectly right, though, in retrospect, delicat is hardly the word I would use for the ferocious rapids of the Rhône.

So on the twentieth day we reached the approaches to Lyons. The wide empty stretches gave way to oil-storage tanks and factories. The river narrowed, hills rose from it studded with houses and soon with fully built-up terraces and streets. Fanny was taking a turn at the wheel and I was sitting behind her paying no attention to our course, but idly watching the vistas of the city as they unfolded round the bends. Suddenly, out of the corner of my eye, I saw a thin stake sticking straight up out of the water. What was that doing right in the centre of the river? Simultaneously a passing bus blew a tremendous blast on his horn (perhaps he was warning us?). There was an ugly crunch. We were aground.

I leapt up and had the engine off in a flash. There is one thing about a Z-drive, the prop hits before the bottom of the boat does. It may be safer, but it's more expensive. We floated off. Gingerly I reversed out. There were two small—in my opinion far too small—cigar-shaped buoys marking the channel. Fanny had missed them—just as I had missed the channel in Chichester Harbour some weeks before and done exactly the same thing. There I had ruined our first propeller. Now our spare had gone. Well, to go aground happens to all of us some time or other. Soon we got going again, but there was a nasty vibration. Evidently the prop was damaged.

It was tough, after all those hundreds of miles, to have a bad break in the last few hundred yards. But not to worry! We crawled downstream and tied up at the Port de Plaisance in the heart of Lyons.

*   *   *

The Port de Plaisance is in no sense a 'port'. It is simply a section of the fine stone quays that contain the river Saône as it flows through the city. In spite of the fact that all craft going up and down river throw their wash against the yachts moored there, it is a good berth. Right opposite is the fine old church of St. Jean (with its remarkable calendar clock), floodlit at night. Above on the hill-top stands the cathedral with all ancient Lyons tucked in below it. There is a splendid funicular up to this with antique hauling machinery which must date from the period of the Crystal Palace and looks as if it will still be good for another century. Behind the port on the upper quays, under the shade of a double avenue of magnificent plane trees, is an open-air market which must be one of the most attractive in France.

But for me what gave the place its special quality was the presiding genius of the port—Michel. This young man, living in a houseboat moored at the quay, was the personification of intelligent, tireless service. From six in the morning till eleven at night he never stopped attending to the hundred and one needs of the yachts which, passing up and down river, called in with every kind of trouble or requirement. At one moment he was in a wet suit repairing a damaged propeller under water, at the next off in his shaky old truck fetching washing from the Laundrymat. Even-tempered, resourceful, humorous, he organised the pool of official pilots taking boats up and down the Rhône, knew every agent and workshop in the city, provided hot showers in his own apartment, changed money, called in the fuel float, and, just to top it off, had a fluent command of English and German.

Within an hour of my arrival he had my propeller off. When we saw it was really too badly damaged to be beaten out he said:

'What is the price of a new propeller in England?'

'About £15.'

'Here it will cost you £40.'

'Forty!'

'Yes. Duty. You are not in the Common Market, M'*sieu*, and the French are greedy, you know. It will be cheaper to air-freight one from the U.K.'

Within half an hour we were through to my son in London who arranged to send out two propellers. As they were replacements, they came through the Customs without duty. Both, including the air-freight charges, cost me £35!

But beyond this and constant consideration and kindness I have to thank Michel for indirectly solving the Mystery of the Sticking Throttle.

* * *

The Mystery of the Sticking Throttle is really quite a saga in itself, with all sorts of overtones of morality, responsibility and commercial integrity, to say nothing of expense, frustration and actual danger at sea to my wife, my boat and myself. Although a book is not the place to beef about one's troubles, unless I briefly outline what happened much of what follows will be meaningless. For, while we solved the mystery in Lyons, it was far from being the end of the story, as you will see.

Prosilios was almost completed in September 1968. It was then too late to set out on a long cruise, so we laid her up at the yard for the winter. Everything was protected against rust, the tanks were filled to avoid condensation and a tarpaulin was put over her to keep out the worst of the English winter. She was not put in the water till April 1969.

During the winter the Boat Show had brought a boom in business to the yard. They were very busy. My boat was a hangover from quieter days and it was plain that all they wanted to see of me was my back. It became quite a struggle to get the last jobs done. Finally the boat was taken out on its 'sea trials'.

These were a mockery, a half-hour's run in which nothing was tested or examined. All I knew was that the boat floated and the propeller went round, but I noticed that the throttle was very stiff and rough in movement. Assured that this was just because the boat was 'new', I took *Prosilios* away to Newhaven.

Then my wife went down with pneumonia and our scheduled May departure was delayed for two months until she recovered sufficiently for us to make a start. During that time we ran the boat around whenever weather permitted and soon the throttle trouble grew very much worse. Pulling back the lever did not slow the engine; it ran on at its previous speed. Sometimes both lever and throttle jammed. This could happen anywhere on the range from tickover to full out; but it didn't *always happen*—that was the mystery. For days it was quite normal, and then, without warning, often just coming in to berth, it would stick and we rammed the jetty or another boat.

Perkins mechanics went over the engine: it was perfect. We called in CAV fuel-pump specialists: they could find nothing wrong. I blamed it on the Teleflex controls: they promptly renewed the whole installation. After all this it seemed that the trouble, though we still hadn't really found it, must have been eliminated. We set out for Calais.

After ten hours at sea we were approaching the harbour in a Force 4 following sea. A dinghy club was racing outside. About forty boats were battling it out in a tricky wind and naturally I started to manœuvre to give way. I closed the throttle. Nothing happened! We went slap through the fleet at eight knots with the crews yelling blue murder—and nothing whatever to be done about it. I pulled on the lever with all my strength. This time it was jammed. It wouldn't move. I pushed it wider to try to free it that way. No good.

So we charged into Calais harbour (which I had never seen except from the ferry), shot through the crowded boat anchorage and, sweating with anxiety, finally pulled the plug and came to rest near a wharf. There a friendly Belgian yacht took us in tow and moored us behind another boat.

It is an alarming experience, when you are as much of an amateur as I am, to have your boat out of control, but it is far worse when you have no idea what is causing it. Clearly to attempt the canals until we had solved the problem was out of the question.

So now the Perkins agent from Boulogne was called in. He took part of the pump to pieces and found that a small pin (which controlled the flow of fuel) had a speck of varnish on it. It was this, he declared, that had caused the trouble. He had never seen anything like it before and would report it to the makers. When he had cleaned it up he assured me that we should have no more trouble from now on, nothing to worry about. So we set off.

But during those long miles south the jamming slowly returned. Not so severely as before, but there was clearly something still very wrong and I took the precaution every time before I started up to work the throttle vigorously back and forth to free whatever was causing it to stick. So without further mishaps we reached Lyons.

There would be some days' delay before the new propellers arrived, so I thought we must once more try to solve the mystery. Michel called in the local CAV pump expert. Now you may ask, why not call in Perkins. It was their engine, after all, new, under guarantee. They should have replaced the whole pump, the whole engine if necessary. Alas, in the marine world it is not so simple as that. The fuel pump is not made by Perkins, it is subcontracted to CAV and under separate guarantee. (So, for that matter, is the dynamo, and that is under separate guarantee!) Imagine buying a car whose components were not guaranteed by its maker! It sounds a ridiculous situation, but there it is. Once you are abroad all these things become 100 per cent more difficult. You are stuck where you are and have to do the best you can to keep going.

The Breton pump expert at Lyons was the first man who had any sense of that most vital element in service and repair—diagnosis. All the others (and I too) had only looked at the pump. He went straight for the fuel filter. I expostulated. It was the pump that was wrong.

'A moment, M'sieu!'

He unscrewed the filter and removed the element. Then he held up the bowl for my inspection. At the bottom lay half a cupful of water!

*　　*　　*

I stared at it aghast. I couldn't believe my eyes. Over a year before, when the boat was building I had said to my wife: 'There is only one thing that can stop a diesel engine and that's water in the fuel. I don't intend us to get caught with that.' So

I had fitted a special oversize filter (such as aircraft use) with such a fine element that neither rust flakes nor water could possibly get through.

'There is your trouble, M'sieu. Your pump sticks because it is rusty.'

Then, of course, I saw it at once. That idiot at Boulogne with his 'speck of varnish'! It was rust. Perkins were not to blame, CAV were not to blame, Teleflex was not to blame. The blame rested fairly and squarely on the shoulders of the yard, who, after a winter lay up, delivering a new boat, had failed to check the state of the tanks and fuel.

It seems to me that boatbuilders are in a class by themselves. The product they sell is designed to be used in a dangerous place—the sea. Today, such is the boom in the yachtbuilding industry, a great many inexperienced people are taking to the sea. So a great responsibility falls on the yards. Many of them are headed by men who know the sea—and nobody who knows it can fail to respect it. But those who build boats and are only anxious to get them away, not giving a damn what happens afterwards, are a pretty poor lot and in the end it is not even good business. A customer who has been let down talks—and never forgets.

Of course, there are ignorant and foolish owners who think a boat is just a car on the water; the sea will soon eliminate them. But the serious owner who has spent some thousands of pounds on his boat expects a reasonable degree of integrity from the man who sells it. In the end, of course, he learns what every sailor learns: you can trust nobody but yourself and blame nobody but yourself. If you find yourself in difficulties that are not your fault, curse the blighter who landed you there and put it down to experience. You won't make that mistake again!

In this case the standard precautions had been taken, the tanks had been filled to the brim with fuel. I had checked that myself. But in my inexperience I had assumed that that having been done, there could be no condensation, no water, no rust. It never entered my head—in spite of the Perkins Manual which says that after the winter lay-up 'The fuel tanks should be drained and the interior of the tank thoroughly cleaned'. It hadn't been done. Now here was the result.

The pump was removed, cleaned, sealed and returned next day with a new guarantee. A few hours' work, but the bill was £20. When we dismantled the filter we saw that it had been swamped. The entire eight-inch element was clogged with red rust. We pumped the tanks dry. There were two-foot-square patches of rust on the bottom. For two days, on our knees, head down in the bilges, with the temperature around ninety degrees, we scraped and mopped up and dried. But it didn't matter. We didn't even grumble. It was such a relief to have solved the mystery.

From that day on we had no more trouble with a sticking throttle, nor with water in the fuel, nor with rust; but one thing leads to another and had we known it we certainly should not have been in that carefree mood in which we set off down the Rhône.

It was a week later. The new propellers had arrived, one had been fitted, the tanks had been filled, the franc devalued and the bills paid. The Loon, a twin-screw Coronet, with two men and a girl on board, had agreed to share the cost of a pilot (£45) and at 7.30 a.m. on August 10th, exactly a month after leaving the U.K., we slipped our mooring and, calling goodbye to the excellent Michel ('Write to me every day!'), slid under the last of the Lyons bridges, passed the confluence of the Saône and the Rhône without noticing it and, aided by a four-knot current, were soon well on our way down the seventy-five-mile stretch we intended to cover by nightfall.

It was easy going. Our monosyllabic pilot, M. Guillet, took the wheel, leaving us nothing to do but admire the boring scenery and feed him. Our consort Coronet, capable of seventeen knots, had settled down dead astern ticking over at our modest seven, we were glad to escape from the furnace of Lyons, it was cool on the water and all was well.

General de Gaulle, in his thirst for atomic power and ambition to put France in the nuclear-arms race, determined to pour vast sums into harnessing the Rhône for this project. The resultant series of hydroelectric stations and locks had transformed and tamed the greater part of that savage river, produced a glut of cheap electricity for French industry and created the most ambitious and remarkable natural power supply in Europe, its final lock, the Mondragon, being the deepest in the world.

The admirable Dr. Pilkington has given a full account of the history of this remarkable river in the olden days when barges were towed upstream by a team of forty horses and the rapids made even the downstream trip a hazardous undertaking. Now the fierce gradients have been largely ironed out into a series of giant steps and when the scheme is completed the need for a pilot on the Rhône will be no greater than for the upper reaches of the Thames. But the project is not yet finished and there are still quite enough rapids to make navigation in either direction a lively business and to call for 1,000 h.p. engines in the enormous fuel-carrying barges, the Citernas, to drive them upstream.

The modernisation of the Rhône has entirely changed any romantic character it may have had. The scale of the transformation is vast. The river has been broadened, diverted, re-routed over much of its length into endless majestic vistas of smooth-flowing water, punctuated by immense weirs and power plants, spillways and locks. The feeder canals that lead to these locks are almost 150 yards wide, the depth of the locks themselves averages about forty feet and they can lift or drop a dozen barges at a time in the space of six minutes!

Admiring the engineering feat and feeling rather like water beetles on the Amazon, we kept going all day, except for a brief stop at Sablon, M. Guillet's home village, for him to tell his wife when he would be back. We swept in and out of the first four giant locks alone—there happened to be no commercial traffic—except for a party of Scandinavians touring in two sculling fours and a pair of canoes. Moored to the big floating bollards, we felt like flies on the walls of these huge caverns. The water sank under us without the least eddy or movement. Far above, almost invisible in his cabin, the lock-keeper pressed his buttons, the king-size doors lifted, raining on us as we passed beneath to emerge on to the next endless reach. Below the fourth lock (Baix Logis Neuf) we moored for the night. Just before mooring we were warned of trouble to come: our engine revs rose and fell in the way they only do when there is air in the fuel lines. Optimistically we disregarded this, had supper and turned in.

*   *   *

Next morning we were away at six o'clock. Twenty minutes later the engine started hunting. The revs fell alarmingly. Then it stopped for good. We were adrift in the river without steerage way. In a moment the Loon was alongside, warps and springs were made fast, the pilot changed over and the two boats continued downstream at ten knots. It was done so quickly and neatly, and with so little fuss, it was pretty clear that the two boys on board the Loon were extremely competent sailors. Before leaving Lyons we had had no more than a brief chat about sharing costs and time of departure. To us, until that moment, they were just 'the crew of the boat that was with us', now they emerged as examples of the sort of cheerful friendly help which always seemed to turn up and without which we could never have completed our trip.

Without, I hope, any false sentimentality, I felt then—and the feeling grew stronger after similar experiences—that there is a special bond, even an unwritten law, between people of all classes and nationalities, whoever they are, that go to sea. They have all been in trouble themselves at one time or another. They know what it means and they come to the aid of another boat in distress without even thinking about it. It might just as well be them.

Reading about lifeboats putting out in impossible weather, Russian trawlers towed into port by English fishermen, liners changing course to save dismasted yachts and so on, I used to think they were special cases, reported because they were 'beyond the call of duty'. But now I know it isn't like that at all. Any seaman worth his salt will come to the help of any other who needs him. It isn't a question of 'duty'—as the word is generally understood—it is a bond of fellowship and understanding—and it feels pretty good when you are on the receiving end.

That morning, for instance, what should we have done without the Loon? The Rhône runs fast, long stretches are far from any habitation, the banks are deserted. We saw what happens to a boat in trouble when we passed a yacht stranded on her side below a run of fast-moving water. How on earth would they get it repaired and afloat again? It would take weeks, cost hundreds . . .

But the crew of the Loon did more than just lash our two boats together. They both stepped on board Prosilios and took possession of the cockpit.

'I'm Roger Brown and this is John Wild. D'you mind if we have a look?'

It transpired they had sailed together a lot, knew the quirks of a Perkins engine from having had one in their own boat. They lost no time in getting the engine cover off and the floorboards up. All that morning, oblivious of the river, the locks and the heat, they sat with their feet in the bilges, subjecting my fuel lines to a detailed examination. Where was the air getting in? That was the problem and they went at it systematically, section by section, eliminating the possibilities one by one. Finally they ran it to earth.

When we had found the big filter clogged with rust at Lyons we had fitted the spare element I carried and re-assembled it. Now, somewhere, that filter was sucking air. Impossible to test it without taking it apart on the bench. The only thing to do was to bypass it. We found a length of plastic tube, joined the filter outlet and inlet pipes and bound the tube with copper wire at the ends. It took some time to bleed the air out of the system after this, but finally the engine started and after further bleeding ran normally.

All the time M. Guillet, perfectly unperturbed, was taking the two boats down through the rapids at ten knots. His knowledge of the river was remarkable. Unfailingly he aimed for the most turbulent water. When the two boats jostled and fought the whirlpools, swung this way and that, he corrected skilfully and we continued into the next smooth run. He never took his eyes off the water, never left the wheel and we secretly marvelled at his elastic bladder. Never once did he visit the loo!

'Well, that's okay. Shall we separate again and run on?'

M. Guillet came back aboard Prosilios, we cast off the warps and he opened the throttle.

'Clonk!'

The boat shook for a second. The engine raced. Something had gone. We had no drive, no steering. We were out of control, this time in turbulent water. Prosilios swung broadside to the stream and began to spin round. We felt as helpless as if we were in a bad skid. Roger and John, having trouble with one of their own engines, were caught unawares. It took all their skill to get alongside again with only one engine. Finally they made it. M. Guillet phlegmatically changed over to the Loon again. The boys got their other engine running, came aboard our boat and, having verified the fact that this was a real breakdown, something they could do nothing about, opened a bottle of wine. 'Well, cheers! All in the day's work!' Then, having plied M. Guillet with enough wine to make it impossible for him to tell north from south, they left it to him, curled up in the cockpit and went to sleep! M. Guillet steered on unperturbed. He might have been drinking water.

Two of the highlights we had been looking forward to on this leg of the trip were the great Mondragon lock, eighty-three feet deep, and the famous bridge at Avignon. We passed them both that morning and I hardly remember a thing. Our spirits had sunk pretty low. Mishap after mishap seem to dog us all the way. Nothing went right. Struggle after struggle, delay after delay—and the money pouring out. And now? This was evidently something serious. It would need an expert to put it right. We should be stranded at Arles. Where was the nearest Perkins agent? Marseille. That was fifty miles away. A vista of further delay, difficulty and expense stretched before us.

At 2.30 we tied up at the floating pontoon of the Club Nautique above Arles, paid off M. Guillet, who, without making any reference to our breakdown, solemnly wished us a 'pleasant trip' and left. At that moment such a farewell seemed highly ironical. John and Roger apologised for not being able to stand by to see us through. They explained that they really had to get on to Nice in the next three days where they would leave the Loon for another couple of chaps to bring back. We couldn't express our thanks. They had helped us out of trouble so efficiently, so generously and so casually, we just stood there pumping their hands. We certainly wouldn't have reached Arles without them and we wouldn't forget in a hurry. When they cast off, turned and planed away at full speed down the last twenty miles to the sea, we stood on that rickety pontoon of the Club Nautique looking across the river to the old town. It seemed a forlorn and deserted spot to be stranded.

*   *   *

Coming down river after that fateful 'Clonk!', Roger, John and I had studied the Perkins Z-drive Manual. The trouble couldn't be in the engine. That was running well and had gone on doing so after the breakdown. Something must have gone in the drive itself. If there was no power in either forward or reverse, the trouble probably lay in the linkage which operated the dog clutch inside the bulbous casing down by the propeller. That was as far as we would take it. In any case the whole Z-drive would have to be removed, dismantled and examined. Easy enough to do at a boatyard on a bench, but how to manage it afloat with nearly the whole drive under water?

The Canals

I spent the rest of the afternoon trying to get away from Arles where there were no facilities whatever. There was said to be a slipway at Port St. Louis, the mouth of the canal, could I get a tow down there? The factotum at the club drove me round to a bargee with time on his hands. Certainly he would tow me there. The price would be 10,000 francs (£90). It didn't appeal to me. Then I heard there was a yard at Arles in a disused branch canal. It turned out that, owing to the maddening French habit of shutting down the entire nation for the annual summer holiday, the owner was not there and the place closed. What to do? It seemed an absolute deadlock. We should never get away from this place. We turned in that night in almost a state of despair.

In the small hours I woke and began to think. To get the Z-drive off the boat we needed to lift the stern out of the water. This was necessary because there is a 'concertina' covering the shaft where it comes through the transom of the boat and connects with the bevel gears at the top of the drive. Here there is a universal joint permitting the drive to kick up should it strike some underwater obstruction. To keep this universal joint dry and well greased it is enclosed in a tubular rubber concertina which clips over the whole assembly.

So, somehow, we had to get this concertina up, clear of the water and, when we had extracted the drive, plug it in such a way that no water would get in when we lowered the boat back into the water. But how to lift the stern of a five-ton boat without a crane, sheerlegs or a skyhook? That was the problem.

The Rhône is a ferocious river, as I have said. High stone parapets, massive quays or tall banks protect the towns along its course from flooding. The Club Nautique at Arles stood well above the water on such a bank. Beside it a long pontoon lay anchored up and down stream about ten yards offshore, to which it was connected by a bridge, hinged on the bank so that it could rise and fall with the height of the river. Now, after a dry summer, the water was pretty low, so there was good clearance under the bridge. Although it was little more than a glorified 'companion way', less than three feet broad, a welded steel lattice either side formed the handrails and gave it some rigidity and strength. If we could move Prosilios round to the inner side of the pontoon into shallow water and get the stern under the bridge, we might be able to hang a block and tackle on the girders and haul her up—if the bridge didn't give way . . .

At any rate it was an idea and I got on the phone to M. Benoît, the Perkins representative, fifty miles away at Marseille. He was not very enthusiastic. However, when I had convinced him that I had to get away and there was no other possibility, he grudgingly agreed to drive out. He had never been to Arles and had no idea what he was in for, but next morning he turned up with a heavy block and tackle, his tools and bathing trunks. When he saw the set-up, he grew very taciturn and monosyllabic. He was a fine-looking young man who hardly ever smiled.

'This is no way to work,' he kept saying all the time he worked, but he was obviously competent and knew the drive, so I coaxed him to begin by getting down into the water before he did.

First we had to unshackle the long steel hawsers bracing the lower end of the bridge to the shore. We reckoned the bridge would hold without them for an hour. Then we had to manœuvre the boat's stern and make fast lines to hold her in just the right position, that is with the cockpit under the bridge. We rigged the anchor chain double to form a girth round the stern, slipped in tyres to protect the chines, hung the tackle under the bridge (it took two men to carry it and looked as if it could have hoisted the *Queen Mary*). Then we hooked up and spun the chain. She came up like a bird!

Now all we prayed was that one of those damned *peniches* wouldn't come hooting round the bend at about ten knots, making that god-awful wash which would batter the coaming against the bridge. There was only a two-inch clearance.

Quickly and deftly M. Benoît went to work, waist deep in the water. He slipped off the Teleflex control, removed the hinged kick-up plates, slid out the trunnions and, when we had taken the weight of the drive on a rope suspended from the bridge, pulled the splined shaft out of its socket. While I hauled the drive up on to the bridge, M. Benoît inserted a wooden disc in the open end of the concertina—the 'accordion', he called it—tightened up the clip and we lowered the boat into the water. Then we berthed her back against the pontoon, re-shackled the bracing hawsers that held the bridge, and had a drink. The whole job had taken under an hour.

We carried the drive up to an open shed under the club, drained off the oil and began to dismantle it.

'What does it say there?' said M. Benoît, pointing to a notice cast into the casing at the foot of the drive.

'Do not remove,' I told him.

He gave one of his rare smiles. 'Then let us remove it.'

When he got it apart we saw the trouble. The rod connecting the forward and reverse control at the top of the drive to the dog clutch at the bottom had snapped clean in half!

It transpired that a spare part would have to be obtained from Paris. In the U.K. it cost only a few shillings. Perkins Paris said they could replace the part free of charge, but I must pay all the rest of the costs. This sort of French thrift—let us call it by its right name, meanness—is surely out of place in a big international organisation like Perkins? It proved to be so, for when I got through to London, and my son phoned the main offices at Peterborough, the parent company accepted all charges without question.

So M. Benoît put the drive in his van and promised to do his best to get it back as soon as possible. He was as good as his word, but it took a week and left us with time on our hands in Arles.

*　　*　　*

During our hold-up at Lyons, visiting other craft moored along the quays at the Port de Plaisance was one of the evening pleasures. From many countries and of all shapes and sizes, their owners and crews were a cheerful, happy lot always willing—apart from the few snobs on the big boats—to swap adventures and experiences. Some had just come up river and were moving off north through the canals we had just left. We eagerly lapped up their tips about ports and charts in the Med and reciprocated, when we could, with details of our own route down through the canals to those who happened to be taking our way north. But the majority, like us, were moving south. Rather starry-eyed, we gossiped about the cruise we intended to make when, at last, we reached the sea.

Moored right next to us was a solid-looking motor cruiser, June-Ho, flying the American flag. A tall, keen-eyed man, who bore a striking resemblance to Rex Harrison, introduced himself as Howard Hirsch, captain, and his wife June, their three-year-old daughter, Bethany and Salty, her tabby kitten, as crew.

America is too vast a continent to generalise about, but,

having lived there on and off for some years, I must say that I often find their naïveté and self-assurance irritating and their assumption that the American way of life is superior to any other silly and tactless to boast about abroad. At the same time they are usually generous and hospitable and their almost childlike attitude to life is engaging. If only they could combine their openhandedness with some modesty and sophistication what a people they would be! Of course, some of them do. June and Howard were a striking example of it.

Perhaps it was the sea and the sobering wonder of it that made them so quiet and easygoing. Perhaps it was the way they had escaped from New York and their office jobs, weekend after weekend, to build June-Ho with the aim of bringing her somehow, someday, on a long cruise to Europe that had made them so careful and practical. No pie-in-the-sky for them. They had seen their dream boat when she was sunk in the bottom of the harbour and bought her as she was, for a song. They had salvaged her and rebuilt her from the bilges up. Into her had gone all the planning and care born of wide cruising experience. She had grown slowly through years of effort, so she was somehow more than a boat, she was the home of an exceptional family. June-Ho was not a luxury yacht, gadgeted out regardless of expense, but she was fully equipped to meet the unexpected, solid and well found throughout. In any circumstances, one felt, her captain would be able to cope.

But beyond all this Howard had that seamanlike quality I have mentioned earlier. He was always ready, anxious, to help. It was built into his character. Mention a difficulty or a need and up he came immediately with an idea, a possibility or the piece of equipment required. One day he even produced a polystyrene dummy head for Fanny's wig! I don't suppose anyone else in the world could fish up such an unlikely 'spare part' from their yacht equipment.

Their misfortunes coming south made ours look like good luck. When at last they had managed to get away and shipped the boat over to Rotterdam she had been badly crushed when lowered into the water. The seams opened up. She began to leak. The yard recommended specialised in steel and knew nothing about wood. It had taken weeks to get her seaworthy. Then Howard, jumping ashore, had slipped and cracked a bone in his heel. It had to be put in plaster and immobilised him on board. They took on a boy to help them down to Paris. In spite of warnings, he also had jumped ashore on a canal bank and promptly sprained his ankle. June had to cope, almost single handed and feed them all. Somehow they had at last reached Paris, where the American hospital treated Howard's heel and it became possible for him to move around the boat a bit more easily. Now, although he still limped and walked with some pain, it was almost normal and they had made a leisurely trip south.

So when, two days later, we saw *June-Ho* coming smoothly down river and watched her turn in to moor beside us on that rickety pontoon, we were pretty happy to see them and when we found they proposed to stick around in Arles for a day or two, happier still. As Howard and I ran out the 200 yards of cable which would bring the 220-volt power supply down from the club (and was a must for June's electric frying pan and vacuum cleaner) I told him of our latest snag. He listened with his usual sympathy and understanding to the way we had got that Z-drive off.

'There's always a way. All you have to do is find it, and, boy,' he laughed, 'did you find it!' So our acquaintance ripened into something more.

'We might cruise a bit in company when we reach the Med?' I suggested.

'That's exactly what I was thinking,' he rejoined.

*   *   *

But it was ten days before we were able to get away from Arles. We filled them as best we could. There is always something to do on a boat. So, while Fanny spring-cleaned and polished the chrome, I went over the logbook. The engine had now done 250 hours. I faced up, for the fourth time, to the fact that I must change the engine oil.*

The Perkins Manual says that the engine oil should be changed every fifty hours. When you are cruising in a boat which has no sail you depend entirely on your engine. You can't afford to have it go wrong from any laziness or carelessness on your part: that oil has to be changed.

With a car when the time comes for an oil change you simply put it on the hoist, remove the drain plug in the sump, run the oil out into a tin, replace the plug, lower the car and fill up again from the top in the usual way. Easy! But a marine engine lies between bearers down in the bottom of the boat. The sump plug is quite inaccessible and, even if you could get at it, who wants a gallon of used engine oil in their bilges?

Since Perkins sell hundreds of their 4/107 engines every year, it seems impossible they should not be aware of this important practical problem and, to ensure their engines give good service, would have devised some reasonable method of helping the owner to follow their instructions.

* The next few paragraphs are only of interest to the technically minded. Those who don't fall into this category won't miss anything by skipping them.

After all, it is a vital point. All they do (at the time of writing) is to supply a hand pump (as an expensive extra) and a length of rubber hose. The pump itself is a beautifully made article, but when you come to use it you find yourself back in the year 1910.

First you have to fix the end of the rubber hose over the top of the dipstick tube! This is situated way down on the side of the sump, so you have to stand on your head to reach it. Then you find that, to make an airtight fit, the hose is too small to go over the top of this tube until you have softened it in hot water! After ten minutes' fiddling by feel, if you are lucky and have long arms, you may manage to get the tube on. Now you are ready to begin.

Used engine oil is black filthy stuff and has a knack of splashing over everything. Fanny found the best way to deal with it was to put a plastic bag inside a bucket and when we had extracted the oil (or most of it) seal up the bag and, rather ashamedly, dispose of it in the nearest clump of bushes. Not very tidy, but what do you do with the stuff?

So, placing bucket and bag on top of the engine and holding the pump in the left hand, you begin to operate the plunger with the right, directing the nozzle into the bag. The pump has a sudden, squirting action. As it is rather stiff in operation, it isn't easy to keep it steady, so if eighty per cent of the oil ends up in the bag, you are lucky.

Obviously to fit the pump permanently in an accessible position on the engine with its own tube running down to the bottom of the sump would make all the difference. Why such a simple and essential modification has not been made standard on Perkins' best-selling engine, beats me.

This was not the only nutty feature we found in the design. We discovered another, even nuttier, when on the ninth day

M. Benoît returned with the repaired Z-drive and we repeated
the drill of hoisting up the hull under the club bridge. When
it was all in place M. Benoît set about filling the drive with oil.
He found he couldn't do it! The filler cap was obstructed by
the hinged kick-up plates right over it. So, up to his waist in
water and uttering strange Gallic oaths, he removed these
again and while I held them clear he filled up. The correct oil
level is determined by removing a plug in the side of the
casing. When the oil runs out, stop filling, replace the plug
and filler cap. This oil level, says the Manual, should be
checked every twenty hours. We lowered the boat into the
river. The plug was below the water level.

'How can you check the oil level with the plug under
water?' I asked Benoît.

He smiled and shrugged. 'Ask Perkins,' he said.

* * *

From across the river the old town of Arles looks a sleepy
place. It seems as if the dust of centuries has settled over it,
leaving a patina of fawn velvet which heat and light have
somehow baked into stillness. That romantic façade is quickly
shattered when you cross the bridge and thread your way
through the narrow crowded streets, busy with too many
cars, scooters and tourists. The shell of the Roman arena, the
vestiges of an old theatre and a pleasant square of cloisters
have a certain sleepy charm; but, for me, the market was the
best part of Arles. The booths stretch for over a mile along
both sides of a wide boulevard outside the walls and the place
is thronged with people who have come in from the surrounding countryside. It is one of those mammoth, all-purpose
markets where you can buy anything from radios to live

cygnets, from bicycle pumps to wine. The world streams up and down through the stalls at a leisurely pace, the old glad to gossip and the young to parade their flowered shirts and mini-skirts. Trees and awnings filter the glare and the heat, barkers shout the virtues of cheap crockery, housewives finger the plumpness of live poultry, old men in Turkish trousers and turbans sell lottery tickets, tourists choose dolls and buy postcards, shafts of sunlight strike naked plastic babies and cheap cotton goods dance in the wind.

The wind! It was our first experience of the Mistral. It burst on us suddenly and built up quickly to gale force. The trees along the river bank turned their backs and shivered, bent double before its force, their foliage streaming out, shuddering and swaying under an onslaught of blows, repeated and repeated, hour after hour, day after day. It is the sort of wind you never meet in the north, where gales bring clouds and rain. This *bourrasque* struck out of a clear, cloudless sky. It never let up. Funnelled between the mountains guarding the river valley, it swept by with a relentless, continuous pressure as if the earth had stopped rotating and the whole sky were rushing wildly over it. The pontoon heaved and ground its shackles, the boats nagged at their fenders and chafed their lines. Now we knew why sailors are wary of the Gulf of Lyons and the Bouches du Rhône. The Mistral is not to be trifled with.

Out in the Camargue it seemed more violent still. Here the vast flat marshes and heaths let it thunder over unchecked. It whirled into the arena of the bullring and we feared that the boys, timing their run in to snatch a rosette from those vicious charging horns, might be caught in some gust and impaled. But they were very nimble on their feet, or perhaps the bulls themselves, irritated by the dust and too often baited, had grown half-hearted, bored by the whole affair.

Some of them indeed refused to charge and turned away, making comical attempts to jump the barrier and return to the peace of their stalls. The famous wild white horses, a miserable and bedraggled herd, could hardly be induced to gallop as they were driven by. The wind indeed had taken the heart out of everything. It whisked the picnic baskets off the tables, slammed the chalet doors, lifted the girls' skirts while sober matrons leaned against it, holding their hats on as they tottered towards their cars. Cowed by its onslaught, we grew nervy and short-tempered and prayed for it to stop.

On the ninth day, as suddenly as it had come, it was gone. A marvellous stillness stole into the sky. We basked, relieved, relaxed and grateful. Then, fearing its return, we quickly cast off and headed for the sea. Now, at last, our troubles were over.

In close company we slid down over the empty waterway, past the featureless banks, looking for the kilometre markers hidden in the trees. An occasional seagull crowned the posts along the channel, a solitary yacht passed us, going north. After three hours we sighted a cluster of houses and turned into the last lock at Port St. Louis. Nobody seemed to take much notice of our arrival and only after repeated blasts on the horn did a lock-keeper appear. Port St. Louis has not, strictly speaking, got a lock. There is just a gate thrown across the wide basin at one end and a lift bridge at the other. There is no difference in water level and the place exists simply as a point to check incoming and outgoing traffic. We showed our papers, received the accolade of the all-powerful rubber stamp and moved out into the final stretch of canal. Now it was only two miles to the sea. Almost at the end lies a little yacht basin, crowded with boats, lonely and isolated under the huge dome of the sky.

And then! Over the guardian dykes we saw the shore

sweeping away in a great curve northwards to hold the Gulf of Fos. On its eastern arm a line of mountains beckoned us. The sea turned from green to that marvellous blue of which we had dreamed. It was a moment of great elation. Like the returning Greeks, long imprisoned in the mountains, we waved to June and Howard, shouting, 'Thálassa! Thálassa!' The sea! The sea!

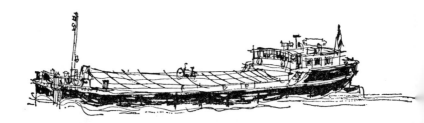

2

The Mediterranean

2

The Mediterranean

THAT first day was the Mediterranean we had dreamed of, the call of sun and blue seas, the reason we had made the trip. In spite of a week of gales, within twenty-four hours the sea had quite subsided and was now flat calm and deep violet blue. Under the cloudless sky we set course across the Gulf of Fos. A buoyed channel showed the way. Tankers were making up towards the Port de Bouc and when we had rounded Cape Couronne we hugged the coastline along towards Marseille, trying to check the landmarks from the Admiralty Pilot.

This proved almost impossible because of the spate of building that has taken place since the Pilot was compiled. The 'isolated tower on a hill', the 'pink farmhouse prominent from seaward' have now been obscured or dwarfed by blocks of apartment houses, clusters of villas or whole new settlements along that populous coast. The building goes on so fast that no guide can hope to keep up with it.

The Admiralty Pilot, which, after all, covers every coastline in the world, must be the most comprehensive and remarkable aid to navigation ever conceived and one of the most valuable legacies that British sea power has bequeathed to the world. It is only in the populous built-up coasts that it cannot keep pace, but we found, for instance, on the east coast of Italy, where little development has taken place, that its directions were astonishingly accurate, even on that featureless coastline.

Of course the sailing directions are intended for the use of large vessels. Its warnings of 'off-lying dangers', shoals, rocks and currents, often seem formidable to the owners of small craft.

'If you read the Pilot, you will never go to sea!' is an opinion I have often heard expressed. But a yacht sails blithely over the 'sunken rock at three fathoms' which would wreck a tanker and the sometimes sombre warnings must be read in that context. 'Better safe than sorry' must be the text pinned up over the desk of the Hydrographer of the Royal Navy.

But what a formidable task these dark blue volumes represent! Almost a century of tireless collection, collation and sifting of information from an army of observers on every coast in the world, continually revised, republished and annotated and somehow reduced to a uniform style, impersonal, terse, factual and containing a mine of accurate information. The Pilot is not light reading and often seems almost meaningless till you are on the spot. Then, navigating your way through some channel or making up towards a strange harbour, all the salient points fall into place and you are warned, informed and reassured. If you follow the Pilot you are most unlikely to find yourself in trouble.

To get some idea of the difficulties, try to do it yourself. Try to describe in words what you see, a coastline or the approaches to some harbour. Only then will you face the difficulties of reducing the changing visual image to concise directions. The Pilot does it all, clearly and simply and, in conjunction with the Admiralty charts (which represent another world-wide undertaking every bit as formidable), gives bearings, buoys, lights, hazards, soundings and throws in local information from port authorities on pilotage, quays, refuelling and water points, hospitals, provisions and even 'de-ratting'. Taken together, charts and sailing directions represent a monumental effort that our country offers freely to the world.

*   *   *

It was four o'clock that afternoon before the outlines of Marseille emerged from the evening haze that lay thick over the coast. The town is huge and the entrance to the Old Port, through the outer breakwater, narrow. A brisk chop was building up as we jostled with a score of fishing boats, trawlers, yachts and pleasure steamers coming in and out through the gap, but when we rounded the old forts we were amazed.

Le Vieux Port of Marseille must be unique in the world. An immense rectangular basin, surrounded by quays and backed by tall buildings of regular height, built, most of them, I imagine, in the nineteenth century, it is a 'city' port. Buses, cars and scooters whirl round it. Ships' chandlers, restaurants, cafés line the crowded streets. At the far end trawlers come dashing in to disgorge their catch for selling right there on the quay. Jutting out into the basin are dozens of floating pontoons to which are moored every kind of craft. Motor cruisers, yachts, speedboats, fishing craft sway and roll with every passing wash. There must be 4,000 boats parked in the basin.

The whole scene is full of movement, animated, gay and exciting. We followed June-Ho and hung around while she moored, seeking a berth nearby. It was the first time we had had to moor stern to the quay and a fresh cross-breeze made it tricky. However, we were directed to pick up a buoy which Fanny, rather to her own surprise, managed to do first shot. Then we backed in at the end of the pontoon (where later we found the wash most violent) and made fast.

We went aboard June-Ho to celebrate our first day in the Med with iced champagne. A thin mist came up, gauzing the lights as night fell. We sat on the bridge deck, enchanted. It seemed the most romantic port we had ever seen.

* * *

But next morning the sky was crystal clear and a wind had sprung up from the north-west. The Mistral was with us again. At first we made light of it. There was plenty to do. The womenfolk set off on those interminable shopping expeditions, looking for the market, finding the best bakery, comparing prices and railing at the iniquitous cost of everything in France. Meanwhile Howard and I went off in search of ships' chandlers and bonded stores, browsed round among displays of ropes and cleats, dropped into the Yacht Club—a large, well-appointed houseboat—for the weather forecast and then strolled along the quays, appraising the hundreds of fine craft in the harbour.

The fascination of a water-front never fails to cast its spell. Masts sway, burgees flutter, the water slaps and popples against white hulls, it is more vivid and lively than any other scene

I know. There is always so much going on, so much to see. Here is a fisherman mending his nets, threading his shuttle so quickly and deftly you can't really make out how the knot is tied. Here is a deckhand polishing the bright work of an immaculate yawl and another hosing foaming detergent off a laid teak deck. On the next pontoon an engineer is cosseting the motors of three twin-screw speedboats, kept, so we are told, for the weekend use of the directors of an insurance company. On the far side of the port, opposite the Town Hall, lies a huge 100-ton schooner with a mast eighty feet high and a boom like a tree-trunk: she hasn't been off her moorings for two years. Up there near the fuel pumps is the Pilots' Club and next to it the berths of the deep-sea trawlers, nets swinging from yards, rusty streaks below the chainplates. In a corner a cleaner with a grid-like spade is fishing out the flotsam and jetsam of empty bottles, floating tins and all the dirty rubbish that fouls up every harbour.

For nowadays there isn't a port in the world that isn't ruined by a scum of black oil. 'The internal combustion engine,' it has been said, 'was expressly invented to drive men mad.' But nobody would dream of giving up the madness. In the non-tidal waters of the Mediterranean there is no movement to disperse the greasy film that slops its filth round the waterlines of the smartest craft, making them look tatty and uncared for. As fast as you clean it off it comes back again. How many hours did we spend in a clean bay, swimming round our boat laboriously scrubbing it off! But there it is. Nothing to be done. We too had an engine and although we were meticulously careful not to spill a drop of oil overboard, I suppose, like everyone else, we did, and so added to the general mess.

The charm of the Vieux Port began to wear off after two

days. Marseille seemed to grow noisier, dirtier and more expensive the longer we stayed. The Mistral continued to blow with unabated fury. Three, four, five days passed and still it blew. Halliards slapped against masts in a continual tattoo which drove one mad, the movement in the harbour never stopped, Prosilios rolled day and night. The fish market at the end of the quays was deserted, not a trawler dared venture out. So it went on. Six, seven, eight days passed and still the cloudless sky hurled the air south. Now the total time we had lost en route was over three weeks. August was almost over. The season was getting late. Should we make Greece by Christmas?

* * *

How well we remembered that Christmas in Corfu! We had been guests of the big family sitting round the table at tea. When it was over Emlyn said: 'Do you think your mother would like me to do a Christmas piece for her?'

The old lady has had a thrombosis and her life has only just been saved. Now she is slowly recovering, lying quietly upstairs in her simple room. Everyone is excited, delighted at the unexpected idea. We file upstairs, past the trap-door (which can still be lowered in case of attack by pirates) and go quietly in. She is lying propped up with pillows, white hair hanging in two severe plaits, hands folded on the counterpane. Everything about her is very still. She is composed, almost as if in prayer. Only her eyes smile at us all, big, luminous. In the corner a small fire flickers in the sort of cast-iron grate that belongs to the time of Victorian nurseries.

We greet her, settle down, and Emlyn, straddling a chair and leaning his arms on its back, begins in such an ordinary voice it seems just a continuation of his conversation. But

Dylan Thomas is a weaver of spells and soon we are all
bemused, the children's eyes sparkle and the words, vibrating
in our ears, call up for each of us the memories of other days,
other faces, evoking a host of ghostlike echoes, scenes of
faraway, cut now by death or time, forgotten till that moment,
now alive again . . .

She looks so frail in the plain iron bed on the bare wood
floor, so frail, yet so alive, so happy. We sit spellbound in the
trance woven by a great artist, woven for her in that tiny room,
so simply, so spontaneously, it almost seems as if it were an
improvisation, never heard before . . .

Outside the moon makes a glittering roadway over the sea
and the little church where all her sons have been baptised
stands black against it.

*   *   *

On the morning of the 30th we were up at 4 a.m. The
wind, as forecast by the locals, had dropped on the ninth day.
Even though the swells might not have abated, we decided to
make a dash for it. Once we could get round the corner, only
twelve miles away, we should be protected from the worst of
the weather. An hour and a half of discomfort, we said, and
then a clear run. So we left our moorings at 6.30 in company
with June-Ho and Athos, a German motor cruiser, belonging to
a rather talkative dentist we had met the day before. We
assumed he had gained his loquacity from having to keep up
a monologue to his gagged patients. But he was a good chap—
besides, he had a slimline crew on board of such light displacement and superb lines that, had we not been sure of our
navigation, she could easily have lured us off course . . .

The kick seemed to have gone out of the swell. The lee of
the offshore islands protected us. We passed the Château d'If,

mecca of the five-franc pleasure boats, and an hour later rounded the island of Le Maire and turned east. Here, protected from the north-westerly swell, the sea was flat calm. Fishermen laid nets, dolphins leaped and we ran inside the islands, the three of us in close company, enjoying the dramatic scenery and the beautiful morning. The auto pilot was functioning perfectly. It was wonderful to be at sea again and to escape the blessings of civilisation.

At 9.30 precisely, three hours out, my engine note suddenly changed and the revs dropped to 2,000. I whipped off the hatch cover to be greeted by a spray of diesel oil. Kneeling over the engine I saw it low down, spurting out of one of the unions to the fuel pump. There was clearly no future in that. I signalled to the others and stopped the engine, devoutly grateful that, for the second time, there were friends around when we were in trouble.

Athos was nearest. She threw me a line and, as soon as we were safely in tow, I went back to the engine. Loosening up the nut where the fuel had been spraying out, I found the aluminium 'olive' (which seals the joint on the end of the line) quite loose on the tube. Luckily the mechanic at Lyons had given me half a dozen olives he happened to have in his pocket as spares, so I slipped the loose one off and a new one on, tightened up, spun the starter and we were back in business. When I saw the revs remained normal and there was no sign of a leak, I signalled *Athos* and we cast off the tow, shouting our thanks, and all three of us continued on our way. The repair had taken twenty minutes.

Now we were approaching Cap Sicie, the sombre cliff-face over 1,000 feet high that guards the western approaches to Toulon. We had been warned that if there was any bad weather about this was the place for it. The swell had been slowly rising over the last hour, but it was astern, and as we ran east about three miles offshore we were soon planing on the crests and could only judge its strength by the way one or two yachts plugging west were bucking into it. *Athos*, rolling rather heavily, hurried on to get out of the bad water and was soon a mile ahead. *June-Ho* came up alongside and shouted she was going into Le Mandrier. I yelled that I would continue to Porquerolles, not wanting to waste the day. We had been running two hours since my breakdown, all was well and it was only eleven o'clock. Howard shouted back that he would press on, catch up *Athos* and tell her not to lose me. As he forged ahead I wondered if he would ever do so, the German seemed to have the legs of both of us. When *June-Ho* seemed pretty well hull down on the horizon my engine died right out. We broached to and rolled helplessly in the swell . . .

What now?

It seemed an age before Howard saw we were again in trouble. He turned and the sight of him turning to rescue us is one I shall never forget. We got a tow made fast and proceeded at three knots into the Bay of Toulon. Once in the lee of the land, the swell abated and by 1.30 we were both safely berthed in the little port of Le Mandrier. It had been quite a morning.

*   *   *

The new marina at Le Mandrier is one of many the French have developed to encourage the great get-away-from-it-all yachting boom. Such ventures are strictly commercial and depend on the fees charged for berthing to recoup their costs. This depends upon the number of visitors the port attracts and this, in turn, upon the 'atmosphere' of the place, the personnel, the public relations. The word soon gets around.

It is probably not fair to judge Le Mandrier by its atmosphere the day we happened to drop in, for they were holding some international dinghy race the next day (Sunday) and the whole place was in a flap, festooned with racing boats and crowds of teenage crews. The officious young lady who ran Le Mandrier was suffering from frigidity—at least as far as visiting yachts was concerned.

However, the Port Captain was a friendly type—most port captains are—and when he had listened to my story, and told me I should never raise the Perkins agent on a Saturday afternoon, I was resigned to wait over till Monday. Then two young men appeared. They didn't claim to be Perkins experts, but said they had experience of the engine. I told them the story, the water, the air, the rust in the tank.

'And do you suppose you are the only yacht in the Mediterranean with rust in her tank, M'sieu?' said one, rather pityingly. 'Everybody has rust in their tanks. Fit a fibreglass tank, M'sieu, if you want to get rid of rust.'

Of course it was true; obvious when you come to think of it, in a fibreglass boat. No reason at all why existing bulkheads should not be divided to hold fuel and water, covered over and incorporated into the mould of the hull. Besides, far more fuel and water could be carried this way, making use of the wasted space in the bilges, and nothing could rust! That was the great point. Some firms have already tumbled to this. Of course, there are alternatives, stainless steel or the 'hot-water bottle' type of tank made of some rubber compound which takes up the shape of the hull where it is placed. One thing is certain, as far as I am concerned, I would never again go to sea with an iron tank. So take my advice, and if you happen to be buying a boat, and the builder tries to sell you one, kiss him goodbye and tell him you have read Turn Right for Corfu.

The boys bled my engine for the nth time, got it running and pronounced it okay, but I wasn't really satisfied. The air was getting in again somewhere and I felt that nagging 'mystery' feeling coming on. Something was wrong. You could put it right for a day, but that was useless. We still had hundreds of miles to cover. We couldn't go on like this.

*   *   *

The morning's experience had alarmed us. Supposing we had been alone, as we well might have been, then where should we have ended up? On the very sharp rocks of Les Deux Frères, or, at best, wallowing around in a heavy swell launching the dinghy or waiting for someone to pick us up.

Did I mention that we had a dinghy aboard *Prosilios*? Well, anyway, we did. It was an eight-foot six-inch Campari with a folding floor. It packed up into a pillow case and lay, unused and unsung, stowed away in the cockpit. I had always thought of dinghies as last-resort escape routes. Heroics! 'She's going! Take to the boats!'—and all that sort of thing. You've struck a rock. It's Force 9. You're badly holed. She's flooding. You throw the wife, the flares, the cigarettes, matches and a tin of corned beef into the dinghy. You shove off. And as you do so, the poor old girl rears up, her fine prow defying the sea to the last, and plunges below the waves. 'Well, she was a fine ship,' you say between clenched teeth as you pull the wife aboard. (You didn't throw her quite straight.) Then—you'll never know how you did it (and nor will anyone else)—with one oar—the other has been bitten in two by a shark—drenched with spray and at the end of your tether, you manage with superhuman skill to drive the dinghy straight on to the next rock. As a matter of fact, it comes up through the bottom. 'Well, that solves the mooring problem,' you laugh lightly (not wanting your wife to know the situation is desperate). And then, as the seas redouble their fury, the miracle happens. The lifeboat appears. They can't reach you, but they yell over the tremendous seas, 'We'll shoot you a line!' They do, and their aim is so good it goes right through the side of the dinghy. Out goes the air, out goes your last hope. You are floundering in the water. The man-eating sharks are flexing their dentures—and the next thing you know you're lying in a clean bed in the hospital. 'It's a miracle you're alive' says the nurse. You wave her aside. 'Get my broker on the line!' you shout. 'I want a new boat. I must get to sea!'

In somewhat more sober moments I had come to the conclusion that an inflatable dinghy was strictly a duckpond vehicle to be used only for getting ashore when you were starving in a tropical lagoon—where it didn't matter if you fell in. True, I had a good friend who always carried his, half inflated, on his coachroof. When I asked him why, he said: 'When she blows up, I might just have time to throw it overboard.' Somehow the mental picture of this elderly, excellent mariner, hurled into the air by his exploding vessel, grimly hanging on to the painter of a half-inflated dinghy, was something which, in spite of my respect for him, I found it hard to take seriously. But there it is. They come all sizes and shapes at sea.

But to return to our inflatable. We had only used it once. That was in Calais. You may remember I described earlier how we careered into harbour with a runaway engine. When we had tied up and calmed down a bit I realised that we had better let someone know of our predicament. The tide was rising. In about three hours the gates of the yacht basin would open, and somehow or other we had to get inside. But how? At that moment those gates stood in the middle of a twenty-foot wall over the top of which cars were passing. We were about 100 yards away, and beyond the wall, I presumed, lay the marina. It was raining heavily. We were soaked to the skin, we'd been ten hours at sea and crossed the Channel—which for us at that time was about equivalent to the Atlantic.

'I must go ashore in the dinghy,' I announced.

Now at that time my wife had never seen an inflatable dinghy. I had never seen this one. It was still securely packed in its carton. Somehow or other we got it out, screwed the collapsible oars together, unrolled the rubber bundle and spread it across the cockpit, found the way, after several false starts, to get the wooden folding floor to lie flat, and then pulled out our magic Japanese electric dinghy inflator. I had bought this as a sort of joke, never imagining it would really work. But it did. As the rain pelted down, we plugged it in, discovered how to attach it to the valve and switched on. The little motor screamed away like an infuriated hornet, the pump on the end of it shot the air in and the dinghy began to come to life. Half of it swelled like some anaesthetised grampus and took on its sausage shape. We repeated the dose on the other side, screwed down the valves and there she was in five minutes—ready for sea. (You will have noted the subtle difference. An inflatable is 'it' when folded, 'she' when inflated.)

'What do we do with it now?' said Fanny.

'Just throw her overboard,' I said in as offhand a manner as I could manage with the rain pouring down my nose.

'Won't it float away?' asked Fanny.

'Of course she won't. There's the painter.'

'The painter?' Fanny looked vaguely around, as if she

expected some interior decorator to materialise from over the side to hold the dinghy for us.

I unravelled the neatly coiled painter ('What a beautiful clothes line it would make,' said Fanny) and secured the end of it firmly to a cleat. Then I gave Fanny the oars to hold and threw the dinghy overboard. She slid into the water with a satisfactory flap and bobbed around looking rather pleased with herself. We were rather pleased too. Getting it together for the first time under these conditions was, we thought, quite a feat. Now all I had to do was to get aboard and pull for the shore.

Easier said than done. For it didn't take me a second to realise that it was next to impossible to get that dinghy to stay still. She waltzed around, she slid away, she came bobbling up to the side and cannoned off. She behaved as coyly—if you will forgive the analogy—as a young bride being invited to get into bed on her wedding night.

The side of our cockpit in *Prosilios* is about three feet above the water. When I sat on it, feet overboard, I could just touch the side of the dinghy with my toes. Standing six foot four and weighing fifteen stone, as soon as I put any weight on, she shot away from under me. This sort of situation is one which puts Fanny in her element. She was full of ingenuity, clutched one end of the clothes line to pull the dinghy in short, got hold of her favourite light collapsible boathook and grabbed the dinghy lifeline (which runs round it) and somehow managed to get our jelly baby—for that's what she looked like—to lie alongside. By this time Fanny (who is only just over five feet) was, of course, spread-eagled over the side, arms stretched wide, holding both ends.

'Now, love,' she said, 'I think I've got it.'

I could see what was going to happen. If I didn't get my

weight fair and square in the middle, this young lady was going to put skids under me. More or less sitting on Fanny's head, I decided I'd better make a bold movement and just get in. As my weight came on, the boathook slipped, the dinghy shot away. I lost my balance, fell in the boat and lay on my back floundering. It was the sort of thing which would have sent bystanders at a marina into hysterics. At the time I didn't think it particularly funny. I managed to lever myself up into a sitting position and told Fanny to haul me in. It seemed the least movement would tip me overboard and though I was wet through already, the waters of Calais harbour were not my idea of the end of a perfect day. Somehow or other, between us we managed to thread the oars through their eyes (called rowlocks), Fanny cast off and I began to try to row. The diminutive oars were no more than paddles. Pull on one more than the other and round you skid in a circle. It took me ten minutes to do those hundred yards and I'd been half round the harbour before I got to the jetty. There a small boy tied me up and I rolled ashore in a prone position with one leg left in the air as the wretched dinghy shot out from under me.

I think I have said enough to make it clear that nothing short of fire would have made us take to the dinghy. But still, all the pleasure of our trip was being marred by this constant anxiety. We set out waiting for the motor to stop. Every time our troubles seemed to be over—until the next time. We went through rapid cycles of depression and optimism. Now we were in a trough. 'If I could sell the boat tomorrow,' I wrote to my son, 'even if I dropped a thousand on it, I'd gladly do so.'

But, of course, we couldn't sell her. We had been through this plenty of times. Leave her where we happened to be, in some yard, to be . . . sold? Who could you trust? In the

autumn it might be six months before you found a purchaser
and she would deteriorate hopelessly without care. Stop and
winter with the boat where it was? In this dump! No thanks;
we were bound for Corfu. Then why not ship her there and
forget the trip? And what would that cost? So, inevitably, we
came back to the same answer—we were stuck with it and had
to see it through. Secretly some part of me responded to this
challenge. I didn't want the thing to beat me. I felt that somehow or other we had to get through these troubles. I wanted
to sail into Corfu, coute qui coute.

*   *   *

The weather forecast that evening was not encouraging. A
Levanter was promised. A neighbour in the next berth warned:
'Look out for that wind. Worse than the Mistral. It raises a
nasty swell.' Harbours, I've decided, are full of types like
these.

'I wouldn't go today . . . You ought to have gone yesterday . . . Wait for it to settle . . . I wouldn't trust the forecast.
Get going, now: it's money for jam . . . Believe me, I know
the local signs . . . I can smell a storm . . . Hang on for a day or
two . . .' So it goes. And what is the result? Harbour rot sets in
and harbour rot is a disease from which fifty per cent of all
yachts in marinas suffer. You see beautiful boats lying there
week after week throughout the season—and they never go to
sea! Some owners have spent tens of thousands on them,
equipped them like an electronic wedding cake, and all they
do is come down for Sunday tea in the cockpit during a
heatwave.

So I never listen to these Jonahs. I go straight to the fisherman to get the local conditions and take his advice. I've never

known it wrong. Unfortunately fishermen don't haunt yacht marinas. To find them you have to dig them out in the old port—where it doesn't cost £1 a night to tie up.

That day the port seemed too far away, so in company with June-Ho, we set off eastwards across Le Grand Rade de Toulon in the direction of Porquerolles. Once we were out in the open mouth of the bay, the Levanter made itself felt. An hour before it had been calm, now it was a healthy chop that was steadily building up. Squalls blackened the water. There were no fishing craft out—always an ominous sign. We altered course so as not to take it right on the nose and edged round the eastern arm of the bay, hoping to sneak into Salettes, our 'alternative' refuge port, if the going got tricky.

As we came up to Point Carqueiranne we passed a little port with a few masts and a row of houses, but failed to identify it. Funny how if a port isn't marked on the map you somehow can't believe it exists. You almost prefer to trust the map to your eyes. But there it was all right. We pushed on round the point. Then we took the full force of the Levanter square on our bows. We bashed into the crests and set course for Australia in the hollows. The boat was riding fine, but the motion was terrific. I looked over to June-Ho, usually so sedate and composed, she too was showing her undersides and dropping her straight stem pretty well down to the deck in the troughs. I imagined the motion on the high bridge deck aft would be worse than ours. Anyway, I opted out of this form of smash and grab, turned to make for the little unknown port and was relieved when I saw Howard do the same. We came up to the place gingerly. I only draw two feet six inches, so there is usually plenty of water for me, but June-Ho draws five feet or more and has to watch it.

There were not a lot of craft in the harbour and they were

all small. The Levanter, whistling round the point, was sending brisk squalls of wind across the water. We managed to drop a kedge aft and get the bows snugged in and went ashore to help June-Ho who had to stay on the seaward end of the pontoon. When she was safely moored we were confronted by the Port Captain in a beautiful uniform evidently designed by himself. He volubly and emphatically told us to go away.

'Tell him to go away,' said Howard, 'that's a better plan.'

The Port Captain informed us that the port was not open. It was under construction. When the new breakwater was completed, then . . . Meanwhile it was a port for small boats. It was full up (this was manifestly untrue) and we would do far better to return to Toulon where we should be much more comfortable. 'It is for your own good, M'sieu, for your own good.' He was formal and perfectly polite, but he wanted no part in us.

It's a curious thing when you are making a cruise and have an objective, how you don't like going back. As far as I was concerned, this little port of Les Oursinières represented another ten miles gained in the direction of Corfu and I damned well wasn't going to lose it. We might only be hanging on by our eyelids, but the Captain's decision is final as to when the weather is suitable for his ship to go to sea, and, as far as I was concerned, this weather wasn't suitable, so here I was and here I was going to stay. I told the Port Captain so, using a somewhat less direct phraseology. He shrugged and left. We stayed.

*   *   *

Next morning, after doing the usual daily check of oil level, batteries and water, I started up the engine. It ran irregularly, one cylinder was out. When I opened up the hatch there was

that same fine mist of diesel. This time it was leaking from a
union where the fuel line entered the injector. I tightened up
the nut, the spray was worse. It was no good. I shut off the
engine and sat on the hatch, a prey to gloomy dejection. It
seemed we would never come to the end of our troubles. It
was hopeless to drag on from port to port in a state of continual anxiety. The whole engine and fuel lines must be
completely overhauled before we moved another inch.

I talked it over with Howard. 'You'd be crazy to go to sea
with a dicky motor. You must get it fixed.' So we should have
to part company, for he had friends waiting for him in St.
Tropez and had to get there as soon as possible. The Levanter
was still blowing, but it wasn't too bad. 'I'll phone you
tonight to tell you where I am and, as soon as you're fixed,
join us in St. Raphael. I'll wait for you there.'

We helped June-Ho cast off and sadly waved her crew farewell
as they turned the point. Now we were on our own. We
shouldn't have the reassuring sight of that good solid hull
with June's bicycle on the forehatch sitting steady on our
quarter, the pleasure of making port together, meeting up for
the evening drink, chewing the rag on the day's trip, browsing
over charts and planning the next run.

'I don't suppose we'll ever see them again,' said Fanny as we
turned away.

'Of course we shall. They're going to winter in Menton or
San Remo, so we're bound to overtake them somewhere.'

But privately I thought how easy it would be to miss
them—and how sorry I should be if we did. Well . . . The best
antidote to depression is action. Better get on with the problem
of the engine. After all, Toulon wasn't fifteen miles away and
there was supposed to be a good Perkins agent there.

In my fluent but ungrammatical French I explained all the

symptoms on the phone. Whoever I was talking to evidently
knew his business. 'I will send a man out to you at once,
M'sieu. He will leave in a quarter of an hour.'

I thought that meant we might see him after lunch, but
within an hour a van drew up and a quiet competent-looking
chap came aboard. We sat down in the cockpit and I told him
the whole story.

'You have been bleeding those lines far too much, M'sieu.
Every time you loosen them you break the seal and, if you go
on doing it, it is natural for them to leak. If you have air in the
system, you must bleed it at the filter and by the nut on the
side of the pump. *Never touch the injector unions.* If you want the
engine to run, *leave it alone!*'

I told him I would be only too happy to leave it alone,
but . . .

'Now, the water. You say there was rust on the bottom of
the tank. How did it get there, that rust?'

'From the water in the fuel.'

'But rust is an oxide of iron. It comes from the iron being
in contact with *air*. What air can there be when the water is
under the diesel? No, M'sieu. It does not make sense. That tank
must have been rusty when it was put in your boat. Before it
was filled.'

'But it was a new tank.'

He shrugged. 'Maybe. But how long had it been lying about
before it was fitted? Perhaps in the open air. Perhaps in your
English rain . . . You say you cleaned it, your tank, at Lyons?'

'As well as we could.'

'Do not derange yourself about the rust. If there is any left,
the filters will catch it. Now the filters. Let me see the filters.'

I showed him the filters. 'It is a big filter that extra one you
have fitted. Perhaps it is a very good filter. But now you have

three filters in the line. So the pump must work harder to pull the fuel through. I do not say it will not do it, but it is better to trust to the filters that are recommended by Perkins. They know the engine. They have experience.'

He opened his toolbox and brought out a complete set of fuel lines, each protected by its own plastic bag. He dismantled the old lines, shaking his head. 'These lines have been forced, M'sieu. Distorted. It is essential they should fit absolutely square to the unions. They are specially bent for this purpose.'

I thought of the man who had repaired the pump at Lyons. It was 7.30 at night before he finished. The temperature was ninety. He was in a hurry, hot, tired. So maybe that was it.

Very carefully and slowly he fitted the new lines.

'You will have no more trouble there, M'sieu, if you leave them alone.'

'I will leave them alone.'

'Now the fuel line. Let me see.' And he pulled off the length of plastic tube by which we had bypassed the extra filter that day coming down the Rhône and carefully examined the ends.

'Here is the trouble, M'sieu. Here is where your air is coming in.' And he offered the tube for my inspection.

For the non-technically minded, I should explain that there exists in the U.K. an excellent fitting called a Jubilee Clip for joining hose to metal. But these fittings are not made in small diameters. At Arles, to replace the copper wire John Wild had twisted round the plastic tube coming down the river, I managed to get hold of two small clips of inferior design and fitted them. Now I saw they had pinched the tube unequally, leaving a slight kink through which a minute quantity of air could pass. So the engine would run smoothly for two or three hours, then the amount of air in the system would slowly build up and it would stop. Bleed off that air and it would be good for another two or three hours and so on. From such small things can you have a breakdown at sea.

From his toolkit this lifesaving man produced a new type of miniature flexible clip I had never seen before. He also produced a new length of rubber hose. He fitted four clips, two at each end, and tightened up. 'No air will get in there now, M'sieu. It is quite safe.'

After further checks on the filters, and bleeding the lines to get out the air which had been let in by taking it all apart, the engine caught at the first turn of the starter.

'Now, if you leave it alone, M'sieu, you will have no further trouble.'

He sat down to write out his bill. I paid him £20 and he receipted it, shook my hand and left.

Since that day I have never touched the engine—except for routine maintenance—and it has run perfectly.

*   *   *

But, of course, that day I did not know it would. The Levanter had grown angry during the day and now was sending vicious squalls across the bay. Howard phoned in the evening as he had promised.

'Fine run to Porquerolles,' his faraway voice came weak over the line, 'and what d'you think we met on the way? A guy adrift with air in his fuel lines! We gave him a tow into harbour.' So I wasn't the only one! Somehow it was typical he should have been around to give a helping hand. 'But then it started to blow up and we had to put into Lavandou. Got really bad that last half-hour. This Levanter certainly packs a punch. Call me tomorrow at St. Raphael and tell me how you've made out.'

But next day it was worse. Squall after squall blackened the bay, dust clouds flew, the trees bent double, not a boat at sea. We held another of our dismal councils. First it had been the Mistral from the west, now it was the Levanter from the east. If we weren't held up by breakdowns, we were held up by weather. It was getting late in the year. We were already in September and there were still a lot of miles to cover and obviously it was a bad season. We bore a grudge against this famous picture-postcard coast for not living up to our dream of blue skies and calm seas.

'I'd like to skip the lot, right down past Genoa. Why don't we hire a railway truck and ship the boat to Spezia?'

'Well,' said Fanny, 'let's see how it is tomorrow.'

The next day the wind lived up to the forecast of the locals. It blew even harder and when I asked how long this east wind could keep it up, they shrugged, 'Sometimes for a fortnight.'

I set out by bus for the Toulon railway station.

*   *   *

I once heard of a Kenya farmer who kept a grey parrot as a pet. He used to take it everywhere with him. When he went off in his truck round the farm he used to tether it to the canopy. Apparently the bird didn't think much of these trips and every so often, not realising he was tied by the leg, tried to take off back to the woods. Of course, this came to an abrupt and ignominious end when he reached the limit of the string and he fluttered down, complaining vociferously. Thereupon the farmer laughed, fussed him and set him back on his perch, muttering.

I'd never thought of this story as having any allegorical significance until the other day when I began trying to recall the curious incidents of this trip. The more I thought about it, the more I was forced to the conclusion that 'something' had taken a hand throughout. I'd always been willing to believe, in principle, that 'There's a divinity that shapes our ends, rough hew them how we may', as Shakespeare put it. But I had never really applied it practically. Now I was forced to. For instance, we had made that ten-hour Channel crossing with enough rust and water in our tanks to have stopped us a dozen times. In retrospect it made my hair curl. But we hadn't stopped. We might have been in a first-class mess on the Rhône if we hadn't had to wait a week there for another propeller and so happened to meet John and Roger, who came to our rescue when we broke down. That delay at Lyons was when we happened to meet Howard and June. Where should we have been without them when the engine packed up off Cap Sicie? We continually complained of our bad luck, but, in fact, it had always been balanced, and overbalanced, by good luck. Something—call it destiny for want of a better word— seemed throughout to be 'shaping our ends'. Our frenzied attempts to 'do' something about our difficulties were, so to speak, taken for granted. We had to act as we did because we were the sort of people we were. But it was incidental and even irrelevant to the overall shape of the trip. This went on growing from day to day on its own unforeseen lines and the best thing to do was to let it alone. But, of course, not understanding what was going on, we couldn't let it alone. We were always meddling with it. Usually that didn't much matter. It was only when we made a determined effort to strike out in another direction that, like the parrot, we were abruptly stopped and set back on our truck. Of course, all this can easily be put down to circumstances, chance, coincidence and all the rest of the mish-mash that people spout who fear for their famous 'free will'. They may be right, but the older I grow, the more my faith grows in some divine order of things that I don't at all understand, but which, if I could let it alone, would at least save me wasting a tremendous lot of energy.

Anyway, that morning all my energies were centred on hiring a truck. It was something I had never tried to do before and it took me to the freight offices of the French National Railways. How much, I enquired, would it cost me to freight my boat to Spezia? Having given all the details of length, breadth, height, weight, etc., the clerk made his calculations.

'It will cost you about five hundred francs to send it to the frontier at Ventimiglia,' he announced.

'But I don't want to send it to Ventimiglia, I want to send it to Spezia.'

'Of course. It can continue to Spezia. I am telling you the price to Ventimiglia.'

'But I don't want the price to Ventimiglia, I want the price to Spezia.'

'Ah, that I cannot tell you, M'sieu. I am telling you the price to Ventimiglia. Now the price from Ventimiglia to Spezia, that is a matter for the Italian State Railways and no doubt they will inform you about that when your boat arrives at the frontier.'

I was amazed. 'At the frontier! You mean to tell me that you have no idea of the Italian freight rates?'

'Here we are in France and we deal with the French rates. In Italy they will give you the Italian rates.'

'Listen,' I said to him, 'you belong to the Common Market, so does Italy. You export goods to Italy. How can a French merchant send goods to Italy if he does not know what it will cost him?'

He shrugged. 'He will inform himself as to the Italian rates by approaching the Italian authorities.'

This conversation really made me feel I was in a madhouse. It continued for a quarter of an hour and got absolutely nowhere. Talk about American isolationism, French isolationism had it looking silly.

At last I was conducted through to another office where I explained the problem all over again. To me it seemed a perfectly simple matter, like buying a railway ticket to go abroad. What would a traveller to Paris say if he were told at Victoria that he could only get a ticket to Calais and must inquire the price in France when he got there! The thing was ludicrous, farcical.

The head of the freight department was a bit more co-operative.

'It is true, M'sieu, that I do not know the Italian rates. For that I must phone to Paris. They will give me the rates. Then I shall be able to tell you what it will cost to take your boat to Spezia. Have the goodness to come back in half an hour.'

I went, did some shopping and returned. Yes, I was told, Paris had informed him of the rates. It would cost approximately £100 to send the boat to Spezia.

'And now, M'sieu, as to the question of lifting the boat out of the water and placing it on the truck and—naturellement—lifting it off the truck at Spezia and putting it back in the water?'

For this, I was informed, I must present myself at the offices of an agent who was experienced in such matters and he would undertake the work. All I should have to do was to bring the boat alongside a quay at Toulon, the crane would be ready, the truck would be at my disposal and the train would then leave. And how long would it take?

'Let us say four days. The line to Spezia is direct, via Genoa.'

After further telephone calls to the loading agents my rough calculation was that the whole job would cost £150 plus.

'And when will you require the truck, M'sieu?'

'I must discuss the matter with my wife. It is very expensive. I will return tomorrow.'

I got the bus back to Les Oursinieres about 6 p.m. It was still blowing a gale.

*   *   *

At half past three next morning I was wakened by the silence. The never-ending tattoo of halliards against masts had stopped, the gusty breathing of the wind as it came over the hill back of the little port had ceased. It was absolutely still. Dawn would come in an hour. Should we have a go? It was only about twelve miles on to Porquerolles, surely we could get that far before the wind sprang up again? Every mile to the east was a mile gained. To snatch even that much out of the eye of the wind before it woke up would be a victory. The hell with railway trucks, the delay, the expense, and, above all, the feeling of being defeated. . . . I woke Fanny.

'The wind's dropped. Let's have a go!'

I quickly dressed and, as soon as I put my head out, saw why it was so quiet. A thick mist enveloped everything, bringing that sense of extra stillness that always seems to come when you cannot see. Down the hill came two yellow eyes, slowly feeling their way. The car stopped. Doors slammed. Two men got out. Fishermen.

'What do you think?' I asked.

They looked up into the mist in a contemplative sort of way.

'If you are going, go now. The wind will lift the mist when the sun comes up.'

I went back on board to find Fanny already up and the water boiling. We always have something hot before starting the day's run and have found that at sea a system of two-hourly feeds works best. Chocolate, biscuits, coffee are the usual snacks that punctuate the day. We find we can keep going for eleven or twelve hours that way and have a wonderful appetite for supper. As we ate we discussed getting out of the little harbour. It was shallow and so narrow that we had come in to moor bow first, dropping a kedge behind us. Now we should have to haul out backwards on the kedge, get it in, swivel round and pick our way out through the close file of boats. Perfectly easy, even in the dark, provided we both know the plan. If we don't do this we find it usually ends in chaos. Under the helmsman's canopy, with the engine running, you cannot hear a word of anything said on the foredeck and if I want to be heard when I'm at the wheel I have to be careful to put my head out and shout.

That morning it all went smoothly. We cast off at 5.30 and, once we were past the breakwater, I set the auto pilot on a safe course out across the bay and left the engine ticking over, which just gave us steerage way. This, we found, was the best way to free us both to coil down the lines, wind up the anchor warp on its spool (which needs both of us on the fore-deck), get in the fenders and generally make ready for sea. On Prosilios the side decks are narrow and even with a slight chop the movement soon gets sharpish, so we try to avoid leaving the cockpit at sea. Indeed, there is no reason to do so.

But when we put about to weather the group of large naval buoys moored off the point I realised for the first time that we had really put to sea in a fog! It wasn't a real pea-souper, but it was pretty thick. Looking along the coast before we had turned, you could see the misty haloes round streetlights perhaps 200 yards away, but at sea there are no streetlights and it's extremely difficult to know how far you really can see. But with the dawn I hoped the visibility would increase. So we set course across the Gulf of Giens for Point Escampobariou. A heading of 135°M would clear the point nicely, but it would also mean we should be leaving an isolated rock, Les Fourmigues, fine on our starboard bow. In other words, if we were too much to the east, we should run into the mainland; if we were too much to the west, we might do a cannon off the rock. On a fine day there was bags of room, but this wasn't a fine day. It was jolly thick with the fag end of the swell that had been racing west for the last three days and a grey curtain all round us through which we peered harder and harder as the minutes ticked by and we knew the outline of something jolly sharp might come up far too suddenly. Dead reckoning told us that we ought to strike—or, shall we say, come abreast of—that isolated rock in exactly thirty minutes. But, in the way it always happens in moments of anxiety, as it came up to twenty-five minutes, I began to wonder. Had I done my chart work accurately? It was alleged my compass had no deviation, but had it? A degree would be enough. Why hadn't I plotted a course well to the west of the wretched rock and avoided all this? Because there was plenty of room. But not in a fog. But who expects to run into fog in the Mediterranean? It really was the end. Either there was so much wind we couldn't move out of port or there was so much fog we couldn't see where we were going when we did! So it went as we peered round the side of the canopy (for the windows had long ago misted up), our eyes pricking.

We never saw Les Fourmigues, the thirty minutes was up. Thirty-one, thirty-two, thirty-three; still no sign, and then suddenly Fanny shouted so loudly it made me jump. 'Look! Rocks! Over there!' She pointed over on the port bow and I could just see them, darker mist in the mist, a vague outline, coming clearer as we stared. They were rocks, all right, the off-lying rocks called La Ratonière, which lay about a mile to the north of Point Escampobariou and a quarter of a mile offshore. Dimly behind them we now made out the high cliffs that backed them. Evidently we must have been heading about a quarter of a degree east of our plotted course and this had put us just that fraction nearer the coast. When I examined the chart later it was clear that the actual width between the two sets of rocks was less than half a mile. It was crazy and most unseamanlike to take such a risk in a fog, but at the time we didn't pay much attention to that. We kept our eyes glued on those rocks, quickly checked the depths on the chart with the echo-sounder and edged in a bit nearer to our turning point, Cape Escampobariou. As long as we could see that—and it was coming clearer through the mist every moment—at least we knew where we were.

Actually this passage between the Presque Île of Giens and the island of Porquerolles is quite narrow, just over a mile wide, and there is an island, called Ribaud, almost in the middle of it; but you don't reach these hazards for about two miles after passing the main cape. Ribaud lies on the northern side of the passage and a chain of rocks and islets runs back to the mainland, so you have to leave it well away to port and shape a course for the lighthouse on the eastern tip of Porquerolles itself. There are three lights to give you a check on this at night and the landmarks are clear by day, but in this sort of weather neither lights nor landmarks were any good. The sea had gone dead calm. There wasn't a breath of wind and the fog was, if anything, thicker. We held our course for another ten minutes and then turned on to a course to bring the Porquerolles light dead ahead. It did.

We had been ploughing on for twenty minutes without any idea of where we were, trusting our compass and hoping that the rising sun would lift the murk—which it didn't—when Fanny gave another of her alarming shouts: 'I can see the bottom!'

I had the engine off pretty quick and we both peered over the side. There, sure enough, under the pure clean water, emerald over the sand, was the bottom. The echo-sounder read thirty feet. We looked up. The square squat tower of the lighthouse was almost overhead!

It was a splendid bit of navigation and I said as much to the Mate.

'You're wonderful, darling! Another fifteen seconds and we should have hit it!'

Now what to do? The northern coast of Porquerolles is low-lying and indented with a number of bays. There are depths of two fathoms and more quite close in, so we set out to do a bit of coastal navigation. With the engine at tickover, using the echo-sounder and our eyes on the bottom, we crawled along the shore in the dead-still water. Sometimes a flat rock would appear not twenty feet away. We edged off. Then everything would be lost again in the fog. We turned in closer. We contoured round the bays and headlands, coming on fishermen silent over their rods, who seemed huge, quite out of scale with the dim outline of the coast, which, through the mist, seemed hundreds of yards away.

For half an hour or more this strange ghosting continued. It was anxious, exciting and I suppose in a way unique to reach one of the most beautiful islands in the Med in such a dreamlike way. At last a trawler loomed up out of the mist. The helmsman evidently knew exactly where he was going and waved us on as he passed. We lost no time in following him. Then minutes later we were tied up in the marina at Porquerolles and as if to celebrate our arrival the mist suddenly lifted clear away to unveil a perfect day. It was still only quarter to eight!

*　　*　　*

Planning our trip through the Mediterranean the year before, we were determined to make it a leisurely passage. Living on board would be economical. We should have enough cash to stop off for a few days here and there, take shore trips to places we wanted to see or indulge in the odd evening out to enjoy a meal which the Mate had not had to cook. Leaving in May, we should have the whole summer before us and there was absolutely no hurry. Fanny had brought along a couple of evening dresses and I had a shore rig which would not disgrace her. But there is a great discrepancy between dreams and reality. Sometimes it is so subtle we fail to notice it, sometimes when it 'turns out' differently we cheat and pretend to ourselves (and others) that was what we had intended, but in this case the original plan had foundered so completely it could be said that, apart from the intention to reach Corfu, there was no plan at all. We had started three months late. Breakdowns and weather had baulked any hope of 'keeping to schedule'. Our slender resources, put aside for living it up, had all been soaked up by repairs and delays. We had learned what all cruising men learn, that the best you can do is to press on and play it by ear.

Porquerolles was, I suppose, the most obvious casualty to our need to press on. In the charming square, with its shaded shops and intimate little restaurants, we browsed around for an hour, buying food and exchanging gas bottles, but the idea of staying over for a few days in the dreamy, easy-going place, although it had been a 'must' before we left, never entered our heads. It was a lovely morning and that meant we could keep going eastward, so within two hours we were away again, running along the coast to the Cap des Mèdes. Before making the seven-mile hop back over to the mainland, and leaving the shelter of the islands, we 'sniffed the air', so to speak. The sea heaved quietly as if it were breathing asleep, a sort of misty luminosity left by the morning fog pervaded the sky. It was like floating inside a pearl.

'It will never be more perfect than this,' said Fanny. I agreed and we set course for Cap Blanc. The coastline of the mainland seemed hazy still and we referred to the Pilot for help. 'Cap de Bregancon' (we read), 'is the south-western extremity of Rocher de Bregancon, a rocky islet crowned with a fort and connected with the mainland by a mole. From Cap de Bregancon the coast is high and trends about two miles eastward to Cap Blanc, so called from the colour of its rocks which can be identified from some distance to seaward. Cap Benat, situated about four and a half cables north-eastward of Cap Blanc, is the south-eastern extremity of a large rounded and rugged hill, 607 feet high.'

I quote direct from the Pilot here because it is typical of the concise, terse information it offers. Read in conjunction with the chart it gives you definite things to identify, the rocky islet, the rounded hill. But, nevertheless, seen from seaward that misty morning, the whole coastline remained a blur, a featureless range flat against the horizon. To be safe, we were shooting for Cap Blanc in the middle of it, but not until an hour later, when we closed the land, did it begin to have shape. We identified the rocky islet and the mole dimly through the mist away to port and, rather doubtfully, the white cliffs of Cap Blanc, somewhat overgrown with veins of greenery, dead ahead. But as we turned east the rounded hill of Cap Benat was unmistakable, with the white beacon on the rock, Ilôt Cristaux, at its foot.

By the time we had Cap Benat abeam, all the mists had evaporated and the morning grew into a sparkling day. A light breeze ruffled the blue water. Far away across the curve of the Rade des Bormes lay shining beaches backed by the mountains, Rocher de Landon, Croix d'Île, over a thousand feet high. Ahead lay another Fourmigues, an isolated rock well out in the bay, but this one, we could see, thank heaven, embroidered with a fringe of cruisers and day boats anchored there, fishing. The whole scene, alive with power boats scurrying here and there and white sails filling to the light breeze, seemed to us that morning quite glorious, full of joy.

Now we had to decide whether to keep going for another four hours to reach St. Tropez or put into Cavalaire, the only other reasonable port on the way. We should probably never even get a berth in overcrowded, expensive St. Tropez, so, as we'd been up since four o'clock and it was getting on for midday, we opted for Cavalaire. Our adventure with the fog had been quite enough for one day, why tempt Providence further? So, gradually closing the land, we rounded Cap Cavalaire and came into the pretty busy harbour to find a berth. It was one o'clock and time for a well-earned lunch.

*　　*　　*

The coastline between Cavalaire and the Gulf of St. Tropez is a sort of spiky nob in outline. Sunken rocks guard the spikes, that is the capes, and if you look at the chart and read the Pilot it seems a stretch where it is wiser to stand well out to seaward. Leaving Cavalaire at 7.30 next morning, we were across to the first spike, Cap Lardier, in half an hour. In the perfect morning visibility the offshore rocks were easy to see, and an hour later, after passing Cap Taillat on its isthmus, we approached Cap Camarat. Here there is a chain of rocks pointing eastwards which extend almost three-quarters of a mile offshore. We gave these a wide berth and when they were abeam shaped a course at 16°M for St. Raphael. An hour later we were abreast of the Cape of St. Tropez itself where there is an even more formidable chain of rocks extending north-eastwards. But it is easy to clear these if you keep the nice hefty tower of La Moutte, which stands on the last rock, well on the port beam.

Now the whole Gulf of St. Tropez began to open up and invite us in.

'I haven't seen it for years. It used to be very pretty. Tiny harbour, little cafés, very romantic.'

'By all acounts it's ruined now.'

'June and Howard might be there still . . .'

'They might . . . Well, I s'pose we shan't come this way again. Might as well see it. After all, it's early still. We've got plenty of time.'

So we rounded the tower of La Moutte and made for another one which warns you off the hazard of Les Rabiou. Somehow I hadn't expected the Citadel, with its high solid walls, which is all you see of St. Tropez as you approach from the east. Beyond, two miles in, at the head of the Gulf, stand huge factories and the coastline of the whole broad sheet of

water is thick with rashes of villas and villages, right round to
St. Maxime on the northern shore. It is typical 'south of
France' coastline and that morning, with the blue sea, busy
with dozens of pleasure craft skating over it in all directions,
it was real picture-postcard stuff. We put our nose into the
harbour to case the joint.

'Gosh! What have they done to it? It's quite different.'

Different or not, it was simply stuffed with yachts. Big
ostentatious Bagliettos from Italy, massive steam yachts with
gold scrolling along their bows and coats of arms on their
funnels, sleek American ketches airing their sails. It was
millionaire's row, all right; but there, in a corner, I caught
sight of that unmistakable bicycle on the foredeck. June-Ho!
What luck!

We turned and hailed them excitedly and they came shooting out of their deckhouse. The reunion was so noisy it
brought the owners on nearby boats out to goof. Our obvious
pleasure had them all smiling and we snugged in against
June-Ho and went aboard to swap news and have coffee.

*   *   *

Perhaps the recipe for a successful party—too many people
crowded into too small a space—accounts for the popularity
of St. Tropez. Once a small idyllic fishing village, it has
become blown up into the sex symbol of our permissive
society on holiday. Everybody wants to go to St. Tropez. God
knows why. Walking past the luxury yachts, through the
narrow crowded streets with their outrageous boutiques and
shabby cafés, the whole thing seemed, as Fanny put it,
'Absolutely dotty'. It is not simply the haunt of the rich and
idle. There were evidently plenty who were idle but certainly

not rich. 'I find these dirty young men with their long hair and acne absolutely repulsive,' said Fanny. I agreed. As for the girls, there were far prettier and more attractive ones to be seen any Saturday morning on Oxford Street.

'It isn't just their appearance, it's the atmosphere I find so depressing,' Fanny went on. 'I mean, if the young were gay and carefree—you know, just feckless, frivolous, bubbling over with vitality—then one could say okay, it's just the exuberance of youth and that's normal, after all. Why not? But it's all so sad, so listless, so dull.'

And indeed the roles did seem to be reversed. It was the girls who swaggered and showed off, like the models in fashion magazines, in those aggressive, fighting postures. It was the men who lolled aimlessly against doorways with fags drooping from their wet lips.

The praying mantis may eat her partner after intercourse, but I was not brought up in a matriarchal society. To me this paradox, this reversal of roles, is one of the things which most deeply divides generations today. It isn't that we older men are less interested in sex or have less inclination to indulge in it, it is simply that we believe it is a man's place to take the initiative. But more than this, if you want something to be 'yours', essentially personal and different from the experience of another, then keep it to yourself. When everything is on display there won't be much in the stockroom.

Perhaps it's a bit unfair to pin all this moralising on St. Tropez, which is probably no better or worse than a hundred other 'pleasure resorts'. Certainly the conversation in the deck-house aboard June-Ho that morning was not concerned with morality. It turned on much simpler and more mundane topics: the fight Howard had had to get berthed in Lavandou where there wasn't any room, our 'bottom' fog navigation into Porquerolles, how our engines were running, how much time the girls needed to shop, whether we should drop in to St. Raphael or go straight on to Cannes—or did they want to stay on in St. Tropez?

'Not me,' said Howard. 'Let's get to sea!'

So, in less than two hours after our arrival, we were on our way out in the Gulf heading up towards St. Raphael.

* * *

It was a short run, little more than an hour along the coast up into the Gulf of Fréjus, at the head of which stands the old port of St. Raphael. We had chosen the old port rather than the new marina (situated about half a mile south of it on the eastern shore of the Gulf) to avoid the harbour dues in these new French marinas which are sometimes exorbitant. In this case it was probably a mistake.

Of the old port at St. Raphael, the Pilot says: 'The port is inaccessible in bad weather, north-westerly winds causing a choppy sea in the harbour and southerly winds sending in much surf.' Although the morning we arrived was pretty well perfect, there was a light breeze from the south-west, but even this was enough to set the whole harbour in movement. A dreadful rickety old pontoon connected our berth with the quay, some of its sections almost three feet apart and held together by chains. These sections danced about like boats, so getting ashore was quite an acrobatic feat. St. Raphael was certainly the most uncomfortable berth on the whole trip. All that day, and all the night following, *Prosilios* rolled and rolled. The motion was so sharp it gave Fanny a headache and almost threw us out of our bunks. The old port is not to be recommended.

The French daily forecasts for mariners—which, by the way, are gabbled off at such a pace that if your French is not pretty good they will be meaningless—take St. Raphael as the dividing point, as far as weather is concerned, along the Côte d'Azur. To the west, towards Marseille and Les Bouches du Rhône, is one area; east, as far as the frontier, is the other. As a broad generality, the frequency of high winds and storms seems to lessen as you move eastwards towards Italy.

Certainly that next morning, the 5th September, was as near perfect as one could wish for, a little high cloud, a calm sea and the sort of sleepy haze which promises heat to come. We were glad enough to get away from our wretched berth just about six o'clock and, with June-Ho keeping close company, we ran down the eastern shores of the Gulf and after clearing a complex of rocks called Les Lions turned east. In the early-morning sun the coast looked splendid and soon we were abreast of the huge red cliffs of Cap Drammont, lifting sheer from the sea with the dramatic little stage-set fortress at their base on the Île d'Or.

I don't know why that little fortress should have reminded me of the tiny churches that bejewel a hundred vantage points on the hillsides of Corfu. They stand white out of the olive groves, like rocks in a green sea. Indeed, the whole island seems almost submerged in a veil of misty green. In autumn, when the brushwood round their trunks has been cut, cleared and burned, the smoke makes blue smudges along the terraces and you see vistas of dark twisted trunks, looming ghostlike through their scented drifts. The sun comes through in palpable shafts of light or scatters under the dapple of a million leaves. It is a very special light, almost like being underwater, living in a strange primeval world. Under the olives all go silently, not to disturb their meditation.

To the Greeks from time immemorial the olive is sacred, the very staff of life—seeing it bears its crop of black fruit steadily for over 2,000 years. The olive is wealth, living wealth. If you own a hundred olives you will never starve.

Stefanos will talk of olives by the hour; of the sixty-nine different varieties, olives for eating, olives for pickling, olives for oil, Spanish olives, Italian olives, the olive in Athens that was bearing when Plato wrote The Republic. 'There were three-quarters of a million trees on Corfu when the Venetians came,' he says. 'They offered a golden thaler for every new tree planted. The Greeks know a good thing when they see it, so now there are four million trees on the island. But they were greedy. They planted them close, too close, so they grew upward and now you can't climb up to get the crop and the branches are too heavy to shake—so you have to wait until they fall. That is why we clean and burn the undergrowth: we should never find them if we didn't. From November till May the girls return to the trees again and again, picking the olives from the ground. It is a slow business. When I was a boy they used to sing together as they picked. It was most beautiful. Now they all have transistor radios. I don't find it an improvement . . .

'Our Corfu olives are different from all others because of this. We have tried to think of ways to pick them mechanically; machines to shake the branches, vacuum cleaners to suck them up. There was even a man who had six hedgehogs and proposed rolling them about to impale the olives on their spines. . . . But none of the methods work. Our hillsides are too steep. . . .

'Nothing is wasted. First there is the oil. Then, from the cake that remains after crushing, residual oil is extracted chemically and made into soap. The bran that is left after that is mixed with coal dust for briquettes. The leaves make fodder for the cattle, the small wood is cut for burning, the trunks make beautiful furniture—but you must not cut an olive without permission. . . .'

We visit the olive press to see Stefanos at work. It is hot and heavy with the smell of oil and steam. Three-foot stone wheels are grinding round and round in a huge stone bowl. The men are pouring in sacks of fruit. You can hear the olive stones crunching and bursting. Slowly it changes to a thick brown paste. Other men are spreading this paste on large circular mats with a hole in the middle and slipping them one by one on a tall steel tube, till it is loaded with layer upon layer of mats and paste, like a gigantic sandwich. Then the hydraulic pumps start up. The mats are slowly compressed from below, while steam jets ooze out from the tube to warm the paste. Now the oil starts trickling out mixed with water and runs away into channels below. The pale yellow emulsion is fed through a separator. Out of its spout comes that glorious golden liquid, the pure oil. Stefanos dips a piece of bread under the stream and eats with relish. . . .

*   *   *

To get the most out of a cruise like ours we find it best to stand about a mile offshore. This usually clears the off-lying rocks, islands and buoys, but is close enough to be able to follow the Pilot's landmarks and, with glasses, to enjoy the little coves, private harbours and villas that fringe this magnificent coast. We were pushing along at a steady seven knots and an hour after leaving St. Raphael had passed the Agay Road and the red and white tower called Le Chretianne which lies about three-quarters of a mile offshore beyond it. Now, as we turned more to the north, and came up towards Cap de l'Esquillon, the whole vista of the Côte d'Azur opened up, receding away to the north-easterly horizon. Ahead lay the Gulf of Napoule, with Cannes at its head, to the right the two low Îles des Lerins, beyond them the hills above Antibes, with Nice and Villefranche below the far mountainous horizon.

This is a part of the world where one quickly runs out of superlatives, so I will just say that morning it looked pretty good. Soaked with sun, brown, fit and feeling absolutely on the top line, we made 'How about this?' waves to June-Ho and got them back with interest. All the alarums and excursions that had so frustrated us were left behind. This was the way we had dreamt it would be and, in a way, we felt we had earned it. So, an hour and a half later, we came in sight of the solid breakwaters that guard the port of Cannes.

Cannes port is very large, well organised and expensive, full of powerful yachts and motor cruisers, among which little Prosilios looked like a rowboat. But we were not to be intimidated. Elegant houris, sunbathing on the upper decks of enormous craft to right and left, might look down on us superciliously as if we were something just emerged from under a stone, smart crews might shout as they backed in, bursting their engines, to let down their chromed gangplanks for the delicate feet of the owners, but the hell with them. Small as we were, we flew the Blue Ensign and the R.A.F. Burgee, we'd come all the way from the U.K., and they could stuff it.

I must say I go for Cannes. I like the clean broad esplanade that backs the harbour, with its flower beds, hotels and smart shops. I like the sandy beach to bathe from right on the other side of the harbour mole. The port itself has character, the old town coming close to the quays on its western side, the street restaurants look chic and not too expensive and the whole place has an air of being well run and cared for. The organisation of the port itself is extremely efficient. 'Runners' on the quays keep in touch with the office on walkie-talkies. The name, nationality and berth of all boats and their arrivals and departures are kept right up to date. Harbour dues go by footage and though it cost us £1 to stay one night there, it was worth it. Of all the Mediterranean ports we put into, Cannes was tops.

*   *   *

My log entry for the next day (September 6th) starts: 'This was the most perfect run of the trip, so far.' It was also the last we should cruise in company with June-Ho, for she was going to winter in Menton and our good company and warm companionship would end—for a time, anyway. It was one of those hazy autumn mornings with mist over the sea that you know will lift into the sparkling radiance of hot sun on blue water. What a day to be at sea!

At 6.30 we moved slowly out of Cannes southward, a bit preoccupied about the point at which we should turn east to cross the shallows between the mainland and the Îles de Lerins. It was tricky, with only a fathom of water in places. This meant that, although we should be all right, June-Ho would have less than a foot of water under her keel. We felt our way slowly, aiming for a channel of slightly deeper water that angles south towards the old castle on the northern shore of Marguerite, the closer island of the two. For ten minutes we were watching Howard closely, but when we saw he kept steadily moving on, we knew we were through the danger spot and opened up to cross the Gulf of Juan. Here stood another rock, our third called La Fourmigue, and when we had passed this and weathered the cape we turned north along the coast towards Antibes. Not being familiar with the south of France, I had always thought of Antibes as just another pleasure resort and was quite unprepared for the splendid battlements of the old town, shining gold in the low morning sun, the breakers (from a mile offshore) seeming to foam at their feet.

Now a fresh northerly breeze came spinning down from the mountains. Whitecaps flecked the dark water and we turned on to 065°M to keep the seas on our port bow. We were shooting for Cape Malalongue, which stands on the southern tip of a tongue of land projecting south beyond Villefranche Bay. Our course took us clear across the Bay of Angels. The town of Nice lay four miles away in the curl of the northern shore, backed by its hills rising to Mount Calvo, 3,000 feet above, and all the Alps beyond. In the magnificent morning the whole panorama looked like a musical-comedy backdrop and all we needed was Julie Andrews to appear, walking on the water, singing 'Edelweiss'.

However, when she failed to materialise I noticed aircraft coming in to land on the Nice airstrip and my mind snapped back twenty-two years. How well I remembered that strip! At Martigues a young French air smuggler in his Messerschmitt had offered to lead me through the driving rainstorms to Nice. His aircraft was fifty miles an hour faster than the Miles Gemini in which I was en route for South Africa. Skilfully he led the way through the swinging grey curtains of rain, circling back to fetch me when his speed took him too far ahead and at last diving down through a cloud gap with me on his tail to land on the Nice runway against which the seas were breaking. It was in the austerity years of 1947 and I was allowed only £10 to get through France. These precious pounds I had naturally black-marketed in Paris to get a higher rate of exchange. When the little weasel of a French Customs official heard of this—for I made no secret of it—he flew into a rage and declared he would report the hotel that had infringed the regulations. I still remembered with pleasure how I had given him the name of another hotel. He had written it down with such venomous zeal; but he was going to be made a fool of later, for the name I had given him was a place then being used as an American hostel! I had diddled him, glory be! Then I had quickly taken off over the sea, skirting the mountains, and, climbing over their peaks, swung down to the sunlit Lombardy plain to land at Milan. From there it had been a sad pilgrimage back to my villa on the Lago Maggiore, to take leave of people and places I was never to see again. . . . All that had been my life too, but so long ago it might have been another's. . . .

From this melancholy reverie of faraway, I was jerked back into the present by seeing, a mile off Cape Malalongue, a large black tower in the sea. I looked again and grabbed the chart. There was nothing of the kind marked. 'Hey, Fanny,' I called, 'get the glasses. What's that big black tower there?' I pointed and she looked. A pause. Then:

'I don't know, darling, but I think it's moving!'

'Moving! How can a tower be moving?'

'I think it is. Look!'

She handed me the glasses. I focussed. Sure enough, it was moving and in the opposite direction to us. Then I knew it could only be one thing.

'Gosh! It must be a nuclear submarine!'

The huge black sinister tower slid by us quietly. Now we had identified it, we could see two tiny white figures on top of it and make out the line of the superstructure just awash. We kept the glasses on it, fascinated. I don't know whether it was the contrast between it and the smiling sunny landscape, but it sent shivers down my spine. Then, like some Jules Verne monster, it stealthily submerged, leaving us with a very queer feeling—that dark shadow, moving unseen below the innocent sea, was the symbol of wars to come.

Once across St. Hospice Bay beyond the cape, the coastline grew more and more spectacular. The mountains strode forward through the haze to frown at the sea. On their tremendous flanks we sighted (and then could not take our eyes off) one tiny village, insubstantial in the mists, growing out of a sharp isolated peak. The clustering houses looked so precarious we felt they must be stuck to the rocks with glue! This was Eze and what a site its founders had chosen! What labour to have built it! How proud and defiant its citizens must have been to have made themselves so impregnable against the surging armies of the petty princelings and marauding corsairs of the Middle Ages! The place stood like a monument to the will to survive!

By now the morning breeze had quite died out and we were furrowing through a glassy sea that only heaved gently as if it were contained beneath a film of cellophane. The southern cliffs of Monaco came into view and we gaped at their palace façade. So gracious, so elegant, such a noble fantasy of architectural imagination, it set the key for the whole place as it came into view round the point. We throttled down, seaborne tourists come to see the sights.

The closely built city rose in a steep amphitheatre (like some hollow sea-washed shell in pastel pinks and yellows) above the harbour below. I understood why it has so long been allowed to remain an anachronism, something special, a tiny self-contained state within a state, quite unique. Nice hygienic Grace had certainly picked the last remaining prince with a romantic kingdom. Monte Carlo, no doubt about it, was the koh-i-noor of the Mediterranean.

After that all was anticlimax. We rounded Cap Martin and at 10.45 were safely berthed in the brand-new marina at Menton Garavan.

*　　*　　*

'Safely berthed'—there is a satisfying finality about the phrase. I feel sure that such a lot could not have been written about berthing if many others besides ourselves had not found it quite a trauma. How to berth upwind, how to berth downwind, how to berth with the wind abeam. . . . Books, articles, diagrams have gone over the whole business again and again. We often felt our problem was how to berth at all. It is quite remarkable what a mess you can get into while hardly moving 2 m.p.h.

The Mediterranean habit of berthing stern to presents additional hazards when you have an outboard drive, for the possibility of bashing it to bits against the quay is very real. How many times, carefully backing in between two other yachts in a crowded harbour, have I called to the Mate: 'Let go!' and heard our anchor splash down. Then, as we reached heaving distance, some quayside lounger would turn up, catch the line and pull on it as if he were bringing in the Queen Mary. In a second our prop will bash into the stone. I yell to the Mate: 'Check! Check!! For God's sake, check!!!'

'I am checking,' she yells back, outraged, and I see her arms being pretty well pulled out of her shoulders. We pull up, thank God, about six inches from the jetty.

If it weren't for the cat's cradle of chains and hawsers on the bottom of crowded harbours, I would still prefer dropping an

I

anchor to picking up a mooring. An anchor's your own, after all, and you know it from the flukes up, but strange buoys are a snare and a delusion. They may look very pink and pretty bobbing about invitingly, either too near in or too far out, but the one you choose is almost certain to be wrong. You should have taken the smaller one to the left or the big one further over. The little football-size ones look easy and innocent, but the light line you pull up is just a prelude to giving yourself a double hernia by finding a battleship-size ton of links on its back end; while the big ones, with a rod and ring sticking out of the top, often lead you to a joust of boathook-tent-pegging which leads to frayed tempers and recriminations every time the eye bobs away the very moment you're ready to grab it.

'For God's sake!'

'I can't *reach* it. I've told you a dozen times, I've got short arms.'

'Then lean out more.'

'How can I? I'm pretty well overboard as it is. Why can't you bring her up properly? If you'd only steer straight we'd have had it first time.'

'I told you her head blows off in this cross-wind.'

'I must have a lighter boathook or I shall just fall in . . . Oh, there's a man telling us to go away. *Bon soir, M'sieu. Il fait beau, n'est ce pas? Quoi? Pas ici? La bas? Ah, très bien, M'sieu, très bien.* The old bastard wants to move us, darling, just as I was getting used to the idea of this buoy. . . .' As you prepare to move off, a wrinkled type in a broad-brimmed hat and a dinghy comes by, takes your line, ties you up, hails another wrinkled type on the wharf. '*Hey, Gaston!*' He catches your stern lines and in a jiffy the whole thing comes right and you're moored. But you didn't moor, they moored you.

'Ought we to tip them?'

' 'Course not, darling. They like doing it. Besides, you never know, probably one of them owns the Casino. . . .'

'That Gaston looks a bit like a croupier, come to think of it. . . .'

'Anyway, we're moored, love, that's the great thing.'

The new French marinas have taken the devil out of all this —and, I should add, the French are way ahead, in catering for the needs of yachts, of any other country in Europe. French marina designers have certainly done their part in contributing to the yachting boom.

Of course, being in practically non-tidal waters, their problem is simplified. Their 'pontoons' do not have to float, rising and falling with the tide, they are simply concrete platforms standing on legs, their tops about eighteen inches above the water. These stand out, at right angles to the main wharf, at about 100-foot intervals and each one berths about twenty yachts, stern to, on either side. Each jetty has fresh water and electric power points (with separate take-offs for each boat) set along it at intervals and, covered with a non-slip type of red tarmac, the whole thing looks neat, inviting and efficient.

At Menton Garavan the new marina is a narrow rectangle running along the shore below the main coastal esplanade. A motor drive runs right round it, beyond which stands shops and cafés and a number of small flatlets for the use of those with permanent berths, stores, showers, etc. At the eastern end is the narrow, well-protected entrance, with crane and fuel point, ship's chandler, workshops and the control tower with the Port Captain's office below it. The whole complex is self-contained and most efficiently laid out. It was, I thought, a model of how a modern marina should be designed and I have described it in some detail because if we ever get around to building marinas in England this is the way to do it.

But now to come back to the method of mooring which has done away with dropping anchors, picking up buoys and all those messy complications of old-style ports and, for me at any rate, solved the problem to perfection. This is how it is done. At each (numbered) berth there are rings set into the concrete sides of the jetty to take stern lines in the usual way, but to one ring a light line is attached. It is weighted at intervals with lead clips and drops down straight to the bottom. If you didn't know, you would never notice it was there. But when you have backed in, if you pick it up with a boathook and walk forward with it, you find at the other end a mooring chain. You simply lift this in over the stemhead, make fast and you are moored. So each berth has its own 'built-in' mooring chain and all these chains are, in turn, shackled to a main chain which runs out along the bottom between each pair of jetties. The initial outlay in chain for a 500-yacht marina must be heavy—that is why the dues are high—but the convenience to the yachtsman is immense. No more tangles of old hawsers and discarded anchors on the bottom, no more lines running in all directions to get your propeller fouled up in. When you want to get away, cast off your stern lines and simply drop your chain which falls to the bottom ready for the next visitor.

The morning we arrived at Port Garavan one of the marina staff gave us a jetty and berth number as we passed the control point at the entrance. Then he got on his moped and was waiting to take our stern lines as we came in. He pointed out the method of mooring, the water and the power points, took the name of our boat, inquired how long we should be staying and left. The whole thing didn't take ten minutes.

We stayed over the weekend at Port Garavan. Then, after taking affectionate leave of June and Howard, with plans to meet the following spring, set out along the coast to Genoa. Five minutes after leaving the port we were in Italian waters, for the frontier is only a few hundred yards beyond the marina. So we lowered our French courtesy ensign and hoisted the Italian. There is an immediate change, more felt than seen at first, when you reach Italy. The Italians, on the whole, are not keen sailors and yachtsmen and there is nothing like the general interest in small boats and sailing to be found in France. Besides, after the varied and interesting contours of the French Riviera, with its islands, gulfs and bays, the coast-line from the Italian frontier northwards, right up to Genoa and beyond, is far less attractive. It does not offer the same scope to the small-boat owner as France and, in spite of the mountains which front the sea, it is dull. This is, no doubt, why the small ports up the coast are so little known.

We only made a two-hour run as far as San Remo that first day on our own, partly to get our papers put in order by calling at the first Italian port, partly to look San Remo over to report back to Howard who was considering it as an alternative to Menton for his winter quarters. San Remo is quite a big, busy port, full of a wide variety of craft, all parked in a free-and-easy style among a sprinkling of buoys, hawsers and anchor chains running in all directions. The wharf where we parked (after some difficulty) was high and we found it awkward to get ashore; but, all the same, it was a relief to be in cheerful, voluble Italy again. A long walk round the busy wharves brought us to the Port Captain's office, a noble old building with an outside staircase, where two Italian marines, in spotless white, dealt with our papers smartly and typed us out details of the Italian marine weather forecasts. This done, we strolled back to find a shady table and a nice cool beer.

It was then we noticed the railway line, completely slicing off the town from the port. A full-sized string of coaches clattered in, towering above the cafés. It was very surprising. After all, San Remo is a 'resort' and the intrusion could hardly be called an amenity. Crowds built up at the level crossings, hammock seats at open cafés were set right against the line, but everyone seemed to accept the situation without fuss. A railway, I suppose, is less of a menance than a motorway. Holiday-makers strolled about enveloped in an audible cloud of round-vowelled, volatile Italian which delighted us after weeks of intellectual, sophisticated French. So we wandered off happily through the markets to shop and get our Italian back into gear after years of rusting. It was good to be back again.

Of course, as a yacht port, San Remo has nothing to offer in the way of facilities compared with any French marina. No water to hand, no electricity laid on, the place is as it has been for probably a century or more, just a sound working port for fishing and the coastal trade; just the friendly, untidy, vigorous, noisy, happy, go-as-you-please Italy we loved. Plenty of character and no mod cons.

*　　*　　*

This striking difference between France and Italy reminded me forcibly of the theory of a friend of mine. He declared that people *are what they eat*. Diet, he said, was the basis of character. The French are French because French soil produces a certain kind of wheat, a certain kind of meat, wine, vegetables and fruit that is essentially 'French'. The same with the Italians,

Spaniards, Greeks. He brushed aside all the other influences, religion, culture, social customs, etc., as secondary. 'This is merely what societies have produced over the centuries: it is what people *do*, it is not what they *are*.'

It sounded a bit cock-eyed at first, but it led straight to a question that is often asked but which I had never heard answered this way. How do different sorts of people, 'nations', as we call them today, arise? Why did a whole group of peoples round one inland sea like the Mediterranean become so individual, so varied? The two great basics of the area are grapes and olives. Ought they not all to be the same?

'Not at all. You can't compare French wine with Italian wine or Spanish wine. They're quite different. Any olive merchant who couldn't tell the difference between a Greek olive and an Italian olive would soon be out of business. To put it down to climate, soil, rainfall, temperature, and so on, is just to come back to the same point. All that has an obvious effect on what each country grows, therefore on those who consume it. Therefore, I repeat, people are what they eat. The northerner is phlegmatic and heavy because he is brought up on potatoes and porridge. The southerner is volatile and slippery because he relies on wine and olive oil. The northerner is tough because he has to work harder to grow his potatoes, the southerner is indolent because it is easier for him to harvest his wine. . . . When you happen to come across isolated pockets of people who for some reason or other have had to subsist solely on what their own soil produces, you always find they have a distinct and special character, something that makes them essentially themselves—like the Hunzas, for instance. . . . But today all this is changing. Why do you suppose people are less individual, more impressionable, more subject to hysteria, to illness, less able to stand up to the manifest evils and failures of our so-called civilisation? It is because they no longer eat their own food. They eat anything from anywhere. Look at us English! Meat from the Argentine, wheat from Canada, bacon from Denmark, butter from New Zealand, fruit from South Africa, tea from India, coffee from Brazil! What can you expect? England was great while she lived on what England could produce. But this amorphous diet, this hybrid food, does what all hybridisation does—produces an increase of vigour for the first generation and then a race of runts. And that goes for all European countries as well. The export and import of food should be banned by law.'

'Then we should all starve.'

'In 1830 the population of England was fifteen million. It was big enough to build the British Empire. Now it's fifty million plus and what good has it done us? The population explosion is due entirely to our lack of character, our lack of self-discipline, and that goes straight back to our lousy diet. But Nature has her own equations. She will take steps, either by war or pestilence, to cut us down to size—if we can't do it for ourselves. . . .'

Nonsense? Perhaps. But life would be dull without fanatics.

*　　*　　*

We had already enjoyed six days of near-perfect weather. It seemed to have settled down into a sort of mellow glory and we pushed on next morning eager to make the most of it. This section of the Italian coastline, in spite of one or two resorts, cannot properly be called its Riviera, which is relatively short —for it does not start till you near Portofino and is virtually over by the time you get to Spezia. From San Remo northwards the yachtsman is presented with an endless barrier of high mountains fronting the sea and we simply set the auto pilot to take us from cape to cape. Our log for that day, the 9th September, reads:

0610 Left San Remo. Set course 080°M.
0630 Capo dell'Arma abeam. Altered course to 070°M.
0720 Capo San Lorenzo abeam.
0740 Porto Maurizio abeam.
0750 Imperia abeam.
0805 Capo Berta abeam. Altered course to 055°M.
0835 Capo Cervo abeam.
0900 Capo delle Mele abeam. Altered course to 010°M.
0915 Alassio abeam.
0930 Capo Santo Croce abeam. Altered course to 026°M.
0935 Isola Gallinaria abeam.
0945 Capo Lena abeam. Altered course to 010°M.

By this time a big thunderhead was gathering with the usual squalls beneath it, so we headed for the next port, of which I had never heard, called Loano. Wind and sea and lashings of real Italian rain pretty well blinded us as we made our entrance, as usual, unprepared, trying to berth and get our oilskins on at the same time. But being drenched to the skin doesn't much matter in the summer and soon the sun was out again and everything was steaming as we dried off. So we spent an hour having a cheerful lunch and second hour searching for non-existent diesel with the aid of a friendly passing motorist. Everybody in Loano seemed to siesta from eleven to three, so we poured our five-gallon jerrycan into the tanks which were getting a bit low, and pushed off again, the thunderclouds having moved on to drench the next village and left us in clear blue.

After an hour we noted in passing a little port called Finale

Ligure that the skull and crossbones was flying from a mast on the mole and we thought this might be a danger signal. (It turned out later to be the emblem of the local dinghy club.) Finale Ligure is small and pretty shallow, but its Port Captain whistled up twenty-five gallons of fuel in as many minutes from the local garage. So an hour later, with profuse thanks to the friendly personnel at the little place, we pushed off yet again and coast crawled up to Capo di Noli. It was such a perfect evening we decided to keep going as long as we could. So we headed straight out from the curve of the coast, passing the big commercial ports, Vado and Savona, well out to sea. At 1830 hours we entered Varazze harbour. We had been eight hours at sea. It was, we thought, a fair working day.

*　　*　　*

Varazze is the home port of Baglietto, a name famous in the luxury motor-cruiser world and a strictly Italian phenomenon. His factories line the coast and we could hardly find room in the port, which was full of dozens of his boats either newly off the production line or back for servicing. By modest English standards, they are massive, sea-going cruisers, averaging fifty to sixty feet in length, powered by twin engines of anything up to 3,000 h.p., giving them speeds of fifteen to thirty knots. They are fitted with every kind of electronic aid, luxuriously equipped in accommodation and deckhouse furnishing and extremely elegant. These boats can cost anything up to £150,000 and Baglietto is to be congratulated on having found a formula that seems pretty well irresistible to Italian millionaires intent on keeping up with other Italian millionaires.

What is astonishing is the number of them. In every sizable

Italian port you find them moored by the dozen. There, with professional crews of anything up to five seamen, immaculately kept, competently handled, their crews live it up on board waiting for the owner and his weekend parties. Their dinghies are fitted with outboards powerful enough for water-skiing, their cabin roofs covered with sorbo mattresses big enough for mass sunbathing. Come the weekend, decorative houris appear to display themselves in poses arresting enough to make any fashion photographer's mouth water. Baglietto has become the symbol of the sea-going *Dolce Vita*.

On the whole the Italians do not like the sea and are frightened of the water; but they like dashing about and showing off, for which purpose a Baglietto is ideal. It is fast enough to beat any sudden deterioration in weather, big enough to feel safe. Not that the owners go in for any extensive cruising. Mostly the boats are used for day picnics or quick coastal dashes from port to port. On Sunday evenings the big Alfa Romeos and Maseratis appear, roar away the guests and all is quiet till next Friday.

Where else in Europe can people afford this sort of thing? Paid crews are not cheap, even in Italy. The air of ostentation and luxury seems quite at variance with the political and economic unrest that fills Italian papers. In the general levelling up (or levelling down) of life today, a certain class in Italy seems to have power to manipulate the tax laws very conveniently or else to be making so much money that the £10,000 a year needed to keep such craft in commission means nothing. Of course, in every country there is a class of *nouveaux riches*. What is so surprising, I repeat, is the size of the class in Italy. It doesn't seem possible today that so many people have so much money. As examples of marine design and construction Baglietto and his rival Benetti are in the top

class; but as usual Fanny put her finger on it when she said:
'I wouldn't want to go cruising on one of those things. You'd
never have any fun.'

*　　*　　*

The day-to-day record of a trip like ours can rapidly become
a bore. No words can really convey the special quality of being
at sea in your own boat, a certain sense of responsibility, a
satisfaction at sighting landmarks, taking fixes, keeping an eye
on the weather, an alertness to meet any emergency that may
arise, coupled with—in our case—a certain subconscious
anxiety. For although our engine was now performing splendidly, we still could not quite forget how many times it had
stopped. Then, at the end of the day, the satisfaction at the
distance run, the relaxation with the boat safely moored and
the interest of a new port to explore.

These are the pleasures of cruising, but when it is all 'plain
sailing' there is really little to say, unless you happen to be an
historian, able to conjure up (and make interesting) stories of
old days, old conflicts and wars in which the Mediterranean
has been plunged for more than two millennia. Having no such
erudition, I ought, I suppose, to be grateful to those irrespons-
ible types back in the U.K. who, unwittingly, by providing
most of our troubles and misfortunes, gave us something (in
retrospect) to shout about.

This middle section of our journey, with its spell of perfect
weather, was, had we known it, running out. There were only
to be ten days altogether and we had already had seven. But,
not knowing this, we somehow imagined it would last for
ever. We had long ago given up waiting to hear the morning
forecast (given, by the way, in Italy, at excellent slow dictation
speed) and set off from the sleek Bagliettos of Varazze at 0630

on the morning of September 10th on the most memorable day of the whole trip.

By now we were almost up to the head of the Gulf of Genoa and swung off eastward, cutting the corner, to make for the city. A vicious maestrale suddenly swept down from the mountains above Voltri. In ten minutes the sea was showing white teeth, with black squalls racing, and I kept a very sharp eye to windward, remembering how I had left Genoa for New York in 1937 on board the *Rex*, the great prestige symbol of Mussolini's Fascist Italy, and how before we were out of the Gulf of Genoa the rails on the boat deck had been flattened by a storm that had blown up from nowhere to full gale in a few hours. However, that morning the dog was only giving a sleepy growl without leaving his kennel and once across the bay the wind died out and left us to the oily swells that wash the coast off Genoa.

The seafront of this city is over eight miles long and at least six of these consist of the formidable dykes that have been built to protect the runway of the Cristofero Colombo Airport, itself a massive pier, jutting out into the sea and then turning to run parallel to the coast. The scale of these works, which have all been completed since the war, is very impressive. The Italians have lost none of their old genius for building. (After all, half New York is built by them.) But the effect of these protective dykes is to keep shipping well out to sea. Genoa lay almost hidden that day, the rising sun behind her dazzled us and the morning mists and industrial haze completely blurred all the outlines of the miles of built-up areas that crowd the waterfront. Genoa used to be called 'la superba' and even now you can see why, for there is something superb about the way she is massed over the coastal hills.

But seeing all this over the endless black wall of the dykes cut off the feet of the city, so to speak, and left us plugging on for over an hour in a sea of yellow oil. Yellow, and I mean yellow not just tinged with it, oil discharged from tankers in the approaches to this great harbour. It must have been an inch thick. The ports of the world, as I have already said, are all made filthy by a scum of oil, but this was the first and only time we met it well out to sea. It smoothed off the waves as if the water had been covered with a sheet of elastic and our bows turned it away in scrolls of sickly green-yellow. It turned our stomachs too, for it smelled foul. There was something obscene about defiling the Mediterranean blue this way. Of course, there are heavy fines imposed on any ship found discharging oil at sea, but it also costs a lot to steam offshore to areas where oil may be discharged. So, as the offence is difficult to detect and prove (with so much oil about already), tankers take the risk. Either way it may cost them money.

So we were glad when, at last, the south-eastern extremity of the last mole, called Molo Duca di Galliera, was behind us and we could look back into the vast harbour with its misty vistas of cranes and shipping. There is, I should add, for those who like the bustle of big ports, a special yacht basin, just behind this mole, called the Portocciole Duca degli Abruzzi. From the charts it looks protected from all winds and seas and it is said that water, electricity and even telephones are laid on to the jetties. However, we did not stop to verify all this, for the water was beginning to turn blue again. We had been at sea for two and a half hours and hoped to make Portofino for lunch.

The south-easterly sweep of the coast below Genoa is broken by the Promontorio di Portofino, which the Pilot calls 'the most prominent of the numerous projections on the north-western coast of Italy'—in other words it makes a very large

wart on the chart. Shaped something like a child's idea of a
boot, the toe points down south-east and the heel up to the
north-west and between these two lies the sole, a bold and
splendid four miles of coast. It was for the heel we were
making, called Punta della Chiappa. We could see the
silhouette of the peak called Monte Portofino rising above it, a
2,000-foot nose of rock on the water. We passed Nervi and
old Camogli (which both have small summer ports) too far
out to see them clearly and another two hours later, at 10.35,
rounded the point and came close inshore to enjoy the scene.
All over the sunny water wherever you looked were pleasure
craft, motor cruisers, rowing boats, inflatables. Most of them
were running right in against the cliffs where the water lay
heavy in great hunks of lapis lazuli. They were making for the
old Doria monastery at the head of a small bay called San
Fruttuoso or, more exactly, for the restaurants that cling to the
cliff there, to enjoy the luxury lobsters. We resisted the temptation and held on towards the lighthouse on the point, where
the church and castle dominate the saddle of the hill and look
down to the open sea on one side and the harbour of Portofino
on the other. Once round the point we picked our way
between bathing parties swimming from villas neatly fitted
into the wooded rocks and entered the port. It has, for me, a
special Italian magic. There is nothing like it anywhere in the
world. It remains, in spite of the luxury yachts that crowd the
harbour, in spite of the rivers of tourists, in spite of being an
international beauty spot, the realisation of some dream we all
of us carry in different ways, the dream of reaching one day,
somehow, somewhere, a perfect and peaceful harbour, safe
from all winds and all seas, and there to drop the hook.
Portofino translates that longing into bricks and water and
throws in romantic beauty for good measure. The houses rise

protectingly round the quays, holding the sea, as it were, in the curled palm of the hand, the shops lie deep in shadow under their arched feet and there is nothing more pleasant in life than to sit at a sunlit table on the quayside and lunch royally on *frutto di mare* and peaches.

At any rate, it seemed so to us that day. We dressed up for it in what my mother used to call our 'bits of best' and played for an hour the opulent, indolent role of tourists on holiday. In fact an hour was not enough, we played it from eleven till three when, still somewhat misty with good wine, we managed to get the hook up and steer ourselves out into the Gulf of Marconi.

*   *   *

Marconi! I remember seeing him once, almost fifty years ago when we were starting the B.B.C., being shown round the new studios at Savoy Hill in 1923. I remember a broad forehead and bright, intelligent Italian eyes. I also remember the bewildered look on his face as Round, our chief engineer, who had already outstripped him in technical development, explained to the Master what he was up to. If anyone ever sowed Dragon's Teeth it was Marconi. . . .

Well, I thought, as we crossed the bay, they had named a fine stretch of water after him, anyway. There was Santa Marguerita, its harbour, as full of masts as a pincushion, the best port on the coast. There was Rapallo, with its discreet hotels where the ghost of Max Beerbohm still potters about. Away across the water was the new yacht basin at Chiavari. The Gulf of Marconi was the high spot of the Italian Riviera, that afternoon at its best, the sky blue, the sun hot, the sea dancing. We set course for Sestri Levanti.

Sestri Levanti is a small isthmus with an East/West axis

terminating in two hills. The neck of the isthmus is scooped out on both sides, a shallow bay on the northern side offering protection from southerly winds and a deeper, better-protected harbour on the southern side, safe from anything that blows from the north. The place has not been 'developed' so much as other ports in the area and has a sleepy, countrified air. As there was a light northerly breeze, we came round the point and tied up to a buoy in the southern bay. A big thunderhead was massing overhead. We thought we would wait to see if it would burst or not and meanwhile have a bathe and get some of the Genoese oil off the waterline by swimming round the boat with a scrubbing brush. We spent an energetic hour doing this in the clear warm water and then had tea. The thunderhead was dispersing with evening. It was five o'clock. Another two hours of daylight. Why not press on? We could make the Cinque Terre by nightfall.

For many years to visit the Cinque Terre had been a wish I had never been able to realise. It is a short stretch of coast with mountains dropping practically sheer into the sea. In their clefts five little villages have wedged themselves. There is no room for a road along the precipices and the villages are only connected with the outside world by a railway which emerges from practically continuous tunnels at each village and then disappears underground again. So the Cinque Terre have remained as they are for centuries, practically unknown except to a handful of discerning visitors, isolated village citadels clinging to the clefts of the cliffs, incredibly picturesque and, of course, made more romantic by being very hard to reach.

The main motor road from Spezia to Genoa climbs high into the mountains. When you reach the top you can some-times catch a glimpse (if you dare take your eyes off the twisty road) of steep valleys vee-ing down to the misty sea, 2,000 feet below. There at the bottom lie the clustering roofs of the villages of the Cinque Terre. That was as near as I had got; but now! To approach them by sea on a summer evening! It was too good to be true.

But there was something more, a bonus that had fallen into our laps the night before when we moored at Varazze. An English voice had hailed us as we backed in and its owner, Charles Elkington, and Barbara, his charming Austrian wife, had invited us to have a drink on board their boat, a fine steel ketch, *Cetos*. Elkington was bound west to winter in Menton and only the day before had made the run we were now making in reverse. In the course of swapping news of our trips, he told us of the hideout he had discovered in the Cinque Terre. 'It isn't in any of the books. Just a mile or so below Monte Rosso. It's called Vernazza. Not much bigger than a tennis court. But you can just about squeeze in. There's plenty of water and it's well protected.'

So now, two hours later, we were rounding the Punta Mesco, the last cape before the Cinque Terre. The sun was setting down into the sea in a cloudless sky, the precipices before us were golden in the marvellous evening light. 'As soon as you're round the point, steer due east,' Elkington had said. 'You'll see Monte Rosso tucked into the bay to the north, but Vernazza is right ahead. There are a couple of towers over the place, but they're not easy to see. . . .' The sun had already set before we had covered the last two miles. We could see the village all right. A spur of rock jutted out to the south of it. But the port itself remained quite invisible. Then we saw a fishing boat emerge from what looked like the face of the cliff itself, north of the spur. We made for the place, but could still see nothing. It was not until we were less than 200 yards away that a breakwater, perfectly camouflaged against the cliff, detached itself and we sneaked in through the opening, not thirty yards wide, to moor in the Shangri-La of the Italian Riviera.

What a place! The breakwater was good and solid to protect the little port from the westerly gales. On the other side it was sheer cliff. A minute church hung over the water. Above that you could just see the black ellipse of the railway tunnel. The breakwater, not fifty yards long, ran into the rock spur and turned into the cleft. There the village started. Houses were piled on top of each other up the precipices, tiny crazy houses with gardens on their roofs, reached by a maze of narrow stairways twisting upwards level above level. We made our way through a tunnel to reach the diminutive piazza at the head of the harbour. Under a few faded umbrellas people were having supper before the Trattoria. Lights began to come on. The one village street, narrow and cobbled, overhung with the high houses, was like some mysterious canyon, disappearing into the shadows. We sat down at a table to take our ease. After eleven hours at sea, it was like reaching the world's end. Grilled fish and a litre of the local wine was set before us. It was quite enough. We did not discover the famous potency of the Cinque Terre wines till we got up to go down to the boat and turn in. Then it was plain our balance was impaired. We lurched and rolled down through the tunnel to the quay. We sat on the edge of it and had a long discussion on how best to get aboard. *Prosilios* was at least four feet away and the whole thing seemed very difficult. At last, somehow, we managed it, fell on to our bunks and slept like logs.

*   *   *

We didn't wake very early next morning. Why not take it easy and just loiter down to Porto Venere? It was only four miles away. It seemed a good idea, so we spent an hour clambering up and down the stairway streets of Vernazza exploring the maze of fascinating little secret passages and whitewashed walls, climbing up to the towers to look down on the patchwork of pink and umber roofs below, the cherished gardens six feet square, the toy harbour and the sea ruled at the horizon by a silver line dividing blue from blue.

Then we had to leave and pottered off below the precipices. They were only sheer for about a hundred feet. Sombre, almost black, rocks rose straight out of the sea or receded a yard or two to leave minute inaccessible beaches and coves. Above the precipices the mountains began. They were terraced solidly right up to their 2,000-foot summits. Hundreds upon hundreds of terraces, lining and scalloping the contours of the slopes. Here grew the famous wines that had so speedily seduced our semicircular canals. Seen from the water looking steeply up, the ribs of shadow lightly etched across their flanks, one could see that the whole place was one vast sun-catching amphitheatre of terraces. No wonder it grew such sweet and potent wine. But the labour that had gone into it! It must have taken centuries to build those miles of walls—and every bunch of grapes, harvested by hand, had to be carried on the head along those dizzying slopes, where one false step (or one glass too much) could start you on a one-way trip to a vintner's paradise.

The villages, Corniglia, Riomaggiore, Campiglia, clustered at the lower edges of this green ribbing, seemed like crude patches of embroidery done with a child's needle between the black and green. . . . When we had pottered along all this for an hour we saw at the end of it all what looked like the entrance of the narrow channel that divides the mainland from the island of Palmaria. We turned into it to find, at the far (eastern) end, the pretty harbour of Porto Venere, backed by a typical façade of tall narrow houses, complete with fortifications, a black and white sandwich church and busy ferries plying to Spezia.

*　　*　　*

Although the Italians have a genius for building their cities and towns with an eye to public occasions, contriving broad flights of steps and spacious piazzas, the ceremonies themselves always seem to me a bit too pretentious, splendid 'shows' lacking that 'common touch' which makes Greek feast days so endearing. In Corfu, for instance, when they carry Saint Spiridon, their patron saint, round the town to show him to the people (which they do four times a year) it is an excuse for an outburst of great rejoicing. Saint Spiridon, after all, is a Corfiot. He belongs to them. He is one of the family. So the whole population turns out. The Saint has worked many miracles, saved the lives of many sailors at sea, half the male children in Corfu are called after him and he is beloved in that special Greek way, not holy or mystical, but as if he were one of them, a father, an elder brother, for whom respect and affection is natural, a part of life.

So, being a Greek saint, if he is part of life, he will naturally wish to share the temporal side of it also, so this is not just a religious celebration, it is a worldly occasion too.

The procession forms up in the narrow market streets and, preceded by banners and giant candles, files of choirboys and priests, the canopy shading the holy remains is borne along. Bishops and archbishops, weighted down with age and their robes, with preposterous hats and sensational beards, shuffle slowly past, looking as if they had stepped straight out of the pages of some medieval fairy-tale. One reads from a holy book, one swings a censer. They look like living ikons, statuesque, magnificent, remote from earthly life. The crowds that line the streets greet the Saint simply and reverently, crossing themselves, watching every detail with those darting Greek eyes. But so that it should not grow too heavy or melancholy, the bands come strutting quickly on the holy heels.

Sounds of their evening practice in upper rooms have deafened the cafés for weeks, now they play gay Tum-te-tum-ta tunes, resplendent in blue tunics and white plumed hats, lifting the mouths of the trumpets, clashing their cymbals, beating their drums and obviously enjoying the whole thing enormously. Platoons of soldiers follow, detachments of sailors, troops of Boy Scouts and Girl Guides, squads of university students in blue serge suits and white gloves. The townspeople bring up the rear, and the whole crocodile, resplendent robes and blaring bands, streams out into the November sunshine of the Plateia. Guns fire a salute, crowds mill round, greeting each other, lifting children on to their shoulders, chattering, gossiping, and there is an extraordinary feeling of lightness and gaiety, all suffused by the clarity of the warm winter sunshine. Somehow there is nothing irreverent or tawdry about it. It is a moment of pure joy. The feeling is inescapable, if you want to 'air' a saint and bring him back into the heart of life, this is the way to do it.

*   *   *

A light westerly breeze sprang up and grew stronger as the day went on. This kept us steadily rolling and we were glad enough of half an hour's respite when three hours after leaving Porto Venere we could put into Viareggio to fill up with diesel.

In spite of being a busy commercial port, Viareggio doesn't look much seaward. The flat country hides the size of the town and the casual visitor would not suspect that a large part of the tonnage for the Italian coastal trade is built here. Once inside the outer breakwater an open area of water appears. This seems to be more or less empty except for one or two dredgers and is really a protective cushion against the westerly winds, which, so the Pilot told us, raise an uncomfortable swell. On the eastern side of the outer harbour the basins begin. There are four of them and at first, as you approach, it is quite difficult to see how to get in. The impression left after our brief visit is of an overcrowded busy jumble of boats of all kinds. We could find nowhere to berth in any of the basins, the yachts were moored so closely. There wasn't a hope of getting to the fuelling station and eventually we tied up in the fairway between two basins. A hundred feet of hose was run out to us from a pump. We filled up and got away as soon as we could. Viareggio seemed no place to linger in.

We plugged on south on the next twenty-mile stretch to Livorno. The coast, as far as Viareggio, had been flat, but at least there was human habitation. Now it was an absolute desolation. Low plantations of stunted pines ran back from the dunes that fringed the shore. Not a house in sight. A cormorant on a stake that marked the sandbanks off the mouth of the River Serchio was the most prominent landmark we noted in the next five miles.

But still it was a glorious day, cloudless sky, hot sun and a light westerly breeze, so as it was 12.30, and we had been going for five hours, we decided to anchor for lunch. It was then we saw a row of curious black walls, isolated moles running along the coast about a hundred yards offshore, forming a protected lagoon behind them. What could they be? We came in carefully through a gap to investigate.

It looked like a graveyard of buried hopes. Evidently someone had started to develop a resort here. There were the remains of one or two bathing shacks, a palisade at the back of the beach. The moles had been put down to break the force of the westerlies. One day there would be a hotel, a casino, and a marina perhaps. . . . But one only had to look fifty yards inland to see why it had been abandoned. There the seaward edge of the pine plantations had been absolutely blasted by the force of the winter gales. The tree-trunks were bent way over, dead, petrified with white salt, like rows and rows of warning skeletons. It was, even on this hot summer day, the most forlorn and desolate place I have ever seen. Still, inside the walls there was about six feet of water over a perfect sandy bottom. It was just like a South Sea lagoon without the coral. So we dropped the hook and plunged in for a gorgeous bathe. Away to the south was a rowboat. Two figures were fishing. To the north a single speedboat was anchored. Otherwise we were quite alone on this, the saddest beach in Italy. There was something eerie and ghostlike about it and I was reminded of a moonlight visit to a deserted mining village in California where the shells of white houses stood watching, their open doors swinging and creaking. In the moonlight one half expected the people who had once lived there to slide out from those gaunt shacks to gaze greedily at our cheerful barbecue in an old backyard. For an hour we had tried to fight off the desolation of the place, but it was too much for us and we were glad to get away.

I don't suppose many people have ever taken it into their

heads to wonder where the River Arno enters the sea. After the glories of the Ponte Vecchio and the leaning tower of Pisa (I'd even forgotten it flowed through Pisa) it comes out on this coast of the damned at a dump called Marina di Pisa, the city itself being only a few miles inland. The Pilot told us that the river is navigable for sixty miles, right up to Florence, by 'boats', but gave no indication of the depth of the channel. It could have been a pleasant diversion to have gone up to Florence by river, but . . . well, as usual, there was the next port, Livorno, coming up on the southern horizon. We had better keep going.

It was probably a mistake not to have finished our day's run in the little yacht basin of Nazario Sauro, which lies at the southern end of the big dykes that protect the main commercial port of the city of Livorno. It is a pretty big and impressive place. We had come right through the port between the breakwaters and the wharves to escape the tiring swell which had been rolling us all day, but after the good luck of finding Vernazza we hoped that one of the three tiny ports south of the city might repeat the pleasure. So we came close in to inspect Ardenza and Antignano. They turned out to be nothing but shallow dinghy ports in the suburbs of Livorno. So we kept going and rounding the Torre of Calefuria came to the last little harbour, Quercianella. There we had to stop, for there wasn't another port for twenty-five miles.

There was nothing in Quercianella but a lot of rowing boats and a rabble of small boys bathing. It was so shallow behind the little mole that, once I had a stern line ashore, we wound up the Z-drive to be safe from the rocks on the bottom. But it was quite snug and peaceful once the bathers had retired to supper. Before turning in, I called to Fanny to come out and look at the sky. She was busy at something in the saloon and demurred with a reply which almost became the title of this book: 'I can't see the stars without my glasses!'

*   *   *

Next morning before sunrise the sky was like the Japanese flag. Bands of high cirrus radiated out of the east, arched right over the zenith and drew together again at the western horizon. Whatever it might be doing down at sea level, up there was a windy sky if ever I saw one. But as, usually, the winds at forty or fifty thousand feet don't get down to earth in much under twelve hours, we pushed off down the coast. There was a light offshore breeze, the sea was calm; but the rising sun did not disperse the cloud, which gradually hazed over. Three hours later there was a complete overcast, a watery sun and, although the sea still remained calm, a certain tension in the air. Something was going to happen. The coast was low-lying, featureless and uninteresting, but ahead was the nob of hills which form the north-easterly side of the Straits of Piombino. Fine on our starboard bow we could make out the northerly tip of Elba, but the visibility was getting less, the whole horizon was misty and a light southerly breeze came up just as we drew abreast of Porto Barati. But there was still nothing to worry about and we headed out a bit to the west, making for Elba.

Ten minutes later the whole picture had altered. The light southerly rapidly built up into a fresh south-easterly breeze, whipping up that short sharp typical Mediterranean sea, the servant of any wind that passes, rising obediently to a storm and falling away to calm again in a few hours at the whim of its invisible master. At this moment the master was angry and quickly getting angrier. Goodbye to Elba! It would have to be

Piombino. Miserable Piombino we had so much hoped to avoid!

The town lies on the southern tip of a hilly promontory of the same name, but the harbour is 'round the corner' on the eastern side. If the place did not happen to be the terminal for the ferries bound for Elba, nobody would ever have heard of Piombino and rightly, for the smelting works and rolling mills have chimneys that belch heavy red-brown smoke all day. The entire surrounding countryside is covered with their soot. Commercially the town no doubt has its place; aesthetically, no doubt, it has none.

However, it has a good protected port and for the moment that outweighed all other considerations. By now it was clear the south-easterly meant business. Ribs of white caps raced up through the strait, the spray flying from their crests. *Prosilios* was bashing and smashing into them, sheets of flying water hit the cockpit windows, our Blue Ensign stood out like a board. As we rounded the low cliffs on which the town stands, we could see the breakers bursting at their feet. Gradually as the seas came abeam we started to roll and held on to the grab rails, swaying and lurching with the movement, looking (a bit anxiously I must admit) for the beacons that marked the extremities of the breakwaters. But we need not have worried. *Prosilios* remained resilient and buoyant in the snappy cross-seas, light as a cork, mastering each crest gleefully as a puppy and keeping moving. Whether we were enjoying it or not, she was clearly having a whale of a time and seemed to settle down regretfully to the smooth harbour water. What a pity the romp was over!

The best berth we could find was right next to the ferry terminal wharf and fifty yards from the hydrofoil Aliscafo speedboats that do the trip to Elba in twenty minutes. There was a good deal of movement and a constant roar of cars coming on and off the ferry. A thick black cream of oil, driven into this corner of the harbour by the wind, slopped its filth round the boat. And then it started to rain.

It caught us (once again) unawares. We always travel with the hood dismantled at sea, so the rain poured into the open cockpit, bringing down with it all the soot of Piombino. Our sorbo cushions soaked it up like sponges. (They were so heavy next day we could hardly lift them.) The whole boat was a filthy mess.

The south-easterly gradually moved through south to south-west and continued to blow. All next day it blew while we did our best to clean ship and sat on our five big three by two-foot cushions one by one to try to squeeze the water out of them. Then, when I started up the engine to charge the batteries, our next trauma made its first appearance. The ammeter needle stayed on zero; the batteries were not charging.

*   *   *

As the engine had only run 300 hours it seemed impossible for there to be anything serious the matter. But the local Piombino electrician, while admitting he knew nothing of the Prestolite alternator we had fitted, disabused us of the hope that it was just a loose connection. No current was coming out of it. It would have to be dismantled. Luckily, with a diesel engine, batteries are only necessary to start up. So, as our batteries were fully charged when we came into Piombino, there would be enough power for a few more starts anyway. The best thing was to press on to the nearest Perkins agent, fifty miles to the south at Porto Santo Stefano. I never like going to sea with a vital part of equipment out of order, but in this case there was no option, so next morning, before dawn, we set off.

Before dawn because we noticed that, although the wind was getting up to Force 4 or 5 by midday, it usually fell before midnight. Dawn was calm and then gradually it built up again during the day. So we found we could snatch a few hours of reasonable weather if we started early. This became a pattern which we followed from Piombino on.

'*Si puo andare. Si puo andare,*' said the fisherman whose advice I took before setting off. '*Al meno tre ore di bel tempo. E ce sempre il portoccioli di Punta Ala per rifugiarsi!*'

This was good news, because the Pilot says that this little harbour, called the Cala del Pozzo, had been abandoned.

'Of course it hasn't,' said the fisherman cheerfully. 'Plenty of yachts there and at least two metres of water.'

It was only a two-hour run across the Gulf of Follonica to Punto Ala. The dawn grew into a sunny morning. The breeze hardly developed and we put into the little port to see how the day would go. It was, as the fisherman had said, full of yachts. They were dotted all over the harbour, moored anyhow, and we had to go carefully to avoid getting our prop snarled up in the cat's cradle of lines that criss-crossed in all directions. Once moored, we had leisure to look round.

The little harbour is sited very prettily, well protected from all winds in the southern sector. The moles are not much more than banks of stones and the place would be untenable in north-westerlies. Under the hill and the big fort which give it protection from the south are a couple of low, rather dreary-looking hotels on the sandy beach. Their black shutters gave the place a rather sad air, but, as the fisherman had said, it is a good refuge. I mention Punto Ala here because it is not to be found in any of the harbour books and could be useful to others who happen to come this way.

As the breeze did not appear to be increasing, we pushed off again later on our next hop, a port called Castiglione della Pescaia. Once round the sharp rocks that lie off Punto Ala, we met quite a heavy swell rolling onshore; but, as it was only an hour's run, we decided to carry on, making the best of it.

Castiglione della Pescaia stands on the side of a canal. The harbour entrance is in fact the seaward end of it. The port is shaped like a cricket bat, handle towards the sea. This handle, where you enter between the breakwaters, is not more than fifty yards wide. With an onshore swell, such as we had that day, the big rollers surge straight down through the entrance. As we approached the place, with its fine castle and hill-top town, we noticed a sailing yawl ahead of us come up to the entrance, turn round and circle out to seaward again. Then she made another approach and ran in. Why had she hesitated like that? We were soon to find out.

As we approached the heads of the breakwaters, we saw that the swell, fairly long and easy in deep water, was far deeper and steeper than we had realised. Most of the crests were breaking into big foamy rollers as the water shallowed. Quite a crowd had gathered on the pierheads to watch boats coming in and a dozen pairs of glasses were trained on us. By the time I realised the danger it was too late to do anything about it. We were coming down along the coast beam to the swell. When we turned in, it would be right astern. Some sub-conscious kind of judgment from old flying days came to my aid. As we began to turn, I aimed for the southerly mole. The crest of a twelve-foot roller caught us and swept us towards the narrow entrance. We were just about to broach to, but full throttle and the wheel right over to port saved us and we shot through the pierheads like a Hawaiian surf-rider, dead centre, doing about twenty knots! It was a pretty exciting and exhilarating thirty seconds, the more so because we hadn't expected it. But all's well that ends well. We mentally fanned ourselves and cooled off as we eased into still water. It was a relief to get our lines ashore halfway down the calm blade of the cricket bat. But whew! That flying entrance is something we shall never forget.

*   *   *

When you are abroad and something goes wrong you feel absolutely lost. The nearest firm who knows anything about your equipment may be miles away. The telephones never seem to work and even when you do get through there is the language difficulty. I speak fairly fluent Italian, but when it comes to electrical technicalities, brushes, transistors, relays and the like, I rapidly get out of my depth. But, apart from all that, in any breakdown there are bound, in any case, to be transport costs, service charges and delays. If it's your own fault, if you go aground and damage a propeller, as we did at Lyons, then you just pay up and look pleasant; but if the breakdown is due to a mechanical fault in equipment under guarantee, then I confess I get very angry at being asked to shoulder all the costs of putting it right.

The whole question of service after sales must be a headache to every exporter. The best gear can go wrong, but the firm's reputation rests on how quickly and efficiently it can be put right. So the choice of a good agent is crucial. But the first question he asks is: 'How much business shall I do with the agency and at what profit?' If the exporting firm gives an optimistic reply, the agent may be disillusioned later and give up; if it gives a pessimistic reply, he won't even start. Big firms, like Perkins, carry a good sprinkling of agents in Europe (and indeed all over the world), but as all of them obviously can't carry a complete range of spares, you are always involved in delays while the parts are obtained from some central depot.

But when the faulty part is, as in our case, not under their direct guarantee, then the complications are very much worse. Our alternator turned out to be an American product, Prestolite. It was up to Prestolite to implement the guarantee and there seemed to be no representative of the firm nearer than Milan, which was over 500 miles away!

A long-distance call to the Director there sent up my blood pressure. How did he know the engine was under guarantee? How could he forward a new alternator (which cost £50) without payment, in the hope that Perkins would reimburse him? They might not. Then he would be making me a present of the thing. It took a quarter of an hour to persuade him that he was not dealing with a crook, that he could safely forward the unit to the official Perkins agent on sale or return. But at last he agreed. The call cost £3.

On sale or return because I still hoped that the fault was a minor one and repairable. If it was only some small component, fuse or brush, then it could be easily dealt with by any competent electrician. But, of course, to find out what is wrong you have first to test the gear and to do that you have to get it out of the boat.

All this began to unfold at Talamone, a very pretty little walled town overlooking a secluded bay, with a tiny harbour. We had been driven in there by a south-westerly gale. When it showed no signs of letting up it seemed sensible to use the enforced delay to deal with our breakdown. In reponse to a telephone call, the Perkins agent appeared with a mechanic who got the alternator off. He insisted on taking it to Grosseto, a town twenty miles away, to have it tested. There they took it to pieces, put it together and shook their heads. There was nothing wrong with it—only it didn't charge! So back we came to the boat again to remount it. This was essential because the same belt that drives the alternator drives the water pump and without that we couldn't go to sea. All the costs so far had been wasted money.

At Porto Santo Stefano, three days later, the same process was repeated; but here things were different. Santo Stefano is a picturesque, busy port. The quays are broad, packed with fine yachts. The fishmarket is the cleanest we found in Italy. It is actually walled in white tiles, and the fish you buy, instead of being wrapped in yesterday's *Corriere della Sera*, is handed to you in a smart plastic bag! But more than all this, to the yachtsman, the port boasts a big, fully equipped and excellently run boat-yard—the Cantiere Argentario.

From its Managing Director, Commandante Gasperi, I got the lowdown. The Perkins agent at Porto Santo Stefano had been an engineer of high ability whom everybody respected, but unfortunately he had died the year before and the agency had been inherited by his sons. They were doing their best, but lacking their father's technical knowledge they had simply involved me in a fruitless journey to Grosseto. I put the thing in Gasperi's hands.

Again the alternator came off. Gasperi's electrician took half an hour to find the fault—the field windings had burned out. That meant a new alternator.

'Look!' said the electrician, sweeping his arm round the workshop. 'Prestolite alternators!' There they lay, the carcasses of at least a dozen generators. He shrugged in that typical Italian way, far more expressive than any words.

'I would advise you to buy a Fiat. Here, in Italy, it is twenty pounds cheaper than the Prestolite.'

This was true, but I did not see why I should buy anything. Prestolite were bound by guarantee. So, another long-distance call, another laboured conversation ending in a flat refusal. 'If you want the alternator, you must pay for it. How do I know if Perkins will agree to reimburse me? If you don't want it, send it back and pay the freight.'

I suppose I should have refused, got in touch with Perkins, complained, insisted and all the rest. But there comes a point when the effort isn't worth making. It wasn't till months later I found out that Perkins had just terminated the Prestolite contract! That accounted for everything. At the time, all I could do was fume against the way the owner always had to pay. The manufacturer and his agent took jolly good care to see that they were in the clear. The customer, who had bought in good faith, found, when it came to the clinch, nothing but an imprecise muddle of pass-the-buck guarantees. The letters I wrote to Perkins at the time and, no doubt, many others they must have received in a similar vein, may have woken them up to the fact that they must put all this on a firmer footing. At any rate, a new form of guarantee is said to be on the way.

Meanwhile the bills started coming in. Perkins agent wanted to be paid for his time and transport costs, all of which had been useless. I paid his bill and sent it on to Perkins headquarters in England. To their credit it must be said that they at once repaid me. I also paid the bill for fitting a new generator, a Fiat. That took care of all the rest of our 'good time' money—and it was still another 650 miles to Corfu.

*　　*　　*

What a sheaf of memories we had of the place! The maddening way they let everything fall to pieces and then, at the very last moment, bodged it together with bits of string! The intensely original way they tackled a problem, never going by the book. The way they were warmly religious, yet not at all devout. Their violent, explosive conversations and splendid gestures. Their deep respect for tradition, for the old ways. Their bold eyes, frank greetings, their warmth, their homeliness.

We are sitting in the old kitchen. Copper pans gleam from the racks. Our shadows on the walls are huge, grotesque in the lamplight. A cauldron steams over the charcoal. Georgina is stirring it—winter feed for Stefano's bees. The mixture scents the air.

'What makes it smell so good?'

'Quite a lot of things. Cinammon, mint, geranium, carnation, mountain tea, jasmine essence, orange essence and the essence of rose petals . . .'

'Sounds more like scent for a harem!'

'Don't you feed your bees like that?'

'No! Just plain syrup and water for British bees!'

Georgina is breaking eggs, seven of them, into the mixture, Stefano adds five pints of milk and a teaspoonful of terramycin.

'We do that to combat disease. Pity it's artificial . . .'

Georgina goes on stirring. 'The rest is sugar and water. Twice as much sugar as water.' He lifts the big pan off the stove.

'Now we can let it cool. Tomorrow we will feed it to the hives, warm, at dusk for their supper.'

'Supper! It's a feast!'

'Yes, it is, really. Perhaps that is why our Greek bees are the tamest in the world. We look after them in winter and they look after us in summer!'

The next evening we file out to the apiary. The hives are set neatly in a dell beneath a huge eucalyptus tree. Lifting the covers gently, one by one, Stefanos pours the warm stuff into the feeder hole. When they have all been fed we pick up the jugs and funnel and walk back through the orange trees to the big house.

*   *   *

In 1940 it happened that I was seconded, as a R.A.F. liaison officer, to a naval headquarters at Portsmouth. The mess maintained its pre-war standards, the long dining room was spacious, comfortable and warm. At breakfast every officer found a wire stand at his place on which to rest his morning paper. It was part of mess etiquette that nobody spoke. The silence was only punctuated by the sound of teaspoons clinking in cups and the ruminative crunching of toast while forty or fifty officers caught up with the news. The news at that time was quite something to catch up on. Norway had been overrun, the Nazi spearhead was sweeping through Europe like an irresistible avalanche. It looked as if nothing could stop it. One morning, late for breakfast, I found myself alone at the table with the Commanding Officer, a Rear-Admiral and a pretty tough, taciturn type. Having finished his breakfast, the great man pushed aside his paper stand and glared across at me in an aggressive, yet somehow bewildered manner. 'Well, Lewis,' he growled, 'and how do you appreciate the situation?'

This technical use of the word 'appreciate' had me quite flummoxed, never having heard it before. I wanted to say that I didn't appreciate it at all; I thought it stank. But clearly such a flippant reply would have been out of place. It took me some time to wake up to the fact that the Top Brass spent quite a lot of their time sitting round tables, rubbing their chins, poring over maps and 'appreciating the situation'. So, to this day, when things look bad, muddled and full of question marks and I haven't a clue what to do next, I remember the old Admiral and try to take his impartial stand. 'Lewis,' I say to myself, 'how do you appreciate the situation?'

How did I appreciate it? We had cruised about 1,000 miles since leaving Newhaven. We had left on July 10th. It was now September 20th. Sixty-two days. An average of about sixteen miles a day. True, we had lost well over a month in bad weather and mechanical breakdowns, but, assuming we still had another 650 miles to go and could not improve on this average, it would take us six weeks more to reach Corfu. That meant arrival some time during the first week of November. It was late, too late. Especially as that last sixty miles of open water across the Straits of Otranto would come at the end of it.

Mechanically, I felt pretty sure we had got through our teething troubles. The engine had run perfectly for the last 400 miles; we might reasonably hope to double the daily average— but then there was the weather. The Mediterranean is pretty unpredictable at any time, but at the change of seasons, the equinoxes, it could easily hold us up for weeks.

Besides this we were, after all, making the cruise for fun. We weren't out to prove anything to ourselves or anyone else. Being cold and thrown about interminably in rough seas for the next six weeks didn't tempt us in the least. I was no Chichester stifling a yawn at anything under Force 7, I was strictly a Force 2 man. I know that there are people to whom tough weather is the very essence of cruising: this is what they like, what they go to sea for. But we do not. We love cruising, we love the sea; but we have far too much respect for it to want to take it on when it gets mad. This is partly age, partly inexperience—and partly the boat.

Anyone who knows anything about it will, of course, long ago have come to the conclusion that we were mad. To make a long cruise in a boat with only one engine is asking for trouble. If it fails, what do you do? We hadn't even an out-board for auxiliary power in case of breakdown. Even if we had had sails, or a steadying sail at least, we should have some means of locomotion in emergency. We had nothing. Because fools step in where angels fear to tread, we had set off blithely, perfectly confident that our engine would never break down, that our boat was ideal for the cruise, but experience had taught us otherwise. I think it would take quite a lot to sink Prosilios, for, as I have said, she rides the seas as lightly and buoyantly as a cork, but the motion is sharp and gets very tiring after a few hours. She would wear out her crew long before she was in any danger herself—or, at any rate, an elderly crew of two. A spanking young crew of four might make light of it.

So I had come to the conclusion that she was not really the right boat for the job. I longed for a boat with a good keel that would hold steady in a seaway. I longed for sails to act as a damper to the motion. I longed, in other words, for a motor sailer. Prosilios had done us proud. She was roomy, comfortable, a wonderful little floating home, and very pleasant at sea, provided you could pick the weather. But now we were getting towards the season when good weather would become increasingly hard to pick. In addition, apart from a short stretch around Naples, the coast for the rest of the way was, on the whole, boring and dull, the same sort of interminable, featureless stuff we had met south of Spezia. If it wasn't that, it was the lonely precipitous coast from Paestum down to Reggio with hardly a harbour worth putting in to for eighty miles. Maybe if we'd been more dedicated, younger, more experienced, more courageous, we would have decided otherwise. As it was, after arguing it back and forth for hours, we came to the conclusion that it wasn't on.

So we cheated.

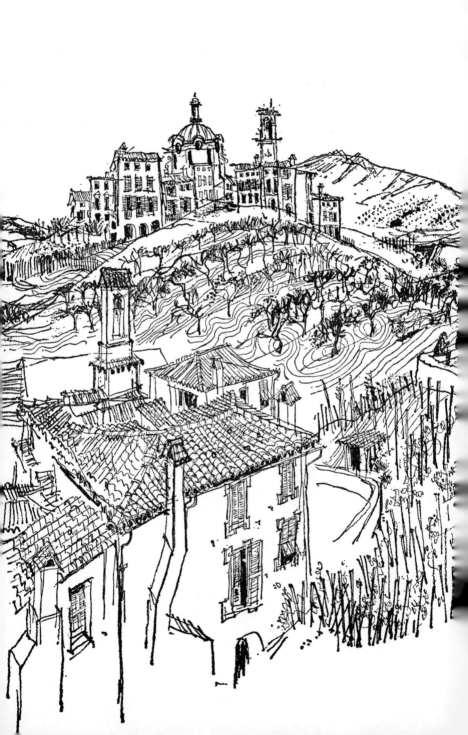

3
The Adriatic

3
The Adriatic

THE cheat was a simple one. We would simply hoist *Prosilios* on to a truck and take her overland to the Adriatic and put her back in the water there. This would save us about 400 sea miles and leave us with a modest 200 miles to complete the trip before winter set in. The question of where to put the boat into Adriatic waters was limited by finding a port where there was a suitable mobile crane to do the job. Italian ports, particularly on the east coast, are not equipped to deal with yachts. There are hardly any pleasure boats, harbours being geared solely to the needs of trawlers and fishing. The only possibilities seemed to be Ancona and Bari, but Ancona was too far north and would have left us with 400 miles to cover. Bari was too far south, it meant a long overland journey; but at least it was in the right direction. So we set about trying to get a truck to convey us to Bari.

Our first attempt was a fiasco. A driver appeared saying he had an eighteen-foot truck and was willing to do the job. I objected that at least eight feet of Prosilios would be waving in the air, but he brushed this aside. It was nothing. He had often conveyed boats longer than his truck. As long as they were firmly secured there was no need to worry. I allowed myself to be persuaded. The mobile crane was laid on (at a cost of £30), the truck drew up on the wharf and Prosilios was slowly hoisted out of the water. When the driver saw her bulk (although he had visited the boat and been on board the previous day) he suddenly got very cold feet: nothing would induce him to load her. Everyone swore at him, the Italians for not knowing better the capacity of his truck and I for wasting the cost of the crane. But there was nothing to be done. In fact I agreed with him. His truck was far too small—but it was a bit late to find it out. We slowly lowered Prosilios back into the water.

Our next ploy was very different. The Cantiere Argentario produced a six-wheel lorry with a thirty-foot deck and knocked up a cradle for Prosilios. When she was loaded her prow fitted neatly up to the driver's cabin and her transom was well within the tailboard. The lorry was perfect for the job and the boat was so well secured that at the end of the 300-mile trip she had not moved an inch. The two drivers, Alberto and Franco, were the sort of men I thought had disappeared from Italy. Courteous, quiet, good-humoured, with kindly simple manners. Although we only knew them for two days, they imprinted themselves clearly on my memory. In some strange way I remember them as friends.

Commandante Gasperi and his yard also did something that only the very best firms know how to do. He took any amount of trouble to help a customer from whom he could not hope for any considerable business, giving unstinting help and advice and committing his firm to an amount in excess of £200 entirely on credit without any enquiry into my bona fides or even asking for my address. (When, in fact, the whole bill was paid within the month, he professed himself astounded at the promptness and efficiency of the British firm that passed him the amount.)

So we were off, the four of us packed into the cab of the lorry (quite against regulations), and *Prosilios* looking down her nose at us from behind. The imperturbable Alberto was driving, Franco straddled the engine, I had the offside seat and Fanny was curled up on the bed, which ran across the cab, behind the seats. It was a beautiful morning and we were all in good spirits and, as soon as we got on to the main roads, made good time. But, as the hours wore on, we began to realise that the lorry was not really very well sprung, the seats were not too comfortable and could we, in fact, continue like this for twenty-four hours? By the time we got to Rome, I decided we could not.

Lorries are not allowed on the Autostrada that connects Rome with its Fiumincino airport, but on a feeder road, Franco leapt out of the cab, crossed the traffic lane, flagged down a car and within seconds we were across, shouting our farewells and agreeing to meet them on the mole of the old port at Bari next morning. The driver of the car, hearing that we had only ten minutes to catch our plane, stepped the speed up to about ninety and, as it happened he was an airport official, we shot into the departure wing and up to the ticket desk, breathlessly begging for two seats on the Bari plane.

The ticket clerk got on the blower to reservations. It appeared that the plane was full.

'Surely,' I said, attempting to use the only sort of 'influence' that came to my mind at that moment, 'surely, you can find a couple of seats for a veteran pilot?'

The clerk beamed at me. 'But on which side?' he enquired.

We all burst out laughing. He gave us our seats and next morning at eight o'clock we found Franco and Alberto waiting with the boat on the St. Agostino mole at Bari.

*   *   *

Now we were in southern Italy and the difference was at once apparent. The northern Italian, with a strong mixture of French, Swiss and German blood in his veins, is hardworking, tough and reliable. On him the prosperity and industry of his country depends. Having lived in the north on and off for twenty years, it was quite a shock when during the war I was posted to command R.A.F. staging posts in Sicily and Bari. Here the Italians were quite different. They were unreliable, untruthful, lazy—and great thieves. Much of this may have been due to climate, to poverty and to lack of work. Many of them seemed to spend their day lounging about with absolutely nothing to do. Since the war a great deal has been done to open up this forgotten area of Italy south of Naples. Places I remembered as hillside villages in 1944 boasted skyscraper skylines in 1967. Herds of water buffaloes roam the Pontine Marshes. Great strides have been made in putting through splendid roads—the mountains right down to Reggio are as fine as anything in all Italy—tourism is on the increase, there is some industry and so on. But for all this a curious, shiftless atmosphere remains.

On the boat it was particularly noticeable. All down the west coast, at every port, we had been just a cruising yacht, one among hundreds. The locals, out for their evening stroll along the wharves, would pause for a moment to read the name on the stern and admire the Blue Ensign and move on. But here at Bari and at every port south to Brindisi knots of people would collect and stand staring at us for hours. They watched every move we made, peered at us as we took our meals, passed comments on our appearance and made jokes at our expense. We might have been visitors from another planet. All this was not exactly unfriendly, but neither was it friendly.

'We might be monkeys in a cage,' said Fanny. And this was exactly it. We were objects of idle curiosity—and it became a great bore. We never liked leaving the boat.

*　　　*　　　*

Our first impression on leaving Bari next morning was that the Adriatic was not the Mediterranean. It seemed quite a different sea. It is, of course, a stretch of water that is comparatively narrow and very deep. From the mountains to the north of it violent winds spring up, producing the famous Bora, which is, by all accounts, a very angry customer. It whistles through the chains of Yugoslav islands, which seem to act on it like a Venturi tube, speeding it up as it passes and even in summer is not to be trifled with. Although we did not, thank heaven, encounter a Bora, we were plagued all down the coast with a heavy residual swell of northerly winds.

We had escaped from Bari as quickly as possible and dropped into Mola di Bari, the next port down the coast, to catch up on our shopping and have a look round. The port is strictly functional, the home of quite a large fleet of deep-sea trawlers, some of which are built on the open ways at the southern side of the harbour. These are fast heavy vessels and the wash they set up coming in is enough to make any berth against the long moles very unpleasant. The smaller port within the main harbour is really only good for rowing boats. It was full of them, but they made a place for us when the wind blew up and we decided to stop overnight.

We set out to explore the town. It proved much more interesting than the waterfront. A maze of narrow lanes and cul-de-sacs flanked by tall houses, all whitewashed and scrupulously clean, with hundreds of balconies festooned with flowers and washing, it was exceedingly picturesque. The quality of the shops was poor, but the fishmarket was attended by a crowd of at least 500 men, milling around the open-air stalls. Nearby a vintner was pressing the wine of local peasants, bringing in their grapes on donkey carts or three-wheel trucklets. They insisted we try a glass of the fresh unfermented juice. It was very sweet and pleasant, but would, they assured me, rapidly make you 'choc'—dialect, in the north, for drunk.

The main road to Brindisi runs right along the water's edge and a continual stream of heavy lorries does not add to the amenities of the harbour. But on the Braccio de Levanti the shipyards are fascinating. One trawler building on the ways was of about 100 tons burthern. Ships always look larger ashore than afloat and this one towered up into the sky, her heavy double oak beams, spaced at about fifteen-inch centres, making her practically solid before the planking went on. This was held in place by thick five-inch galvanised nails, driven deep into the countersunk holes (previously drilled) with sledgehammers and then plugged with dowelling. The

1,000 h.p. engine drove a shining three-foot bronze propeller and the hatchways covered refrigerated holds for ten tons of fish. These boats with their complete electronic equipment and crew of twelve had cruised in company, three of them, right over to Columbia and back. Looking at the fine lines of the schooner bows, the full midsection and clean run, one felt they were certainly built to keep the sea. Builders and owners clustered there on the quay looking up were proud of their handiwork and it felt good in this plastic age to see something being fashioned in the open air with the simplest tools, holding its own against all the mechanisation.

*　　*　　*

The actual coastline from Mola di Bari southwards consists of low sandstone cliffs, about thirty feet high, sometimes with shallow beaches at their feet, sometimes with shoals and rocks offshore, an occasional island, a ruined fortress, a white village and, of course, the inevitable massive Spanish watch-towers, relics of the days when Spain ruled Italy and even deposed the Pope!

It is a dreary prospect, and Monopoli, the next port south, on the morning we arrived there seemed quite abandoned. Apart from a couple of small coastal steamers, it was empty of all shipping. A long mole, the Diga Tramontana, protects it from the northerlies, while the shorter Mola Marguerita juts out northwards from the old town, holding off the Levantas and making an inner harbour, safe from all winds. We tied up here for an hour. It was nine o'clock in the morning, but nothing moved. It all seemed sad and deserted, so we had a cup of coffee and cast off, heading south for Savelletri.

This little 'village' port is, in layout, an exact replica of

Monopoli in miniature, but here there were plenty of boats. A few fishermen sitting about seemed, for once, singularly uninterested in our arrival and made no move to take our lines. However, when we were safely moored, one of them told us we were in the middle of the trawler berths and would have to move. We did so and manœuvred, with some difficulty, into a place opposite a large restaurant (patronised at weekends by escapees from Brindisi for its excellent cooking and seafood). By now the north wind was blowing up again. The sea was flecked with white. We decided to call it a day and, if the early forecast was favourable, to make a dawn start next morning.

It was already the 28th of September. The days were drawing in. So a start at 0545 next day was an hour before light came. The evening forecast had prophesied Force 3 from the northern sector, but we left in a windless swell and it was not until dawn came that the wind began to get up. It was only a four-and-a-half-hour run to Brindisi, but there was no shelter on the way and, once committed to it, there was nothing to do but to keep going as the wind and sea rose. It developed into the most strenuous and anxious leg of the cruise. There was a misty overcast, reducing the visibility and blurring the outline of the low-lying coast ahead. We peered somewhat anxiously into this, trying to pick up the next tower, San Leonardo, Villanova, Pozzelli, which always seemed to be standing in the sea and, by some optical illusion, far larger on the horizon than it turned out to be as we approached. Optimistically putting our dead-reckoning position ahead of our actual one, we imagined each one to be the outline of the cracking plant at Brindisi and when it shrank to just another tower, Vacito, Testa, Penna, the journey began to seem endless. This was chiefly owing to the cockscrew motion which was violent enough to keep us hanging on to avoid being thrown across the cockpit. The auto pilot had long ago given up and I struggled with the wheel, correcting every breaking swell that overtook us. The wind was practically due north and our course of 120°M meant that we were running with it on our port quarter. It was now, when I had time to look, somewhere around Force 5 and seemed bent on forcing Prosilios to broach to. Steering became a tussle and, as the hours wore on, I began to feel like the Flying Dutchman doomed to labour endlessly through the storms of the world. There was nothing to distract the attention—in fact it required all I had got to hold the course. No shipping was at sea. We only passed one heavy fishing vessel with her trawl out. Rising and falling with the swell, with a steadiness I envied, the crew laughed and waved vigorously as we passed them close. They could evidently see we were having a bit of a battle and their encouragement cheered us. I felt in what now seems a rather exaggerated way that this was the companionship of the sea. My spirits rose, and I began to find a rhythm between the sea and the wheel easing the tensions which were no doubt adding to my fatigue. Only an hour to go now. The coast began to curl out to seaward, forcing us to follow suit and take the seas more on the beam. This was Capo Gallo that protected the approaches to Brindisi. We had been told by fishermen that the weather was always worst just off the Cape—and they were right. We were rolling heavily. A jagged line of rocks just awash protected the harbour approach. We kept well clear as we rounded them to steer south. Now we started planing on the following crests. A big rusty merchantman was heaving and tugging at her anchor in the outer roads, a long black plume of smoke was being carried away horizontally from the slender chimney of the cracking plant. The wind blowing straight into the mouth of the outer harbour pursued us through the light structures on the breakwaters. Even inside it was not easy at once to make out the entrance to the inner harbour. But the enormous war memorial was a landmark and we gratefully turned towards it. Small fishing boats heading out to sea were standing on end and crashing down, even inside the harbour. Not until we had passed through the narrow canal (Pigonate) into the inner 'port' did we find it calm. We were thankful to tie up opposite the Hotel Internazionale. Four and a quarter hours at the wheel had been enough for me. It took me twenty-four hours to recover from the fatigue.

*　　*　　*

Brindisi has always been the main terminus in the Eastern Mediterranean. A Roman column marks the end of the Appian way. The big, completely land-locked port can handle ocean liners and the huge cracking plant and fuel depot (set in another arm of the harbour well away from the town) must be one of the most important in Europe. In the days when the route to India lay through the Suez Canal, Brindisi was the overland terminus for all Europeans travelling to and from India. The Hotel Internazionale, the only decent hotel in the town, owes its existence to this traffic. Then, in the early days of civil aviation, the Sunderland flying boats used the big sheltered stretches of protected water as the ships had done earlier.

Now although the centre of gravity has changed one would have thought all this would have left some stamp of dignity and antiquity on the place. In fact, except for a good waterfront, the layout is cramped and, unlike even small Italian towns, lacks their usual dignity of fine open squares, churches and public buildings. The life centres on one street running back from the quays and this is crowded with people and festooned with neon signs more Greek than Latin, for Brindisi has now shrunk to handling little more than the regular ferries taking cars and tourists to Greece or Yugoslavia and a few small cargo vessels plying the same routes. There is nothing to commend the place except a good market. The country round about, although it produces quantities of wine, olives, tomatoes and so on, is flat, dreary and featureless. From the yachtsman's point of view the place is a dead loss, a broken-down shipyard on the inaccessible side of the harbour, no special area set aside for pleasure boats, no moorings and very expensive water. Over it all that lazy, shiftless attitude to everything I have referred to earlier.

From Brindisi the ferries take off daily for Corfu, covering the 110 miles in about eight hours—a speed of around fifteen knots. The direct trip, at half the speed, was out of the question for us. We had the fuel, but as we had already found out, if there were any sort of sea we shouldn't have the endurance. However, there was nothing to stop us carrying on, coastwise, southward for about forty-two miles, till we reached Otranto. Here there was a harbour. This would shorten the actual open-sea passage across to Fano, the first outlying island off Corfu, to about forty-five miles. From there it was only another forty miles on to Corfu town itself. So, adding it up, we should have three legs of about six hours each, or a little more. Nothing particularly formidable in that, but I did not feel I could tackle it without help. My wife was really too inexperienced to handle the boat in a seaway and I knew already that four hours in quite a 'gentlemanly' blow was pretty fatiguing. How would six be? The actual open-sea crossing was also an anxiety. Owing to the slow speed of the boat we could not count on a good forecast at departure lasting through the trip. A lot can happen in the Med in six hours—and at this season of the year it very often does!

So we needed help. Even if we succeeded in finding that, we also needed weather. We had been two and a half months on the trip. In spite of our 'cheat' across Italy, it was already September 29th and although Corfu can be wonderful in the autumn, calm and serene for weeks on end, it can also be the opposite. In other words, one could not reasonably count on the weather.

Then, as if to emphasise this, the north-easter started to blow day after day from a clear sky, never less than Force 5 and often up to six or seven. Twice we put our nose out, but even in the outer harbour we saw it was no sort of weather to battle with, for us anyway, so, tired of the interminable delays, which were now, after all, legitimate and to be expected at this season, we decided to put *Prosilios* on the ferry for Corfu.

But how? A trailer, of course, was the obvious answer. I scoured the port for any signs of one. Nothing. A ten-foot speedboat, yes; but a five-ton cruiser, not a hope. Then a lorry? But it would be 'exported' to Greece. What about their Customs regulations? What about the Italian regulations when it came back? The Italians shook their heads. And cost? About £60 to take it over and £30 to bring it back. Terrible. But what could we do? We had to get there. And then, of course, another cradle would have to be made. Cost £20 plus. And a crane to load it? I managed to find one. Cost another £15. Swallowing all this, in a sort of desperation, the next thing was to find out the cost of hiring a truck for the job. I spent all one morning on this. Answer, about £65. So now we were up to about £200. Of course it was ridiculous. We must sail. And there was the horizontal plume of smoke from the cracking plant, the white-capped swell rolling in, the north wind booming through the bending palms. . . . Well, we should have to accept it—and, to cap it all, there wasn't a truck!

There wasn't a truck. Literally, not one. It was vendemmia. For miles around the grape harvest was being got in. Along the roadsides stood the big hampers of grapes from square miles of vineyards. They had to be got in—otherwise they would go bad. The whole area was working flat out. The presses were running twenty-four hours a day. Every available piece of transport was in use. In a fortnight perhaps, they said, when the heat was off. . . . But now, nothing. I went to the Italian Automobile Club. A truck? Easy. The Director started phoning. He found out what I had found out already.

'Your only hope is Naples. Rome. But at this time of year . . .' He phoned again. Long distance. 'It is impossible. They are all working the vendemmia.' He got up, shook hands. 'I am very sorry,' he said. So was I.

So it went on for a week. During that time we had searched for trucks, chased a low-loader for half an hour through the suburbs of the town (only to find its owner was in Turin) and tried to load the boat on a small cargo vessel, the *Potamos*. When her derrick started to bend like a flyrod, we had given that up and we were back to square one. The American Navy had moved in, forcing us to leave our comfortable mooring and move to the other side of the port, the wind continued to blow and even the 5,000-ton *Appia*, with her stabilisers, was pitching as we cleared the harbour. Well, it wasn't for want of trying . . . Perhaps we weren't *meant* to get to Corfu.

And then I had an idea. In Greece there was no vendemmia. There were plenty of trucks in Corfu. If we took an Italian truck it would go over full and come back empty. If we found a Greek truck it would come over empty and go back full. No difference. In Greece we had good friends who would help us. Could they raise a truck? There was only one way to find out, go over and see. So, reluctantly, we climbed aboard the ferry.

It was a bit humiliating. All our friends knew we were sailing out. Many of them had been expecting us since the beginning of September. My son had driven my car down and we were to have spent his holiday together. Other friends were due in from the U.K., from Israel. We had missed them all and finally arrived, like any tourist, on the ferry! What a come-down!

'You'll not get a truck,' said Theodore, owner of the biggest garage in the town. 'Or, if you do, it'll cost you a lot of money. They're all working on building. Hotels going up all over the place. We've sold some of our land for one. But—I've got a big trailer. How long is your boat?'

From that moment Theodore put all his drive and in-genuity to the problem of adapting his trailer, which was not good for more than two tons and fifteen feet, to carrying a boat of five tons and twenty-six feet. We brought the trailer from the country to town, discussed welding on another axle, fitting another pair of wheels, strengthening the chassis, making a cradle, arranging for the Customs to pass it out without duty, provided it returned; but as the days passed, it became clear that it wouldn't do. The Greeks are wonderfully ingenious, but this was getting more and more expensive— and, even if we could complete the lash-up, it wouldn't have been safe.

I tried unsuccessfully to borrow a good trailer, which would have done the job, from an American tourist, but he refused. I tried asking one or two good sailors in the island to come back with me and make the run, but they knew the water too well to land themselves into that at this time of the year. So, leaving Fanny on Corfu, pretty dejected and really seeing no way to get the boat over, I boarded the ferry back to Brindisi. I'd been five days in Corfu.

* * *

My friend Stan Symons met the boat.
'No luck?' he questioned, seeing my face.
'No luck.'
'What are you going to do?'
'See if Fugazzo can help.'
We agreed to meet for supper. Stan would stay the night on board and we could talk it over. I repaired to the office of Mr. Fugazzo, Managing Director of Orientmar. He was the only man I had met in Brindisi with what might be called normal efficiency. A short, rotund little man, speaking perfect English with a slight lisp and a charming accent, he listened to my story.
'What about the *Rhumba*?' he asked.
'The *Rhumba*?'
'She has been working the Otranto–Corfu run all the summer. From today the *Appia** goes out of service and I have arranged for the *Rhumba* to alternate with the *Egnatia* from now on. I know the owner well. He will do what I say.'
We went into details of the size and weight of the boat, he picked up the phone, spoke with the owner and a few minutes later we were in his car, motoring round the harbour to a quay on the far side where the *Rhumba* was lying.

* *Appia* and *Egnatia* are 5,000-ton car ferries, belonging to Italy and Greece respectively, that run between Brindisi, Corfu, Igoumenitza and Patras during the summer months.

She was an old ship, adapted as a ferry by cutting a hole in her side through which cars could be loaded. *Prosilios* was too high to go through this, but could be easily loaded on deck.

'We must come back tomorrow morning. There is nobody here now. We can then talk with the engineer about a crane and with the bosun about stowage. There will be no difficulty.'

We agreed to meet on the following morning at 9.30.

After supper that night Stan and I had a long talk.

'It'd be pretty dicey getting her up on that deck,' I explained, 'It's about twelve feet above the quay and their crane looks awfully ropey. The engine was in bits this evening when we got there.'

'What's the deck like?'

'There's just room, I think, if we can get her loaded athwartships.'

'What about a cradle?'

'D'you think it would matter if she just lay on deck with tyres under her chines? After all, it's only for twelve hours.'

'Depends on the weather. If there's no movement you might get away with it, but in anything like a sea . . .'

'I've got the templates for a cradle, but it's the awful expense, Stan. It just goes on and on.'

'I know. I still think if you held on, the weather's bound to break and you can sail her over.'

'I really don't think I dare risk it alone. I suppose you can't come?'

' 'Fraid not. My wife's arriving tomorrow, on the train, sometime, I don't exactly know when. I shall have to hang about at the railway station till she turns up. . . . And then I can't just push off directly she arrives . . .'

'Of course not. . . .'

There was a long silence while we both thought it over.

'Supposing you could get her loaded on the Rhumba, what about unloading at Corfu?'

'That's another snag. There isn't a crane of any kind there.'

'Nothing?'

'Nothing. There's a big dredger with a crane working out by the harbour mole, but imagine trying to divert that, getting it in alongside, holding up the ship for hours—apart from the cost. . . .'

'Then I don't see the point of loading her at all.'

'There isn't really. But the Greeks are awfully ingenious in things like this. I wouldn't put it past them to organise a gang of fifty men and lift her off!'

'That I'd really like to see!' laughed Stan.

'I feel if I go at it hard enough, something's bound to give. There must be a way, and I must find it.'

'I know, but, keeping the other options open, what about that boy who's crewing on the *Spirit of Saint Louis*?'

'Brett? He's awfully young and inexperienced.'

'All you want is someone to take a trick at the wheel.'

'He doesn't strike me as, well, I don't know, trustworthy. Can't say why. Is he free, anyway?'

'I believe so. The crew turned up today. The owner's left. I imagine he's laid off and looking for work. . . .'

The *Spirit of Saint Louis* had been lying alongside us ever since we came into Brindisi. She was a hefty-looking sloop with a steel hull made in Holland, fitted out in the American style with everything that opens and shuts. Her owner and his wife had been cruising in the Med for some time. They had been very hospitable to Fanny and me, and it was Brett, the boy who had been crewing for them, Stan was referring to. Now they had to return to the States and had hired some professional crew to sail the boat back to the West Indies, so the boy would be free . . . But I didn't like the way he idled about when the owners weren't aboard and the way he spoke of them. 'The boss is no sailor.' To my mind, even if it's true, that's no way to talk. Still, I should only be hiring him for forty-eight hours. . . .

Next morning I asked Stan to help me untie to run over to the refuelling pump and fill up.

'What d'you want to do that for? It'll add another quarter of a ton to the weight that crane's got to lift.'

'Well, I know . . . But I don't like her tanks being almost empty. Quarter of a ton doesn't make much difference.'

'Okay then. Let's go. I must get up to the station.'

We crossed the harbour to the pump. The Spirit of Saint Louis was lying nearby. She too was waiting to refuel. Brett was there, hanging around. We all hung around. The man who worked the pump hadn't turned up. Stan took leave of us.

'Must get up and meet the wife.'

'Call by and see me when you're passing.'

'I will. Good luck with the crane!'

Stan hurried off to his car. I strolled over to the Spirit of Saint Louis. Only one of the 'professional' crew was on deck.

'When are you off?

'As soon as we've got the hang of the taps. The thing's stiff with taps.' It was a very English voice that spoke, breezy, cheerful. 'The skipper's down in the hold with the old granite crusher,' he added. I could see a back bent over the big diesel that lay under the open hatches.

'Seen the fuel man?'

'No, but you know these Ities—slow starters in the morning.'

I looked at my watch. It was half past nine. My appointment

with Fugazzo. I mustn't miss that. I turned to Brett. 'Could you do me a favour?'

'Sure.'

'When the bloke comes with the fuel tell him to put 150 litres in my tank. I've got an appointment I mustn't miss.'

'Okay. Where's the fuel cap?'

I showed him. 'Here's 10,000 lire.' I passed him the note. 'It ought to be somewhere around 6,000. Give me the change when I get back.'

'Okay.'

I hurried off, saw Fugazzo, and, when he had arranged for me to meet the engineer in charge of the yard, took a taxi round to the Rhumba.

There the trouble started. It was easy enough to load the boat, but how would they unload at Corfu? They went round and round it. The ship's derricks weren't strong enough. Suppose (I suggested) we made a rough axle with two wheels and rolled her down planks on to the quay? And if she ran off the planks? Then why not two U-section steel girders. There were several lying about the yard. That would keep the wheels straight. How would they get the wheels up into the channels? With chocks. Supposing the girders slipped back on the quay as she was going down? Put a sleeper across them with some men on either end to weight it. What about a cradle? Have you got a cradle? I had not. We must make do with tyres. They shrugged. It was plain the whole thing was too much trouble. If the boat was damaged, there might be all sorts of trouble with claims. They couldn't be bothered. I hoped that the challenge of difficulties (which were perfectly valid and real) might arouse their enthusiasm, that they might want to overcome them. But they were southern Italians. It didn't. It meant effort and risk and, above all, work. After two hours I gave it up. They agreed to think it over. They would find some way. I wasn't to worry. I went back to Prosilios. I knew they wouldn't help. Everything seemed closed against me. There was no way. But I had to find one.

The tanks had been filled up. No signs of Brett. I enquired of the English crew. Had they seen him? No, but some of his stuff was still aboard. They supposed he'd be back later. I took Prosilios back across the harbour to her mooring and tied up. I made myself some lunch and tried to take a siesta, knowing that nobody would be moving till about five. But I couldn't rest. The thing went round and round in my head. And then I had a brilliant idea.

We couldn't unload the boat without a crane. Then why not take one with us on board the Rhumba? There was a mobile crane over there at the yard. Hire it. Hoist it on board with Prosilios. Then at Corfu let it unload the boat and return with the Rhumba to Brindisi. Why not? That was a perfectly simple and feasible solution. I wasn't going to be beaten.

I took the ferry back across the harbour and stopped by at the Spirit of Saint Louis. Had they seen Brett? No, but they could have missed him. His stuff was gone. He hadn't left anything with them? He owed me about 4,000 lire. No; but in that case surely he'd be back. I walked up the main street where the cafés were. I'd often seen Brett sitting there with his friends, the lounging youths of the town. No signs of him. Vaguely worried and upset about it, I went on to Fugazzo and unfolded my brilliant idea. He listened with his usual patient kindness. Then he started phoning, explaining. 'Come back in an hour. I'll have the answer then. I think it'll be all right. It's a good idea. They ought to have thought of it.'

I went back to the main street and walked up and down it looking for Brett. I went into all the cafés, the shops where I'd seen him. But there was no sign of him. I felt it was the last straw. There'd been something said about him taking a plane to London, I remembered. I was now quite sure he'd gone, taking my 4,000 lire with him. It wasn't the money, it was the principle of the thing. The bloody young marine layabout, it was really too much. Had he paid for the fuel at all? I'd heard the pump man wanted to see me. Had he walked off with the whole ten thousand? I wouldn't have put it past him. I'd never trusted the chap, as I'd said to Stan. Fuming, I walked back to Fugazzo's office. He wasn't there. But he'd left a message. They were sorry, but they couldn't load the crane. It weighed six tons and the deck wasn't strong enough.

I remember I sat down with my head in my hands. Nothing seemed to go right. Everything was against me. One of Fugazzo's assistants, sympathetic and smiling, pushed a little majolica plaque across his desk. The Italians have lots of these things. On them are written trite little mottoes, the sort of thing you find in Christmas crackers: 'Guests are like fish; after three days they stink', 'What will be, will be', and things like that. I looked at this one. Roughly translated, it read: 'An ounce of luck is worth a ton of effort.'

I excused myself, said I would be back in the morning and walked back along the quays, very dejected. The *Spirit of Saint Louis* was still lying beyond the big American depot ships moored opposite the hotel. An idle crowd of evening strollers were gazing up at them. I'd just pass by once more to see if I'd been wrong and if Brett had called by and left my change.

The skipper came out of the deckhouse and introduced himself as Peter Haward. A tall, lanky chap with a fine forehead, he looked more like an intellectual than a sailor. No, they'd seen no signs of him; but could I, if I knew the town, tell them of some pub where they could get an evening meal?

The others then came out on deck. Freddy Castle, whom I'd met earlier in the day, and Martin Rubin, an American. I took them along to a place off the main street and asked if they'd mind if I joined them. It was better than dining alone. They'd be glad if I would, they said. Perhaps, if I knew the language, I could help them with all that double dutch on the menu. They were all very cheery and relaxed.

We talked of their trip, Malta, Gib, then down to the Canaries and across to the West Indies. To me it seemed a hell of a long way, but it didn't seem to worry them. I began to see what a heavy responsibility delivery crews carry and to respect Peter, who spoke of it all in such a practical, assured way. He must know his business, I reflected, and it was a hell of a profession, after all, taking a strange boat half across the world, meeting whatever came. As the meal progressed and we all relaxed a bit, they asked about my trip and I told them of all the delays and troubles we'd had and how, now, I was at my wits' end, not knowing how I could get over the last 130 miles after coming all this way. The conversation turned to other things, the canals, the shortcomings of Z-drives, the climate in Corfu. Then Peter, who had been silent for a few minutes, turned to me and said:

'How would it be if I put one of my chaps on board your boat and went round by Corfu? I don't suppose the owner would mind.'

I didn't really take it in. Somehow, with all the other plans I'd had still going round and round in my head, I couldn't focus it. I said, 'That would be wonderful.' But, inside, I didn't really believe it.

'We're leaving at dawn. Are your tanks full?'

Well, there's a coincidence for you, I thought! Why had I been so sure I must have my tank filled?

We walked back along the quays and Peter took me aside.

'Look,' he said, 'I don't want anything for myself, but it would be something for these chaps of mine, if you could pay me something. . . .'

With all the costs of the last days turning in my head, rather frightened at what he might ask, I answered: 'I couldn't afford more than a hundred.'

'I thought forty-eight would be fair,' said Peter.

I was overwhelmed. Now at last I began to believe it. 'An ounce of luck is worth a ton of effort.'

'I'll put Fred Castle on board with you. He's a pretty sound chap.'

'I'd like that.'

We went back on board the *Spirit of Saint Louis* and cast off to cross the harbour. Peter moored alongside *Prosilios* and we discussed times and pored over charts.

'If the weather blows up, we'll put into Otranto till it clears. If it's okay we'll run down to Otranto and then go straight across.'

'If we want to get in to Fano before dark,' I said, 'we ought to leave, let's see, put it at six knots, that's thirteen hours. It's dark at 1830. We ought to leave at 0530.'

'Okay. I'll set the alarm for 0430.'

*　　*　　*

If I say that I turned in with a prayer of thankfulness in my heart, it is not an exaggeration. Suddenly all the gloom of struggle and worry had cleared—and all because Brett had walked off with a few of my lire! I ought to be grateful to him. And I was. To have a man with me who knew more about the sea than I should ever know—and to have an escort, skippered by a man like Peter . . . It was beyond my wildest hopes. Only twenty-four hours ago I had got back to Brindisi without any idea of how I was going to solve what seemed an insoluble problem. Now it had solved itself.

Looking back on it all now I see that our whole cruise was really a perfectly ordinary one. Plenty of people have brought boats out to Greece. There had been a few anxious moments, but in effect nothing really serious happened. Our lives were never in danger. We never encountered really bad weather. Every time things looked a bit dicey good friends had somehow materialised and helped us. But you have to put all this against the measure of our own inexperience and if I have made mountains out of molehills it is because molehills were mountains to us.

I was reminded of this pretty forcibly only yesterday when a letter turned up from Freddy, safe home for Christmas with his family in Solihull. The *Spirit of Saint Louis* had reached Grenada in good order. They'd had a few days in Malta and a few days in Gib. Then—I quote from Freddy's letter:

'At Gib Peter ran across an old customer, Sam, M.B.—a portrait painter of distinction. He has an Illingworth 10-10 sloop—24 ft. waterline. Sam wanted to go to Barbados with his wife so I was again seconded to command—with Peter sailing in convoy. We had headwinds, of course, and I used the small diesel to make progress, but just past Cape Spartel, the prop dropped off! Peter towed us for two days until the wind freed, after which we had some hairy sailing. Sam wasn't too nimble so I did all the deck work and we steered watch and watch. Sam's wife was sick for four days and the other crew member, a one-eyed black cat, missed his dirt box more often than not (which wasn't surprising in the conditions). We had all sorts of fun, but Peter stuck to us well, which was a comfort. The last night out Sam fell in the cockpit and fractured a rib. His wife took the helm and I eventually got him into the quarter berth and we got into Las Palmas that day at 3 p.m.—seven days out of Gib. I was all in. . . .

'From then on we ran into headwinds which culminated in a thirty-six-hour gale from the S.W.—very interesting. The winds were disappointing on the whole. We had light variables from 28° to 50°W in all latitudes, 15° to 18°N. When we couldn't sail we used the old granite crusher and it wasn't till the twentieth day out of Las Palmas that the Trades set in, which gave us five exhilarating days of downhill sailing and 140 miles odd per day. We spent a few days at Grenada and flew home Friday night.'

*   *   *

I confess to a quite childish pleasure at leaving port in the dark! The feeling of being awake and on the move when everyone else is asleep, a feeling of secrecy, of slipping away unobserved, all this adds up to a sense of romantic adventure which may be naïve, but all the same I like it very much. The rich detail of the daylight landscape is reduced to the barest minimum, the black masses of buildings and harbour walls, a few streetlights and out ahead the swinging beams of the port lighthouses, the winking of leading lights and the slow beginning of movement as the sea starts to bring life to the boat; this wonderful counterpoint of movement on movement, accompanied by the hum of the motor and the rhythmic splash, splash, splash of the bow-wave spray. Then, as you reach the harbour mouth, you begin to feel more than see the weight of the swell, judging it by the response of the ship. The strength of the wind and its direction is telegraphed to you from the way it strikes your shoulders and face. Looking down on the glowing compass, you turn the wheel till the course lines up on the grid, spin the sensing unit till the tell-tale lights flash red and green, cut in the auto pilot and feel the spokes moving uncannily under your hand. Now you are on course and have time to begin to scan the eastern horizon for that first greying out which precedes the dawn. . . .

Such are my memories of clearing Brindisi harbour at 0530 on the 14th of October. *Spirit of Saint Louis* followed us closely, her nav lights glowing. Freddy was below, checking our course out to the beacon which lies south-east of the harbour, marking the limit of a shoal. We could see it winking way out to sea. The heavy swell I expected to encounter as we left harbour had died down and was comparatively light, the northerly breeze was hardly awake. It looked as if we might have an easy run south.

'Alter course on to 142°M when we've rounded the buoy.' Freddy had popped his cheerful head round the cabin door. 'Shall I brew up some coffee?'

'Fine. You'll find some biscuits in the rack.'

We rounded the beacon at 0614, set the new course and tuned in the morning weather forecast. It prophesied winds of Force 2 from the N.N.E., seven-eighths overcast and good visibility. It was light now and we were running down the coast about three miles out. *Spirit of Saint Louis* had set her main and genoa, but there was hardly enough wind to fill them. The day bettered the forecast, the swell was going down, the sun began to come through. I got out our folding deck-chair and Freddy and I occupied it at intervals, taking hour-on, hour-off spells, not at the wheel, which was looking after itself, but in the helmsman's seat. We began to natter about our lives and found that we were both old pilots. Freddy had flown over sixty different types of aircraft in the Second World War, beating me, who had only flown fifty-three different types in the First! At intervals he took bearings. We were off the Saint Cataldo light at 0915 and Porto Otranto was abeam at 11.35, six hours out of Brindisi. We estimated our speed at just under seven knots. We were well up to schedule.

Now for the dreaded Otranto Strait which had been my bugbear for weeks! We ran on for another three-quarters of an hour till we picked up the big light structure on Cape Otranto. It stands 176 feet above the sea and its white mass on the side of the mountainous cape is quite unmistakable. There was nothing to stop us carrying on. The wind had quite died out, the sea was almost calm, so when Freddy had got a satisfactory stern bearing on the Cape we turned on to 113°M, making for the island of Fano, the first and largest of the outlying islands north of Corfu.

It was a most beautiful afternoon. Above, it looked as if the higher winds were undecided. Wisps of cirrus swirled this way and that, bubbles of cumulus floated about aimlessly, the visibility, which should have thrown up the mountains of Albania and the island ahead, thickened to a haze and it wasn't till 1430 that Freddy, standing up forrard in the pulpit, shouted 'Landho!' He had sighted the flank of Fano through the mist.

By now the sea was flat calm, a marvellous mirror of opal, out of which, disturbed by our arrival, flying fishes took off and, letting down their tails every so often, wiggled them energetically to keep up their air speed and sailed away over the shining plains of water sometimes for three or four hundred yards before they plopped in again.

We estimated that we had picked up Fano about twenty-five

miles out and, as the afternoon wore on, and the island seemed to grow no nearer, it seemed as if we were becalmed in a cocoon of golden mists. The whole Adriatic was taking a deep siesta and only our wake and the comfortable sight of *Spirit of Saint Louis* dead astern reassured us that we must be, in fact, making our steady seven knots towards land. But with the coming of evening, behind us over the heel of Italy a huge and ominous black star of cloud reached out. A big storm was building up there, sixty miles away. Flashes of lightning came from the heart of it. But we didn't need, thank heaven, to worry about that. We were nearing the island, the light was going fast, we switched on our nav lights and came close inshore, waiting for the beacon on the south-westerly side of the bay to appear. Before it did the light had quite gone and the steep cliffs of the island lay like a block of ebony above the black glass of the sea.

The Pilot warned us that, although there was a harbour, the entrance to it was tortuous. There were shoals, rocks. It was no place to find in the dark. So, probing the shore with our lights, we felt our way into the bay, engines ticking over.

'My echo sounder's U.S.,' Peter shouted across the water. 'What have you got?'

'Three fathoms.'

'That'll do. I'm going to drop the hook. Why don't you tie up alongside?'

With the engine off, we could just hear the surf on the beach. There were a few lights in cottages along the shore, the headlights of a car appeared, a torch shone for a moment right up at the mountain top, the pulse of the lighthouse beyond the hill swelled and died like a heart beating. It was quite still. We were in Greek waters. At last!

*   *   *

For me it was quite an occasion. I fished out a bottle of whisky. Peter whipped up a savoury mess of eggs, cheese and God knows what else in the huge electric frying pan. We had an hilarious supper. For me it was a real Thanksgiving feast. The nightmare of the last ten days, the threat of the strait and all my anxieties had vanished, as so many nightmares do, in the light of reality. I was grateful, more than I could easily express, to these men I had not known three days ago, laughing and talking in the glow of the saloon. I was tired too, fourteen hours at sea, however perfect, was enough for one day. So, leaving them talking, I returned to *Prosilios* and turned in.

But not for long. At 01 30 I woke. A swell was surging into the bay from the south-west. The boats, tied together, were heaving and chafing at the fenders. We decided to separate. So, casting off, we circled and dropped our own hook about a hundred yards away. The swell was building up rapidly. We didn't know what the holding ground was like.

'We'd better keep an anchor watch,' said Freddy.

I was wide awake now. 'You turn in,' I said. 'I'll wake you at four.'

'Keep an eye on that light on the shore and the loom of the beam there over the hill. If the bearings change, call me. We don't want to drag in this. It's onshore.'

Freddy went below and I settled down in the cockpit. *Prosilios* was lifting to the swells, rising and falling comfortably. I could see the masthead light on *Spirit of Saint Louis* doing the same. I began to find it wonderful being there in the cockpit at night, alone. There were no stars. It was very dark. The waves lifted the boat on their shoulders and swept on, growling deeply as they broke on the beach. I felt myself swaying to the rhythm of the boat, up and down, up and down, as if the sea were breathing. And then the swinging beam of the lighthouse. That had another rhythm. Day and night that was also a rhythm; and the seasons, the very orbit of the earth, was a rhythm. . . . I began to see rhythms in everything. How strange it was! . . .

A glow on the sea over to starboard roused me out of this reverie. It was some light shining up on the mainsail of a caique. It moved slowly inshore, feeling for the harbour. Then the movement ceased. The light went out. She was moored. I checked on our position again. The bearings hadn't changed. Evidently the anchor was holding, though the swell was still rising. At 0415 I called Freddy. He came on deck and I turned in.

An hour later I was rudely awakened. A big swell had broken right under us, throwing some loose stuff across the cabin, smashing the wireless. I was quickly out in the cockpit. Dawn was breaking, a grey, heavy dawn. The swells were now riding hard on each other's heels, right into the bay. Looking shoreward, we could see our position. We were anchored not a hundred yards off the beach against which the rollers were surging and breaking angrily. *Prosilios* was pitching violently. We were in that classic situation—storm on a lee shore.

'Got a safety harness?' said Freddy. 'I think we'd better get out of this.'

I got out the harness. 'What are you going to do?'

'Get the anchor up. Get the engine running and just take the weight off the line when I yell.'

Freddy put on my cheater and the harness and—for some obscure reason, known only to him—my panama hat. It gave him an irresistibly comic appearance at a moment when some light relief was welcome.

'What are the swells? About fourteen feet?' *Prosilios* was pitching madly.

Freddy surveyed the angry sea. 'Not more than twelve,' was all he would allow.

He climbed carefully out of the cockpit, clipped on the hook and moved slowly forward, step by step. 'Start the engine,' he called.

I did so and watched him anxiously as he made his way to the foredeck. It was something I was glad I didn't have to do. Arrived there and well fastened to the pulpit, he sat down and began to get the line in. . . .

There was little wind, so the pull on it wasn't much. Plunging up and down in the bows, Freddy hauled steadily on the line. Now he had got the chain—the last three fathoms. 'She's clear!' he yelled. 'Slow ahead!'

Keeping her head into the swells, I slowly worked our way into deeper water. Somehow or other Freddy managed to get the anchor stowed, the line coiled down and all made fast.

'Get over to the others,' he yelled. 'Wake the buggers up!'

Spirit of Saint Louis was riding the swells like a porpoise, her red undersides showing on every crest. But there was no sign of life aboard. It was pretty cool, I thought, sleeping through this. At last our yells woke them. Peter's head appeared.

'We're getting out!' I yelled at him. 'I don't like it!'

'You'll be all right!' he yelled back. 'We'll follow. Keep south, close into the shore, till you're well clear.'

We forged slowly ahead. *Prosilios* rode the swells splendidly, lifting to them buoyantly, never taking a drop aboard. Once in deeper water the sharp breaking curl went out of them and we felt easier. *Spirit of Saint Louis* at last got under way and we could see her moving south to clear the shoals. Then she turned to follow us east. The swells were still quite heavy, but we had them on the starboard quarter now and rode them easily, putting up the revs.

'Must be that storm we saw over Italy last night,' I suggested.

'I shouldn't wonder,' said Freddy. He was busy taking bearings. 'Better keep on 095,' he said. 'There's a shoal off the north coast. We don't want to tangle with that.'

Once we were in the lee of the islands, Samothrace and Diaplo, the sea went down. Soon it was almost calm and we ran along the north coast of Corfu, making for the Cape St. Katerina. To port lay the island of Merlera, beyond the high ranges of Albania. It all had that gaunt and glorious grandeur I remembered from two years ago. The ferry, the *Egnatia*, was coming up through the channel heading for Brindisi. There were many friends of ours aboard, but we were too far off for them to see us. At 0935 we rounded the cape, close inshore. We had been four and a half hours at sea.

It turned into a sparkling morning. The sun was out and the sea was dancing. I looked up the gaunt flanks of the northern mountains, to the long ridge and summit of Pantocrator, 3,000 feet above. A million olive trees clothed the lower slopes in a sombre mist of grey-green, lonely, austere. Among them here and there wisps of smoke were rising in the still air. They were burning the brushwood below the trees to clear the ground for the olive fall that would begin next month and last right through till May. The coast was indented with many coves, most of them deserted or with one or two white cottages above the water. The sea was a real Greek blue. To port, the barren mountains of Albania slid down to a stony foreshore and curled out towards Corfu, leaving a channel less than two miles wide. Indeed, as we turned south towards these narrows, it was difficult to see a way through. We swept out past the old Venetian seamark which still stands there, while a caique, knowing the water, foamed through right against the shore.

'Shall I take the wheel for a bit?' asked Freddy.

'I've planned this morning for two years and battled for it for the last three months,' I told him. 'I'm taking her in.'

Freddy laughed. 'Okay,' he said. Then looking up, 'What an island! It's gorgeous! I understand how you feel!'

And indeed I was feeling a good deal, because I'd often wondered whether we should ever make it and here it was! Feeling a good deal of feeling not at all clear, a sort of composite emotion picture of what the place meant to me, where its hold lay, why I wanted, needed, to come back, a mosaic of memory chips, forming and reforming in my head, small prosaic things that, added up, made the taste of the place unique. . . . Would that old girl in the cottage next to the hotel still be calling her turkeys, Peep, peep, peep? . . . Would that child still be riding down through the oranges on her donkey, faithfully followed by two sheep and a lamb? . . . Would the 'ugly duchess', as we called her, still be sitting side-saddle, back straight, white kerchief on her head, with her bags of olives on the donkey, her husband trudging behind? . . . And what about the rich kitchen smells of the hot food on the charcoal, and blind Yanni in his cigarette kiosk—you couldn't fool him, he knew every pack, every coin and every note by touch—and the fish sellers on their motor-bikes and the two brother butchers who had quarrelled and divided their shop in half and wouldn't speak to one another, and the madhouse with the broken fence that let the idiots out and everyone gentle and compassionate with them, and the Pappas coming round to bless every house at Epiphany with his sprig of rosemary and holy water and the church bells and the first stylosa iris, January jewels, and the peace along the terraces under the waltzing olives, slow, stately and still they waltzed, but you could never quite catch them at it, and the cheerful greeting from strangers on the road and the grapefruit hanging from the trees like golden footballs and the man who came every week to drink the water from one particular well? . . . All this and a lot more was in the mosaic and it added up to the sunset of a simple life, not yet gone, but fast melting under the sweet saliva of packaged tours and gift shops. . . .

In the tiny bay of Kouloura our two boats came together. We shut off the engines to say goodbye. Freddy shook hands and climbed back aboard the *Spirit of Saint Louis*. Peter and I shook hands across the sea. 'Pass me your camera,' he said. 'Let me take some shots. One never seems to have any of one's own boat!'

I handed it over and cavorted about while Peter snapped away. Then we came alongside again and Martin Rubin passed back the camera on the end of his boathook.

'We'll escort you down to harbour and see you safely tied up,' said Peter.

Now, as we cleared the narrows, the shores opened out to form an inland sea. To starboard the coast made a great bay, Pyrghi, Ipsos and Comena Head, and then, due south as we cut across, we could see the town of Corfu with its noble tatty façade, the old fort and the low island that protects the quays. It all looked a bit down-at-heel, home-made, with the extraordinary charm that old things have, worn but mellowed by the life that has been lived through them. It had that elusive quality that we dub 'character'. It was the most perfect small island capital in the world.

We rounded into harbour. I made for the Customs wharf behind the detached mole. *Spirit of Saint Louis* stood off waiting, faithful to the end. When I was safely moored I stood on the foredeck, clasping my hands above my head, in a gesture of thanks and farewell. . . .

*   *   *

I stepped ashore, slightly rolling from the motion, very tired, for I'd been nineteen hours at sea with about two hours' sleep. Fanny met me, jubilant at my so swift, safe return. We drove off to the villa where friends were waiting. Fanny was opening the post. Suddenly she burst out laughing. 'I can't believe it!' she said. 'Here's a letter from America. They must be mad. Look!' She handed it to me.

'In recognition of your outstanding contribution to literature, you have been elected this day

A KNIGHT OF MARK TWAIN'

It was only some months later that, somewhat crestfallen, I realised I had been mistaken for the Poet Laureate.

Corfu. Spring/70

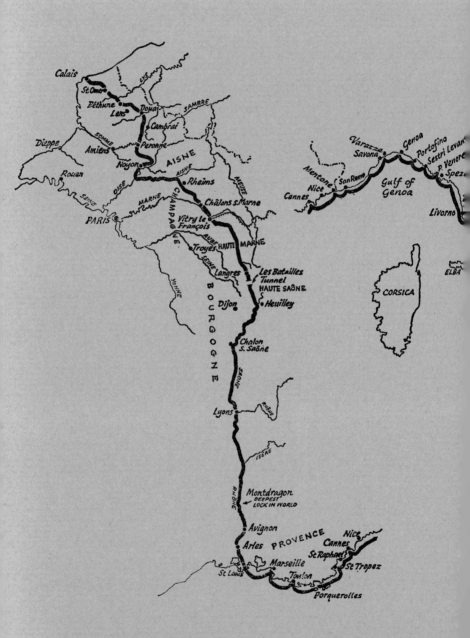